The *Type & Learn*™ Advantage

Type and Learn C is part of the *Type and Learn* series of books, brought to you by Programmers Press. The designers of the *Type and Learn* series understand that there are numerous obstacles to learning how to program. So we worked with one of the industry's finest authors, Tom Swan, to develop a learning method for you, the first-time programmer. The *Type and Learn* series is the result of extensive research and testing on the part of Tom Swan and IDG Books Worldwide.

The formula for the book is simple: Learn by doing. It's been proven that a hands-on approach not only speeds learning, but also helps you to remember what you learn. When you can perform an action and see the results, you'll remember what you did *and* why you did it.

Professional programmers often say that reading about programming is nice, but writing code is better. The fact is it's fundamental to your success. That's why each book includes software. This software is not casual filler; it is strategically linked to the content and topic of a book so you can begin programming immediately.

We believe that the author has the experience to teach programming as well as the skill to present complex topics to first-time programmers. We know that you will benefit from the informal, hands-on approach. When you finish this book, you will not only understand how a program works, but you'll have written several programs, and you'll be prepared to move on to the next programming level.

— Chris Williams
Publisher, IDG Programmers Press

Type and Learn C

by Tom Swan

Programmers Press

**IDG
BOOKS**

An International Data Group Company

San Mateo, California ✦ Indianapolis, Indiana ✦ Boston, Massachusetts

Type and Learn C

Published by
IDG Books Worldwide, Inc.
An International Data Group Company
155 Bovet Rd., Suite 310
San Mateo, CA 94402

For editorial queries, please write to:
IDG Programmers Press
140 Wood Road, Suite 200
Braintree, MA 02184

Library of Congress Catalog Card No.: 94-75049

ISBN: 1-56884-073-X

Printed in the United States of America

10 9 8 7 6 5 4 3 2

2C/QT/SV/ZU

Distributed in the United States by IDG Books Worldwide, Inc.

Distributed in Canada by Macmillan of Canada, a Division of Canada Publishing Corporation; by Computer and Technical Books in Miami, Florida, for South America and the Caribbean; by Longman Singapore in Singapore, Malaysia, Thailand, and Korea; by Toppan Co. Ltd. in Japan; by Asia Computerworld in Hong Kong; by Woodslane Pty. Ltd. in Australia and New Zealand; and by Transword Publishers Ltd. in the U.K. and Europe.

For general information on IDG Books in the U.S., including information on discounts and premiums, contact IDG Books at 800-762-2974 or 415-312-0650.

For information on where to purchase IDG Books outside the U.S., contact Christina Turner at 415-312-0633.

For information on translations, contact Marc Jeffrey Mikulich, Foreign Rights Manager, at IDG Books Worldwide; FAX NUMBER 415-358-1260.

For sales inquiries and special prices for bulk quantities, write to the address above or call IDG Books Worldwide at 415-312-0650.

 are registered trademarks of IDG Books Worldwide, Inc.

 The text in this book is printed on recycled paper.

About the Author

Tom Swan is a well-known author of over 25 best-selling books and hundreds of articles on computer programming. He has worked as a programmer and a consultant, and is a recognized expert in several programming languages. Tom's regular columns appear in *Dr. Dobb's Journal* ("Algorithm Alley") and in *PC Techniques* ("Shades of Windows").

When not at their home base in Pennsylvania, Tom Swan and his wife Anne live aboard their sailboat, *Gypsy Venus,* and are presently exploring the watery parts of the east coast of the United States. Meanwhile, Tom is hard at work revising his classic nautical text, *Programming at C.* (Just kidding, says Tom.)

Why Readers Prefer Tom Swan's Books

. . . Thank you very much for taking the time to write such a clear, interesting, easily comprehended work that is in the book *Mastering Borland C++*. I am a complete novice to the IBM world and am having an incredible blast with learning to program in C! I have found that not only is your book an excellent tutor, but it is filled with very specific advice (I hate books that are too general about things) and is loaded with humor to boot. I guess what I am *really* trying to say is, thanks for taking the time to *do it right*!

—Bob Page

I just purchased your new *Inside Windows File Formats.* This kind of book was long overdue! I've been wanting to write a .GRP editor for months now, but between the errata in Microsoft's documentation and the 20-point type in "PC Magazine" on the .GRP format (20-point type makes everything look hard, doesn't it?), I just gave up—until I saw your book . . . On a personal note, your books are excellent; I enjoy reading them.

—Jim Haentzschel

. . . thank you for writing that book of yours. You make learning assembly easy . . . When my instructor picked your book as a text book, he picked well. I find it easy to read, explanations are precise, and difficult aspects are picked apart bit by bit (no pun intended), so as to make easier for the reader to understand . . . Keep up the good work, I really enjoy reading your book. The class is barely into chapter 5; I'm already in chapter 8 . . . Take care and keep writing!

—Geoff Stanford

Tom, am attempting to teach myself C by using your book. Not knowing anything about it, I bought Borland Turbo C++ for Windows as my compiler. Your book appears to be written for use with DOS, but I have had little difficulty translating into the compiler version I have. I find that your book is very thorough and am enjoying the experience . . . I am really enjoying your book and this new hobby of mine.

—Paul Fish

I am enjoying your book (*Borland Pascal 7.0 Programming for Windows*). I could have used it four months ago when I started converting my DOS-based utility program (shareware, "Disk-at-a-Glance") to Windows . . . Thanks for writing the book. Good stuff!

—Steve Leonard

About IDG Books Worldwide

Welcome to the world of IDG Books Worldwide.

IDG Books Worldwide, Inc., is a subsidiary of International Data Group, the world's largest publisher of computer-related information and the leading global provider of information services on information technology. International Data Group publishes over 195 computer publications in 62 countries. Forty million people read one or more International Data Group publications each month

If you use personal computers, IDG Books is committed to publishing quality books that meet your needs. We rely on our extensive network of publications, including such leading periodicals as *Macworld, InfoWorld, PC World, Computerworld, Publish, Network World,* and *SunWorld,* to help us make informed and timely decisions in creating useful computer books that meet your needs.

Every IDG book strives to bring extra value and skill-building instructions to the reader. Our books are written by experts, with the backing of IDG periodicals, and with careful thought devoted to issues such as audience, interior design, use of icons, and illustrations. Our editorial staff is a careful mix of high-tech journalists and experienced book people. Our close contact with the makers of computer products helps ensure accuracy and thorough coverage. Our heavy use of personal computers at every step in production means we can deliver books in the most timely manner.

We are delivering books of high quality at competitive prices on topics customers want. At IDG, we believe in quality, and we have been delivering quality for over 25 years. You'll find no better book on a subject than an IDG book.

John Kilkullen
President and C.E.O.
IDG Books Worldwide, Inc.

IDG Books Worldwide, Inc. is a subsidiary of International Data Group. The officers are Patrick J. McGovern, Founder and Board Chairman; Walter Boyd, President. International Data Group's publications include: **ARGENTINA'S** Computerworld Argentina, Infoworld Argentina; **ASIA'S** Computerworld Hong Kong, PC World Hong Kong, Computerworld Southeast Asia, PC World Singapore, Computerworld Malaysia, PC World Malaysia; **AUSTRALIA'S** Computerworld Australia, Australian PC World, Australian Macworld, Network World, Mobile Business Australia, Reseller, IDG Sources; **AUSTRIA'S** Computerwelt Oesterreich, PC Test; **BRAZIL'S** Computerworld, Gamepro, Game Power, Mundo IBM, Mundo Unix, PC World, Super Game; **BELGIUM'S** Data News (CW) **BULGARIA'S** Computerworld Bulgaria, Ediworld, PC & Mac World Bulgaria, Network World Bulgaria; **CANADA'S** CIO Canada, Computerworld Canada, Graduate Computerworld, InfoCanada, Network World Canada; **CHILE'S** Computerworld Chile, Informatica; **COLOMBIA'S** Computerworld Colombia; **CZECH REPUBLIC'S** Computerworld, Elektronika, PC World; **DENMARK'S** CAD/CAM WORLD, Communications World, Computerworld Danmark, LOTUS World, Macintosh Produktkatalog, Macworld Danmark, PC World Danmark, PC World Produktguide, Windows World; **ECUADOR'S** PC World Ecuador; **EGYPT'S** Computerworld (CW) Middle East, PC World Middle East; **FINLAND'S** MikroPC, Tietoviikko, Tietoverkko; **FRANCE'S** Distributique, GOLDEN MAC, InfoPC, Languages & Systems, Le Guide du Monde Informatique, Le Monde Informatique, Telecoms & Reseaux; **GERMANY'S** Computerwoche, Computerwoche Focus, Computerwoche Extra, Computerwoche Karriere, Information Management, Macwelt, Netzwelt, PC Welt, PC Woche, Publish, Unit; **GREECE'S** Infoworld, PC Games; **HUNGARY'S** Computerworld SZT, PC World; **INDIA'S** Computers & Communications; **IRELAND'S** Computerscope; **ISRAEL'S** Computerworld Israel, PC World Israel; **ITALY'S** Computerworld Italia, Lotus Magazine, Macworld Italia, Networking Italia, PC Shopping Italy, PC World Italia; **JAPAN'S** Computerworld Today, Information Systems World, Macworld Japan, Nikkei Personal Computing, SunWorld Japan, Windows World; **KENYA'S** East African Computer News; **KOREA'S** Computerworld Korea, Macworld Korea, PC World Korea; **MEXICO'S** Compu Edicion, Compu Manufactura, Computacion/Punto de Venta, Computerworld Mexico, MacWorld, Mundo Unix, PC World, Windows; **THE NETHERLANDS'** Computer! Totaal, Computable (CW), LAN Magazine, MacWorld, Totaal "Windows"; **NEW ZEALAND'S** Computer Listings, Computerworld New Zealand, New Zealand PC World; **NIGERIA'S** PC World Africa; **NORWAY'S** Computerworld Norge, C/World, Lotusworld Norge, Macworld Norge, Networld, PC World Ekspress, PC World Norge, PC World's Produktguide, Publish& Multimedia World, Student Data, Unix World, Windowsworld; IDG Direct Response; **PANAMA'S** PC World Panama; **PERU'S** Computerworld Peru, PC World; **PEOPLE'S REPUBLIC OF CHINA'S** China Computerworld, China Infoworld, PC World China, Electronics International, Electronic Product World, China Network World; IDG HIGH TECH BEIJING'S New Product World; IDG SHENZHEN'S Computer News Digest; **PHILIPPINES'** Computerworld Philippines, PC Digest (PCW); **POLAND'S** Computerworld Poland, PC World/Komputer; **PORTUGAL'S** Cerebro/PC World, Correio Informatico/Computerworld, MacIn; **ROMANIA'S** Computerworld, PC World; **RUSSIA'S** Computerworld-Moscow, Mir - PC, Sety; **SLOVENIA'S** Monitor Magazine; **SOUTH AFRICA'S** Computer Mail (CIO),Computing S.A.,Network World S.A.; **SPAIN'S** Amiga World, Computerworld Espana, Communicaciones World, Macworld Espana, NeXTWORLD, Super Juegos Magazine (GamePro), PC World Espana, Publish, Sunworld; **SWEDEN'S** Attack, ComputerSweden, Corporate Computing, Lokala Natverk/LAN, Lotus World, MAC&PC, Macworld, Mikrodatorn, PC World, Publishing & Design (CAP), DataIngenjoren, Maxi Data,Windows World; **SWITZERLAND'S** Computerworld Schweiz, Macworld Schweiz, PC Katalog, PC & Workstation; **TAIWAN'S** Computerworld Taiwan, Global Computer Express, PC World Taiwan; **THAILAND'S** Thai Computerworld; **TURKEY'S** Computerworld Monitor, Macworld Turkiye, PC World Turkiye; **UKRAINE'S** Computerworld; **UNITED KINGDOM'S** Computing /Computerworld, Connexion/Network World, Lotus Magazine, Macworld, Open Computing/Sunworld; **UNITED STATES'** AmigaWorld, Cable in the Classroom, CD Review, CIO, Computerworld, Desktop Video World, DOS Resource Guide, Electronic Entertainment Magazine, Federal Computer Week, Federal Integrator, GamePro, IDG Books, Infoworld, Infoworld Direct, Laser Event, Macworld, Multimedia World, Network World, NeXTWORLD, PC Letter, PC World, PlayRight, Power PC World, Publish, SunWorld, SWATPro, Video Event; **VENEZUELA'S** Computerworld Venezuela, MicroComputerworld Venezuela; **VIETNAM'S** PC World Vietnam

Dedication

To Barry and Mary Ellen Beville for the inspiration to "just do it," and especially for reminding me that *Anything's Possible.*

Acknowledgments

I owe special thanks to many who helped make this book possible. At IDG, Chris Williams, John Kilcullen, and David Solomon believed in this book's concept and lent their support at every step along the way. Editor Erik Dafforn read every word (probably six times), caught many errors, and made numerous suggestions. My wife Anne helped edit the text, ran errands, mailed chapters, cooked dinner, and even cleaned the bilge on our floating home and sailboat, "Gypsy Venus." (I wrote most of the manuscript while traveling from Maryland to Florida on the Intracoastal Waterway.) Thanks also to my agent, Bill Gladstone, and his capable staff at Waterside Productions for keeping this project afloat, and to Technical Editor Greg Guntle, for his helpful comments and suggestions in the text and listings. Others who contributed to the editing and production of *Type and Learn C* include Barb Potter, Marta Partington, Cindy Phipps, Beth Jenkins, Tony Augsburger, Valery Bourke, Mary Breidenbach, Chris Collins, Sherry Gomoll, Drew Moore, Kathie Schnorr and Gina Scott.

The publisher would like to give special thanks to Patrick J. McGovern, without whom this book would not have been possible.

Credits

Publisher
Chris Williams

Senior Editor
Trudy Neuhaus

Production Director
Beth Jenkins

Production Coordinator
Cindy L. Phipps

Project Editor
Erik Dafforn

Editors
Barbara Potter
Marta Partington

Technical Reviewer
Greg Guntle

Production Staff
Tony Augsburger
Valery Bourke
Mary Breidenbach
Chris Collins
Sherry Gomoll
Drew R. Moore
Kathie Schnorr
Gina Scott

Proofreader
Charles A. Hutchinson

Indexer
Anne Leach

Book Design
Beth Jenkins

Cover Illustration
Steve Lyons

Cover Design
Kavish + Kavish
TonBo Design

Contents at a Glance

Table of Contents

Part 3. Standard Function Library 227

Preface

In writing this book, the first in a planned series of *Type and Learn* programming tutorials for beginners, I tried to keep one word in mind: *accessibility.* I set out to write a book that anyone, young or *experienced* (you are never too old) can use to learn C.

Too often, beginning programming books create more puzzles than they solve. When you are first learning to program in C, you need a book that tells you *exactly* what's going on at every step along the way. You want a book that also has everything you need to get started. *Type and Learn C* includes a special edition of Borland's world-famous Turbo C++ compiler. Simply install the supplied disk, turn to Chapter 1, and get ready to dig into C.

Why C? Because it's popular, available on most computer systems, and relatively easy to learn. C is not a big language — it has only a few native commands, so there's not much to memorize. In fact, this book introduces most of C in just three chapters. Despite its relative simplicity, however, C is a highly capable language for writing computer programs. Indeed, most of the world's software is written in C, a trend that is expected to continue for years to come.

Spend one day with my *Type and Learn* method introduced in Part 1, and you'll learn enough about C to write your own programs. Best of all, you'll discover whether C is the right choice for you — whether you are planning a career in programming, or just want to know more about how computer software works inside.

But enough sales talk. If you decide to use this book as your introduction to C programming, drop a postcard in the mail in care of the publisher and let me know of your experiences. It's an exciting time to learn how to program, and nothing would please me more than to hear this book helped you begin.

Here's what's here

Type and Learn C is divided into four parts. Part 1 introduces C and explains how to use my *Type and Learn* method. Then, after you master the supplied special first edition of Borland's Turbo C++, you take a fast tour of C's main features.

Part 2 examines all aspects of C programming *inside and out.* By the time you finish the chapters in this part, you'll be ready to develop your own software in C.

Part 3 adds *standard functions* to your repertoire. You learn input and output operations, string handling, math functions, memory techniques, and more.

Part 4 rounds out your C education with *algorithms* — methods for solving a variety of problems such as sorting, searching, and self-referential data structures. All algorithms are explained using sample programs written in C. Also included is a mailing list database manager that demonstrates file-handling techniques.

Conventions used in this book

To help you better access information, this book contains several helpful icons:

 Notes give you important additional information about the current topic.

 Warnings help you avert disaster before it strikes.

 Tips offer time-saving advice for better, more efficient programming.

Hints show programming alternatives you might not have thought of.

Step-by-Steps prepare you for the Type and Learn lessons found throughout the book. They appear in this format:

Step-by-Steps®

1. Step-by-Steps appear apart from normal text.

2. They tell you which program listing to open, from those provided on disk.

3. Finally, they show you where to begin the Type and Learn lesson.

Part 1

Introduction: C Basics

So, you've decided to learn C, and here you are, ready to begin an exciting journey into the world of programming — a trip that may change your life. You might be a student taking a course in the computer sciences, or perhaps you plan to tackle programming in your spare time. Maybe you already know another programming language, and you need to learn C in a hurry. Or, perhaps you just want to discover why C has become the number one choice of programming languages among professional software developers.

Whatever your reasons for wanting to learn how to program in C, you've come to the right place. In Chapter 1, you meet the C language, its history, purpose, and value to programmers. I also introduce my *Type and Learn* method — a fast and easy way to learn programming. You install a special edition of Borland's Turbo C++ compiler included with this book — there's nothing else to buy. (Until I can figure out how to package a PC in a book, however, *you* supply the computer.) Finally, just to whet your appetite for what's to come, you try out two sample *Type and Learn* programs.

Chapter 2 covers Turbo C++ operations — the editor, compiler, debugger, and options. If you have some PC experience, you probably can zoom through this chapter. The *integrated development environment* in Turbo C++, or IDE, provides a one-stop C programming system with everything you need to write, run, and debug the sample programs in this book. Of course, all listings are also included on disk.

With those basics under your belt, in Chapter 3 you tour the C programming language. In one chapter, you meet every important aspect of C. After finishing Chapter 3, if you decide that C is right for your needs, you are ready to move on to Part 2, where you dig more deeply into the world of C.

Ready? Turn the page, and let's get started.

Chapter 1

The Type and Learn Method

This book has a simple theme: *If you can type, you can learn how to program in C.*

It doesn't matter whether you're a keyboard speed demon or a typing turtle. Regardless of your typing skills, by entering highlighted listings into the special edition of Borland's Turbo C++ included on disk, you can learn how to program in C faster with my *Type and Learn* method than with any other system.

I make that bold claim for a simple reason. Not long ago, in my *PC Techniques* column, "Shades of Windows," I complained that "nobody types listings from magazines anymore." I then challenged readers to enter the article's listings anyway, and to let me know if I was wrong.

To my surprise, they did, and I was forced to swallow my words. Months later, I was still receiving letters from readers who nine times out of ten told me that even if program listings are available on disk, they still type them into their editors. Why? "Because typing listings," they said, "helps us learn how programs operate."

Inspired by that idea, I developed a teaching method using specially designed program listings that, when entered into a computer, can help anyone learn C with a minimum of effort. The result is a quick and easy way to learn C programming — and more important, *to remember what you learn.* Here's how my *Type and Learn* method works.

Type Once; Learn Forever

You've probably done this. At the grocery store, you reach into your pocket and discover that you left your carefully prepared list on the kitchen table. You don't have time to return home, so you complete your shopping from memory. To your amazement, you manage to purchase nearly every item on the list. How is that possible?

The answer is obvious: *Just writing things down improves your ability to learn and remember.*

My *Type and Learn* method is founded on that basic concept. In each of this book's chapters, you read about a programming term or process—how a function works, for example. Next, you load a partially completed listing from disk into your computer. Then, following the chapter's instructions, you complete the program by typing specially highlighted statements printed in this book. You also type *snippets* (portions of programs) into program shells. I carefully selected each marked section and snippet to help you focus on the subject at hand. By typing into prepared listings, you save time while you master new programming topics. You ignore other parts of programs until you are ready for them.

Why Use C?

The purpose of a programming language is to make life easier for programmers. If it weren't for C, software would have to be written as it was in the old days — by toggling individual bits in memory on and off. Obviously, that would hardly be practical in today's high-powered world of software development (it probably wasn't much fun even way back then). Today, programmers use languages like C to write all kinds of computer programs.

C offers programmers three key advantages:

▶ C is a *general-purpose programming language.* You can write games, business software, utilities, mathematical models, word processors, spreadsheets, and other kinds of software in C.

▶ C is a *structured programming language.* It uses structured statements such as `while` and `for` loops in place of `goto` statements that are too easily misused, causing bugs to creep into programs written in unstructured languages such as BASIC and assembly language.

▶ C is a *standardized programming language.* In general, when programmers say C, they mean ANSI C, the recognized standard for the C programming language. The software supplied with this book is a special Turbo C++ compiler that you can use to program in ANSI C and C++.

Some of the best reasons for learning C are its popularity and widespread use. All career programmers should be familiar with C — it's the rare programming shop that doesn't use C for software development. Countless books, references, and software collections include programs written in C. For learning other languages, C also provides an excellent training ground. After you master C, you will have little trouble picking up additional programming languages on your own.

What Is a Compiler?

I'll answer that question in a second, but first consider what a *computer language* is. People don't speak it. Its words aren't in the dictionary — or, at least, they have different meanings in a program. You don't write home to your mother in C. (If you do, you and Mom should get out more often.)

If C isn't a conventional language, what is it? And what in the world is a C compiler? First things first. Calling C a *language* is a mistake in terms. C is really a *symbolic instruction code,* a set of commands that perform actions on a computer. Writing text to the display, adding two numbers, transferring data to disk — all of these actions and countless others can be programmed using C *statements,* constructed according to C's rules and regulations — in other words, its *syntax.* Here's a sampling of a few statements in C:

```
int count = 0;
while (count < 100)
{
  printf("count == %d\n", count);
  count++;
}
```

Don't be concerned if that looks like mush — eventually, statements like those will be as easy to read as the Sunday comics. Notice, however, that even if you don't understand the statements, you can spot an integer (abbreviated `int`) named `count` and a statement in between braces that does something *while* `count` is less than 100. The braces collect statements into a *block,* which in this example prints the value of `count` and increases it, eventually causing the `while` loop to end. As you can tell, even if you don't understand every detail, C's readability is one of its major conveniences. With C, you write programs in *your* language, not the computer's.

A C *compiler's* purpose in life is to read symbolic statements written in the C language and translate those statements into a finished program (see Figure 1-1). This process is called *compiling* or *compilation.* When you *compile* a program's source file — a plain ASCII text file that contains the program's instructions — you create executable code that, due to your skill (and a bit of luck), performs exactly as you want. After compilation, the program runs as an independent application from an operating system such as DOS or Windows.

Not all programming languages are designed to be compiled. Many forms of BASIC, for example, use an interpreter that translates a program's statements into actions each time the program runs (see Figure 1-2). Because BASIC interprets programs, it must be started along with the program. Interpretation takes time, and therefore, compiled programs generally run faster than interpreted programs because the compiled code is in native, machine language form. On the other hand, interpreted instructions are ready to use as soon as you write them; programs written in C require compilation, which adds time to the program's development. Even so, professional programmers prefer compiled languages like C because it lets them write *high-level statements* that humans can understand, but produce compiled *low-level code* that runs quickly on a computer.

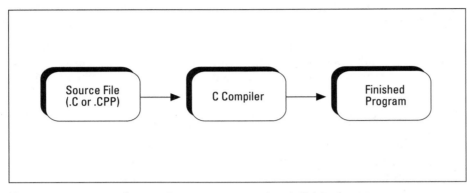

Figure 1-1 ▶ A compiler translates C statements into a finished program.

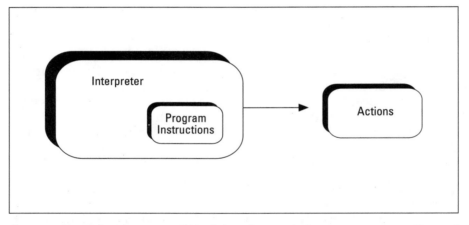

Figure 1-2 ▶ An interpreter translates instructions each time a program runs. To run the program, you first have to start the interpreter.

What Is a Linker?

I didn't tell the whole truth in the preceding section. A compiler actually produces raw code, known as *object code,* usually stored in a file ending in .OBJ. Before object code can be fed to the CPU, it must be *linked* to other components, creating *executable code,* typically stored in a file ending in .EXE. Compiling a C program is only half of the story. You also have to *link* the object code to create an executable code file (see Figure 1-3).

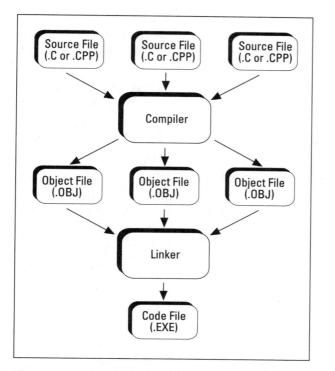

Figure 1-3 ▶ A compiler translates source files into object code; a linker combines object code files into a finished executable code file.

A linker also binds a program's object code with startup and shutdown instructions required by the operating system, and with other pieces of programming provided with a compiler. The linker's primary job is to construct a single executable code file from multiple object code modules. This lets you write large programs one piece at a time, whittling down the most demanding tasks to manageable size.

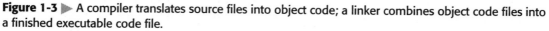

For now, don't worry about how to run the compiler and linker. Just be aware of their roles. You'll learn more about compiling and linking as you try out this book's sample programs.

A Few Good Terms

To master C programming, you need to become familiar with a variety of new terms. I'll define various words as we go along (I introduced a few in the preceding sections), but here are some important terms used in this book that you need to know right away:

▶ *Keywords* are words that are reserved by a programming language. Because the words `while` and `if` are reserved, for instance, you can't use them for your own purposes. Unlike some languages that have massive keyword lists, C reserves only a few keywords, all of which you will meet in this book.

▶ *Syntax* refers to the rules you must follow when typing statements and other constructions. To avoid errors in programs, you must adhere religiously to C syntax. (Never fear, the compiler tells you if you make a mistake in syntax.)

▶ *Semantics* refers to the meanings behind C's rules of syntax. The purpose of this book is to explain not only the syntax of C, but also its semantics so you can learn how to apply the language for writing programs that perform specific tasks.

▶ *Algorithms* are best defined as "methods of solution." An algorithm is a step-by-step description of the solution to a problem — the steps required to sort a list of names alphabetically, for example. Algorithms are usually written in *pseudocode* — informal descriptions of a program's steps that resemble actual programming — that programmers can translate more or less directly into C statements.

▶ *Library functions* extend a programming language's native capabilities. The standard library functions provided with this book include hundreds of subroutines for mathematics, string handling, file processing, date and time operations, memory management, and many other tasks.

▶ *Source code* files contain a program's statements in plain ASCII text form. You may create and edit source code files using any plain-text editor such as the one built into Turbo C++. Source code files may end with the filename extensions .C or .CPP.

▶ *Object code* files contain the program's raw instruction codes. The compiler reads one or more source code files, processes any statements it finds, and generates object code, storing the results in files ending with the filename extension .OBJ.

▶ *Executable code* files are created by linking one or more object code files, producing a new file ending with the extension .EXE. Sometimes, you might be tempted to literally execute a program that doesn't work correctly, but in general, *executing a program* simply means to run it (not to kill it), usually by typing its name at a DOS prompt. You can also execute programs directly from Turbo C++.

▶ *Compile time* refers to the time during which the compiler reads source code files and generates object code. A *compile-time error* is a mistake in syntax discovered during compilation.

▶ *Runtime* refers to the time during which a program runs. A *runtime error* is a mistake in the program's logic — displaying output in the wrong location on-screen, for example, or computing a formula incorrectly.

▶ *Debugging* is the process of locating and fixing a program's runtime errors, or *bugs*. The version of Turbo C++ supplied with this book has a built-in debugger that helps you analyze programs and investigate the causes of operational problems. Use the debugger to step slowly through a program's statements, to examine variables, and to halt a program at a strategic location.

A Brief History of C

Knowing some of C's history will give you a better appreciation of the language and why it has evolved into its present form as explained in this book. C was originally designed as a symbolic code that formalized programming practices in use at that time. In other words, C was created to do what was needed and little more. Today, C remains true to its origins. It is a language written by programmers for programmers, and its terse design is still one of its key strengths.

In 1978, C blossomed into what was to become the most popular computer programming language ever. That year saw the publication of *The C Programming Language,* written by Brian W. Kernighan and Dennis M. Ritchie, a book that established the standard by which all C compilers were judged for almost a decade.

That version of C, known today as *K&R C,* was the direct descendant of a C dialect written by Dennis Ritchie for the UNIX operating system running on a DEC PDP-11 computer. Actually, UNIX, its tools, and C were developed more or less simultaneously, with each part in the system inspiring changes to the others. C literally grew up with UNIX, but the C language has since left the nest and is now available on just about every computer system around.

K&R C traces its ancestory back even further to another language called BCPL (Basic Combined Programming Language) written by Martin Richards in 1969 at Cambridge University. As computer languages go, BCPL was extremely low level — that is, its elements corresponded directly to the computer's architecture. In 1970, Ken Thompson wrote a BCPL-like language for an early UNIX operating system running on a DEC PDP-7 computer. In the spirit of the times, when small memory cores forced programmers to jealously conserve RAM, Thompson named the language B, "saving" three letters.

BCPL and B were *typeless* languages in which variables were simply words in memory. The languages served the needs of their times, and were still in heavy use ten years after their creation. As software tasks grew more demanding, however, it became clear that something better had to be invented. Programmers needed a *structured programming language* with *data types* that would enable them to use integers (whole numbers like 100 and –99), floating-point values (fractional values like 3.14159 and –0.5), and characters (letters, digits, and punctuation) in relatively safe ways.

That language was K&R C, which added functions, integers, floating-point values, characters, dozens of operators, and other components to B. As the story goes, the name C was borrowed from the second letter in BCPL. Others say C's name arose because C is alphabetically "higher" than B, raising the question among trivia buffs of whether C's next incarnation will be named *D* or *P*. (C's authors won't say.)

Whatever the source of its name, K&R C was a smash hit. Soon after the publication of *The C Programming Language,* C compilers began to pop up like buds in a flower show. Possibly due to the book's existence, most of these implementations were largely compatible, meaning that a program written for one computer required only minor changes to be transferred, or *ported,* to another system. C's widespread use and its relative compatibility among implementations led directly to the language's next and more formal stage.

In recognition of C's growing use — and, probably, in fear of losing control over the de facto standard that had evolved independently among C compiler authors — in 1983, the American National Standards Institute charged the C Programming Language Committee X3J11 to adopt a rigorous standard for C implementors to follow. In five years of grueling work and dueling egos, the committee accomplished the impossible: they cleaned C's house of quirks, conflicts, and ambiguities, and they added a few carefully selected features, resisting attempts to bloat the language with capabilities from countless proposals received during the evaluation period.

The result was ANSI C, a standard that remains virtually unchanged since its adoption in 1988. The publication of the ANSI C standard also marked the end of K&R C, which quickly faded from the scene and is rarely used today. Nevertheless, many compilers continue to support the older K&R syntax and ANSI C, among them the version of Turbo C++ packed with this book. If you run across older K&R code, you can use it with Turbo C++. New programs, however, should be written to conform to the ANSI C standard as are all programs in this book.

The Next Generation

The story of C is not yet over. During the time when the X3J11 committee moved steadily toward producing the ANSI C standard, another researcher, Bjarne Stroustrup of Bell Laboratories, began experimenting with an *object-oriented* flavor of C that he called *C++* (pronounced *C plus plus*). C++ extended C, and according to Stroustrup, refined the language, making C++ in his words "a better C."

Apparently, the X3J11 committee agreed, if not completely, and they adopted some of Stroustrup's proposals into the ANSI C standard. Subsequently, a new committee was formed to investigate a standard for ANSI C++, which is just now being readied for publication. Does this new standard mean that ANSI C is destined to join its ancestors BCPL, B, and K&R C on the heap of discarded programming languages?

The answer is a solid *no.* Frankly, C++ isn't for everyone. When learning C, it's best to stick to the basics, and you are well advised to ignore some of the more advanced elements found in C++. For example, C++ provides classes for *object-oriented programming,* or OOP as it is known. Until you know C, you aren't ready for OOP.

On the other hand, because C++ is based on ANSI C, you may as well use modern next-generation compilers like Turbo C++ to write C programs. That way, you can take advantage of both worlds. After you finish *Type and Learn C,* you'll be ready to tackle OOP and other advanced C++ subjects.

And, if you get really good at C programming, you might want to send in the coupon in the back of the book and upgrade to the latest edition of Borland C++. You receive double the price of this book back as a discount. How's that for a bargain?

How to Install Turbo C++

Follow these steps to install this first special edition of Turbo C++ (created for **Type and Learn C**) and all of this book's program listings onto your PC's hard drive. You need about 3MB of disk space to install Turbo C++. In addition, you need about 1MB of space for this book's sample listings.

1. Insert the diskette labeled *Type and Learn C* into drive A: or B:. Close all open programs and save any unsaved files in other applications before continuing.

2. To install Turbo C++ from a DOS prompt (open a DOS window if you are running Microsoft Windows), first change to the drive containing the diskette by entering **A:** or **B:**.

3. Enter **install c:**. Turbo C++ automatically creates the directory TCLITE in your root directory.

4. To install this book's sample listings, copy the self-extracting archive file TLC.EXE to the installation directory. For example, enter a command such as

   ```
   copy a:\tlc.exe c:\tclite
   ```

5. The TLC.EXE file contains the book's listings in compressed form. To unpack the files, change to the installation directory and run the TLC.EXE program. For example, enter these commands:

   ```
   c:
   cd \tclite
   tlc
   ```

6. Running TLC creates PART1, PART2, PART3, and PART4 directories (plus other subdirectories) in the current path. All sample listing files are stored in these directories. After unpacking, you may delete TLC.EXE (keep a copy on floppy disk, however, in case you want to reinstall the files).

7. Next, configure Turbo C++. Edit or create a plain-text CONFIG.SYS file in the root directory, usually C:\. You may use the Turbo C++ editor, the DOS EDIT utility, or a word processor capable of creating plain ASCII text files. Make sure CONFIG.SYS has a FILES command set to at least 20:

   ```
   FILES=20
   ```

8. Also edit or create a plain-text AUTOEXEC.BAT file in the root directory, and add the directory C:\TCLITE\BIN to a PATH statement. For example, insert this command *exactly* as shown (change C:\TCLITE if you installed Turbo C++ to another path):

   ```
   PATH C:\DOS;C:\WINDOWS;C:\TCLITE\BIN
   ```

9. Reboot your computer by pressing Ctrl+Alt+Del. After rebooting, you should be able to run Turbo C++ (type **tc**). If you receive an error message, make sure the PATH statement in step 8 specifies the drive and directory that holds the file TC.EXE. If you run Windows, start it now and open a DOS prompt window, then type **tc** to start Turbo C++.

Be sure to add C:\TCLITE\BIN, *not* the base installation directory, to the PATH. *BIN* stands for *binaries,* the directory where Turbo C++ stores its binary executable code files. If you add only C:\TCLITE to the PATH, you will not be able to run Turbo C++.

Your First C Program

That's enough background and preparation. Let's write a program. Follow the instructions under *Step-by-Steps* to finish Listing 1-1, FIRST.CPP, and then turn to the discussion that follows the listing.

Step-by-Steps

1. If you are running Microsoft Windows, first open a DOS prompt window. You may open the window in text or graphics mode. DOS users: go straight to step 2.

2. Change to the C:\TCLITE\PART1 directory (type **cd c:\tclite\part1**). From now on, I'll refer to this directory simply as PART1.

3. Start Turbo C++ by typing **tc**. If that doesn't work, you didn't install the compiler correctly, or the PATH isn't set to the right directory. Type **path** to check its setting.

4. Use the Turbo C++ **F**ile|**O**pen... command (or press F3) to open the file FIRST.CPP. You should see the program listing in a window.

5. Enter *only* the highlighted instructions in Listing 1-1 where shown here. (If you get stuck or accidentally delete something, the completed FIRST.CPP program is stored in the PART1\FINISHED directory. All completed listings are stored in similar FINISHED directories for each part of the book.)

6. Press Ctrl+F9 to compile, link, and run the program.

7. Follow instructions on-screen.

Listing 1-1: *FIRST.CPP*

```
/* Your first C program */

#include <stdio.h>
#include <conio.h>

char Pause(void)
{
  char c;
  printf("\nPress Enter to continue...");
  while ((c = getchar()) != '\n') { }
  return c;
```

```
}

int main()
{
  char name[80];  /* A place to hold input */

  clrscr();
  puts("What is your name? ");
  gets(name);
  puts("");
  puts("Your name is:");
  puts(name);

  Pause();  /* Wait for Enter key */
  return 0;  /* "no errors detected" */
}
```

The six lines you typed are examples of *input and output,* or I/O, statements — some of the most important operations that nearly all computer programs perform. First, `clrscr()` clears the screen. (The empty parentheses after `clrscr()` tell the compiler this is a function — a subroutine that performs an action — and not something else.) Next, the `puts` function *put*s a *s*tring of text, surrounded by double quotes, onto the standard output — in other words, the display. The `gets` function *get*s a *s*tring of text from the standard input — namely the keyboard. The *s* in `puts` and `gets` stands for *string.* When you press Enter, `gets` deposits that text into the object `name` inside parentheses. Another `puts` statement writes the text stored in `name` — a fact that you can easily verify by running the program. Do that and enter your name. Compare the output on-screen with the statements in the listing.

Get in the habit of reading listings, and pay special attention to the highlighted lines printed here. Compare output on-screen with the program statements that produce that output. Resist the urge to skip over the listings — they will become easier to read as you learn more about C. *Remember to focus on the highlighted statements.* You can read the unhighlighted sections if you want, but you don't have to.

Never mind what the other lines do for the moment — focus only on the highlighted text that you entered. By typing those lines, you now know how to

▶ Use the `clrscr` function to clear the display.

▶ Use the `puts` function to display a quoted string.

▶ Use the `gets` function to input a string.

▶ Use the `puts` function to display a *variable* such as `name`.

Your Second C Program

The second and final sample program in this chapter demonstrates how to use *expressions* to compute formulas similar to those you might enter into a pocket calculator. As you did with FIRST.CPP, follow the instructions under "Step-by-Steps" to complete Listing 1-2, SECOND.CPP. I assume you know how to open a DOS window (if you are running Microsoft Windows) and start Turbo C++, so I won't repeat those steps. Compare the program's output to the instructions you typed and then turn to the discussion following the listing to learn how the program works.

Step-by-Steps

1. Change to the PART1 directory. If you completed Listing 1-1, you are already there.

2. Open the source code file, SECOND.CPP. (Shortcut: press F3 and select the filename.)

3. Enter *only* the highlighted instructions in Listing 1-2.

4. Press Ctrl+F9 to compile, link, and run the program.

5. When prompted, enter an amount such as 123.45 and a discount rate (0.15, for example). The program displays the discounted price.

Listing 1-2: SECOND.CPP

```
/* Your second C program */

#include <stdio.h>
#include <stdlib.h>
#include <conio.h>

char Pause(void)
{
  char c;
  printf("\nPress Enter to continue...");
  while ((c = getchar()) != '\n') { }
  return c;
}
```

```c
float GetFloat(void)
{
  char buffer[80];
  gets(buffer);
  return strtod(buffer, NULL);
}

int main()
{
  float amount, discount, result;

  clrscr();
  printf("Enter amount (ex. 123.45): ");
  amount = GetFloat();
  discount = 1.0;
  while (discount >= 1.0) {
    printf("Enter discount rate (ex. 0.15): ");
    discount = GetFloat();
    if (discount >= 1.0)
      puts("Error: discount must be less than zero");
  }
  result = amount - (amount * discount);
  printf("Discounted amount == %.2f\n", result);

  Pause();   /* Wait for Enter key */
  return 0;  /* "no errors detected" */
}
```

Help! If you receive an error when compiling Listing 1-2, it's probably due to a typing mistake. Carefully check your typing. It sometimes also helps to have someone *else* go over the lines. Be especially careful to type double quotes and other punctuation *exactly* as shown. Every character must be perfect — when it comes to being finicky, compilers are worse than cats.

Let's go through what you typed line by line. There are several new elements here. The first line declares three *variables* named amount, discount, and result. A variable is a reserved place in memory that can store information of a certain type — in this case, of type float. The variables amount, discount, and result can hold *floating-point values* — data the program processes.

The first statement in the program clears the screen by calling the clrscr() function, just as in FIRST.CPP. The next line calls a C library function curiously named printf. The f in printf stands for *formatted*. The printf function outputs a formatted line of text, in this case prompting you to enter an amount. Unlike puts, which you saw in FIRST.CPP, printf does not start a new output line, so when you run the program, the cursor remains positioned after the colon and one extra space for a more natural-looking prompt.

To see the difference between the two functions, change the first instance of printf to puts; then recompile and run the program. You now enter text on the line below the prompt. If that's not what you want, change puts back to printf before continuing. Get used to making small changes like these to programs, rerun the modified code, and see what happens. *Learn to teach yourself new topics* by using the compiler to investigate a statement's semantics — in other words, the meaning or effect that a statement has.

The next line that you entered assigns the result of another function, GetFloat(), to a variable named amount. This is called an *assignment statement*:

```
amount = GetFloat();
```

Function GetFloat isn't part of the standard C library — scan SECOND.CPP and you'll find it near the middle of the listing. This is an example of a function that the program provides, but it's too early to discuss writing your own functions. For now, think of GetFloat as a *magic box* that lets users enter a floating-point value. That entry is *returned* by GetFloat and is assigned to the amount variable for use in the program.

Another variable, discount, holds the amount you enter for the discount rate. Locate the statement

```
discount = GetFloat();
```

That's another example of an assigment statement, but here, the value returned by GetFloat is deposited in discount. You have just witnessed an important principle in C programming — *the reuse of a function.* The same function, GetFloat, is used to input two values, amount and discount, into the program.

SECOND.CPP also demonstrates how to check for errors — something that even the fanciest calculators don't usually do very well. A while loop repeats the instructions between the braces, { and }, over and over *while* the value of discount is greater than or equal to 1.0. Have you ever entered a percentage, such as 25, into a calculator only to discover that you should have entered 0.25? SECOND.CPP prevents that kind of mistake by testing the value of discount. If that value is greater than or equal to 1.0, the program *repeats the prompt,* requesting that you enter a correct discount rate. Run the program and enter 25 for the discount rate to see the resulting error message.

The last two highlighted statements compute and display the result of an *expression* in another assignment statement:

```
result = amount - (amount * discount);
```

The parentheses around the subexpression, (amount * discount), force that part of the expression to be evaluated first. During evaluation, amount is multiplied times discount, and then that result is subtracted from amount. The result of *that* operation is assigned to the result variable to the left of the equal sign. C always performs multiplication and division before addition and subtraction, so you could write the preceding statement like this and it would still be correct:

```
result = amount - amount * discount;
```

The extra parentheses in the original make the expression clearer to my eyes, but you can leave them out if you wish. The compiler doesn't care one way or another.

Last but not least, the program displays the computed answer, using another printf statement with some funny-looking stuff inside the parentheses:

```
printf("Discounted amount == %.2f\n", result);
```

Remember: printf displays *formatted output.* It does that by interpreting (yes, just like a BASIC interpreter) *embedded formatting instructions* inside the first quoted string in parentheses. Look closely at that string. First comes some plain old text: *Discounted amount ==.* (A double-equal sign, ==, in C means *equals* and should not be confused with the single equal sign, which as you have seen, stands for *assignment.*) After the plain text are some weird characters that resemble the output of a modem gone bananas:

```
%.2f\n
```

Is it any wonder that C sometimes has a reputation for being cryptic? In time, you'll get used to expressions like that, but they are admittedly difficult to comprehend. Even experienced C programmers have trouble getting printf to do their bidding.

Here, the instruction %.2f literally means "format a floating-point value at this location having any number of whole number digits rounded to two decimal places." (I *told* you C was a terse language!) The \n after this instruction is a *newline escape code.* It inserts a carriage return and a line feed into the output to start a new line at the end of this one.

Look one final time at the printf statement. The formatting string is followed by a comma and the result variable:

```
printf("Discounted amount == %.2f\n", result);
```

For each formatting instruction such as %2.f embedded in the preceding string, C *inserts the value of a variable.* That statement then *inserts* the value of result at the place where the %2.f instruction appears, formatting the value according to the instruction's demands. The formatted ouput looks something like this:

```
Discounted amount == 104.93
```

That finishes this chapter's introduction to C programming and the *Type and Learn* method. In the chapters to come, you'll learn much more about C's elements, and you'll complete many more sample listings. Before turning the page, take a moment to go back through the instructions you typed in FIRST.CPP and SECOND.CPP, and be sure you understand them. In the next chapter, you learn your way around the Turbo C++ integrated environment, a necessary step before learning more about programming with C.

Chapter 2

First Things First

When programmers talk about the environment, they are not referring to holes in the ozone layer. A *programming environment* consists of editors, compilers, linkers, and other software tools used to construct programs. Before going further into C programming, you need to spend a little time getting in tune with your system's environment.

This chapter tours the Turbo C++ *integrated development environment,* or IDE, supplied with this book. It's an *integrated* environment because it rolls an editor, compiler, linker, debugger, and other tools into one ball of wax. If you know your way around PCs, you can skim this chapter — most IDE commands are intuitive, and you can easily learn them as you enter this book's sample programs. You don't have to memorize every IDE command. Just go over the ones mentioned here, and take a few moments to become familiar with the IDE's main operations.

 If you didn't install Turbo C++, follow the instructions under "How to Install Turbo C++" in Chapter 1 before continuing.

Configurations

Figure 2-1 labels the IDE's main elements. Command menus are along the top. Function key labels and messages appear in the status bar at the bottom. In between those lines, edit windows hold file contents. The sample window shows some of the lines from FIRST.CPP, which you completed in Chapter 1.

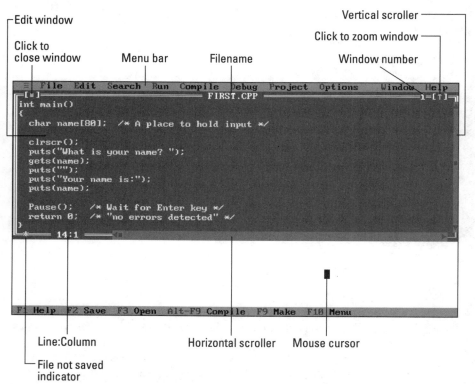

Figure 2-1 ▶ The Turbo C++ integrated development environment.

Online help

Press F1 for online help, and use the arrow keys (or a mouse if you have one) to scroll the help window's text. The IDE has extensive online help — remember to use it if you can't remember a keystroke or a command. To close the online help window, press Esc or use the mouse to click the window's close button at upper left.

The IDE also supports *context-sensitive help.* To demonstrate this feature, move the cursor to any character of the word while and either press Ctrl+F1 or click the *right* mouse button. You then receive help about C's while statement. Get in the habit of using online help to investigate unfamiliar parts of programs — it's a great way to get answers fast.

Menus and commands

Press F10 and use the arrow keys to open menus and highlight commands. As you do that, read the messages along the bottom of the screen for brief descriptions about what each command does.

To select a command, highlight it and press Enter. Or you can use the mouse's left button to open a menu and then click a command to select an operation. If you don't want to perform a command, click the mouse pointer in another menu or window, or press Esc to close a menu and return to what you were doing before.

Another way to open a menu is to press Alt and the menu's highlighted letter. For example, press Alt+F to open the *File* menu. After that, you can press a highlighted command letter (don't press Alt again, though). To use the *Get info...* command in the *File* menu, for example, press Alt+F and then G. Press Esc to close the resulting window.

Remember to press Esc if you get stuck, or if the editor misbehaves. Pressing Esc one or more times cancels any operations you may have started by accident.

You can also press selected function keys to perform commands. Function keys such as F8 and Alt+F7 are shown to the right of their menu items. Press those and other function keys to execute their commands without opening a menu. Try to memorize function keys associated with often-used commands.

The IDE can open multiple windows — press F3, for example, and open another file, SECOND.CPP. To arrange windows, drag their borders or click and drag the size button at lower left. Also try commands in the *Window* menu. You can *Zoom* windows to full screen, *Tile* multiple windows side by side, and *Cascade* them like a fanned-out deck of cards. The window with double-line borders is active — any typing or commands are directed at the active window's contents. Press F6 to make another window active, or click anywhere inside an inactive window.

If you have a mouse, you can double-click a window's top border to zoom it to a full screen. Do that a second time to restore a window to its previous size.

Directory options

The IDE has several options that you can select to customize your programming environment. Using the *Options* menu, select the *Directories...* command, displaying the dialog box (often just called a *dialog*) shown in Figure 2-2. Press the Tab key to move from field to field in this and in all other dialog windows you encounter. (You know a menu command displays a dialog if it ends with an ellipsis. *File\Open...* displays a dialog; *File\Save* does not.)

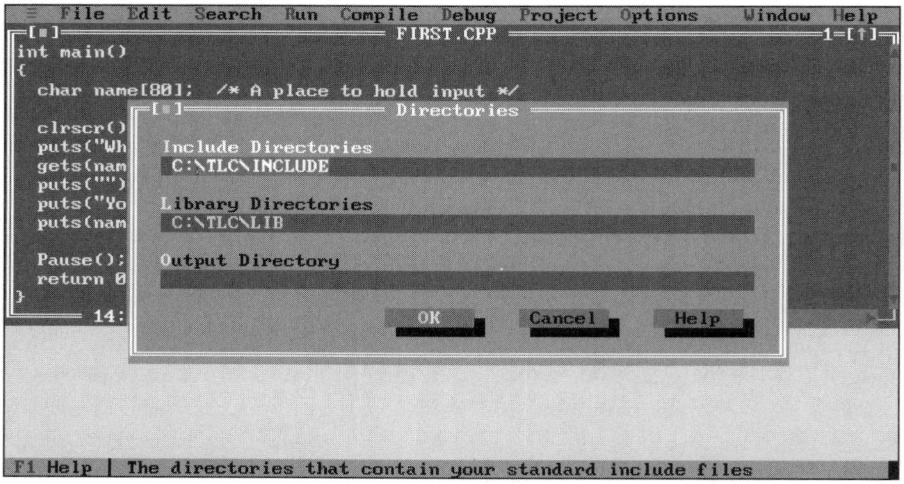

Figure 2-2 ▶ The Directories dialog box.

The first directory option, *Include Directories*, tells the compiler where to find *header files.* As you will learn in future chapters, header files contain declarations for the standard C library. Make sure the directory is set as shown here. Substitute an alternate drive and pathname if you did not install the compiler to C:\TLC.

The second directory option, *Library Directories*, tells the compiler where to find the standard C library's compiled object files. One or more of these files are linked to every C program's finished .EXE code files.

If you receive errors when compiling the programs in this book, the most likely cause is a bad pathname in one or both of the preceding directory settings. Always check those settings if the compiler reports "Unable to open include file" or if the linker complains that it can't find .OBJ files. These common problems are usually due to an improperly configured environment.

The third and final directory option, *Output Directory*, is usually blank. Enter a drive and pathname here if you want the compiler and linker to create object and executable code files in another directory. If this directory is blank, output files are placed in the current directory.

In any of those directory settings, separate multiple-directory pathnames with semicolons. *Don't insert any extra spaces.* For example, a three-directory setting (using fictitious pathnames) might look like this:

```
C:\TLC\INCLUDE;C:\HEADERS;D:\MYSTUFF\INCLUDE
```

Don't enter that now. Use a similar format in the future if you need to store header and .OBJ files in multiple locations.

Click the **OK** button or press Enter to accept your directory settings and close the *Directories* dialog. Click Cancel or press Esc to close the dialog and *not* save changes. Click *Help* or press F1 for online help about this dialog. Most dialogs have similar buttons.

Environment options

Use the *Options\Environment* command and select *Preferences...* to display another dialog, listing several options for configuring the display. If your computer has an EGA or VGA display, you might want to set Screen Size to *43/50* lines (43 lines in EGA mode; 50 for VGA). That way, you can see more of a program and you can fit more windows into the IDE.

Try other *Environment* commands to configure the mouse and editor. I won't go into each command here — the default settings are probably OK for most people. After you gain experience, use this command to set up the IDE to suit your tastes. Use the *Help* button or press F1 for descriptions about options that are unclear.

Use the *Environment\Preferences...* command in the Options menu to select which kinds of files you want the IDE to save automatically. For safety, enable *Editor files* to save changes to windows every time you select the *Run\Run* or *File\DOS* shell commands. Your selected options are saved automatically when you quit the IDE, but you also can use *Options\Save* to record them at any time.

Directory Commands

Open the *File* menu and examine the bottom five commands. Select *Change dir...* to change directories. When I suggest changing to a directory such as PART1, this is the command to use. The next command, *Print*, prints the contents of the active window. Of course, you need a printer to use the command (but you didn't need me to tell you that, right?).

Select *Get info...* to see various facts and figures about the current directory, file, and memory configuration. Programmers working on very large applications need to monitor this window. Until you get to that stage in programming, you can ignore this information.

The *DOS shell...* command is, perhaps, one of the most useful in the *File* menu. Select it to return temporarily to the DOS prompt. You can run programs, delete and copy files, format disks, and perform other chores. Meanwhile, back at the ranch, the IDE waits patiently to be reactivated. To return, type **exit**.

Don't forget to return to the IDE by typing **exit**. If you switch off your system while the IDE is still in RAM, you will lose any typing that you didn't save.

Lastly, the *File* menu's *Quit* command does the expected — it exits the IDE and returns to the DOS prompt. Experienced IDE users usually press Alt+X to quit — it's faster than selecting the menu command.

The Editor

The IDE sports a full-featured text editor with all necessary commands to write programs large and small. To try out the editor, first close all windows. (Answer *No* if you are asked to save changes.) Press F3 and select FIRST.CPP to open that file. To prevent accidentally changing the original file, copy it to a new file by selecting *File\Save as....* Type **temp** and press Enter. The editor automatically appends .CPP to the name you enter and shows the final filename at the top of the window.

To enter text in a window, just type. Move the flashing cursor by pressing the arrow keys, or click the mouse where you want to begin typing. Press Ins to toggle between inserting and overtyping. The cursor grows tall for overtyping; it shrinks down when inserting. Don't worry about hurting anything. You are typing into a temporary copy of the program, and you don't have to be too careful.

Before moving the cursor away from a line, use the *Edit\Restore line* command to undo changes to that line.

Table 2-1 lists common IDE editing keys. Try these on the sample window. Most of these same keys were used by the WordStar word processor, which was all the rage years ago in the early days of desktop computing. Although WordStar isn't used much anymore, the program's keystrokes are positioned for fast typing on keyboards with Ctrl keys to the left of A. (Many other keyboards have an option to reposition Ctrl at that location.)

Select any edit window and press F1 for a complete online list of editing keys and operations.

Here are some other hints for using the IDE editor:

▶ Hold down the Shift key while moving the cursor to highlight text. Or click and drag the mouse pointer. Double-click a line to select it. After selecting some text, use the *Edit\Cut* command to delete it to an internal buffer called the clipboard; then move the cursor to a new position and use *Edit\Paste* to reinsert the text.

▶ To copy a line (useful for typing multiple statements that differ in only a few characters), select a line and use *Edit\Copy* to save the text to the clipboard. Move the cursor and select *Edit\Paste* to insert the copied text. The text stays in the clipboard so you can paste it multiple times to different locations.

Table 2-1 ▶ IDE Editing Keys

Cursor Movement Commands

Action	Keystrokes	Alternate Function Key
Character left	Ctrl+S	Left arrow
Character right	Ctrl+D	Right arrow
Word left	Ctrl+A	none
Word right	Ctrl+F	none
Line up	Ctrl+E	Up arrow
Line down	Ctrl+X	Down arrow
Scroll up	Ctrl+W	none
Scroll down	Ctrl+Z	none
Page up	Ctrl+R	PgUp
Page down	Ctrl+C	PgDn

Insert and Delete Commands

Action	Keystrokes	Alternate Function Key
Insert mode on/off	Ctrl+V	Ins
Insert line	Ctrl+N	none
Delete line	Ctrl+Y	none
Delete to end of line	Ctrl+Q Y	none
Delete character left	Ctrl+H	Backspace
Delete character	Ctrl+G	Del
Delete word right	Ctrl+Y	none

▶ To see the text most recently cut or copied to the clipboard, select *Edit\Show clipboard*. You can use the resulting window as you can any other edit window, but the clipboard text isn't saved in a file.

▶ Press F2 frequently to save a window's contents to disk. It is especially important to save your typing before compiling and running a program. If the program *crashes* (a most unhappy event), you might have to reboot, in which case any unsaved text is gone for good.

When a window's text is not saved, an asterisk appears at the lower left corner (see Figure 2-1). To see this mark, open a new window with *File\New* and then type some text while you watch the window's bottom border.

▶ To close a window, click its close button at upper left. Or select the *Window\Close* command (or press Alt+F3). If the window contains unsaved text, a message asks permission to save the file. Answer Yes to preserve your changes; answer No to toss them away. Select Cancel if you don't want to close the window after all.

▶ To start a new file, use the *File\New* command. The file is initially named NONAME00.CPP (or something similar). To give it a more descriptive name, save the file by pressing F2 and type any name you want.

The Compiler

There are several ways to run the Turbo C++ compiler built into the IDE. You already know how to use the simplest method. Load a program into a window and press Ctrl+F9 to compile, link, and run the program. Do the same for most programs in this book.

The Compile menu is mostly for multifile projects (see the section titled "Projects" in this chapter), but the menu's commands can also be used with single file examples such as most of the programs in this book. Use *Compile to OBJ* to generate object code but not to create a finished executable file. Use *Make EXE file* to compile and link a program. Select *Link EXE file* to link object files created by the first command. Use *Build all* to recompile and link all files from scratch.

Press F9 to compile and link, but not run, a program; this is useful when you just want to check for typing errors.

The Debugger

Professional software designers wouldn't dream of programming without a good debugger at their elbows, and it's a good idea to get used to using one now. The IDE includes a built-in debugger that can help you investigate how programs work. Trust me: you won't regret the time you spend learning this important programming tool.

Think of the debugger as a kind of microscope that lets you peer inside a running program. Use the debugger's commands to examine values in memory, single-step program statements, halt programs at strategic locations, evaluate expressions, and more. As you can probably guess, a debugger's main job is helping programmers track down bugs. But a debugger also makes an ideal self-teaching tool that reveals how programs operate deep inside.

Let's try some debugger commands. First, close all open windows and then open the SECOND.CPP source file you completed in Chapter 1.

Open file SECOND.CPP in the PART1\FINISHED directory if you didn't complete that program in Chapter 1.

Don't run the program just yet. Instead, press Alt+F5 to view the output screen. Consider this to be a "read only" picture of the program's output. It *looks* like a DOS text screen (it even has a flashing cursor), but you can't type into it or issue commands here. Press Enter or another key to return to the IDE.

Single-stepping

Press F8 to compile the program if necessary and *single-step* through program statements. In a moment, you should see the first line of the program at function main highlighted. The program is now revving its engine, and the code is ready to roll as soon as you wave the green flag. Press F8 once more. Now the clrscr statement is highlighted. Press Alt+F5 to view the read-only output screen, and press any key to return to the IDE. Press F8 to execute the clrscr statement; then press Alt+F5 to view the output screen again. It is now clear.

You just observed the result of the clrscr statement by *single-stepping the program* — executing an individual command and viewing its effect. This marvelous technique slows a program's actions so you can investigate what each statement does.

For heaven's sake, don't wait for me to tell you to single step through this book's sample listings. You can press F8 to run *any* program one step at a time, slowing down the code so you can watch how it works.

If you are looking at a blank screen, press Enter to get back to the IDE. Try pressing F8 once more, followed by Alt+F5. You should see this prompt displayed by the printf statement:

```
Enter amount (ex. 123.45):
```

Press Enter to get back to the IDE. The following statement should be highlighted:

```
amount = GetFloat();
```

If not, select *Run\Program reset* (or press Ctrl+F2) to start over and then press F8 four times or until the preceding statement is selected. You'll probably have to restart programs this way from time to time after running experiments. Remember: *If you get lost, start fresh* — good advice also for other activities, not just programming.

Watching variables

To view a variable's value, insert it into a *Watch* window. First, use the arrow keys to move the flashing cursor to any character in the amount variable on the currently highlighted line. Then select the *Debug* menu's *Watches* command, which has several subcommands. Select *Add watch*. (You can execute all those commands in one easy motion by pressing Ctrl+F7.) The word amount should be listed in the *Watch Expression* input line. If not, type amount. Then press Enter to insert that variable into the *Watch* window.

If the Watch window obscures the program's statements, adjust the window sizes (use *Window\Tile*, for example) so you can see both windows at the same time.

The Watch window lists variables or other items you want to observe. At this point, the window should have a single line, amount. Let's add two more. Press Ctrl+F7, type discount, and press Enter. Do it again and add result. The window should now look like the one in Figure 2-3.

Statement to be executed next

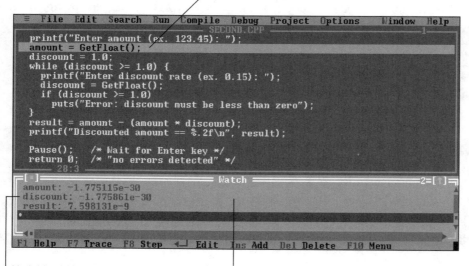

Variables being watched   Watch window

Figure 2-3 ▶ The Turbo C++ IDE with the Watch window activated.

The Watch window shows the program's three variables: amount, discount, and result. By watching these variables, you can view how statements affect them. The *Watch* window works like a magnifying lens that reveals the insides of values in memory. It's a great way to discover whether a program is storing values where you think they should go, and also for examining the results of expressions that are otherwise invisible.

Press F8 to execute the highlighted assignment statement. The output screen appears, and the program waits for you to enter an amount. Do that and press Enter. Again, the IDE reappears. Look at the amount variable in the *Watch* window. It equals the value you just entered, verifying that the assignment statement deposited its result in the correct location.

The next highlighted statement assigns the value 1.0 to discount. Keep your eye on the discount variable in the Watch window as you press F8 one time to execute the assignment. You just saw the program assign 1.0 to discount.

The program is now poised at the beginning of the `while` statement that checks whether `discount` is an appropriate value. Press F8 twice to step into this loop and execute another `printf` statement. Press Alt+F5 to examine the new prompt that statement displays. Because you are viewing the read-only output screen, you can't *respond* to the prompt; you can only view it. Press Enter to return to the IDE. You should see this highlighted statement:

```
discount = GetFloat();
```

If the preceding statement isn't highlighted, reset the program with Ctrl+F2 and press F8 until reaching that line.

Instead of pressing F8, this time you will *step into* the `GetFloat` function, which returns a floating-point value entered at the keyboard. To step into a function, press F7. The first line of `GetFloat` is now highlighted. Press F8 twice to step through this function's statements. When the output screen reappears, enter a discount rate and press Enter. Then press F8 twice more to finish the function and return to the main program.

As these steps demonstrate, the debugger automatically switches to the output screen to show the results of I/O statements. At times, the screen flashes briefly when the debugger rapidly switches screens. The flashes are normal — ignore them.

Press F8 a couple more times until this assignment to `result` is highlighted:

```
result = amount - (amount * discount);
```

Train your sights on `result` in the *Watch* window, and press F8 to evaluate and assign the expression to `result`. Finally, press F8 to execute the subsequent `printf` statement. Use Alt+F5 to view the output screen. Press Enter to return to the IDE.

Evaluating expressions

Rather than evaluate expressions as you just did by single-stepping program statements, it's often useful to enter them into the debugger's *expression evaluator*. This tool works like a programmer's calculator. To use it, press Ctrl+F4, displaying the *Evaluate and Modify* window in Figure 2-4.

Enter any expression into the *Expression* input line. For example, enter `amount` and press Enter to see that variable's value in the *Result* line. Press Tab to move to the *New Value* line, and enter a value to insert into `amount`. To accept that change, select the *Modify* button and then close the window by pressing Esc or selecting Cancel. Remember this method for inserting temporary values into variables while you investigate a program's operation.

```
≡  File  Edit  Search  Run  Compile  Debug  Project  Options    Window  Help
┌─[■]════════════════════════ SECOND.CPP ═══════════════════════2=[↑]─┐
│ float amount, discount, result;                                      │
│                                                                      │
│ clrscr();                                                            │
│ printf("E┌─[■]═══════════════ Evaluate and Modify ═══════════┐      │
│ amount = │                                                    │      │
│ discount │  Expression                                        │      │
│ while (di│  ┌───────────────────────────────┐┌─┐ ┌────────┐  │      │
│   printf(│  │ amount-(amount*0.16)          │↓ │ │Evaluate│  │      │
│   discoun│  └───────────────────────────────┘└─┘ └────────┘  │      │
│   if (dis│  Result                                            │      │
│     puts(│  ┌───────────────────────────────┐    ┌────────┐  │      │
│ }        │  │ 103.697997436523              │    │Modify  │  │      │
│ result = │  └───────────────────────────────┘    └────────┘  │      │
│ printf("D│  New Value                                         │      │
│ ═══ 32:1 │  ┌───────────────────────────────┐┌─┐ ┌────────┐  │      │
│          │  │                               │↓ │ │Cancel  │  │      │
│          │  └───────────────────────────────┘└─┘ └────────┘  │      │
│ amount: 12                                     ┌────────┐    ─1──   │
│ discount:                                      │Help    │          │
│ result: 7.598131e-9                            └────────┘          │
│ •                                                                  │
└────────────────────────────────────────────────────────────────────┘
 F1 Help │ Enter expression to evaluate
```

Figure 2-4 ▶ The IDE debugger's Evaluate and Modify window.

You can also enter complex expressions. If you closed the window, press Ctrl+F4 to bring it back, and enter `amount*discount` into the *Expression* line. When you press Enter, the *Result* line shows you the product of those two variables. You can also enter literal values in expressions. Try `amount*0.25`. The evaluator can handle any C expression.

Click the small downward-pointing arrows next to the window's input lines to open a *history list*. Rather than retype expressions, you can select them from this historical account of your recent entries. Other windows in the IDE also have history lists that work similarly.

Press Esc to close the *Evaluate and Modify* window if it's open. If you want, you may run the program to completion by pressing Ctrl+F9 — the same keys you normally press to compile, link, and run programs. The IDE knows that the program is already partially completed, so when you press Ctrl+F9 this time, the program simply continues from where it stopped. Instead of continuing a partially executed program, you can also press Ctrl+F2 to reset. In either case, notice that the function keys on the status line change to their startup settings — a good way to tell if a program is no longer operating under control of the debugger.

If you make any changes to a program while running it with the debugger, you might receive a warning that the source was modified. Answer Yes to rebuild (that is, recompile) and start over. If the change you made was inconsequential, answer No and continue debugging.

Setting breakpoints

A breakpoint stops a program at a planned location. To debug an errant program or to investigate how it operates, you can set a breakpoint at any statement. When you execute the program, it runs up to the breakpoint and halts. You can then examine variables and inspect the program's output.

> You can't set breakpoints at any *line* in a program, only at a *statement* that does something.

Let's set two breakpoints to demonstrate how they work. Load SECOND.CPP into the IDE. If that file is already open, press Ctrl+F2 to reset. Press F6 if necessary to activate the edit window. Move the cursor to the second `printf` statement — the one that prompts for a discount rate just after `while`. To set a breakpoint at that location, select the *Debug\Toggle breakpoint* command, or press Ctrl+F8. The line should turn bright red (or a shade of pale on a monochrome display). To remove a breakpoint, repeat the same command. (Press Ctrl+F8 twice to test this feature. Make sure the breakpoint is set before going on.)

Move the cursor down a few lines and set another breakpoint at the assignment to `result` above the final `printf` statement. You can set as many breakpoints as you like — there's no practical limit, but you'll rarely use more than a handful.

Now, run the program in the usual way by pressing Ctrl+F9. (The IDE compiles the program if necessary.) Enter an amount when prompted and press Enter. The program immediately halts at the first breakpoint location, pausing *before* executing the `printf` statement. Take this opportunity to add the program's three variables to the *Watch* window unless they are already there. If they aren't, press Ctrl+F7 to enter `amount`, `discount`, and `result`.

You will next execute the `printf` statement and the assignment that calls `GetFloat` so you can enter a value into `discount`. You could press F8 to do that, but try this instead: cursor down to the `if` statement two lines below, and press F4. Enter a discount rate, and press Enter. The program halts when reaching the statement at the cursor — a handy way to run a few lines and stop.

To continue running the program to the next breakpoint, press Crtl+F9. The program stops at the assignment statement. To execute that statement, press F8, and watch the value in `result` change.

> Setting a breakpoint, pressing Ctrl+F9 to run the program to that point, and pressing F8 to single-step from that location are all typical ways to debug programs piece by piece. Try these steps a few times on different statements in SECOND.CPP, and remember this technique for investigating the inner workings of programs to come.

Don't make the common mistake of assuming that debuggers are useful only for chasing bugs. As the preceding experiments demonstrate, a debugger also makes an extremely valuable tool for investigating programs and acquiring a deeper understanding of how their statements operate. You might want to go back through this section once more and repeat the step-by-step experiments. Memorize or jot down the keystrokes for stepping through statements, inserting watches, and setting breakpoints. Then, the next time you come across a program statement that looks like goon-talk from Mars, don't ponder the code; use the debugger to take it apart and see what makes it tick.

Projects

Finally, two words about projects: *ignore them* — at least, that is, for the time being. The IDE's *Project* menu is for programming multifile applications written in separate modules, an advanced technique that won't do you any good just now. While learning C, it's best to write programs in single files, so I'll postpone describing projects until later.

You might want to use the *Project* menu, however, to open files ending in .PRJ on this book's disk and from other sources. After doing that, press Ctrl+F9 to compile and link the program's individual pieces, and then run the finished code file. Use the *Close project* command to close the project before loading other programs.

 Projects store settings from the *Options* menu. After opening a .PRJ file, if you can't compile the program, make sure the Include and Library directories are set as described in this chapter.

Chapter 3

Programming with C

Learning a programming language like C can be frustrating, especially if you have to wade through a lot of definitions, rules, and references. To help you avoid "tutorial tedium," this chapter presents C snapshots in the form of *code snippets* that you enter into a program shell. As you type and compile each snippet, you learn a variety of C techniques firsthand without having to memorize a lot of details.

Start the IDE and follow the instructions in this chapter for a complete overview of the C programming language. You meet all of C's high points — enough to begin writing your own programs.

 To the armchair programmers in the audience who might be reading this book by the fireside, maybe with the TV on in the background: Sorry, friends, but you can't learn C that way. You might pick up some pointers here and there, but to get your money's worth from this book, *you must type, compile, and run the sample listings.* Invest an hour or so with this chapter to find out whether C is the right choice for you and to prepare for more advanced subjects to come.

About *main*

The main part of every C program is a *function* named `main`. Here's what the `main` function looks like when stripped to the bone:

```
int main()
{
}
```

Try this: Open a new window and type the preceding three lines. Press F2 and save the file as MAIN.CPP; then press Ctrl+F9 to compile and run. You just entered, compiled, linked, and ran a complete C program. Nothing seems to happen because the program doesn't do anything, but the source code is *syntactically* complete.

Always write syntactically complete programs. That way, even if the program's operations are unfinished, you can compile and debug other parts that are done.

The empty parentheses after `main` identify it as a function — a collection of statements surrounded by braces. Inside the braces, you can insert statements that perform the program's operations. When you run a C program, it always begins at `main`. Modify your sample program to look like this:

```
int main()
{
   return 0;
}
```

The keyword `int` stands for `integer`, an example of a C *data type.* The data type `int` can represent whole numbers such as –5, 256, or 2001. Typing `int` before `main` tells the compiler the function returns an `int` value to the process that calls `main`.

That process is the operating system, or other environment, from which you ran the program. The *return statement* inside `main` returns the value 0 to its caller. Traditionally, 0 means "no errors occurred." Any other value tells the caller something went wrong. Under most operating systems, a batch file command (`ERRORLEVEL` in DOS) can be used to retrieve a program's return value.

So far, `main` isn't all that exciting. To give the program more to do, change its lines to

```
#include <stdio.h>
int main()
{
   puts("Type and Learn C");
   return 0;
}
```

Press Ctrl+F9 to compile and run; then press Alt+F5 to view the output screen. You see the message *Type and Learn C* displayed by a `puts` (put string) statement. Press any key to return to the IDE.

You added two new elements to the developing program. First is an *include directive:*

```
#include <stdio.h>
```

That tells the compiler to include — meaning to read and insert — the lines from a file named STDIO.H. The `#include` keyword begins with a pound sign, which the compiler recognizes as a command to perform an action at compile time. The angle brackets around the filename tell the compiler to look for STDIO.H in the directory specified by the IDE's *Options\Directories...* command. Other C compilers have similar commands for specifying default include directories.

STDIO.H declares various input and output functions that most C programs use. In this case, the program calls the `puts` function declared in STDIO.H to display a line of text:

```
puts("Type and Learn C");
```

The `puts` function is not a native C command. It's just a library function. To display text and perform other I/O operations, you must include the STDIO.H header file, which makes functions like `puts` available.

To see the error you receive if you don't include STDIO.H, delete the include directive. Move the cursor to this line and press Ctrl+Y:

```
#include <stdio.h>
```

Press Ctrl+F9 to compile and run. This time, the Compiling window tells you that one or more errors were detected during compilation. When this happens, you must fix the problem before you can run the code. The compiler is the autocrat of C syntax. It won't let syntax errors pass.

Press any key to open a Message window, which states "Function 'puts' should have a prototype in function main()." (Cursor right or use the mouse to view the entire message.) A *prototype,* usually stored in a header file, tells the compiler the name and format of a library function like `puts`. Lacking the STDIO.H header file, the compiler doesn't recognize `puts`, so it issues an error.

Errors are as common as flat tires at a race track. Writing perfectly correct code every time is impossible, and most programmers need the help of a compiler to locate their mistakes. Even after 15 years in programming, it sometimes takes me several tries to find all my goofs. Errors are normal. Don't let them bug you.

Just for practice, fix the error in the program by retyping the include statement on the first line:

```
#include <stdio.h>
```

Recompile and run the program. Remember, press Alt+F5 to see the output screen.

C Shell

Every C program shares many of the same elements, some of which must be written in certain positions or arranged just so. In this section, you create an empty program — call it a *C shell* — that makes a handy test bed for tests and demonstrations. Throughout the rest of this chapter, you insert code snippets into the shell so you can experiment with different C techniques.

Listing 3-1, SHELL.CPP, is located in the PART1 directory. If you want, you can delete that file (another copy of it is in the FINISHED directory), and try your hand at typing the complete listing. This will give you typing practice, but I'll postpone discussing the program's statements until the appropriate time.

Step-by-Steps

1. Change to the PART1 directory.

2. Press F3 and load SHELL.CPP, or

3. Select *File|DOS shell*, delete SHELL.CPP, type **exit** to return, and type the entire listing for practice. Save as SHELL.CPP.

Listing 3-1: SHELL.CPP

```
/* C shell */

#include <stdio.h>
#include <conio.h>

char Pause(void)
{
  char c;
  printf("\nPress Enter to continue...");
  while ((c = getchar()) != '\n') { }
  return c;
}

int main()
{
  clrscr();
/* Insert snippets here */

Pause();
  return 0;
}
```

Although just a shell, SHELL.CPP is a syntactically complete program. You can compile and run it even though the code doesn't perform any useful tasks — it just waits for you to press Enter. From your knowledge of C so far, you should be able to recognize some of the program's elements. Try to identify these parts:

▶ The two header-file include directives

▶ The main function

▶ The main function's return statement

▶ The statement that clears the display

Comments

A *comment* is a note the compiler ignores. SHELL.CPP has several comments surrounded, or *delimited,* by the two-character symbols /* and */. The compiler ignores these symbols and all text inside. Comments are useful for identifying the purpose or name of a program:

```
/* C shell */
```

Comments can extend for several lines. The compiler skips all text between /* and */:

```
/* A relatively lengthy note
   that extends for two lines */
```

Comments often follow statements to describe their purposes. For instance, add comments to the last two statements in SHELL.CPP:

```
Pause();   /* Wait for Enter key */
return 0;  /* End program: no errors detected */
```

Type the highlighted text to describe what each statement does. You don't have to align the comments, but they usually look better that way.

C++ compilers understand a different sort of comment that begins with // and extends to the end of the line. Change the clrscr statement to

```
clrscr();  // Clear screen
```

I prefer to use C++ style comments as shown above. To compile this book's programs with an ANSI C compiler, however, change all comments to the C style shown after the next paragraph.

The comment // Clear screen *must* appear at the end of the line. In ANSI C, the preceding line is written:

```
clrscr();  /* Clear screen */
```

Comments may not be nested. This is an error:

```
/* You can't /* nest */ comments like this */
```

Many programmers insert a large descriptive comment at the beginning of source files. Add the snippet in Listing 3-2 to SHELL.CPP. Feel free to design your own comment style — you don't have to use the one shown here.

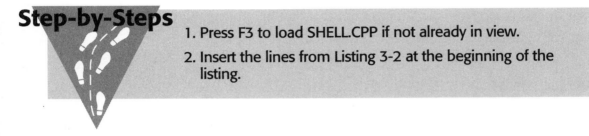

Step-by-Steps

1. Press F3 to load SHELL.CPP if not already in view.

2. Insert the lines from Listing 3-2 at the beginning of the listing.

Listing 3-2: SHELL.CPP (sample comments)

```
/* ------------------------------------------------------------ *\
**   SHELL.CPP -- Empty C program shell for tests and demos     **
** ------------------------------------------------------------ **
**                                                              **
**   Use this space to insert notes, tips, instructions for     **
**   compiling a program, and other information.                **
**                                                              **
**      Copyright (c) 1994 by Tom Swan. All rights reserved.    **
\* ------------------------------------------------------------ */
```

Locate the symbol /* at upper left that begins this large comment. Then locate the symbol */ at lower right that ends it. The compiler skips all text in between.

Variables

A variable is a named location in memory that holds a value. True to its name, a *variable* can be changed by a program statement. Declare a variable by specifying a data type and a name, ending with a semicolon:

```
int count;
```

That declares a variable count of type int, which can hold an integer value. Assign a value to count with an assignment statement. For example, this assigns 10 to count:

```
count = 10;
```

You can do both jobs in one step, declaring the variable and assigning an initial value:

```
int count = 10;
```

That has the same effect as the preceding two statements. Usually, it's a good idea to initialize new variables this way because uninitialized variables have undefined values, and if used in that state, might cause a bug. (An uninitialized variable in an accounting program, for instance, might give new customers a negative balance before they buy anything. How would you feel about being on the wrong end of *that* transaction?)

Add some variables to SHELL.CPP, inserting the snippet from Listing 3-3 after the clrscr statement.

Step-by-Steps

1. Locate the comment *Insert snippets here* in SHELL.CPP.
2. Type the lines from Listing 3-3 below the comment.

Listing 3-3: SHELL.CPP (variables)

```
int count = 10;
printf("count == %d\n", count);
count = 25;
printf("count == %d\n", count);
```

Compile and run the program. On-screen, you see

```
count == 10
count == 25
```

Remember, a double equal sign means "equals" in C. A single equal sign means "assignment." When reading programs, pronounce = as "is assigned."

```
int count = 10;
```

Read that as "int count is assigned the value ten."

Variables declared outside of main are automatically initialized to zero. Add this line just above int main():

```
int global;
```

Next, add these lines inside main() (you may delete the other statements you added from Listing 3-3):

```
printf("global == %d\n", global);
global = 123;
printf("global == %d\n", global);
```

Run the program. On-screen, you see

```
global == 0
global == 123
```

The `global` variable equals zero before it is assigned the value 123. All global variables — that is, all variables outside of `main` or any other function — are given the value 0.

C has a few other data types. For instance, you can declare *floating-point values.* Add these statements to `main` in SHELL.CPP:

```
float pi;
pi = 3.14159;
printf("pi == %f\n", pi);
```

The first line declares a variable `pi` of type `float`, which is designed to represent floating-point values. The second line assigns the fractional value 3.14159 to `pi`, storing that value inside the variable. The final line displays

```
pi == 3.141590
```

A third data type, `char`, can store characters. (Some programmers pronounce `char` as in *charred,* others pronounce it as *care.*) A `char` variable can store any symbol that you can type in your editor. Add these lines to `main()`:

```
char ch;
ch = 'X';
printf("ch == %c\n", ch);
```

The first line declares a variable named `ch` of type `char`. It can hold any symbol in the ASCII character set as commonly used on PCs. The second line assigns the character *X* in single quotes to `ch`. The last line displays the character stored in `ch`.

 Although `int`, `float`, and `char` are different data types, they are used in similar ways.

C has other data types, but with just these three basic types: `int`, `float`, and `char`, you can write lots of interesting programs.

Identifiers

Words like `count` and `pi` are *identifiers.* They are words that you invent, and you can choose any names you please. They must begin with a letter, however, but they may have any combination of letters and digits. Here are some well-formed identifiers:

```
count      average      weight      x99
```

The first three identifiers suggest their purposes; the last is OK but obscure. Always try to invent meaningful identifiers. You may use upper- or lowercase for identifiers:

```
Count     AVERAGE     Weight
```

Traditionally, however, variables are written in lowercase. C distinguishes between identifiers of different case, so these are three different identifiers:

```
Count     COUNT       count
```

Long identifiers may be clearer if broken up with underscores:

```
float distance_to_the_moon;
```

That's certainly more readable than

```
float distancetothemoon;
```

You can also use capital letters to make long identifiers easy to read:

```
float distanceToTheMoon;
```

Reserved Keywords

You can't use C's reserved keywords for your own identifiers. The compiler issues an error if you declare a variable like this:

```
int while;// ???
```

The `while` keyword is reserved for use as a C statement. You can't use it for a variable name.

For a complete list of reserved keywords, select the IDE's Help|Contents command, and choose Keywords under C++ Language. As I said before, you can't use reserved words for your own identifiers.

Symbolic Constants

A constant is a value that never changes during runtime. You've already seen *literal constants* such as these:

```
int count = 123;
float pi = 3.14159;
```

The literal constants 123 and 3.14159 are those you type directly into the program's source code.

Too many literal constants make programs difficult to maintain. Consider a situation where a program has to initialize two variables to the same starting value. First, you declare the two variables:

```
int v1;
int v2;
```

Then, somewhere else in the program, you initialize v1 and v2 with assignment statements:

```
v1 = 7659;
v2 = 7660;
```

There's nothing wrong with that — unless, that is, those statements are buried at lines 720 and 15,231 in an 18,000-line program. So you don't have to hunt for literal values to change them, it's usually best to give them *symbolic names*.

Use a #define directive to create a symbolic constant for any literal value. Like #include directives, #define is a compile-time command that has meaning only when the program is compiled. It doesn't create code or perform any work at runtime. Here's how to create a symbolic constant, START, for the literal value 7659:

```
#define START 7659
```

Only program statements end with semicolons, not directives such as #include and #define.

The compiler replaces every instance of the word START with the associated text. In other words, these statements

```
v1 = START;
v2 = START + 1;
```

are "seen" by the compiler as though they were written

```
v1 = 7659;
v2 = 7659 + 1;
```

To change the starting values of v1 and v2, you simply modify the #define directive and recompile:

```
#define START 99
```

Add a few symbolic constants to SHELL.CPP. For example, insert these three directives just under the second #include directive near the top of the listing:

```
#define PI 3.14159
#define START 9999
#define ASCII_X 'X'
```

The first line associates the digits 3.14159 with the symbol PI. The second specifies a symbolic constant START for 9999. The third identifies a character X by the name ASCII_X. Traditionally, constants are written in uppercase, optionally using underscores in multiword symbols.

When the compiler encounters a symbolic constant, it replaces the symbol with the associated text.

Also add these statements to main:

```
int count = START;
float pi = PI;
char ch = ASCII_X;
```

Each line declares a variable, using the int, float, and char types. Each variable is assigned a symbolic constant. To the compiler, these lines appear as

```
int count = 9999;
float pi = 3.14159;
char ch = 'X';
```

The symbolic constants are replaced with their associated literal values. Finally, add these statements to main, after the three you just typed:

```
printf("count == %d\n", count);
printf("pi == %f\n", pi);
printf("ch == %c\n", ch);
```

Compile and run the program. On-screen, you see

```
count == 9999
pi == 3.141590
ch == X
```

Try changing the literal constants, recompile, and run. Press F8 to single-step the program. Add the variables to a *Watch* window. Insert comments to explain each statement. Experiment!

Statements

A statement is any line in a program that, when compiled, performs a runtime action. Some of these actions have visible effects; others work behind the scenes. Displaying text is the visible result of an output statement. Assigning a value to a variable is also a statement, but its action can't be seen — except, that is, by using a debugger.

An important rule to remember is *every statement must end with a semicolon.* A semicolon *terminates* the statement. Here are three samples:

```
int count;
count = 123;
printf("count == %d\n", count);
```

The first line is a statement. It *defines* a variable `count` at runtime. By "define," I mean to "reserve space for." Technically speaking, the program source *declares* the variable, telling the compiler what `count` is. When the program runs, the statement reserves space in memory to hold `count`'s value.

The second line also is a statement. It assigns the literal value 123 to `count`, replacing any value currently there. This action takes place when the program runs.

The third and final line is a statement as well. It displays the value of `count`, an effect you can easily observe by running the program.

All three lines must end with semicolons, identifying them as statements. Enter the preceding three lines into `main`, then delete one or more semicolons, and compile to see the error you receive if you forget to terminate a statement properly.

The compiler doesn't always tell you that you forgot a semicolon because it doesn't *know* that. It merely gets confused upon continuing to compile source code that appears to belong to the *preceding* statement that wasn't properly terminated. Eventually, the compiler realizes it has gone too far, and it issues an error. If you find that behavior odd, well, so does everyone. It's just the way compilers work. When you receive strange errors, first look for obvious mistakes — misspelling a variable name, leaving out a semicolon, *inserting* a semicolon by mistake after a #define directive, and so on.

Expressions

C's capability to evaluate *expressions* is of utmost importance. An expression is composed of *operands* intermixed with *operators*. In this expression:

```
(a + b * c)
```

objects a, b, and c are operands. They might represent values entered by users or read from disk files. The symbols + (plus) and * (times) are operators. They work like function keys on a calculator.

Lone expressions like the preceding one are meaningless. They just sit there looking pretty. To use an expression, you must consider what happens to its result. One thing you can do with an expression's result is assign it to a variable:

```
answer = (a + b * c);
```

That's better. Now the result of the expression to the right of the equal sign is assigned to answer at left. Compiling the statement produces code that *evaluates the expression* at runtime and, in this case, deposits the result in a variable. That result equals the value of b times c added to a. (Multiplication and division are performed before addition and subtraction.)

Start with a fresh copy of SHELL.CPP from Listing 3-1. (Either reload the file from disk, or delete new lines you typed.) Then add the programming from Listing 3-4 to `main`.

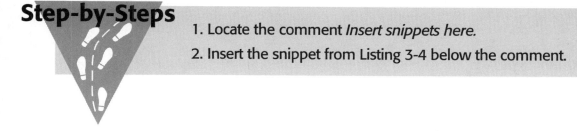

Step-by-Steps

1. Locate the comment *Insert snippets here.*

2. Insert the snippet from Listing 3-4 below the comment.

Listing 3-4: SHELL.CPP (expressions 1)

```
float distance;  // feet
float time;      // seconds

time = 14.5;
distance = 16 * (time * time);
printf("distance = %f feet\n", distance);
```

 By tradition, a single blank line separates variable declarations from other statements. The compiler ignores blank lines, but when strategically placed, they can help make programs more readable.

The lines you typed compute the distance a falling body travels in a certain time, ignoring the effects of friction, terminal velocities, bungee cords, and parachutes. In an elementary physics book, you might find this formula written as follows, with d for distance in feet and t for the time in seconds:

$$d = 16t^2$$

To translate that formula into a C statement, declare a couple of floating-point variables (`distance` and `time` will do nicely). Rewrite the expression in C:

```
distance = 16 * (time * time);
```

Compare the formula and statement. Each multiplies 16 by the square of `time` and assigns the result to `distance`. Translating formulas into C expressions is not difficult if you convert them one step at a time.

Try another formula on your own before looking at the answer in Listing 3-5. The following equation calculates the area of trapezoid A, with h for the height, a for the longer and b for the shorter parallel side:

$$A = \frac{h(a+b)}{2}$$

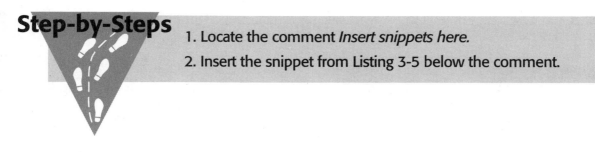

Step-by-Steps

1. Locate the comment *Insert snippets here.*
2. Insert the snippet from Listing 3-5 below the comment.

Listing 3-5: SHELL.CPP (expressions 2)

```
float area;
float height;
float aside;
float bside;

area = 56;
height = 100;
aside = 25;
bside = 14;

area = (height * (aside + bside)) / 2;
printf("area == %f\n", area);
```

As in the preceding listing, the solution declares a few variables and assigns values (change the ones shown here, if you like). The assignment statement and expression, however, are a bit more complex:

```
(height * (aside + bside)) / 2;
```

Compare that to the formula. Both multiply height times the sum of aside plus bside and then divide that product by 2. Because multiplication and division are performed before addition and subtraction, I added extra parentheses to force the correct evaluation order. The most deeply nested subexpressions in parentheses are always evaluated first. To see why parentheses are necessary, consider this *incorrect* solution:

```
height * aside + bside / 2;  // ???
```

C evaluates that expression by multiplying height times aside, then dividing bside by 2, and only then adding the two subresults. Obviously, that's wrong. Always use parentheses to tell the compiler which parts of a complex expression to evaluate first.

I promised not to have too many mathematical expressions in this book, so I'll stop here and move on. Even if math isn't your forte, though, you will undoubtedly need to translate *some* formulas into C. For practice, look up some equations in a text book and test your expression skills using SHELL.CPP.

Functions

A *function* is a collection of statements identified by name. Using a function's name in a statement *calls* the function and runs its instructions.

Functions perform actions and they can return values. Some functions come ready-to-use in the C function library. You can also write your own functions.

You have seen several examples of library functions. For instance, this statement calls clrscr to clear the screen:

```
clrscr();
```

 The clrscr function is supplied with Turbo C++, but not other C compilers. Usually, there's a function similar to clrscr to clear the display, but it may be named something else. The clrscr and other screen functions are declared in the CONIO.H header file, included into SHELL.CPP by an #include directive.

SHELL.CPP calls another function in a similar way to wait for you to press the Enter key:

```
Pause();
```

In this case, however, Pause() is a function that I wrote and inserted into SHELL.CPP. Locate this function above main. Removing its statements just for illustration, Pause() looks like this:

```
char Pause()
{
}
```

All functions, no matter how complex, are written in exactly this same way. First is the function's *return type,* char. The function *returns* a value of that type. The function's name, Pause, is an identifier that I selected. The parentheses tell the compiler Pause is a function, not a variable. The braces form a *code block* into which you can insert the function's statements.

In ANSI C, functions with empty parentheses must be declared with the keyword void. For example, the preceding function's first line must be written:

```
char Pause(void)
```

Because you are using a C++ compiler with this book, you can leave out void. If you use an ANSI C compiler, you may have to add that keyword to prevent a warning.

You can take a look at the statements inside Pause, but don't try to decipher them. You might want to single-step through the statements, however, and observe their actions. Follow these steps:

1. Set a breakpoint (Ctrl+F8) on the Pause statement near the end of main.

2. Run the program (Ctrl+F9).

3. When it stops at Pause, press F7 to *step into* the function.

4. Press F8 to single-step through Pause's statements.

In step 3, if you press F8, the debugger calls Pause, but it does not step inside the function. Press F7 to trace into a function's statements. Press F8 to call a function and stop at the next statement. Repeat step 3 both ways to see the difference.

Functions like clrscr and Pause are convenient because you can use them at many different places. To clear the screen, write

```
clrscr();
```

Similarly, to wait for a user to press Enter, insert a Pause statement:

```
Pause();
```

If you capitalize your own functions, as I did here for Pause, you tell them apart from standard library functions, all of which are spelled in lowercase.

Function Parameters and Arguments

Functions can compute expressions and return values. To alter the initial values that a function uses, you can pass it *arguments.*

Consider the typical problem of converting values among different units. For example, one nautical mile, or *knot,* equals about 1.151 statute miles. C functions can use that formula to convert between miles and knots.

Start with a fresh copy of SHELL.CPP. Add the two functions in Listing 3-6 just above int main(). All functions must be inserted outside of main and other functions. C does not permit one function to be inserted inside another.

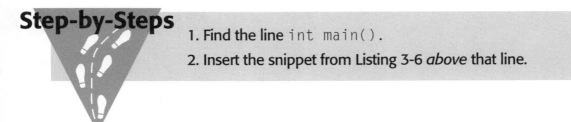

Step-by-Steps

1. Find the line int main().

2. Insert the snippet from Listing 3-6 *above* that line.

Listing 3-6: SHELL.CPP (functions 1)

```
float MilesToKnots(float miles)
{
  return miles * 0.8684;
}

float KnotsToMiles(float knots)
{
  return knots * 1.1516;
}
```

The two functions `MilesToKnots` and `KnotsToMiles` are similar in design to `Pause` but have three main differences. Each returns a `float` value, each has a declaration inside parentheses, and each returns the result of an expression.

Declarations inside a function's parentheses are called *parameters.* `MilesToKnots` declares a `float` parameter named `miles`:

```
float MilesToKnots(float miles)
```

The declaration `float miles` looks like a variable declaration, and that's exactly what it is. Inside the function, a statement can use `miles` in an expression as it can any other variable. In this case, the function returns the result of multiplying `miles` by 0.8684:

```
return miles * 0.8684;
```

That computes the equivalent knots for any value stored in `miles`. *That* value comes from another statement that calls the function. For example, insert these lines into `main`:

```
float knots;
knots = MilesToKnots(25);
printf("25 miles == %f knots\n", knots);
```

The first statement declares a `float` variable, `knots`. Next, an assignment statement calls `MilesToKnots`, passing the value 25 as an argument. Passing an argument is like throwing a ball to the function, which "catches" the value in a parameter. In this case, the function receives the argument 25 in its `miles` parameter, multiplies by the conversion factor, and returns the result. That result is stored in the `knots` variable and then displayed. On-screen, you see

```
25 miles == 21.709999 knots
```

`KnotsToMiles` works similarly but uses a different factor to convert nautical to statute miles. Insert these statements into `main`:

```
float miles;
miles = KnotsToMiles(25);
printf("25 knots == %f miles\n", miles);
```

Press F7 in the debugger to *step into* calls to the two functions described here. Add parameters `miles` or `knots` to a Watch window. Try passing different values (change 25 to 45, for example), and repeat the experiment. In each case, the function parameters receive the values you pass as arguments.

Arrays

By stacking multiple variables, you create a structure called an *array.* If you need five integers, you can create them individually:

```
int count1;
int count2;
int count3;
int count4;
int count5;
```

It's easier, however, to create one array that collects five integer values in a single package:

```
int counts[5];
```

That creates an array named `counts` big enough to hold five `int` values. Use an expression like this to assign a value to an array position:

```
counts[0] = 123;
```

The 0 inside square brackets is an *array index.* It refers to the array's first value. This statement assigns a value to the array's *second* position:

```
counts[1] = 321;
```

Some additional statements fill the rest of the array:

```
counts[2] = -1;
counts[3] = 509;
counts[4] = 543;
```

You assign values and use indexed array expressions like `counts[2]` and `counts[4]` in exactly the same way you use individual `int` variables. This, however, is a serious error:

```
counts[5] = 0;  // ???
```

The `counts` array has room for five values at indexed positions 0, 1, 2, 3, and 4 (a *total* of five indexes). The highest allowed index value is always one *less* than the array's total number, thus in this case, `counts[4]` refers to the last array element.

You can create arrays of other types, not just `int`. Here's how to declare an array of 12 `float` values:

```
float profits[12];
```

That array might hold the monthly profits in an accounting program. To display June's profits, use a statement like this:

```
printf("June profits == %.2f\n", profits[5]);
```

Careful readers might wonder if the 5 is an error, but this actually refers to the array's sixth entry. The expression profits[0] refers to the first entry (January), profits[1] to the second (February), and so on. Rather than tempt fate, it's best not to use literal index values. Instead, define a few symbolic constants. I'll do the first three; you do the rest:

```
#define JAN 0
#define FEB 1
#define MAR 2
```

Add those (and the rest of the months if you want) to SHELL.CPP after the #include directives. Then add these statements to main:

```
float profits[12];
profits[JAN] = 450;
profits[FEB] = 1250;
profits[MAR] = 789;
```

The first line declares an array of profits, big enough to hold 12 values of type float. The second line assigns 450 to the first entry in the array. For clarity, that and the next two lines use symbolic constants rather than literal index values.

Finally in main, add three output statements to display the values of each element in profits:

```
printf("January  == %.2f\n", profits[JAN]);
printf("February == %.2f\n", profits[FEB]);
printf("March    == %.2f\n", profits[MAR]);
```

Strings

A string in C is just an array of char values. You declare a string like you do any array. For example, this declares a string of 80 characters:

```
char string[80];
```

C relaxes its array syntax rules to permit assigning strings initial values. For instance, to store the string *Type and Learn C* in string, declare it like this:

```
char string[80] = "Type and Learn C";
```

Strings in C are *null-terminated* — they end with a zero byte, also called a *null character.* C adds this byte automatically to literal strings, but it's sometimes your job to make sure strings are properly terminated.

You can pass string variables to functions such as gets (get string). This waits for a user to enter a string at the keyboard and then deposits the result in string:

```
gets(string);
```

You can also pass `string` to an output function to display its value:

```
puts(string);
```

Try adding these statements to `main` in SHELL.CPP:

```
char string[80] = "Initial string";
puts(string);
printf("Enter another string:");
gets(string);
puts(string);
```

When you run the program, it first displays *Initial string*, and then it prompts you to enter another. After you press Enter, the final statement again displays `string`, showing its new value.

 Run the preceding statements in the debugger as you watch the `string` variable.

Although you may assign a string an initial value, elsewhere in the program, you can't use a similar assignment to change that value. This doesn't work:

```
string = "Not allowed!";   // ???
```

To change the string stored in the `string` array of `char`, you must call a *string function.* First, include the STRING.H header after the existing two `#include` directives:

```
#include <string.h>
```

Next, call `strcpy` to assign a different value to the `string` array:

```
strcpy(string, "New string assignment");
```

Then display `string`'s newly assigned characters:

```
puts(string);
```

These sample statements only scratch the surface of what you can do with strings. The important lessons are that strings in C are just arrays of `char`, and they must be terminated with a zero byte.

Loops

There are several types of *structured loop statements* in C, but it's too early to go into all of them in great detail. Let's take a closer look, however, at one you have seen before, `while`.

A `while` loop repeats one or more statements *while* an expression is true. It's a powerful way to execute multiple statements dozens or even thousands of times. Every `while` loop needs a *control expression* that makes the loop repeat and, most important, ensures that the loop eventually ends.

If a program keeps going when you think it should stop, a runaway loop may be the cause. Try pressing Ctrl+Break. If that doesn't work, you may have to reboot — one good reason to save your source files before running programs under development!

A simple program that counts from 0 to 9 demonstrates how to write a `while` loop. Enter these lines into `main` in a fresh copy of SHELL.CPP:

```
int count = 0;
while (count < 10) {
  printf("count == %d\n", count);
  count = count + 1;
}
```

First, the snippet declares a `count` variable of type `int`, initializing `count` to zero. Next, a `while` loop tests whether `count` is less than 10. If so, the statements in braces following that expression are executed. The first of those statements displays `count`'s value, after which the second statement increases `count` by one. Eventually, `count` becomes equal to 10, ending the loop. On-screen, you see

```
count == 0
count == 1
count == 2
count == 3
count == 4
count == 5
count == 6
count == 7
count == 8
count == 9
```

A `while` loop is frequently useful for calling a function repeatedly, perhaps passing the function different arguments on each loop. To try this, insert the `MilesToKnots` function from earlier into SHELL.CPP (unless it is still there). Add these lines just above `main`:

```
float MilesToKnots(float miles)
{
  return miles * 0.8684;
}
```

Next, add the snippet in Listing 3-7 to `main`.

Step-by-Steps

1. Locate the comment *Insert snippets here.*

2. Insert the snippet from Listing 3-7 below the comment.

Listing 3-7: SHELL.CPP (loops)

```
float miles;
float knots;
int number = 1;

while (number <= 10) {
  miles = number * 4;
  knots = MilesToKnots(miles);
  printf("%.3f miles == %.3f knots\n", miles, knots);
  number = number + 1;
}
```

The program uses three variables and a `while` loop to display a table of miles converted to knots. Running the program produces this output on-screen:

```
4.000 miles == 3.474 knots
8.000 miles == 6.947 knots
12.000 miles == 10.421 knots
16.000 miles == 13.894 knots
20.000 miles == 17.368 knots
24.000 miles == 20.842 knots
28.000 miles == 24.315 knots
32.000 miles == 27.789 knots
36.000 miles == 31.262 knots
40.000 miles == 34.736 knots
```

To produce that table, the snippet's `while` loop repeats *while* variable `number` is less than or equal to 10. Inside the loop, a `float` variable `miles` is assigned the result of the expression `number * 4`. This is typical, and you often will use a loop's control variable such as `number` in an expression inside the loop.

The second statement in the loop calls `MilesToKnots`, passing the value of `miles` as an argument. The function receives that value in its parameter and returns the equivalent value in nautical miles, assigned to a third variable, `knots`. The `while` loop displays both of the values `miles` and `knot` and then adds one to `number`.

Try altering the table's values by changing 10 to another ending value. Or set `number` to 100 initially. Change 4 to 2 or another value to modify the `miles` passed to the function. Try adding 2 to `number` at the bottom of the loop. In each case, consider what you *think* should happen; then run the program to see if you are right. If not, use the debugger to find out why the program didn't behave as you expected.

Good News

You've made it! By following this chapter, you've met most of C's major elements, and you should now be able to write your own simple programs. If you are having trouble with any subjects introduced so far, reread this and the previous two chapters before moving on.

In Part 2, you learn more about the C programming language, starting with data types and variables. As you will see, these basic tools are your primary means of feeding information to programs.

Part 2

C Inside and Out

Now that you've digested the preceding C appetizers, you're ready for the full course meal. In Part 2, you dine on the complete C language, starting with "Data Types and Variables" in Chapter 4, and moving to "Operators and Expressions" in Chapter 5. In these two chapters, you learn all about C's information-storing and processing capabilities.

Chapter 6, "Flow Control Statements and Relational Operators," adds structured statements to your growing knowledge of C. By controlling which statements execute based on various conditions, programs can make decisions, respond to user input, and execute statements in loops.

Chapter 7, "Derived Data Types," and Chapter 8, "Pointers," expand on what you know about data types, showing how to build complex variables, such as arrays, structures, and strings. You also learn about pointers — a subject that confuses and confounds every beginning programmer. Knowing how to use pointers is essential for mastering C, and I devote an entire chapter to this vital subject.

In Chapter 9, you learn how to make "Functions" do your bidding. With functions, you divide complex tasks into pieces so you can write sophisticated software while never working on more than a few relatively simple operations at a time. Chapter 10, "Advanced Programming Techniques," ends Part 2 with an explanation of how C handles directives such as `#include` and `#define`, which you have seen, and others like `#pragma` and `#error` that are new. Chapter 10 also provides additional information about pointers, structures, and variables.

After completing the chapters in Part 2, you will have feasted on most ingredients in the C programming language. So, turn the page and let's dig into the first course — "Data Types and Variables" — a program's primary means for storing and processing information.

Chapter 4

Data Types and Variables

The C programming language has a wide variety of options for storing, manipulating, and supplying facts and figures. This chapter explains C's fundamental data types and variables — a program's basic tools for keeping and using information of all kinds.

 Some sections in this and other chapters in Part 2 suggest entering code snippets into SHELL.CPP, stored in the PART2 directory. Press F3 to load that file (or a copy) into the IDE, and insert the suggested statements after the comment /*Insert snippets here*/. You may delete old additions before adding new ones.

What's in a Data Type?

Nothing, actually. Data types don't *hold* values; they describe a value's *type.* For instance, an *integer* (which goes by the name `int` in C) is the data type for whole numbers such as 1234 and –9999. The two numbers obviously have different values, but they are both integers — that is, *they have the same type.*

Don't go looking for a zillion data types in C. There are only two fundamental kinds: integer and floating-point. Integers are used for whole numbers such as –1 and 2048. Floating-point values represent fractional values such as 3.14159 and –0.06 (sometimes incorrectly termed "real numbers"). Integers can also represent ASCII characters, but in C, a character is just an integer put to special use.

So, with only two data types, C's data storage capabilities must be severely limited, right? Not exactly. Imaginative use of C's data types opens the door for countless applications, and it's your job as a C programmer to find new roles for simple types like integers and characters to play.

C's data types

Too many tables can make a programming tutorial about as interesting to read as a ship's cargo manifest, so I've purposely limited the number of tables in this book. I'll break my rule, however, to list C's data types in Table 4-1. In time, you'll learn how to use each of the table's data types. Don't bother memorizing this information. Just mark this page for future reference.

Table 4-1 ▶ Data Types

Type	Length	Range		
unsigned char	8 bits	0	to	255
char	8 bits	–128	to	127
enum	16 bits	–32,768	to	32,767
unsigned int	16 bits	0	to	65,535
short int	16 bits	–32,768	to	32,767
int	16 bits	–32,768	to	32,767
unsigned long	32 bits	0	to	4,294,967,295
long	32 bits	–2,147,483,648	to	2,147,483,647
float	32 bits	3.4×10^{-38}	to	$3.4 \times 10^{+38}$
double	64 bits	1.7×10^{-308}	to	$1.7 \times 10^{+308}$
long double	80 bits	3.4×10^{-4932}	to	$1.1 \times 10^{+4932}$

There are several key facts to learn from Table 4-1:

▶ Every data type has a name such as `unsigned long` or `double`. Programs use these names to create objects in memory that can hold values of the specified type.

▶ An object of a selected type has a fixed size. The size of a `long` value, for example, is always 32 bits — but the sizes listed in the table are strictly for the compiler supplied with this book. The same types in other versions of C on other computer systems might have different fixed sizes.

▶ Because data types have fixed sizes, they can represent values only within a defined range. A 16-bit `unsigned int` object can represent values from 0 to 65,535. To store larger values requires choosing a different data type with more bits (`unsigned long`, for example).

▶ Integer and character data types may be `signed` or `unsigned`. They are `signed` by default. Unsigned data types can hold positive values and zero; signed data types can hold zero, negative, and positive values.

Variables

Data types are used to define variables. A *variable* holds a value of a certain type. Because it occupies space in memory, a variable is called an *object.* When you *define a variable,* you reserve space for an object of a specified type.

 The term *object* has nothing to do with OOP, or *object-oriented programming,* an advanced programming technique beyond the mandate of this book. In this book, an *object* is just a space in memory big enough to hold a value of a specified type. (C++ compilers add OOP extensions and other refinements to the C language.)

To define a variable, give it a data type and a name. Here's how to define a variable named `count` of the data type `int`:

```
int count;
```

The name of the variable is `count`. Its data type is `int`. Because it's a statement, the line ends with a semicolon, as do all statements in C. Here's another example:

```
float pi;
```

That designates `pi` as a variable of the data type `float`. From Table 4-1, you know that an `int` object occupies 16 bits and can represent values from –32,768 to +32,767. A `float` object occupies 32 bits and can represent floating-point values from 3.4×10^{-38} to $3.4\times10^{+38}$.

At runtime, the declaration instructs the program to reserve space for a value of the specified type. Use an assignment to store a value in that space:

```
count = 1234;
```

You can similarly store a character constant in ch with these declaration and assignment statements:

```
char ch;
ch = 'Q';
```

Since characters are just integers, however, you can also use char variables to store small whole number values:

```
ch = 81;
```

In the ASCII character set, the letter *Q* is represented as the value 81, so the preceding two statements are functionally equivalent. Character symbols like *Q, A, P, %, $,* and + are for human consumption. Internally, they are all just integers.

Try your hand at typing a few variable definitions by completing Listing 4-1, VAR.CPP.

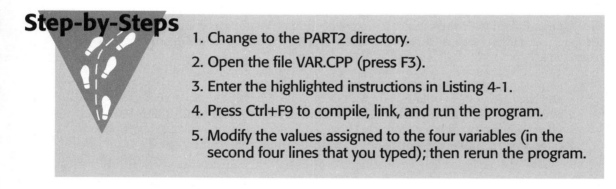

Step-by-Steps

1. Change to the PART2 directory.

2. Open the file VAR.CPP (press F3).

3. Enter the highlighted instructions in Listing 4-1.

4. Press Ctrl+F9 to compile, link, and run the program.

5. Modify the values assigned to the four variables (in the second four lines that you typed); then rerun the program.

Listing 4-1: VAR.CPP

```
/* Variables */

#include <stdio.h>
#include <conio.h>

char Pause()
{
  char c;
  printf("\nPress Enter to continue...");
  while ((c = getchar()) != '\n') { }
  return c;
}
```

```
int main()
{
  clrscr();

  int count = 1234;
  float pi = 3.14159;
  char c = 'Q';
  long distance = 45000L;

  printf("count    == %d\n", count);
  printf("pi       == %f\n", pi);
  printf("c        == %c\n", c);
  printf("distance == %ld\n", distance);

  Pause();
  return 0;
}
```

The four lines you typed declare four variables, each of a different type. The variable's names are count, pi, c, and distance. Their types are int, float, char, and long. Each declaration is a statement, so each must end with a semicolon. In addition, the statements initialize each variable using an assignment. Note that the constant 1234 is assigned directly to the int count, and that 45000L (ending in L for long) is assigned to the long distance. End constants in L to tell the compiler they are intended for use with long variables.

Delete the semicolon at the end of a variable declaration and recompile to see the error message the compiler reports. It's a good idea to make mistakes on purpose now so you'll recognize them later when you make the same errors accidentally. Take it from me — you'll make plenty of mistakes (I surely do!).

Great escapes

A char variable may represent a visible symbol like *A* or *%*, or it can specify a *control code* such as a carriage return or a tab. Use a *character escape* to specify control codes in char constants.

Character escapes begin with a backslash followed by a letter that selects a control code. The escape '\n', for instance, specifies a carriage return control code with the ASCII value 13. Table 4-2 lists C's character escape codes.

Table 4-2 ▶ Character Escape Codes

Escape Code	ASCII Value	Description
\a	0x07	Alarm (bell)
\b	0x08	Backspace
\t	0x09	Horizontal tab
\n	0x0A	New line (line feed)
\v	0x0B	Vertical tab
\f	0x0C	New page (form feed)
\r	0x0D	Carriage return
\"	0x22	Double quote (")
\'	0x27	Single quote (')
\?	0x3F	Question mark (?)
\\	0x5C	Backslash (\)
\000	000	Octal value
\xHH	0xHH	Hexadecimal value

Because the backslash is used specially, you must enter *two* backslashes to represent one. Programmers (including yours truly) often forget this fact, leading to all sorts of problems especially for strings that designate file-and pathnames:

```
#define FILENAME "C:\TSWAN\NUMERICS"  // ???
```

That's a mistake because the compiler translates \T as a tab control code and \N as a new line (carriage return or line feed). To enter backslashes explicitly, type them back to back:

```
#define FILENAME "C:\\TSWAN\\NUMERICS"
```

To enter control codes not listed in Table 4-2, use the form '\0ddd' where *ddd* is an octal value, or '\xdd' where *dd* is a hexadecimal value of the control code you want. The following statements each set a char variable ch to the ASCII value 13 decimal, the control code for a carriage return:

```
ch = '\015';  // Octal
ch = '\x0D';  // Hexadecimal
```

You may also embed control code constants in strings. Most commonly, you'll do that to start new lines in printf statements:

```
printf("Display and start new line\n");
```

Ending the quoted string with the symbol \n starts a new line after the statement writes the string to the standard output. To display double-spaced lines, use two control codes:

```
printf("Double spaced output\n\n");
```

Keep in mind that the newline escape code represents a line feed control code, not a carriage return (\r). The two codes are often confused.

A handy trick is to *begin* a string with a new line:

```
printf("\nStart on new line");
printf("\nAlso start on new line");
```

After the second statement, the cursor is positioned after the *e* in *line,* which might be useful for arranging data on-screen just as you want.

Don't confuse string constants with character constants. A string, as you will learn in future chapters, is really an array of char variables, strung together like pearls on a string, and ending with a *null* (ASCII zero). The following are *not* equivalent:

```
#define ACHAR 'A'
#define ASTRING "A"
```

The first line symbolizes a character constant 'A'. The second represents a string "A". They may seem to do the same thing, but the character is a single integer value. The string is a character ending in a null. Internally, "A" is represented as *two* characters: 'A' and the control code '\0x0'. Thus 'A' takes one byte; "A" takes two.

A string might also have no characters, but a char variable always has one. This creates a *null string:*

```
#define NULL_STRING ""
```

Though it may seem silly to have a string with nothing in it, the construction is more useful than you may imagine. For example, you can use a null string to display a blank line with the puts function:

```
puts("");   // Start a new line
```

A *null character* is one that specifies the ASCII control code zero:

```
#define NULL_CHAR '\0x0'
```

Another useful trick is to concatenate string constants simply by writing them side by side. This definition:

```
#define ALPHA_STRING "abc" "def" "ghi"
```

is the same as

```
#define ALPHA_STRING "abcdefghi"
```

You may find concatenation of string constants useful in cases where you need to combine two or more string constants:

```
#define FIRST_NAME "Santa"
#define LAST_NAME "Claus"
```

If you use those two string constants together, the compiler joins them into one string:

```
puts(LAST_NAME ", " FIRST_NAME);
```

Although that statement appears to write three string objects, it actually writes only one, displaying *Claus, Santa* on-screen.

Type qualifiers

Prefacing int with one of four qualifiers specifies short, long, signed, or unsigned data types. The qualifiers short and long may be used alone or in front of the keyword int:

```
short int shortCount;
long int longCount;
```

The first line declares shortCount as type short int. The second line declares longCount as type long int. The int keyword is redundant, so it's usually left out. Most C programmers write the preceding two lines as

```
short shortCount;
long longCount;
```

ANSI C imposes these rules on int, short, and long objects:

▶ A short or int object must occupy at least 16 bits (two bytes).

▶ A long object must occupy at least 32 bits (four bytes).

▶ A short object may be no larger than an int.

▶ An int object may be no larger than a long.

Except for those rules, the exact sizes of int, short, and long objects are up to the compiler author. In one compiler, an int might be 16 bits long. In another, it could occupy 32 bits. Because of the potential for different integer sizes among C compilers, it's best to write programs that do not assume specific sizes for int, short, and long objects. You may do that, however, (and sometimes you must) if you are writing programs for a single computer or operating system.

The int, short, and long data types may additionally be prefaced with the keywords signed or unsigned. Signed values may be positive, zero, or negative. Unsigned values may be only zero or positive. For example, this declares countDown as a signed int variable:

```
signed int countDown;
```

Because the `int`, `short`, and `long` data types are `signed` by default, you'll never use `signed` like that. To declare a `signed` integer, just write

```
int countDown;   // Same as preceding statement
```

To declare an `unsigned` integer, use this statement instead:

```
unsigned int countDown;
```

Integer constants like 1234 and –9876 are signed by default. To specify an unsigned integer constant, end it with a capital *U*:

```
unsigned int level = 5256U;
```

Specify unsigned long constants like this:

```
unsigned long level = 442524UL;
```

Variable names

The variables in VAR.CPP are just for show, but notice how their names suggest their possible uses. Choosing good variable names is something of an art in programming. A variable named `temperature` has an obvious meaning, but the purpose of one named `x29g` is no clearer than a muddy river. Always choose variable names that describe their purposes. Your programs will be easier to maintain and understand, especially years from now when they need revision.

You may use upper- or lowercase letters and digits for variable names, but they must begin with a letter. A variable may be named `colt45`, for instance, but not `96tears`. As a rule, C programmers use lowercase for variable names, but that's only a tradition, not a requirement.

To make long variable names more readable, you may embed underscores in them:

```
int miles_to_go_before_I_sleep;
```

That's certainly more readable than

```
int milestogobeforeIsleep;
```

You might also use a mix of upper- and lowercase letters to make long names more readable. This style is sometimes called *camel caps* because of the "humps" in the capital letters (by tradition, the first letter is still in lowercase):

```
int milesToGoBeforeISleep;
```

Here are some other useful tips for identifiers:

▶ Try to keep names shorter than about 31 or 32 characters. (The compiler packed with this book recognizes names up to 32 characters long.) Early C compilers considered only the first eight characters of an identifier so that `countABC` and `countABCDEFG` were "seen" as identical names. Fortunately, few modern compilers are so restrictive.

▶ Separate multiword identifiers with underscores, or as I have suggested, use capital letters to make long names readable. Any of the following styles is acceptable, but for consistency, choose a favorite and stick to it (I prefer the last one):

```
int averagescore;
int average_score;
int averageScore;
```

▶ Never preface variables with an underscore except to refer to an existing name in the standard library (or one purchased from another vendor). Leading underscores, as in `_argument`, are sometimes used in libraries to minimize conflicts with your own identifiers. If you never precede an identifier with an underscore, you'll never accidentally redefine a name in a library file.

▶ Case is significant in C. The following three statements appear similar, but they create three *different* variable names:

```
int count;
int Count;
int COUNT;
```

Initializing variables

Defining variables merely reserves space for them in memory. Before using variables, you must *initialize* their values; otherwise, they will equal whatever was previously stored in their memory locations. To initialize a variable, assign it a value, as you did in VAR.CPP. This statement assigns the integer value 1234 to the `count` variable:

```
count = 1234;
```

A variable may hold only one value at a time, but that value may change as often as necessary. When you assign a new value to a variable:

```
count = 43;
```

the assignment *replaces* the value currently held by `count`. There is no limit to the number of times you can assign values to variables.

You can also assign the value of one variable to another. Add the following statement to VAR.CPP:

```
distance = count;
```

That assigns `count` to `distance`, after which both variables equal the same value. Make this change, recompile, and run the program. Notice that `distance` and `count` are now equal.

If you received the error message *undefined symbol,* you probably added the preceding statement *before* declaring `distance` or `count`. Variables must be declared before they can be used. To fix the problem, move the statement *below* the declarations.

Values assigned to variables must be *type-compatible.* To see the results of using incompatible data types, change `count`'s assignment to

```
count = distance;
```

When you compile the program, the compiler warns you that the *conversion may lose significant digits.* Take all such warnings seriously! It means you have assigned a value of a relatively large data type to an object of a smaller type. In this case, `distance` holds a 32-bit `long` value. Assigning that value to the 16-bit `int count` is acceptable only if the *value* of `distance` is within the range defined for the `int` data type (refer back to Table 4-1). Because a variable's value is determined at runtime, the compiler can't check whether the assignment is correct, so it issues a warning.

Whenever you receive a warning about a possible loss of significant digits, unless you are 100 percent positive that the assigned value is within the proper range of the target object's data type, you should take steps to correct the error, or a serious bug could develop. One solution is to make both variables the same type:

```
long count;
long distance;
```

You can always safely assign the value of identically typed variables to one another. When it isn't convenient to modify a variable's data type, you can sometimes get around the compiler's warning by using a *type cast expression:*

```
count = (int)distance;
```

Prefacing an object's name with a data type in parentheses tells the compiler to convert the value of the named object to the specified type. You are in effect saying "I know that `distance` is a different type, but treat it as an `int` value anyway." The compiler obeys your command without question — so don't use type casts carelessly!

Speaking of assignments, here's a handy shorthand trick for defining and initializing multiple variables. These statements create three `int` variables:

```
int i;
int j;
int k;
```

Rather than type each definition on a separate line, you can string them together, separating the variable names with commas and ending the statement with a semicolon:

```
int i, j, k;
```

That has the same effect as the preceding three statements. You can also use a similar trick to assign values to multiple variables. Of course, you can initialize i, j, and k to zero in three separate statements:

```
i = 0;
j = 0;
k = 0;
```

But it's easier to assign the identical value to each variable by stringing them together with equal signs:

```
i = j = k = 0;
```

Constants

A *constant* is the exact opposite of a variable. As its name suggests, *a constant is a value that never changes.* It's useful for defining minimum or maximum values, copyright notices, program titles — any data that doesn't change at runtime.

There are three kinds of constants in C — literal, symbolic, and object — described in the next sections.

Literal constants

A *literal constant* is a value typed directly in a program statement or expression. The integer value 1234 is a literal constant. So is 3.14159 and the string "Bumblebees can't fly".

You can choose to create literal constants in a variety of formats. For example, you can use decimal, octal, or hexadecimal notation for integer values. These statements assign the identical value in different forms to an int variable named max:

```
max = 255;    /* decimal */
max = 0xFF;   /* hexadecimal */
max = 0377;   /* octal */
```

Begin decimal (base 10) integers with a digit from 1 to 9. Begin hexadecimal (base 16) integers with 0x or 0X. Begin octal (base 8) integers with a leading zero. Decimal integers, of course, use the digits 0 through 9. Hexadecimal integers use 0 through 9 plus the letters A, B, C, D, E, and F (in upper- or lowercase). Octal integers use the digits 0 through 7.

Long integer constants should end with a capital *L*, distinguishing them from int values:

```
long population;
population = 655982L;
```

You can write floating-point constants in decimal or scientific notations. In decimal, pi might be represented as

```
float pi;
pi = 3.14159;
```

Scientific notation is useful for conveniently expressing very large or small values. Astronomical software, for example, might need to store large distances:

```
float distanceToPlanet;
distanceToPlanet = 4300000000.0;
```

That sets `distanceToPlanet` to four billion, three hundred million miles — just next door in astronomical terms. When your're typing large or small values in decimal, however, a missed or extra zero is literally an error of magnitude. Scientific notation reduces the possibility of making a mistake:

```
distance = 4.3E+09;
```

The expression `4.3E+09` is the same as the mathematical notation 4.3×10^9. To form the decimal equivalent of a value in scientific notation, move the decimal point right by the exponent value — nine places in this example. Move the decimal left for negative exponents. These statements create and set a `float` variable named `measurement` to the value 0.0000000043:

```
float measurement;
measurement = 4.3E-09;
```

A string constant is any text that is surrounded, or *delimited,* by double quote marks. Strings in C require special handling, so I'll skip over them for now. (See Chapter 7, "Derived Data Types," for more about strings.) VAR.CPP uses strings to print labels in its `printf` statements:

```
printf("distance == %ld\n", distance);
```

Character constants are single letters surrounded by single quote marks. These statements define a `char` variable and assign it the letter *Q:*

```
char ch;
ch = 'Q';
```

The `char` data type is actually an integer from 0 to 255 — the full range of extended ASCII values. Because characters are stored internally as integers, you can use `char` to store small values:

```
char byte;
byte = 0x8E;
```

Or you can assign decimal or octal values:

```
byte = 255;
byte = 071;
```

Because characters are represented as integers, they can be signed or unsigned. You might, for example, represent signed bytes in the range of –128 to +127 like this:

```
signed char byte;
byte = -87;
```

Generally, characters should be unsigned; small integers can be signed or unsigned. It doesn't make much sense to represent ASCII characters using `signed char` variables.

For practice with literal values, finish Listing 4-2, LITERAL.CPP.

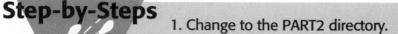

Step-by-Steps

1. Change to the PART2 directory.

2. Open the file LITERAL.CPP.

3. Enter the highlighted instructions in Listing 4-2.

4. Press Ctrl+F9 to compile, link, and run the program.

Listing 4-2: LITERAL.CPP

```
/* Literal Constants */

#include <stdio.h>
#include <conio.h>

char Pause()
{
  char c;
  printf("\nPress Enter to continue...");
  while ((c = getchar()) != '\n') { }
  return c;
}

int main()
{
  clrscr();

  int int1, int2;
  long long1, long2;
  float float1, float2;
  char char1, char2, char3;

  int1 = 99;
  int2 = 0xFF01;

  long1 = -68741L;
  long2 = 0xFFFF0001L;
```

```
    float1 = 3.14159;
    float2 = 1.5E04;

    char1 = 'C';
    char2 = 15;
    char3 = 0xF1;

    printf("int1 == %d\n", int1);
    printf("int2 == %#x\n", int2);
    printf("long1 == %ld\n", long1);
    printf("long2 == %ld\n", long2);
    printf("float1 == %f\n", float1);
    printf("float2 == %E\n", float2);
    printf("char1 == %c\n", char1);
    printf("char2 == %d\n", char2);
    printf("char3 == %c\n", char3);
    Pause();
    return 0;
}
```

Symbolic constants

Perhaps you realize that 3.14159 is the value of pi, but a value like 130000 might mean anything. It's best to give names to values so you can use them symbolically. Do that by using #define directives:

```
#define PI 3.14159
#define ANDROMEDA 130000
```

Those directives give the literal value 3.14159 the name PI, and the literal value 130000 the name ANDROMEDA. These names are not variables — they are just symbols that the compiler understands to mean something else. The symbols can be used anywhere their literal values might be appropriate:

```
long galaxyDiameter;
galaxyDiameter = ANDROMEDA;
```

The symbolic constant ANDROMEDA represents the diameter of the Andromeda galaxy — a fact that you can easily determine just by reading the program's well-chosen names.

A #define directive has three parts: the #define keyword, a name, and a value. The name is traditionally typed in uppercase. One common use for #define is to designate a maximum value:

```
#define MAX 100
```

The program can then use MAX in many places:

```
int i, j, k;
i = MAX;
j = MAX * 2;
k = MAX / 2;
```

To alter the value used in the three expressions, you can simply change the value associated with the MAX symbol:

```
#define MAX 200
```

Recompiling the program automatically inserts 200 into the three expressions. If you had used literal values instead of the symbolic MAX constant, you would have to make three changes instead of one. In large programs with thousands of statements, symbolic constants can save a lot of wasted time and effort.

The #define directive does not "define" an object. It defines a symbolic name for a literal value. When the compiler encounters a symbolic name such as MAX, it replaces that symbol with 200, just as if you had typed the number directly.

Finish Listing 4-3, DEFINE.CPP, for practice entering and using symbolic constants:

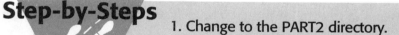

Step-by-Steps

1. Change to the PART2 directory.
2. Open the file DEFINE.CPP (press F3).
3. Enter the highlighted instructions in Listing 4-3.
4. Press Ctrl+F9 to compile, link, and run the program.

Listing 4-3: DEFINE.CPP

```
/* Symbolic constants */

#include <stdio.h>
#include <conio.h>

#define MAX 100
#define PI 3.14159
#define MYNAME "Tom"
#define YOURNAME "Gertrude"
```

```
char Pause()
{
  char c;
  printf("\nPress Enter to continue...");
  while ((c = getchar()) != '\n') { }
  return c;
}

int main()
{
  int count;
  count = MAX;

  clrscr();
  printf("count     == %d\n", count);
  printf("MAX       == %d\n", MAX);
  printf("MYNAME    == %s\n", MYNAME);
  printf("YOURNAME  == %s\n", YOURNAME);
  Pause();
  return 0;
}
```

Object constants

C's third kind of constant doesn't have an official name, but I call them *object constants*. Some programmers call them *typed constants*. They are a cross between a variable and a literal constant. Like variables, they occupy space in memory, but like constants, their values cannot be changed.

Create an object constant by preceding a variable definition with the keyword `const` and assigning an initial value, all in one step:

```
const int Max = 500;
```

The value 500 is stored in a location reserved for an `int` object named `Max`. You may not change that value; you can use it only in "read-only" fashion. For example, you can assign `Max` to an `int` variable:

```
int count;
count = Max;
```

But you can't change `Max` to another value. This is not allowed:

```
Max = 99;  // ???
```

Finish Listing 4-4, OBJECT.CPP, to practice typing and using object constants.

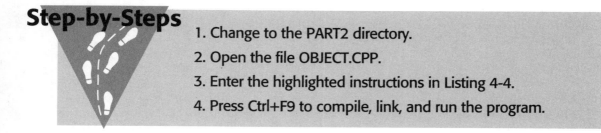

Step-by-Steps

1. Change to the PART2 directory.
2. Open the file OBJECT.CPP.
3. Enter the highlighted instructions in Listing 4-4.
4. Press Ctrl+F9 to compile, link, and run the program.

Listing 4-4: OBJECT.CPP

```
/* Object constants */

#include <stdio.h>
#include <conio.h>

const int Max = 100;
const float Pi = 3.14159;

char Pause()
{
  char c;
  printf("\nPress Enter to continue...");
  while ((c = getchar()) != '\n') { }
  return c;
}

int main()
{
  int count;
  count = Max;

  clrscr();
  printf("count == %d\n", count);
  printf("Max    == %d\n", Max);
  printf("Pi     == %.5f\n", Pi);
  Pause();
  return 0;
}
```

The first line you typed creates an `int` object constant named `Max` and initializes the object to 100; the second line creates a `float` object constant named `Pi` and initializes it to 3.14159. Use object constants anywhere their values might be used. Inside `main`, you created an `int` named `count` to which you assigned the value of the object constant `Max`.

Object constants are particularly valuable when used along with functions — but more on that in another chapter. Most C programmers use symbolic constants created by `#define` rather than object constants as shown here.

Sizes of typed variables

To determine the size of a variable, use the `sizeof` operator, which looks like a function call. Place the target object in parentheses. This statement, for example, assigns the size in bytes of a `long` integer variable `count` to an `int` variable `countSize`:

```
long count;
int countSize;
countSize = sizeof(count);
```

Using the compiler supplied with this book, the last line sets `countSize` to 4, the number of bytes occupied by a `long` integer variable.

As I mentioned, because variables are fixed in size, the values they can hold are limited in range. Include the LIMITS.H header file to determine the minimum and maximum values you can store in a variable of a specific type. The file declares various constants such as `INT_MAX` that you can use to determine the minimum and maximum values for all integer data types. (Unsigned type minimums are zero and therefore have no constants.) For example, these statements set `maxInt` to the maximum value that an `int` variable can represent:

```
#include <limits.h>
int maxInt = INT_MAX;
```

Complete Listing 4-5, LIMITS.CPP, for a useful benchmark program that determines the sizes and value ranges of integer data types for any ANSI C compiler. Figure 4-1 displays the output of LIMITS.CPP.

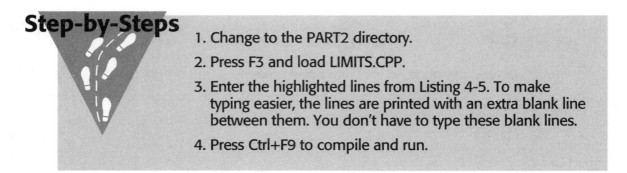

Step-by-Steps

1. Change to the PART2 directory.

2. Press F3 and load LIMITS.CPP.

3. Enter the highlighted lines from Listing 4-5. To make typing easier, the lines are printed with an extra blank line between them. You don't have to type these blank lines.

4. Press Ctrl+F9 to compile and run.

Listing 4-5: LIMITS.CPP

```
/* Limits */

#include <stdio.h>
#include <conio.h>
#include <limits.h>

char Pause()
{
  char c;
  printf("\nPress Enter to continue...");
  while ((c = getchar()) != '\n') { }
  return c;
}

void print(char* s, int size, long min, long max)
{
  printf("%s%7d%13ld  %lu\n", s, size, min, max);
}

int main()
{
  clrscr();

  puts("C Data Types and Sizes\n\n");

  puts("============================================");
  puts("Type              Size      Minimum  Maximum");
  puts("============================================\n");

  print("char          ", sizeof(char), CHAR_MIN, CHAR_MAX);

  print("signed char   ", sizeof(signed char), SCHAR_MIN, SCHAR_MAX);

  print("unsigned char ", sizeof(unsigned char), 0, UCHAR_MAX);

  print("short         ", sizeof(short), SHRT_MIN, SHRT_MAX);

  print("unsigned short", sizeof(unsigned short), 0, USHRT_MAX);
```

```
    print("int             ", sizeof(int), INT_MIN, INT_MAX);

    print("unsigned int   ", sizeof(unsigned int), 0, UINT_MAX);

    print("long            ", sizeof(long), LONG_MIN, LONG_MAX);

    print("unsigned long  ", sizeof(unsigned long), 0, ULONG_MAX);

    Pause();
    return 0;
}
```

```
=================================================
Type              Size     Minimum  Maximum

=================================================
char               1          -128  127
signed char        1          -128  127
unsigned char      1             0  255
short              2        -32768  32767
unsigned short     2             0  65535
int                2        -32768  32767
unsigned int       2             0  65535
long               4   -2147483648  2147483647
unsigned long      4             0  4294967295
```

Figure 4-1 ▶ LIMITS.CPP displays this table of integer sizes and ranges.

Floating-Point Data Types

If math is your forte, you'll probably use C's floating-point types frequently, but everyone should master them. The first rule to remember is that all floating-point types are signed — you can't use the `signed` or `unsigned` keywords to define `float`, `long`, or `long double` variables.

Most of the time, you should use the relatively small, and therefore less precise, `float` data type only for rough approximations, to save space in large arrays, and when accuracy isn't too important. Other times, `double` or `long double` data types provide better precision because, due to their larger sizes, they can represent a greater number of significant digits. Keep in mind, however, that floating-point values are subject to round-off errors. If you count your chickens with floating-point variables, you may get plucked by your customers when the results aren't exact to the last penny. In general, use integers to count things; use floating-point for measurements, fractions, and approximations. Floating-point objects can also hold very large and small values that are beyond the limits of C's integer types.

Define floating-point values as you do other objects:

```
float f1;
double f2;
long double f3;
```

Always use a decimal point to assign literal constants to floating-point objects:

```
f1 = 3.14159;
f2 = 0.5;
f3 = 10.0;
```

As I mentioned, you can also write large and small values more conveniently using scientific notation:

```
f3 = 4E-7;
```

That's equivalent to assigning 4×10^{-7} to f3.

For most programs, the double type offers the best compromise between accuracy and speed. Larger variables take longer to process in expressions, so it's best to reserve the long double type for critical applications where accuracy is essential.

Applications that need to determine the limits of floating-point precision should include the FLOAT.H header file and use its many constants, such as DBL_MIN, LDBL_MAX, and others. These statements, for example, assign the smallest possible positive double value to a variable:

```
#include <float.h>
double f = DBL_MIN;
printf("f == %g", f);
```

The last line displays the minimum value that a double value can accurately represent:

```
f == 2.22507e-308
```

That about does it for data types and variables. In the next chapter, you put two and two together — literally — when you examine how to combine variables using expressions.

Chapter 5

Operators and Expressions

Like Chicago in the roaring twenties, C has more than a few slick operators. You've already seen some of C's most common operators — the assignment operator (=) for example, and the math operators: multiply (*), divide (/), add (+), and subtract (-). Others include unary, increment, decrement, and bitwise operators that you can use to do a "fancy number" on C expressions.

C's Operators

In this chapter, you meet all of C's operators. There are four types:

- ▶ Arithmetic operators (+, -, *, /, and %)
- ▶ Unary operators (+ and -)
- ▶ Increment and decrement operators (++ and - -)
- ▶ Bitwise operators (&, |, ^, <<, >>, and ~)

The following sections introduce C's operators. After that, I show how to use them in expressions.

What do operators do?

Operators perform work on their operands in precisely defined ways. You, of course, realize that that the plus operator (+) adds two values:

```
c = a + b;
```

What some programmers find strange, however, especially with bitwise operators, is that *all* C operators are used similarly. For example, a bitwise SHIFT-LEFT operator (<<) looks odd, but in an expression, it is used just like plus:

```
c = a << b;
```

Rather than add a and b, the << operator shifts the bits in a left by the number of times specified by b. The shifted quantity is then assigned to c.

C also provides several *relational operators,* but I'll postpone talking about them in detail until the next chapter. Relational operators are valuable for determining facts about objects such as whether one value is greater than another. Even so, relational operators are used in the same basic way as all other operators. This statement, for example, assigns false (represented as the integer 0) to c if a is greater than or equal to b, or it assigns true (represented as 1 or another non-zero value) if a is less than b:

```
c = a < b;
```

The < symbol means "less than." If a is less than b, the expression a < b is true. If a is greater than or equal to b, the expression is false.

Arithmetic operators

You've already seen examples of the arithmetic operators: multiply (*), divide (/), add (+), and subtract (-). A fifth operator (%), *modulo,* gives the remainder after division of two integer operands (it can't be used with floating-point objects). This assigns to c the remainder of the division a/b:

```
c = a % b;
```

To experiment with arithmetic operators, load a copy of SHELL.CPP from the PART2 directory into the IDE, and try some of the following expressions. First, declare a couple of variables inside function main below the comment *Insert snippets here:*

```
int result, op1, op2;
```

Use op1 and op2 for operands, and assign the result of an expression to result. For example, add these lines to the program:

```
op1 = 567;
op2 = 16;
result = op1 / op2;
```

To display the division's result, add this line just above the `Pause` statement in SHELL.CPP:

```
printf("result == %d\n", result);
```

Try other expressions, changing / to any arithmetic operator. Experiment with different operand values. You might also use floating-point values:

```
float result, op1, op2;
```

In that case, use this statement to display `result`'s value:

```
printf("result = %f\n", result);
```

Unary operators

Arithmetic operators are *binary* because expressions like a+b require two operands. *Unary operators* operate on single operands. If a and b are integer or floating-point objects, this line assigns the arithmetic negation of a to b:

```
b = -a;
```

If a equals 10, b now equals –10, and a is unchanged. If a equals –123, `-a` equals 123. You can also precede values with unary +:

```
a = +b;
```

That's the same as setting a equal to b, so there's not much point in using unary plus:

```
a = b;   // Same as preceding statement
```

By the way, `sizeof`, which you met in the preceding chapter, is not a function; it's a unary operator, a fact that many programmers don't seem to realize. This assigns the size in bytes of an object b to a:

```
a = sizeof(b);
```

Because it's an operator, `sizeof` can be used without parentheses:

```
a = sizeof b;
```

Usually, however, extra parentheses are added for clarity. Unlike any other operator, a `sizeof` operand may be a data type name:

```
a = sizeof(long);
```

Or it may be a variable:

```
a = sizeof(myCount);
```

Using a fresh copy of SHELL.CPP, try the following snippets to experiment with C's unary operators:

```
int result, op1;
op1 = 123;
result = -op1;   // Unary minus
printf("op1 == %d\n", op1);
printf("result == %d\n", result);
printf("sizeof result == %d\n", sizeof(result));
```

Increment and decrement operators

If there was a popularity contest for elements in C, the increment (++) and decrement (--) operators would win the grand prize. These nifty symbols — you can call them *plus-plus* and *minus-minus* — add or subtract one from their operands in ways that are unique among programming languages.

To add one to an integer object (the operators cannot be used with floating-point values), preface the object's name with ++:

```
int value = 123;
++value;
```

That sets value to 124. To subtract one, preface the object's name with --:

```
int value = 123;
--value;
```

That sets value to 122. In both cases, the examples use *prefix notation* to increment and decrement an operand. You may also use *postfix notation,* attaching the operators behind their operands:

```
int value = 123;
value++;
```

Again, that sets value to 124. This sets it to 122:

```
int value = 123;
value--;
```

When used as shown here, it doesn't matter whether the operators precede or follow their operands. The results are the same. But when those results are assigned to *another* object, operator placement becomes critical. That's because in addition to affecting their operand values, increment and decrement expressions also have values. A few examples demonstrate this important concept. Start with a couple of integer variables:

```
int value;
int result;
```

As you know, you can assign the value of one variable to another:

```
result = value;   // Assign value to result
```

On the one hand, `value` is an object that stores an integer quantity in memory. When written in a statement, however, `value` is more correctly thought of as an *expression* that produces a value. Likewise, in addition to performing work on the `value` object, `++value` and `value++` also have values as expressions. The following assignment, for instance, increments `value` and assigns the incremented integer to `result`:

```
result = ++value;
```

That's functionally equivalent to these individual statements:

```
value = value + 1;   // Increment value by one
result = value;      // Assign value to result
```

Written in prefix notation, `++value` *first* increments `value`; then the expression is evaluated. As an expression, `++value` equals the incremented result. Next, consider this:

```
result = value++;
```

Now, `value` is first assigned to `result`; then `value` is incremented. The statement works as though you had written it using the same two steps as before, but in reverse order:

```
result = value;      // Assign value to result
value = value + 1;   // Increment value by one
```

Using postfix notation, the expression `value++` is evaluated *before* the operand is incremented. As an expression, `value++` equals the unincremented result.

The decrement operator works in the same way, but of course, it subtracts one from its operand. Work through the following samples until you understand them thoroughly. These set `result` to 10 and `value` to 9:

```
value = 10;
result = value--;
```

These set both `value` and `result` to 9:

```
value = 10;
result = --value;
```

For some more practice using increment and decrement operators, add the statements in Listing 5-1 to SHELL.CPP.

Step-by-Steps

1. Locate the comment *Insert snippets here* in SHELL.CPP.

2. Type the lines from Listing 5-1 below the comment.

3. Before running the program, jot down expected values of `result` for each group of expressions; then press Ctrl+F9 to check your guesses.

Listing 5-1: Add to SHELL.CPP

```
value = 10;
result = ++value;
printf("result == %d\n", result);

value = 10;
result = value++;
printf("result == %d\n", result);

value = 10;
result = --value;
printf("result == %d\n", result);

value = 10;
result = value--;
printf("result == %d\n", result);
```

One final note about increment and decrement operators: if the following two lines are equivalent, you may wonder, why use one over the other?

```
result = result + 1;   // Don't do this
result++;              // Do this instead
```

In all cases, the second form is preferred; the first is considered a mark of an amateur C programmer. The second form also helps the compiler generate more efficient code. In the first case, to add one to `result`, the compiler outputs code that does the following:

1. Loads the value of `result` into a register

2. Adds one to the register value

3. Stores the incremented value back to `result` in memory

The two uses of `result` in steps 1 and 3 are inefficient because memory references are relatively costly in processing time. The expression `result++` is more efficient because it generates code that increments `result` directly without loading its value into a register.

C compilers are not required to generate more efficient code for increment and decrement operators, but most of them do, so it's good to use ++ and -- whenever you can. Your programs will run faster, and what's more, nobody can accuse you of being an amateur.

Bitwise operators

C is wise about bits — that is, there are operators in C that make it easy to perform *bitwise operations* on values in memory. Because of C's ability to operate directly on memory bits, some programmers view C as a cross between a low- and high-level language (assembly language, for example, compared to Pascal or BASIC). The terms *high* and *low* refer to how "far away" a language is from the computing machine. C's bitwise operators let you stick your nose into memory if you want, but you can also use higher-level elements (integers, characters, floating-point objects, and so on) to construct software that runs independently of the computer's inner nature. You don't have to be a bit twiddler to use C.

In short, if you plan to write scientific or business software, you may have little use for C's bitwise operators (but skim the following notes anyway). If you are writing system software — programming languages, for instance, or operating systems — you'll undoubtedly use bitwise operators and expressions heavily.

There are six bitwise operators: AND (&), OR (|), XOR (^), SHIFT-LEFT (<<), SHIFT-RIGHT (>>), and COMPLEMENT (~). They are often referred to as *logical operators,* and their names are traditionally written in uppercase. XOR, by the way, stands for *exclusive OR.*

Use & to combine bits according to the rules for a logical AND. Assume that result, op1, and op2 are integer objects (bitwise operators cannot be used with floating-point values). Load a fresh copy of SHELL.CPP into the IDE; then add these variable declarations below the comment *Insert snippets here:*

```
int op1, op2, result;
```

Type a couple of blank lines and then add this statement to display result's final value:

```
printf("result == 0x%04X\n", result);
```

Between those two lines, insert the following snippets to experiment with bitwise operators. These statements assign the bitwise logical AND of op1 and op2 to result:

```
op1 = 0x0F07;
op2 = 0x00FF;
result = op1 & op2;
```

A bit that is 1 in both operands is set to 1 in result. All other bits are set to 0. After the assignment, result equals 0x0007. The expression *masks* the value of op1, permitting the lower eight bits of op1 to *pass through* to the result. The upper eight bits (0x0F) are masked out because 0 bits exist at those positions in op2.

These statements assign the bitwise logical OR of op1 and op2 to result:

```
op1 = 0x0101;
op2 = 0x1001;
result = op1 | op2;
```

Bits that are 1 in *either or both* operands result in a 1 bit in result, so the final statement sets result to 0x1101. The exclusive OR (XOR) operator works a bit differently. Using the same starting values, these statements set result to 0x1100:

```
op1 = 0x0101;
op2 = 0x1001;
result = op1 ^ op2;
```

If a bit in op1 *or* in op2 is 1, but not 1 in both operands, the resulting bit is set to 1. Otherwise, the resulting bit is set to zero. The last statement therefore sets result to 0x1100.

SHIFT-LEFT and SHIFT-RIGHT operators shift bits in objects left and right, shifting in one or more zeros at the other end. Try these statements to shift the bits in op1 four positions:

```
op1 = 0x00FF;
op2 = 4;
result = op1 << op2;
```

That sets result to 0x0FF0 — the bits in op1 are shifted four places left, and zero bits are shifted in at right. The original values of op1 and op2 are unchanged. These statements shift the result to the right:

```
op1 = 0x00FF;
op2 = 4;
result = op1 >> op2;
```

That sets op1 to 0x000F — the bits in op1 are shifted four places to the right, and zero bits are shifted in at left.

Shift operations are useful for multiplying and dividing integer values by powers of two. To understand how this works, think about how you can do the same in decimal by multiplying and dividing by powers of ten. The decimal value 123 times 10 (or 10^1) equals 1230 — the digits shift left one position and a zero shifts in at right. *The exponent indicates the number of shift positions.* Similarly, 1230 divided by 10 equals 123 — the digits shift right one position and a zero shifts in at left (you could write 123 as 0123). Multiplying 123 by 10^3, or 1000, equals 123000 — the digits shift left three places. Likewise, dividing by powers of ten shifts digits right. 123000 divided by 10^2, or 100, equals 1230.

You can perform similar multiplications and divisions using bitwise operators, but because those operators perform work on binary digits (bits), the results are multiplied and divided by powers of two rather than ten. Try these statements in SHELL.CPP:

```
op1 = 4;
result = op1 << 1;
```

That shifts op1 one bit to the left, in effect multiplying 4x2, setting result to 8. In the second line, change 1 to 2 and rerun. Now result equals 0x0010 (16 in decimal), the result of multiplying 4 times 2^2. Shift left by 8 to multiply by 2^8, and so on.

To divide by a power of two, shift bits to the right. For example, use these statements to divide op1 by 2^5, equal to five 2s multiplied together, or 32.

```
op1 = 128;
op2 = 5;
result = op1 >> op2;
```

That sets result to 4, the result of dividing 128 by 32.

When you need to multiply or divide integers by powers of two, always use bitwise shifts. The compiler can generate fast shift instructions that run like blazes compared to the time it takes to evaluate multiplication and division expressions.

Precedence and Evaluation Order

Every C compiler has a built-in expression evaluator that dissects source code expressions and builds instructions in the compiled code to evaluate the expressions' results. The C expression evaluator adheres religiously to rules of precedence and evaluation order (also called *associativity*), which describe the relative importance of elements in a multipart expression. You don't have to memorize all of these rules, but when forming complex expressions, you should be aware of the effects of precedence and evaluation order.

Parentheses

In the absence of parentheses, an expression is evaluated using a set of default rules. An expression like this

```
value = a + b * c;
```

is evaluated by first multiplying b times c, then adding a, before assigning the final result to value. In C, multiplication and division are performed before addition and subtraction. To add a and b *before* multiplying, you must use parentheses to group the expression you want evaluated first:

```
value = (a + b) * c;
```

C always processes items in the innermost parentheses before evaluating other expression parts. Now, the sum of a and b is multiplied by c.

Statements without parentheses are perfectly acceptable but difficult to read:

```
value = a / b * c + d * e;
```

A few parentheses, though technically not needed, make the programmer's intentions perfectly clear:

```
value = ((a / b) * c) + (d * e);
```

In English, a is first divided by b because that subexpression is inside the innermost nested parentheses. That result is multiplied by c. Independently, d is multiplied by e. The two subexpression results are added, and the final result is assigned to value.

Because expressions are evaluated at compile time, extra parentheses cost nothing in performance. The parentheses tell the compiler how to evaluate an expression. They otherwise have no effect on the compiled code.

Default operator precedence

Table 5-1 lists the default operator precedence and evaluation orders for many of C's operators. As I suggested, don't try to memorize this table — in time, you'll learn the default orders for the operators you use most often. You can look up the others as needed.

Table 5-1 ▶ Precedence and Evaluation Order (Partial)

Operators in Precedence Order	Evaluation Order
~ ++ -- + - sizeof	right-left
* / %	left-right
+ -	left-right
<< >>	left-right
&	left-right
^	left-right
|	left-right
= += -= *= /= %= &= ^= |= <<= >>=	right-left

Note to Table 5.1: Unary operators + and - have higher precedence than their binary equivalents.

 Table 5-1 lists only operators explained so far. (The bottom row lists shorthand operators explained in the next section.) See Appendix A for a complete precedence and evaluation table.

The two columns in Table 5-1 show default operator precedence and evaluation orders. Operators on the same line have the same precedence. Operators above have higher precedence than those below. In a multipart expression, C evaluates subexpressions by applying operators in precedence order, higher ones first. In expressions that use two or more operators of the same precedence, C evaluates subexpressions using the default left-to-right or right-to-left order as specified for that operator.

Most of the time, C evaluates expressions from left to right — the same way you read them. Consider this:

```
value = a * b / c * d;
```

Because multiplication and division operators have the same precedence, and because those operators are evaluated from left to right, C processes that expression by multiplying a times b, dividing by c, and multiplying by d. The expression is evaluated as though it had been written

```
value = ((a * b) / c) * d;
```

To multiply the two subexpressions *before* dividing, you must use parentheses to override the default evaluation order:

```
value = (a * b) / (c * d);
```

Parentheses are required because the times and divide operators have the same precedence level, causing the subexpressions to be evaluated from left to right.

A few operators such as unary plus and minus evaluate from right to left. Generally, you don't need to be aware of that fact because the results of unary operators are usually obvious. In this expression:

```
value = (a * -b) / (-c * d);
```

a is multiplied by the negative of b, the negative of c is multiplied by d, and those two subexpression results are then divided.

Combining operators with different default evaluation orders can put you behind the eight ball, so think carefully before writing expressions such as

```
value = -c-- * d;
```

There are programmers who relish figuring out what expressions like that do — but I don't happen to be one of them. What do you think a equals after the program executes these statements?

```
int a, c = 10;
a = -c--;
```

C evaluates -c-- by first applying the unary minus to c. After that's done, the decrement operator is applied. So, in this case, a is set to –10, and c is decremented to 9. The effect is clearer if you separate the statement into individual steps:

```
a = -c;
c = c - 1;
```

If that's not what you intended to do, use parentheses to obtain a different result:

```
int a, c = 10;
a = -(--c);
```

Because --c is encased in parentheses, that subexpression is evaluated *before* the result is negated, thus decrementing c to 9 and setting a to –9. But contrary to what you might expect, this does *not* produce the same result:

```
a = -(c--);
```

Because increment and decrement operators are evaluated from right to left, the postfix subexpression (c--) equals c, not c-1, thus -(c--) and -c-- are exactly equivalent — the parentheses in this case are meaningless. Even so, I prefer to use parentheses to make the intent of the expression as clear as possible and to prevent bugs caused by faulty assumptions about default precedence and evaluation orders. If you have to puzzle through an expression to understand what it does, consider adding a few pairs of parentheses to improve the statement's clarity.

Shorthand operators

Second in popularity only to increment and decrement operators are C's *shorthand operators.* Until you get used to them, they may seem more confusing than helpful, but try to put them into action whenever you can. They help the compiler generate more efficient code (at least in some cases), they save typing, and they keep statements looking neat and trim.

See the last line of Table 5-1 for a complete list of shorthand operators, which have the lowest precedence level (actually, the comma operator, which you meet in the next chapter, is lower). Form a shorthand operator by combining an arithmetic or bitwise operator and the equal sign (+= or /= for example).

Use shorthand operators to avoid duplicate identifiers in expressions such as

```
a = a + b;
```

That's exactly equivalent but possibly less efficient than

```
a += b;
```

Literally translated, the shorthand operator += means "add a to b and then assign the result back to a." Here are some other examples with the equivalent longhand expressions written at right as comments:

```
a /= b;   // a = a / b;
a *= b;   // a = a * b;
a -= b;   // a = a - b;
a %= b;   // a = a % b;
```

You can also use shorthand operators in complex expressions such as

```
a *= (b / c) + d;
```

That's exactly the same as

```
a = a * ((b / c) + d);
```

There are shorthand forms for bitwise operators as well. To logically AND a value a with 0x00FF and store the result back in a, you can write

```
a &= 0x00FF;
```

That's the same as the longhand:

```
a = a & 0x00FF;
```

To try your hand at using shorthand expressions, add the statements in Listing 5-2 to a copy of SHELL.CPP.

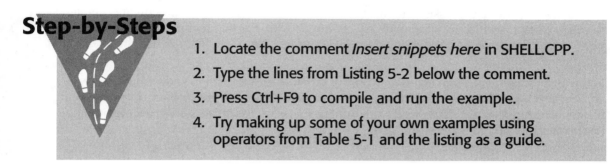

Step-by-Steps

1. Locate the comment *Insert snippets here* in SHELL.CPP.
2. Type the lines from Listing 5-2 below the comment.
3. Press Ctrl+F9 to compile and run the example.
4. Try making up some of your own examples using operators from Table 5-1 and the listing as a guide.

Listing 5-2: Add to SHELL.CPP

```
int v1, v2;

v1 = 7;
printf("v1 == %d\n", v1);
v1 *= 20;
printf("v1 *= 20 == %d\n\n", v1);

v2 = 20;
printf("v1 == %d, v2 == %d\n", v1, v2);
v1 /= v2;
printf("v1 /= v2 == %d\n\n", v1);

v1 = 0x000F;
printf("v1 == 0x%04X\n", v1);
v1 <<= 8;
printf("v1 <<= 8 == 0x%04X\n", v1);
```

Unlike the way it processes increment and decrement operators, C doesn't necessarily create more efficient code for shorthand expressions. In most cases, shorthand operators are merely conveniences that save typing and keep statements looking neat. For complex data structures such as arrays, however, which I cover in a later chapter, statements like this:

```
array[i * j] = array[i * j] * 5;
```

compile to more efficient code if written as

```
array[i * j] *= 5;
```

In both cases, the array element at position i * j is multiplied by 5. The longhand form repeats the multiplication i * j, wasting time. The shorthand version performs the multiplication only once. Some optimizing C compilers (but not the one supplied with this book) can eliminate unnecessary duplicate expressions in that and similar cases. Even so, most programmers prefer to hand-optimize their code rather than rely on the compiler. For that reason, shorthand operators are an essential tool for squeezing as much performance as possible from statements that use complex expressions.

In the next chapter, you learn about *flow control* statements that begin to show what C can really do. You also learn about C's relational operators. Among other jobs, flow control statements and relational operators make decisions and perform loops — two essential tasks you'll perform in just about every program you write.

Chapter 6

Flow Control Statements and Relational Operators

Programming without flow control statements is like depending on the rain for a drink of water. In a house, H_2O is piped in from the local water works or a well and then directed from room to room through pipes and valves. To quench your thirst, you don't stand outside waiting for a cloudburst; you just turn the faucet handle and drink.

In C, *flow control* statements work like plumbing fixtures. They direct the flow of a program by using relational expressions that control which statements execute based on this or that condition, similar to the way valves and spigots control water flow at home.

Good Relations

Flow control statements use relational, equality, and logical operators that compare operands in various ways. All of these operators have the same goal — to produce a value representing true or false that can be used to direct the program's flow.

In C, *false* is represented by the integer 0; *true* equals 1. So you don't have to remember that fact (though it's a good idea to memorize it), define TRUE and FALSE symbols like this:

```
#define FALSE 0
#define TRUE 1
```

 See Appendix A for the precedence and evaluation orders of C's relational, equality, and logical operators.

Relational operators

Relational operators compare the relative values of integer or floating-point operands. C's relational operators are

```
>   >=   <   <=
```

Use the greater than (>), greater than or equal to (>=), less than (<), and less than or equal to (< =) operators to compare values in statements such as

```
if (a >= b)
   statement;
```

If the value of a is greater than or equal to b, the program executes statement. If the expression (a >= b) is false — that is, if a is less than b — the program does *not* execute statement.

 The math symbols ≥ and ≤ are equivalent to the C operators >= and <= respectively.

Equality operators

Often, you need to find out if two values are equal. For that, use one of C's two equality operators:

```
==   !=
```

The first operator, ==, tests whether two operands are equal. Use it like this:

```
if (a == b)
   statement;
```

If a equals b, the program executes `statement`; otherwise, `statement` is skipped. Now, repeat after me: *two equal signs test for equality*. Say it again. *Two equal signs test for equality*. No mistake is made more often in C than this:

```
if (a = b)     // ??? Don't do this!!!
   statement;
```

The *single* equal sign is C's assignment operator — it *assigns* the value of b to a. The *double* equal sign tests for equality — it *compares* the values of a and b. To guard against mistakes, you receive the warning *Possibly incorrect assignment in function* if you accidentally use the assignment operator (=) where an equality operator (==) is most likely intended. Regardless of experience, every programmer (including a certain author of computer books) makes that same mistake over and over, so don't be dismayed if you receive the warning frequently.

To test whether two values are different, use the not-equal operator (!=) like this

```
if (a != b)
   statement;
```

The program executes `statement` if a is not equal to b; otherwise, if a equals b, `statement` is skipped.

Some programming languages use the symbol <> for "not equal." C uses != instead.

Logical operators

You can form complex relational expressions using C's logical operators && (AND) and || (OR). Suppose, for example, you want to execute a statement if a is within the range of values 10 and 25. The obvious solution tests whether a is greater or equal to 10 *AND* whether a is less than or equal to 25:

```
if ((a >= 10) && (a <= 25))
   statement;
```

The logical && operator is applied to the relational expressions (a >= 10) and (a <= 25). Only if both statements are true is `statement` executed. If either statement is false, or if both are false, `statement` is skipped. You'll often see that kind of statement written in a slightly different form:

```
if ((10 <= a) && (a <= 25))
   statement;
```

That does the same but more closely resembles the mathematical expression *10≤v≤25*, commonly used to express a range of values for an object *v*.

Use the logical OR operator (||) to test whether one *OR* another part of a complex expression is true. What do you think this does?

```
if ((a < 10) || (a > 25))
   statement;
```

Putting that into English, the statement tests whether "a is less than 10 *OR* a is greater than 25." If either subexpression is true, or if both are true, statement is executed; otherwise, it's skipped. As a result, statement is executed only if a is *outside* the range 10 to 25.

By the way, because || is lower in precedence than < and > (see Appendix A), the preceding example can be written with only two parentheses:

```
if (a < 10 || a > 25)
   statement;
```

The effect is the same, but if extra parentheses make the statement clearer, don't hesitate to use them.

Don't mistake logical AND (&&) and logical OR (||) for the bitwise AND and OR operators & and |. The symbols are easily confused, usually with disastrous results. You just have to memorize that the double symbols && and || are for use in logical true-or-false expressions. The single symbols & and | perform bitwise AND and OR operations on their operands' bits. From now on in this book, the uppercase words AND and OR refer to logical true-or-false operators && and ||. The phrases *bitwise AND* and *bitwise OR* refer to the bitwise operators & and |.

Reverse logic

Use the logical *NOT* operator (!) to reverse the logic of a true or false expression. It's most typically applied to a variable that holds the results of another expression. For example, suppose you are writing a program that records the air temperature. You want to determine if the temperature is rising. First, define a variable to represent that fact:

```
int rising;
```

The program sets rising to true (1) or false (0) with a statement such as

```
rising = (temp > oldtemp);
```

If temp is greater than oldtemp (two variables initialized elsewhere), rising is set to true; otherwise, it's false. Remember: *all expressions have values.* The value of the expression (temp > oldtemp) is true or false, and since those concepts are represented by 1 and 0, the relational expression can be assigned to an int variable, saving the expression's value for use elsewhere in the program.

You can now use rising to execute a statement if the temperature is rising:

```
if (rising)
   statement;
```

That's exactly the same as

```
if (temp > oldtemp)
   statement;
```

but it doesn't require reevaluating the relational expression. If the program needs to determine whether the temperature is *not* rising, apply the NOT operator to the variable:

```
if (!rising)
   statement;
```

If rising is true, !rising is false. If rising is false, !rising is true. Pronouce !rising as "not rising." The preceding lines execute statement if the temperature is not rising, having the same effect as

```
if (temp <= oldtemp)
   statement;
```

Decisions, Decisions

Now, finally, at long last, and golly gee wiz, isn't it about time, you are ready to begin writing C programs that actually do something useful. With relational operators, you can perform all sorts of magic by making decisions based on this or that value. Though the idea may seem simple, a programming language's decision-making capability is a powerful concept that provides much of the driving force behind all of the world's computer software.

If-else

You've already seen some examples of if statements — they work exactly as expected. *If* an expression is true, *then* a statement (or group of statements) is executed; *else* another statement or group is called to action. *If* you want to experiment with if and if-else statements, *then* load a fresh copy of SHELL.CPP into the IDE and add these statements after the comment *Insert snippets here:*

```
int a, b;
a = 10;
b = 20;
if (a < b)
   printf("a is less than b");
```

Press Ctrl+F9 to compile and run the program. Because a is less than b, you see the sentence *a is less than b.* Change the values of a and b and then rerun. The printf statement is executed only if the relational expression (a < b) is true.

In general terms, if statements are written according to the form

```
if (control expression)
   statement;
```

The `control expression` must evaluate to a true (1) or false (0) value. It must be enclosed in parentheses. The `statement` can be any statement, or it can be a compound group of two or more statements enclosed in braces:

```
if (control expression) {
  statement1;
  statement2;
}
```

You may insert as many statements as you want between the braces. Together, the *compound statement,* also called a *statement block,* is syntactically equivalent to a single statement, but it doesn't end with a semicolon.

An `if` statement may optionally be followed by an `else` clause that selects an alternate statement to execute.

```
if (control expression)
  statement1;
else
  statement2;
```

If the control expression is true, the program executes `statement1`; otherwise, it executes `statement2`. Both statements end with semicolons, as do all statements in C.

You can nest `if` statements, one inside each other like bugs in a rug. In fact, if you're not careful, nested `if` statements are common sources of buggy code. Consider this:

```
if (a < b)
  if (c < d)
    statement1;
  else
    statement2;
```

If `a` is less than `b`, the program executes the next `if` statement. In that case, if `c` is less than `d`, the program executes `statement1`; otherwise, it executes `statement2`. If `a` is greater or equal to `b`, *neither* statement executes because the nested `if` statement is skipped.

But what if you wanted to execute `statement2` if `a` is greater or equal to `b`? To make the `else` go with the correct `if`, use braces like this:

```
if (a < b) {
  if (c < d)
    statement1;
} else
  statement2;
```

Now, if `a` is less than `b`, the nested `if` statement executes `statement1` only if `c` is less than `d`. If `a` is greater than or equal to `b`, the program executes `statement2`. In the absence of braces, the `else` clause goes with the nearest preceding `if`. Use braces to force the else to go with an *earlier* `if`.

There are an endless number of ways to nest if and if-else statements — you'll run into more variations than talk shows on TV. Enter the programming in Listing 6-1 for a demonstration of how to use if-else to test the validity of user input.

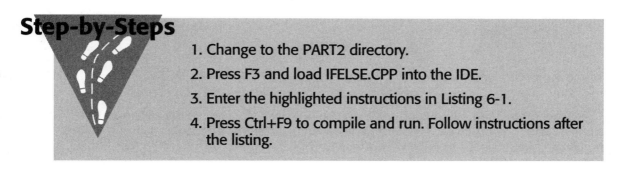

Step-by-Steps

1. Change to the PART2 directory.
2. Press F3 and load IFELSE.CPP into the IDE.
3. Enter the highlighted instructions in Listing 6-1.
4. Press Ctrl+F9 to compile and run. Follow instructions after the listing.

Listing 6-1: IFELSE.CPP

```
/* if-else */

#include <stdio.h>
#include <stdlib.h>
#include <conio.h>

int GetInt()
{
  char answer[80];

  printf("Enter a value between 10 and 20: ");
  gets(answer);
  return atoi(answer);
}

char Pause()
{
  char c;
  printf("\nPress Enter to continue...");
  while ((c = getchar()) != '\n') { }
  return c;
}

int main()
{
  clrscr();
```

```
int v = GetInt();
if ((v < 10) || (v > 20))
  puts("Error: v is out of range!");
else
  puts("Thank you.");

Pause();
return 0;
}
```

The first line you typed calls a function, GetInt, that prompts for and returns an integer value, assigned to an int variable v. (You'll investigate functions later in this book, so I'll postpone explaining how functions like GetInt work.)

After obtaining input, an if statement checks whether v is outside the range 10 to 20. If so, puts displays an error message. If v is OK, a second puts writes *Thank you.* Getting input and testing it for validity is one of the most common uses for if statements.

Try modifying the sample program to display *different* messages if v is too low or too high. Change the range of tested values. Test for *two* ranges (10 to 20 *or* 100 to 200, for example). Make up small *what-if* experiments on your own and try to implement them. What input values would thoroughly test your programming?

Following are some other sample if statements. Suppose you want to convert lowercase letters to uppercase — useful in menu-driven programs, for example, where you ask users to press a key to select an operation. Most often, you'll want lowercase *q* to select the same command as uppercase *Q.* After consulting an ASCII chart, you determine that subtracting 32 from any lowercase letter converts it to uppercase. Of course, you must subtract 32 *only* from letters; you don't want to "convert" digits and punctuation.

Listing 6-2 shows one way to solve the problem. Enter the lines into a fresh copy of SHELL.CPP.

Step-by-Steps

1. Locate the comment *Insert snippets here* in SHELL.CPP in the PART2 directory.

2. Type the lines from Listing 6-2 after the comment.

3. Press Ctrl+F9 to compile and run the example.

Listing 6-2: Add to SHELL.CPP

```
char c, oldc;
printf("Press a character key: ");
c = getche();
oldc = c;
if (c >= 'a' && c <= 'z')
  c = c - 32;
printf("\nUppercase equivalent of %c == %c\n", oldc, c);
```

The first line defines two char variables, c and oldc. After displaying a prompt, the program calls getche ("*get ch*aracter and *e*cho"), a Borland-only function that is useful for obtaining a character without waiting for users to press Enter. (Other C compilers offer similar functions, though not necessarily named getche.) That character is saved in c and in oldc.

Next, an if statement checks whether c holds a lowercase letter. Because ASCII characters are represented as integers, the statement can compare the values of 'a' and 'z' directly. If the character is lowercase, 32 is subtracted from it to convert to uppercase. A printf statement displays the final result.

There are two improvements you might want to make to the sample listing. First, you can call getche and assign its result to c and oldc with a *single* statement:

```
oldc = c = getche();
```

Type that in place of the two assignments in Listing 6-2. In general, you may assign a value to two or more variables like this:

```
a = b = c = 123;
```

That sets a, b, and c to 123, exactly as though you had written

```
a = 123;
b = 123;
c = 123;
```

The second improvement you can make is to use a shorthand operator in the expression that subtracts 32 from c. Replace this statement:

```
c = c - 32;
```

with the equivalent shorthand:

```
c -= 32;
```

One final note about if statements: it's often convenient to use a true-or-false variable as a control expression. For an example, enter Listing 6-3 into a fresh copy of SHELL.CPP.

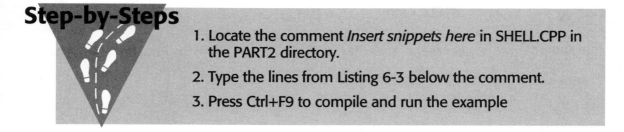

Step-by-Steps

1. Locate the comment *Insert snippets here* in SHELL.CPP in the PART2 directory.
2. Type the lines from Listing 6-3 below the comment.
3. Press Ctrl+F9 to compile and run the example

Listing 6-3: Add to SHELL.CPP

```
char c;
int yes;

printf("Press Y or N: ");
c = getch();
yes = (c == 'Y' || c == 'y');
if (yes)
  printf("Yes!");
else
  printf("No.");
```

The sample program demonstrates how you can display the words *Yes* or *No* when users press *Y* or *N*. (For simplicity, any key other than *Y* is considered a *No* response.) First, the program defines two variables: a char c to hold the input character and an int variable named yes, sometimes called a *Boolean logic variable* because it represents true or false.

The program next uses printf to display the prompt *Press Y or N:*. Then getch ("*get ch*aracter without echo") is called to obtain a keypress, but not display any text on-screen. The character is assigned to c, after which this statement initializes the yes integer variable:

```
yes = (c == 'Y' || c == 'y');
```

Carefully examine that line — you'll use this kind of statement frequently. The expression to the right of the equal sign tests whether the character in c is an upper- or lowercase *Y*. If so, the expression is true (1); if not, it's false (0). The result of that expression — either 1 or 0 — is then assigned to yes. The statement operates like this:

```
if (c == 'Y' || c == 'y')
  yes = TRUE;
else
  yes = FALSE;
```

Because the longer equivalent uses two assignments, it generates slightly larger code, and for that reason, the shorthand is preferred.

Either way, `yes` now indicates whether the user pressed the *Y* key, a fact that an `if` statement can use to select an action — in this case, displaying *Yes* or *No:*

```
if (yes)
  printf("Yes!");
else
  printf("No.");
```

The expression `if (yes)` is exactly the same as

```
if (yes != FALSE)...
```

Or because true and false are represented as 1 and 0:

```
if (yes != 0)...
```

Those statements are perfectly acceptable, but it's important to get used to the common short-hand form:

```
if (yes)...
```

I find it helpful to read that as "if yes is valid" or "if yes is not false." This is not a new expression form; it's merely a consequence of the fact that a variable name written in a program is an expression that produces a value. The `yes` integer variable represents true or false; its value is therefore 1 or 0, and it can be used directly as an `if` statement control expression. Once you learn the technique, however, you can ignore the gory details and write meaningful statements such as:

```
int answerIsCorrect;
...
if (answerIsCorrect)
  statement;
```

The program defines a Boolean logic variable `answerIsCorrect`. Elsewhere, a process (not shown) sets that variable to true or false, a fact that is easily checked with an `if` statement. Notice how clear the code is to read. Obviously, `statement` is executed only if the correct answer was given.

Try always to write code that is understandable on its own without the need for explanatory comments. *Obvious code is good programming.* A good way to make programs readable is to select meaningful true-or-false variable names such as `answerIsCorrect`.

Else-if

Following an `if` statement with an `else` clause that is in turn followed by *another* `if` statement creates a contraption known as a *multiway decision tree*. It works sort of like the mental process some people go through every morning when they awake:

If it's sunny, I'll get up now,

else if it's raining, I'll sleep for another hour,

else if the phone rings, I'll get my wife to answer it,

else I'll sleep until noon!

 If you object to the admittedly sexist suggestion in step three, change `wife` to `husband`, *else if* you are not married, change it to `companion`, *else* delete the line altogether.

There isn't an actual `else-if` statement in C. A multiway decision tree is merely a collection of `if` statements and `else` clauses, optionally followed by a final "catchall" `else`. The general form is

```
if (condition1)
   statement1;
else if (condition2)
   statement2;
else if (condition3)
   statement3;
```

An `if` statement starts the ball rolling, executing `statement1` if `condition1` is true. If `condition2` is true, `statement2` is executed. If `condition3` is true, `statement3` is executed, and so on for as many conditions and statements as you need. Only one of the statements is selected. If none is true, *no* statements are executed. To provide a final catchall statement if all conditions are false, follow the preceding lines with a final `else`:

```
if (condition1)
   statement1;
else if (condition2)
   statement2;
else if (condition3)
   statement3;
else
   statement4;
```

If all conditions are false, `statement4` is executed. When written that way, at least one statement is guaranteed to be selected, ensuring total control over the program's actions for all possible conditions.

Listing 6-4 uses a multiway decision tree to display a message describing the nature of a character.

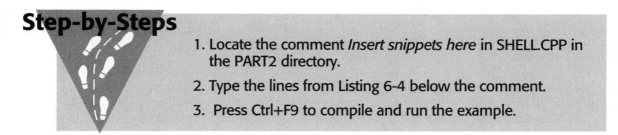

Step-by-Steps

1. Locate the comment *Insert snippets here* in SHELL.CPP in the PART2 directory.

2. Type the lines from Listing 6-4 below the comment.

3. Press Ctrl+F9 to compile and run the example.

Listing 6-4: Add to SHELL.CPP

```
char c;
printf("Press a character key: ");
c = getche();

printf("\nCharacter %c is ", c);
if (c >= '0' && c <= '9')
  puts("a digit");
else if (c >= 'a' && c <= 'z')
  puts("a lowercase letter");
else if (c >= 'A' && c <= 'Z')
  puts("an uppercase letter");
else if (c == ' ')
  puts("a space");
else
  puts("not a digit, letter, or space");
```

The program defines a char variable c, prompts you to press a key, and assigns the entered character from getche to c. After those steps, the program tells you whether the character is a digit, a lowercase letter, an uppercase letter, a space, or none of the above — the case handled by the final else clause.

The programming in Listing 6-4 is a simple form of *parsing,* the process of determining an item's nature or characteristics. A C compiler *parses* an expression, for example, to extract its operators, operands, and other components.

Switch

Some multiway decision trees are more clearly written using a `switch` statement, which looks like this:

```
switch (expression) {
  case const1:
    statement1;
    break;
  case const2:
    statement2;
    break;
  case const3:
    statement3;
    break;
  default
    statement4;
}
```

The keyword `switch` is followed by an expression, which produces a value to be compared to a series of constants as though written as

```
x = expression;
if (x == const1)
  statement1;
else if (x == const2)
  statement2;
else if (x == const3)
  statement3;
else
  statement4;
```

The `switch` statement uses one or more `case` labels, each specifying a different constant (in no particular order) to be compared to the expression. Each label ends with a colon. The expression is typically a variable name, but it could be a function that returns a value, or it might be any other expression that can be compared to the `case` constants. There are two critical facts to remember when using `switch`:

▶ Each case should be ended with a `break` statement, which ends the `switch` statement for a matching `case`.

▶ The default case (equivalent to the final `else` in a multiway decision tree) is optional. If used, it does not have to end with `break`, though it may end that way without harm.

The logic behind `switch` and those two rules is easier to fathom by examining a real-life example. Add the programming in Listing 6-5 to a fresh copy of SHELL.CPP. It demonstrates how to use `switch` to select program operations from a menu — a classic user interface that, even in today's world of graphical windows, remains a valuable programming technique to learn.

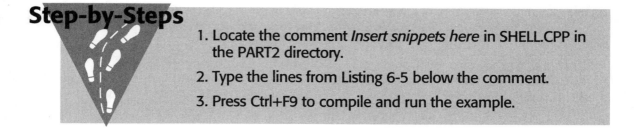

Step-by-Steps

1. Locate the comment *Insert snippets here* in SHELL.CPP in the PART2 directory.

2. Type the lines from Listing 6-5 below the comment.

3. Press Ctrl+F9 to compile and run the example.

Listing 6-5: Add to SHELL.CPP

```
int choice;

printf("Menu: A(dd D(elete S(ort Q(uit: ");
choice = toupper(getche());
puts("");  // Start new line
switch (choice) {
  case 'A':
    printf("You selected Add\n");
    break;
  case 'D':
    printf("You selected Delete\n");
    break;
  case 'S':
    printf("You selected Sort\n");
    break;
  case 'Q':
    printf("You selected Quit\n");
    break;
  default:
    printf("\nIllegal choice!!!\n");
}
```

To hold the user's choice, I defined an `int` variable, `choice`. C programmers typically represent characters as `int` values this way, though you could use `char` instead. The program uses `printf` to display a simple menu with a few fictitious operations and then calls `getche` to obtain a keypress. The statement

```
choice = toupper(getche());
```

calls the `toupper` function, declared in the CTYPE.H header file, to convert to uppercase the character returned by `getche`. That result is then assigned to `choice`.

Next, the program starts a new line by passing a null string to `puts`, after which a `switch` statement compares `choice` with some character constants. Each case in the sample merely confirms your selection. The default case displays an error message. In your own code, you might call functions, compute expressions, or perform any other tasks in the various cases.

To understand the significance of `break` statements in `case` clauses, delete the first one in `case 'A':` and rerun the program. Press A to select the *A(dd* command. On-screen, you see these messages:

```
Menu: A(dd D(elete S(ort Q(uit: a
You selected Add
You selected Delete
```

Because `case 'A':` no longer ends with `break`, pressing the *A* key executes the statement under that case *and also the next statement below.* In other words, in the absence of `break`, a case *falls through* to the next case, a trick that can sometimes be used to select among a number of statements. You might, for example, write a `switch` statement like this:

```
switch (expression) {
  case const1:
    statement1;
  case const2:
    statement2;
  case const3:
    statement3;
    break;
}
```

If `expression` **equals** `const1`, statements 1, 2, and 3 execute (the first case falls through to the second, which falls through to the third). If `expression` equals `const2`, statements 2 and 3 execute (the second statement falls through to the third). If `expression` equals `const3`, only `statement3` is executed.

Don't use the fall-through trick in `switch` statements unless you have excellent reasons for doing so. In general, the technique introduces too much potential for error and is considered a poor programming practice.

Getting Looped

Fortunately for my stomach, I gave up riding roller coasters before engineers discovered that, in addition to going up and down, it was also possible for the cars to go all the way around. I can handle a sailboat at sea, but you'll never get me to "loop the loop." I can't even watch amusement park advertisements without turning a feeble shade of green.

In C, loops perform actions multiple times — a simple concept that has more power than you might imagine (and is far gentler on the tummy). Loops make it possible to program repetitive processes, saving space in code (you have to enter a repeating statement only once no matter how many times it's needed) and performing countless tasks such as displaying tables, reading text files, and sorting databases. If loops didn't exist, you'd have to invent them. Without loops, computer software as we know it simply wouldn't exist.

While

A `while` statement is C's most fundamental loop. It has the general layout

```
while (expression)
   statement;
```

The `expression` must evaluate to a true (1) or false (0) result. While the `expression` is true, the program repeatedly executes `statement`. Sooner or later, `expression` must become false so the loop ends. If `expression` never becomes false, the program will hang, and you may have to reboot to recover.

Most commonly, the `expression` uses a control variable that the `while` loop modifies in some way. For instance, to count up to 10, you can write

```
int count;
count = 1;
while (count <= 10) {
   printf("count == %d\n", count);
   count++;
}
```

Add those lines to a copy of SHELL.CPP, and compile to count up to ten (just what you needed a computer for, right?). The first two lines define and initialize a control variable, `count`, to 1. A `while` loop expression tests whether `count` is less than or equal to 10. If so, the statements inside braces are executed, displaying `count`'s value and incrementing `count`. Then the `while` expression again tests whether `count` is less than or equal to 10. Obviously, because the loop advances `count`'s value, the control variable eventually reaches 11, at which time the `while` loop's expression becomes false, ending the loop and sending the program on its way to the next statement beyond.

Listing 6-6 is a more involved example that shows how to use `while` loops for calculating factorials — equal to an integer series multiplied together. The factorial of 5, for example, equals 1*2*3*4*5, or 120.

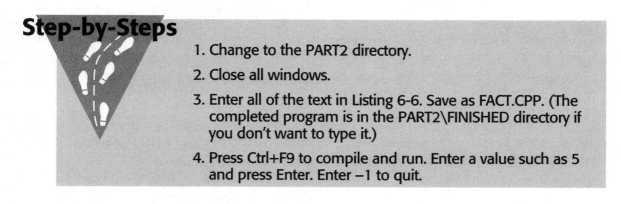

Step-by-Steps

1. Change to the PART2 directory.

2. Close all windows.

3. Enter all of the text in Listing 6-6. Save as FACT.CPP. (The completed program is in the PART2\FINISHED directory if you don't want to type it.)

4. Press Ctrl+F9 to compile and run. Enter a value such as 5 and press Enter. Enter –1 to quit.

Listing 6-6: FACT.CPP

```
/* FACT.CPP */

#include <stdio.h>
#include <stdlib.h>

main()
{
  int value = 0;
  double result;
  char answer[128];

  while (value >= 0) {
    printf("Value? (-1 to quit) ");
    gets(answer);
    value = atoi(answer);
    if (value >= 0) {
      result = 1;
      while (value > 0) {
        result *= value;
        value--;
      }
      printf("Factorial = %f\n", result);
    }
  }
  return 0;
}
```

The program begins by defining a few variables: an integer `value`, which holds the target value, a `double` floating-point variable `result` for the factorial of `value`, and a string `answer` to hold your input.

The first `while` loop in the program tests whether `value` is greater than or equal to zero. If not, the user probably entered –1 to end the program. Doing that requires no special handling — after the `while` loop simply ends, so does the program.

Inside the first `while` loop's braces, three statements prompt for a value. Function `gets` stores your typing in a string. This statement assigns the integer equivalent of that string to `value`:

```
value = atoi(answer);
```

The `atoi` (ASCII to integer) function converts a string to an integer. After that statement, an `if` statement tests whether `value` is greater than or equal to zero. If so, `result` is set to 1 because, by definition, the factorial of zero equals 1.

A second `while` loop next repeats two statements while `value` is greater than zero. The statements multiply `result` times `value` and then subtract one from `value`, eventually decreasing it to zero. At that point, the `while` loop ends, and a `printf` statement displays the final result. The first `while` loop then repeats the prompt for another value.

For a better understanding of FACT.CPP, run the program one step at a time with the IDE's debugger. To do that, press F8 and use the Debug|Watches command to inspect the values of `value` and `result`. (Press Ctrl+F2 if necessary to clear any other program from the debugger's control.) Enter a value when prompted. Press Alt+F5 to view the output screen after the last `printf` statement displays the computed factorial.

The FACT.CPP program demonstrates a subtle — but extremely important — characteristic of `while` loops. If a `while` loop's controlling expression is false, the loop's statements *do not execute, not even once.* Consider this program fragment:

```
int count = 0;
while (count > 0)
   statement;
```

The `statement` never executes because `count` is zero, causing the control expression (`count > 0`) to be false. This is the rule to remember: *A `while` loop's statements may execute zero or more times.*

Do-while

A `do-while` statement is the flip side of a `while`. Use `do-while` to create a loop that always executes its statements at least once. (Pascal programmers in the audience may recognize `do-while` as equivalent to Pascal's `repeat` statements.) The `do-while` has this form:

```
do {
   statement;
} while (expression);
```

The `statement` is executed while `expression` is true. As with `while`, the `statement` should perform some action that causes the `expression` eventually to become false, ending the loop. Technically speaking, the braces are required only if `statement` is compound:

```
do {
   statement1;
   statement2;
   ...
   statementN;
} while (expression);
```

But the braces are typically included anyway because the code seems less clear without them. For practice with `do-while`, enter the program snippet in Listing 6-7 into a fresh copy of SHELL.CPP.

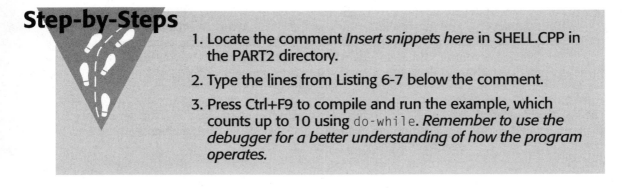

Step-by-Steps

1. Locate the comment *Insert snippets here* in SHELL.CPP in the PART2 directory.

2. Type the lines from Listing 6-7 below the comment.

3. Press Ctrl+F9 to compile and run the example, which counts up to 10 using `do-while`. *Remember to use the debugger for a better understanding of how the program operates.*

Listing 6-7: Add to SHELL.CPP

```
int count;
printf("do-while count\n");
count = 0;
do {
  count++;
  printf("%d\n", count);
} while (count < 10);
```

For

I saved the best for last — the `for` loop. It's as useful as rain and as common as sunshine. You'll probably use `for` loops more than any other feature in C.

The `for` loop has a somewhat odd construction, best learned by typing a couple of examples into SHELL.CPP. Try this sample, which counts up to 10:

```
int count;
for (count = 1; count < 11; count++)
  printf("%i\n", count);
```

Like other loops, `for` typically uses a control variable such as `count`. The keyword `for` is followed by a three-part expression in parentheses, each part separated from the next with a semicolon. In this example, the expression does the following:

▶ Initializes `count` to 1

▶ Tests whether `count` is less than 11

▶ Increments `count` by one each time through the loop

The first step is performed *one time* before the `for` loop's statement executes (`printf` in the example). The second step is performed *every time* before the statement executes. The third step is performed *every time* after the statement executes. In effect, the `for` loop operates exactly the same as a `while` statement written like this:

```
int count;
count = 1;
while (count < 11) {
  printf("%i\n", count);
  count++;
}
```

Here's another sample, this time using a `char` variable as the control. Before you run the code, what do you think it does?

```
char c;
for (c = 'A'; c <= 'Z'; c++)
  putchar(c);
```

The `for` loop initializes a `char` variable c to the letter `'A'`. Each time before executing the loop's `putchar` statement, c is compared to `'Z'`. If the expression c <= `'Z'` is true, `putchar` displays c's current value, after which the statement c++ increments c to the next letter. Eventually, the expression becomes false, ending the loop. As you may have guessed, the program displays the alphabet.

Some interesting variations are possible with `for` loops. For instance, you can write a "do-forever" loop like this, which fills up the screen with x characters faster than you can say *forevermore*:

```
for (;;) printf("x");
```

To end the program, press Ctrl+Break; then press Ctrl+F2 to reset. The odd-looking `for` loop has no statement or expressions, but it is perfectly acceptable. It executes its statement (`printf` here) repeatedly without end — that is, without a *planned* ending. Be aware, however, that unless a do-forever loop executes an input or output instruction, it may be impossible to break out of the loop from the keyboard.

You can also use the comma operator to execute multiple statements and expressions. Here's a `for` loop that initializes and uses two control variables (try it in SHELL.CPP):

```
int i, j;
for (i = 1, j = 10; i < j; i += 2, j++)
  printf("i == %2d, j == %2d\n", i, j);
```

Like all `for` loops, this one has three sections in parentheses. In this case, however, the first section has two initializing statements, separated with a comma, that set i to 1 and j to 10. The second section tests whether i is less than j. The third section also has two parts — one that adds 2 to i and another that increments j by 1. Each time through the loop, i increases more rapidly than j, eventually ending the loop when i catches up to j. On-screen, the program displays

```
i  ==   1,  j  == 10
i  ==   3,  j  == 11
i  ==   5,  j  == 12
i  ==   7,  j  == 13
i  ==   9,  j  == 14
i  ==  11,  j  == 15
i  ==  13,  j  == 16
i  ==  15,  j  == 17
i  ==  17,  j  == 18
```

By the way, the comma operator has the lowest precedence among all operators (see Appendix A). It's sort of an oddball. Using the comma operator, you can write multipart statements such as:

```
i = 10, j = 123, printf("i==%d  j==%d\n", i, j);
```

But don't do that. You gain nothing and the style is too unusual to do any good. Technically, the preceding line is *one* statement, similar in design to a compound statement delimited with braces:

```
{
  i = 10;
  j = 123;
  printf("i==%d  j==%d\n", i, j);
}
```

The comma operator is typically used in `for` loops and variable declarations (including function parameters, but more on that in Chapter 9). For example, this uses comma operators to define and initialize three `int` variables:

```
int i = 1, j = 2, k = 3;
```

Other Statements

That's all the loop statements in C, but there are four related statement varieties you should know about before moving on. You won't use these often (and one of them, `goto`, you should *never* use at all). But they may come in handy at times.

Technically speaking, there's one more flow-control statement not covered in this chapter — `return`. You've seen it used in functions, but I'll postpone discussing `return`'s ins and outs until Chapter 9.

Break

Breaking up is hard to do, but not in C. The `break` statement unconditionally ends the current statement. You already saw it used to end `case`s in a `switch` statement. Use it also with `while`, `do-while`, and `for` to end a loop immediately, perhaps due to an error or another exceptional condition. Listing 6-8 demonstrates how `break` works.

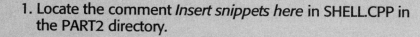

Step-by-Steps

1. Locate the comment *Insert snippets here* in SHELL.CPP in the PART2 directory.

2. Type the lines from Listing 6-8 below the comment.

3. Press Ctrl+F9 to compile and run the example. Follow instructions after the listing.

Listing 6-9: Add to SHELL.CPP

```
int count;

count = 0;
while (++count <= 25) {
  if (count > 10 && count < 18)
    break;
  printf("%d\n", count);
}
```

The `while` loop expression increments `count` by one and tests whether that incremented value is less than or equal to 25. Inside the `while` loop, an `if` statement checks whether `count` is greater than 10 and less than 18 — if so, `break` ends the loop before it would normally end when `count` reaches 26. As a result, the program counts up to 10 and stops, demonstrating how `break` can be used to end a loop due to an exceptional condition.

Continue

A `break` statement's counterpoint is `continue`, which unconditionally restarts a loop at the top skipping any statements that follow the `continue` keyword. You may use `continue` exactly as you do `break`, but not in a `switch` statement. For example, using the same programming from Listing 6-8, change `break` to `continue` and rerun:

```
while (++count <= 25) {
  if (count > 10 && count < 18)
    continue;
  printf("%d\n", count);
}
```

As before, the `while` loop increments `count` and checks whether it is less than or equal to 25. If so, the `if` statement tests whether `count` is between 10 and 18, executing `continue`. Now, instead of stopping when `count` reaches 11, the `continue` statement *skips* the output `printf` statement until `count` equals 18. As a result, the modified program counts up to 10, skips the values from 11 to 17, and then picks up the count at 18, finishing at 25. This demonstrates how `continue` can be used to alter the course of a loop but not end it as with `break`.

Conditional

Some programmers find the `?:` conditional operator confusing, but it's occasionally useful for reducing clutter, especially in code that uses lots of `if-else` statements. The operator has the form

```
logical-OR-expression ? expression : conditional-expression
```

The *logical-OR-expression* must be an expression that can be evaluated as a true or false value. A question mark symbol comes next, followed by another *expression* to be executed if the *logical-OR-expression* is true. A colon follows that expression, after which a *conditional-expression* is supplied for cases where the *logical-OR-expression* is false. In short, the operator works like this:

```
logical-OR-expression ? doThisIfTrue : elseDoThisIfFalse
```

If the *logical-OR-expression* is true, the `doThisIfTrue` statement is executed; otherwise, the `elseDoThisIfFalse` statement is executed.

To learn how to use the conditional operator, type this common `if-else` statement into a copy of SHELL.CPP:

```
int valueA = 10;
int valueB = 20;
printf("valueA ");
if (valueA < valueB)
  printf("<");
else
  printf(">=");
puts(" valueB");
```

The `if-else` statement displays a message that tells you whether `valueA` is less than `valueB`. You can do the same in fewer lines using a conditional operator. Replace the last six lines in the preceding code with these three:

```
printf("valueA ");
(valueA < valueB) ? printf("<") : printf(">=");
puts(" valueB");
```

If the expression (valueA < valueB) is true, the first printf statement displays the symbol <. If the expression is false, the second printf displays >=.

A conditional statement has the value of the statement executed — a fact that you can put to good use by *assigning* that value to an object. For example, you can use the conditional operator to prevent a program from halting due to an integer divide-by-zero error. Add this code to a fresh copy of SHELL.CPP:

```
int i1 = 10;
int i2 = 0;
int iresult = i1 / i2;
printf("iresult == %d\n", iresult);
```

When you press Ctrl+F9 to compile and run the program, it ends without displaying the final result. Press Alt+F5 to discover why — on-screen is the message *Divide error.* Dividing by zero simply isn't allowed. To prevent this unhappy occurrence, you can use an if statement to test whether i2 equals zero:

```
if (i2 == 0)
  iresult = 0;
else
  iresult = i1 / i2;
```

That prevents the error but requires two assignments and, besides, it looks clumsy. You can do the same with one assignment by using a conditional operator. Try these statements in SHELL.CPP:

```
int i1 = 10;
int i2 = 0;
int iresult = (i2 == 0) ? 0 : i1 / i2;
printf("iresult == %d\n", iresult);
```

The third line performs several jobs. First, it defines the integer object iresult. Next, it performs a conditional statement, testing whether the expression (i2 == 0) is true. If so, the value of the conditional expression is 0 (the literal value after the question mark); otherwise, the value equals i1 divided by i2. Either way, the final value — zero or the result of the integer division — is assigned to iresult. Try other values for i1 and i2 until you understand how the statement works.

Goto

It's time for a confession. In the section on for statements, I lied. I didn't save the best for last; I actually saved the *worst* feature in C to end this chapter — goto. Before I show you how to use it, let me recommend that you *never* use goto statements. If you think your program requires a goto, you need to redesign your code. There is nothing goto can do that other, more structured statements such as while and for cannot do as well or better.

So, if goto is useless, why does it exist? Most likely, when C was first invented, many other programming languages had a "jump" or "goto" command (or a "skip over" instruction) to mirror similar control statements in assembly language. It was only natural for C to have a goto as well, even though it wasn't needed. I suspect goto was added to C because that was easier than justifying leaving it out.

A goto statement directs the program to execute a labeled statement. A label is any unused identifier that ends with a colon. It may be placed in front of any statement. To start or restart the program running from that statement, the program issues a goto command to the label. Here's a sample you can try in SHELL.CPP:

```
int count = 1;
TOP:
  printf("%d\n", count);
  count++;
  if (count <= 10) goto TOP;
```

That's probably the worst way to write a loop in C. First, the program defines an integer variable, count, initialized to 1. The label TOP: precedes a printf output statement that displays count's value. After that, count is incremented, and if count is less than or equal to 10, an if statement executes a goto statement, directing the program to run starting at the labeled statement. Eventually, count becomes greater than 10, causing the if statement not to execute the goto and, in this example, ending the program.

There are other rules about goto — for instance, you cannot jump from one function to inside another. But I see no point in discussing further a feature that I would never use in practice. (In fact, I can't recall *ever* using a goto except in examples that explain how it works!) So let's move on to more interesting topics. In the next chapter, you learn how to construct *derived data types* such as arrays and structures. You also examine unions and bit fields — which sound more mysterious than they really are. As you'll discover, C's derived data types make it possible to combine simple types into highly sophisticated objects that can handle a wide variety of information-storage tasks.

Chapter 7

Derived Data Types

Amateur Dr. Frankensteins listen up. Sew legs down there, attach arms over here, insert head on top, press Enter, and what have you got? In fiction, you create a tragic monster. In C, you construct an array, structure, string, or other *derived data type* composed of elements borrowed from C's laboratory of body parts — that is, integers, floating-point values, and characters.

As you learn in this chapter, derived types form the backbones of many applications. Using derived types, you assign symbolic names to enumerated constants, you collect multiple objects in arrays, you build and manipulate character strings, and you fashion complex structures. With this chapter — and your skills on the operating table — perhaps your resulting programs will be more forgiving of you than Mary Shelley's classic monster was of its inventor.

Symbolic Representations

Computers store values numerically as collections of 0 and 1 bits in memory, but it's too difficult to write computer programs on the computer's binary level. Instead, it's clearer and easier to represent values symbolically. A graphics program, for example, might specify an object's color as the symbol red, but in memory, that color and other objects are represented numerically.

Well-chosen symbols add clarity to programs. Suppose you need to store a color value as an integer. You define an `int` variable named `color`:

```
int color;
```

Statements can assign values to `color`, but literal integer constants are meaningless:

```
color = 1;
```

For better clarity, you might define a few symbolic constants that represent color values:

```
#define red 0
#define green 1
#define blue 2
```

The values are arbitrary — they could be any unique integers that the program understands as colors. The symbols can now be used in statements:

```
color = blue;
int background = red;
```

Those statements have obvious meanings. No comments are needed, and the assignments are easily modified. Whenever possible, always use symbols rather than literal values. They can make code read more like good prose than computer programs.

Can You Enumerate on That?

C's enumerated data type defines symbolic constants more or less automatically. Rather than use three definitions:

```
#define red 0
#define green 1
#define blue 2
```

you can do the same by creating an *enumerated type:*

```
enum Colors {red, green, blue};
```

The `enum` keyword identifies `Colors` as a new data type, one that represents a list of items (`red`, `green`, `blue`) in braces, separated by commas. The listed items are integer contants, automatically assigned sequential values starting with 0. So, in this case, `red` represents 0, `green` is 1, and `blue` is 2, just as though you defined them individually. Some programmers capitalize type names like `Colors` to distinguish it from variables and other names, but it could also be spelled `colors` in lowercase.

The enumerated type `Colors` and its listed elements `red`, `green`, and `blue` are *not* variables, and they occupy no space in memory at runtime. Enumerated types are similar to other data types such as `int` and `double`. They are strictly for your convenience in writing code that is clear and easy to understand.

To use an enumerated data type, you must define a variable. Here's a sample:

```
Colors background;
```

That designates `background` as a variable of the enumerated type `Colors`. As a variable of that type, `background` can be assigned any one of the enumeration's listed elements:

```
background = red;
```

Enumerated constants behave like integers, but they permit the compiler to perform type checking on assignments. For instance, suppose you define another enumerated type:

```
enum Temperatures {cold, warm, hot};
```

Later, while modifying your carefully constructed code, one of your less talented associates mistakenly attempts to assign one of `Temperatures`' elements to `background`:

```
background = hot;  // ???
```

Well-designed C compilers (such as the one supplied with this book) warn you that `hot` is not an appropriate value for `background`, even though, internally, `hot`, `warm`, `cold`, `red`, `green`, and `blue` are all just integer values. Using enumerated data types can help prevent errors caused by assigning the wrong types of values to variables.

Fancy enumerations

A sample program, Listing 7-1, MONTHS.CPP, demonstrates a few subtle variations on the preceding theme. The problem to solve is, how can a program best represent the month names *Jan, Feb, Mar, ... Dec?* An enumerated data type offers one possible solution.

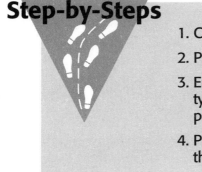

Step-by-Steps

1. Change to the PART2 directory.

2. Press F3 and load MONTHS.CPP into the IDE.

3. Enter the highlighted instructions in Listing 7-1. Be sure to type braces { and } in the `enum` statement, not parentheses!

4. Press Ctrl+F9 to compile and run. Follow instructions after the listing.

Listing 7-1: MONTHS.CPP

```
/* Enumerated Constants */

#include <stdio.h>
#include <conio.h>
#include <ctype.h>

enum Months {Jan, Feb, Mar,
  Apr, May, Jun, Jul, Aug, Sep,
  Oct, Nov, Dec};

char Pause()
{
  char c;
  printf("\nPress Enter to continue...");
  while ((c = getchar()) != '\n') { }
  return c;
}

int main()
{
  Months month;
  int day;
  int year;

  month = Aug;
  day = 12;
  year = 2002;

  clrscr();
  printf("Date is: ");

  switch (month) {
    case Jan: printf("January"); break;
    case Feb: printf("February"); break;
    case Mar: printf("March"); break;
    case Apr: printf("April"); break;
    case May: printf("May"); break;
    case Jun: printf("June"); break;
    case Jul: printf("July"); break;
    case Aug: printf("August"); break;
    case Sep: printf("September"); break;
    case Oct: printf("October"); break;
    case Nov: printf("November"); break;
    case Dec: printf("December"); break;
  }
```

```
    printf(" %d, %d\n", day, year);

    Pause();
    return 0;
}
```

The first three lines you typed define an enumerated data type, `Months`, for the 12 month names, abbreviated to Jan, Feb, Mar, and so on. The program defines a variable of type `Months`:

```
Months month;
```

Other variables, `day` and `year`, are plain `int` values. The program assigns a symbolic month name to `month`:

```
month = Aug;
```

It's important to realize that `Aug` is just a symbol for an integer constant — the word "Aug" isn't stored in the compiled code. Consequently, to display month names for a given `Months` value requires additional work. You might, for example, use a `switch` statement as in the sample code. Each `case` is written on a single line to save space. You could also write them in the usual way:

```
case Jan:
  printf("January");
  break;
case Feb:
...
```

The sample program has an intentional bug, however, that may be hard to spot. When the compiler processes the `Months` enumeration, it assigns sequential values starting with zero to the listed elements. Thus Jan is 0, Feb is 1, and so on. Prove that by inserting this line after the last `printf` statement in the listing:

```
printf("month value == %d\n", month);
```

When you press Ctrl+F9 to compile and run the program, it informs you that

```
month value == 7
```

But August is usually represented as 8, not 7. To fix the problem, assign 1 to `Jan` in the enumeration:

```
enum Months {Jan = 1, Feb, Mar,
  Apr, May, Jun, Jul, Aug, Sep,
  Oct, Nov, Dec};
```

Specifying 1 for `Jan` causes the compiler to assign sequential values *starting from 1* to the other symbols. Thus Feb becomes 2, Mar is 3, and so on. The modified program still displays the word "August" correctly, but it now represents that month internally as the value 8:

```
month value == 8
```

You can assign values similarly to any enumerated constant. For example, you might define `Temperature` like this:

```
enum Temperature {cold = 32, warm = 60, hot = 100};
```

Using typedef aliases

Strict ANSI C compilers require you to use the `enum` keyword to define variables of an enumerated type. For instance, you must define a variable `month` of type `enum Months` by writing

```
enum Months month;
```

The compiler supplied with this book and most other C++ compilers permit you to delete `enum` and simply write

```
Months month;
```

In strict ANSI C, you can acheive a similar brevity of expression by using a `typedef` alias — just a fancy way of creating a name that represents *another* data type. To demonstrate the technique, change the `Months` enumeration in MONTHS.CPP to the following:

```
typedef enum months {Jan = 1, Feb, Mar, Apr, May,
   Jun, Jul, Aug, Sep, Oct, Nov, Dec} Months;
```

The `typedef` statement uses the general form

```
typedef <anytype> Name;
```

The construction associates *Name* with *<anytype>*. In the preceding enumeration, `Months` is symbolically equated to `enum months`; therefore, a statement that defines a variable `month` of type `Months`:

```
Months month;
```

is actually "seen" by the compiler as

```
enum months month;
```

The `typedef` keyword is commonly used with enumerated types and with structures (to be introduced later in this chapter). I prefer the C++ style of *not* using `typedef`, but if you must use an ANSI C-only compiler, you'll need to master the technique. You'll also see the method used in published C listings.

Collecting Data in Arrays

When you have more than one object of a type to store, an array might be the appropriate safekeeping device. Arrays are just blocks of memory big enough to hold one, two, hundreds, even thousands of values, all of the same type. You define an array using square brackets:

```
int numbers[10];
```

That sets aside enough memory to hold ten `int` values. As Figure 7-1 illustrates, all values in an array are adjacent in memory, making it possible for programs to treat the array either as one object or as a collection of individual values.

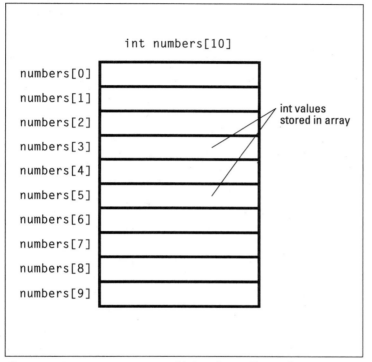

Figure 7-1 ▶ An array stores multiple values adjacent in memory.

To refer to an element in an array, an expression uses square brackets with an *index value* inside. For example, this sets the third array value of `numbers` to 650:

```
numbers[2] = 650;
```

Examine Figure 7-1 to see why it's necessary to use an index value of 2 to refer to the array's third element, sometimes called a "slot." The first element is indexed as 0, the second as 1, the third as 2, and so on. All arrays are similarly indexed starting with 0. For example, here's how to define an array of floating-point values:

```
float sums[100];
```

The array `sums` is large enough to store 100 values of type `float`. Here again, the first element is indexed by the integer 0:

```
sums[0] = 3.14159;
```

That assigns 3.14159 to the array's first element. Index 99 references the last element:

```
sums[99] = 9.9999;
```

The expression `sums[99]`, not `sums[100]`, refers to the one-hundredth value in the array. You can also assign values from the array to another variable. This, for example, copies the fourth value from `sums` to a `float` variable, `copy`:

```
float copy = sums[3];
```

Suppose you want to total the values in `sums`. It's probably easiest to use a `for` statement:

```
int i;
float total = 0;
for (i = 0; i < 100; i++)
    total += sums[i];
```

The final statement, which uses the shorthand `+=` operator, is equivalent to

```
total = total + sums[i];
```

Notice the use of an `int` index, `i`, to refer to all of the array's values, indexed from 0 to 99. It is especially important to limit the index to the range of defined values. This, for instance, is a serious mistake:

```
for (i = 0; i <= 100; i++)  // ???
    total += sums[i];
```

That `for` loop repeats 101 times, setting `i` to the values 0 to 100. On the last repetition, the faulty code adds `sums[100]` to `total` as though you had written

```
total += sums[100];  // ???
```

The expression `sums[100]` is an example of a *boundary error.* It refers to a location in memory outside the array's defined bounds. C does not warn you about boundary errors. It is up to you to prevent them, especially for statements that *assign* values to array positions:

```
sums[105] = 123.456;  // ???
```

The expression `sums[105]` refers to a location in memory that may belong to another variable, the program's stack space, or to compiled code. Obviously, assigning a value to any of those positions is a serious mistake. When using index values, always be sure to play inside the array's yard!

A good way to prevent boundary errors is to define the array's size using a symbolic constant:

```
#define SIZE 100  // Number of array elements
```

You can then use `SIZE` to define the array:

```
float sums[SIZE];  // Array of SIZE float values
```

Subsequent `for` loops and other statements can also use `SIZE` to ensure that index values stay in bounds:

```
int i;
float total = 0;
for (i = 0; i < SIZE; i++)
  total += sums[i];
```

The expression `i < SIZE` limits `i`'s value to one *less* than `SIZE`, or 99. Best of all, you can change the constant to adjust the array's size *and* the `for` loop control expression:

```
#define SIZE 200
```

Simply recompiling the program adjusts the array to hold 200 elements and changes the `for` loop to limit the array index to the values 0 to 199. No other changes to the program are needed.

Using arrays

Listing 7-2, AVERAGE.CPP, demonstrates how to use arrays to store a collection of values. The program sums the values in the array and computes the average value. The demonstration also shows how to call the C library's `rand` function to generate so-called *random numbers.* For example, try running AVERAGE.CPP several times. As you'll see, each run assigns a different set of values to the program's array.

 Technically speaking, there is no such beast as a *random number.* Computers, however, can generate *random sequences* of values that exhibit properties of randomness. That is, successive numbers are not obviously predictable from those already generated. The study of random sequences and their characteristics has fascinated computer scientists for decades. To use random sequences, include the STDLIB.H and TIME.H functions in your programs.

Listing 7-2: AVERAGE.CPP

```
/* Average values in an array */

#include <stdio.h>
#include <conio.h>
#include <stdlib.h>
#include <time.h>

#define SIZE 14
long data[SIZE];
```

```
char Pause()
{
  char c;
  printf("\nPress Enter to continue...");
  while ((c = getchar()) != '\n') { }
  return c;
}


main()
{
  int i;
  long total = 0, average;

  clrscr();
  randomize();
  for (i = 0; i < SIZE; i++)
    data[i] = rand();

  printf("\nArray of values:\n\n");
  for (i = 0; i < SIZE; i++)
    printf("%2d: %ld\n", i, data[i]);

  for (i = 0; i < SIZE; i++)
    total += data[i];
  average = total / SIZE;

  printf("\nTotal ............ %ld\n", total);
  printf("Number of values .. %d\n", SIZE);
  printf("Average value ..... %ld\n", average);

  Pause();
  return 0;
}
```

The sample program defines an array data large enough to hold 14 values of type long. For safety, a #define directive creates a constant, SIZE, that represents the array's size. Notice that the array is defined globally (outside of main or any other function). You can also define arrays inside functions. For example, you may move this statement inside main's braces:

```
long data[SIZE];
```

You next typed some variable definitions: one for an index int named i and another that creates two long variables, total and average, which have obvious purposes. Variable total is initialized to zero, but average is not initialized in its definition because it is assigned a value later.

The next four lines perform startup chores, first clearing the display and then calling `randomize`, which *seeds* the random number generator. Seeding the generator causes it to begin different random sequences on each program run. (The seed is extracted from the computer's clock — the reason for including the TIME.H header file.) If you want the *same* sequence on each run, don't call `randomize`. A `for` loop calls `rand` for a number at random, assigned to each of the array slots from `data[0]` to `data[SIZE-1]`. This statement assigns the value returned by `rand` to the array slot indexed by integer value `i`:

```
data[i] = rand();
```

After those setups, a `printf` statement displays a label. Another `for` loop displays the data in the array. Notice again how the expression `data[i]` refers to individual array values indexed by the value of `i`.

Finally, a third `for` loop sums the values in `data`, storing the result in variable `total`. After that's done, the final statement you typed computes the average value. The `total`, `SIZE`, and `average` values are then displayed for reference (see Figure 7-2).

```
Array of values:

 0: 28298
 1: 25995
 2: 13658
 3: 16057
 4: 1575
 5: 2132
 6: 21478
 7: 5641
 8: 20356
 9: 16210
10: 22179
11: 6346
12: 7311
13: 6490

Total ............ 193726
Number of values .. 14
Average value ..... 13837
```

Figure 7-2 ▶ Sample output from AVERAGE.CPP (Listing 7-2).

Multidimensional arrays

The arrays you have seen so far are *single dimensional*. That is, they store a sequence of values one after the other like a train of boxcars (see also Figure 7-1). Arrays may also have two or more dimensions. Such *multidimensional arrays* form matrixes and are useful for representing data in tabular form.

To create a multidimensional array, specify two or more dimensions in square brackets. For example, this creates a 4-by-5 table of `int` values:

```
int table[4][5]
```

Arrays are stored in row-order, thus the expression `table[0]` represents the first row of 5 values, `table[1]` represents the second row, `table[2]` the third, and so on (see Figure 7-3). The expression `table[0][0]` refers to the upper-left value in the table; `table[2][3]` represents the fourth value in the third row.

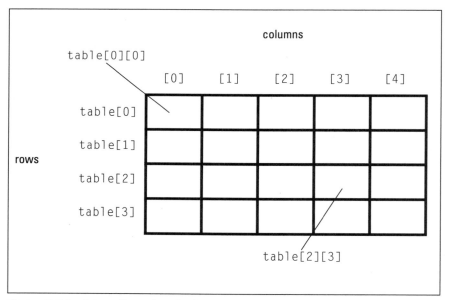

Figure 7-3 ▶ A two-dimensional 4-by-5 array.

Two-dimensional arrays are easily visualized as having rows and columns, but it's often also helpful to think of them as "arrays of arrays." Using this concept, you might view the `table` array as a 4-element array of 5-element arrays, a notion that becomes especially useful when you add more dimensions. This, for example, creates a three-dimensional matrix:

```
int cube[3][5][4];
```

In some applications, it might make sense to visualize cube as an object with three dimensions. The statement

```
int v = cube[2][1][3];
```

assigns to v one value from the cube. In other cases, cube may be thought of as an array of arrays of arrays. It's rare to need more than three dimensions, but you may in theory create multidimensional arrays of as many levels as you need. Remember, however, that the space required to store multidimensional arrays grows very large very fast. A 100-by-100 array of int values occupies 20,000 bytes (assuming two-byte integers). A three-dimensional, 100-by-100-by-100 array requires 2 *million* bytes of storage — too large for the compiler supplied with this book and, indeed, for most compilers to handle.

Multidimensional arrays are frequently used for storing tables of information — hours worked by a company's employees on each day of the week, for example. Listing 7-3, EMPLOYEE.CPP, demonstrates how to construct the necessary data structures.

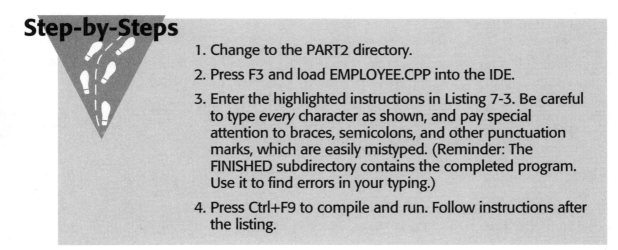

Step-by-Steps

1. Change to the PART2 directory.

2. Press F3 and load EMPLOYEE.CPP into the IDE.

3. Enter the highlighted instructions in Listing 7-3. Be careful to type *every* character as shown, and pay special attention to braces, semicolons, and other punctuation marks, which are easily mistyped. (Reminder: The FINISHED subdirectory contains the completed program. Use it to find errors in your typing.)

4. Press Ctrl+F9 to compile and run. Follow instructions after the listing.

Listing 7-3: EMPLOYEE.CPP

```
/* Multidimensional arrays */

#include <stdio.h>
#include <conio.h>
#include <stdlib.h>
#include <time.h>

#define EMPLOYEES 10
```

```c
enum Days {Sun, Mon, Tue, Wed, Thu, Fri, Sat};

char dayNames[7][4] = {
  "Sun", "Mon", "Tue", "Wed", "Thu", "Fri", "Sat"
};

char Pause()
{
  char c;
  printf("\nPress Enter to continue...");
  while ((c = getchar()) != '\n') { }
  return c;
}

int main()
{
  int hours[EMPLOYEES][7];
  int emp;    // Employee number
  Days day;   // Day name

  printf("Hours worked\n\n");

  clrscr();
  randomize();
  for (emp = 0; emp < EMPLOYEES; emp++)
    for (day = Sun; day <= Sat; day++)
      hours[emp][day] = rand() % 15;   // Maximum 14 hrs per day

  printf("Employee:");
  for (emp = 0; emp < EMPLOYEES; emp++)
    printf(" [%2d]", emp + 1);
  puts("");

  for (day = Sun; day <= Sat; day++) {
    printf("\n    %3s", dayNames[day]);
    for (emp = 0; emp < EMPLOYEES; emp++)
      printf("%5d", hours[emp][day]);
  }

  puts("");
  Pause();
  return 0;
}
```

The program uses a few constants and types for clarity. A symbolic constant, EMPLOYEES, represents the number of workers in the company. An enumerated data type, Days, symbolically represents the days of the week Sun through Sat. A multidimensional array, dayNames, stores character strings for each day. The construction char dayNames[7][4] is literally a seven-element array of four-character arrays — that is, seven *strings,* each large enough for three characters plus a null terminator.

I'll get back to strings in a moment. For now, study how the program initializes the dayNames array, using literal string constants in braces, separated by commas. You may perform a similar trick to initialize any array. For example, this defines an array of ten integers and assigns values to each slot:

```
int array[10] = {10, 20,
   30, 40, 50, 60, 70, 80, 90, 100};
```

Remember to use braces, not parentheses, for the list of constants. You must supply the correct number of values, and you may use this technique only in the array's definition. You may not use the method to assign new array values at runtime.

Getting back to the sample program, function main defines three variables — an array hours with space for seven entries for each employee, an integer index emp, and a second index of the enumerated data type Days, named day. Using the two index values, the expression hours[3][Tue] refers to the number of hours worked by employee number 4 on Tuesday. (The expression hours[0] refers to the first empolyee, so hours[3] refers to employee number 4, not number 3.)

To assign values to the hours array, the program calls the rand function, assigning the expression rand() % 15 to each slot in hours. A nested for loop ensures that every slot is assigned a value.

Similar for loops display the resulting table, a sample of which is illustrated in Figure 7-4. You should be able to understand most of the programming in this section, but some of the notations in the printf statements may seem odd. (You learn more about printf in Chapter 9's discussion of functions and also Chapter 11's look at C's input and output functions.)

```
Employee: [ 1] [ 2] [ 3] [ 4] [ 5] [ 6] [ 7] [ 8] [ 9] [10]
      Sun    5    6    9    3    5    5    2   13   14    7
      Mon    8   13   13   13   13    2    2    0    0   14
      Tue    8    3    9    9    6    9    5    7    0    9
      Wed   12    9    0    7    8    4    6   10    2    2
      Thu    0    0   13    8    2   12   11    2    5    8
      Fri   11   14    0    9    0    5    1   11    5    6
      Sat    5    2    9   13   12    0    7    8    3    6
```

Figure 7-4 ▶ Sample output from EMPLOYEE.CPP (Listing 7-3).

Strings and Other Character Things

Strings in some computer languages are data types in their own right. In C, however, strings are simply arrays of `char` values, with one special rule thrown in for good measure. A C-style string ends with a character value equal to zero, called *the null terminator.* And, no, that's not the name of a gruesome new movie starring Arnold Schwarzenegger. It's just a value that is used to mark the end of a string.

Figure 7-5 illustrates how the string `"Turbo C"` appears in memory. All characters in the string, including the space, are stored next to each other in eight-bit bytes representing ASCII character values. In other words, *the string is an array of* `char` *values.* It ends with a null terminator. Figure 7.6 shows the same string stored in an array that is larger than necessary. The bytes beyond the null terminator still occupy space in memory, but they are not part of the string. Be sure to understand that concept. A string, including its null terminator, may completely fill the `char` array's allocated memory, it may partially fill that space, or it may have *no* characters. Figure 7-7, for example, shows a *null string* — one that has no characters; just a null terminator. The length of this string is zero, but its `char` array still occupies space in memory.

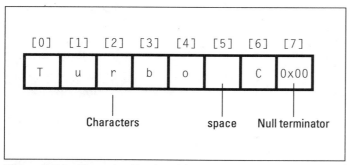

Figure 7-5 ▶ The string `Turbo C` in memory.

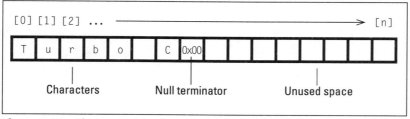

Figure 7-6 ▶ The same string in a larger memory space.

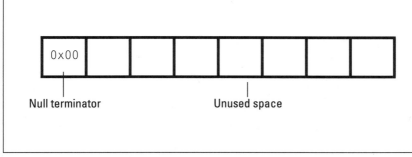

Figure 7-7 ▶ A null string.

String functions

There are many operations you can perform on strings. You can assign characters to them, you can copy them, you can compare two strings, and so on. The following notes introduce a few of the standard library's string functions; others are covered in Chapter 14. First, include the STRING.H header file:

```
#include <string.h>
```

Then define an array of `char` large enough to hold your string. *Remember to add one byte for the string's null terminator.* For example, add the preceding line to a copy of SHELL.CPP from the PART2 directory. (Type the line beneath the other `#include` directives.) Then, below the comment *Insert snippets here,* enter these two statements:

```
char string[20] = "Type and Learn C";
puts(string);
```

The first line defines an array of 20 `char` values and assigns to that space the string `Type and Learn C`. The compiler automatically attaches a null terminator after `C`. If the array isn't large enough to hold the assigned string, you receive the error message *Illegal Initialization.* To see the error, change 20 to 2 and press F9. Change the 2 back to 20 before continuing.

After constructing a string, you might need to determine its length. Do that by calling the `strlen` function, which you can assign to an `int` variable. Add these lines after the preceding two, and press Ctrl+F9 to compile and run the program:

```
int len = strlen(string);
printf("length of string == %d\n", len);
```

The *size* of a `char` array is not the same as the *length* of the string it contains. To display the size of the array in bytes, add these lines to the program:

```
int size = sizeof(string);
printf("size of string == %d\n", size);
```

On-screen, you see

```
Type and Learn C
length of string == 16
size of string == 20
```

The length of the string, 16, equals the number of characters contained in the char array. The size of that array is 20 bytes. Accounting for the null terminator (not included in the string's length), this string has three unused bytes at its end. You can get rid of those bytes by changing the string definition to

```
char string[17] = "Type and Learn C";
```

Press Ctrl+F9 to run the program, which tells you that the string length is 16 and its size is 17 — exactly the right amount of space to store the string and its null terminator.

Rather than count characters manually, you can ask the compiler to create a char array of exactly the correct size. To do that, specify *no* array length:

```
char string[] = "Type and Learn C";
```

When you define strings that way, the compiler sets string to exactly the correct size (17 bytes in this case).

The preceding string initializations are actually shorthand forms of the general array initialization technique introduced earlier in this chapter. The following statement constructs and initializes a string array s to the string ABC plus a null terminator:

```
char s[4] = "ABC";
```

You may do the same by individually setting each character in the array, but in that case, it's your responsibility to provide a null at the end:

```
char s[4] = {
  'A', 'B', 'C', 0x00
};
```

There's no good reason to create strings that way, but you should understand the technique. (Note the semicolon after the declaration.) The technique is permitted only in the variable's definition. You cannot use the same method to assign different strings at runtime. This is not allowed:

```
char string[20] = "Type and Learn C";
string = "Turbo C++";   // ???
```

The first line is OK, but the second attempts to assign different characters to string. To do that at runtime, you must call a *string function,* strcpy. Using a fresh copy of SHELL.CPP from the PART2 directory, enter these lines after the comment *Insert snippets here*:

```
char string[20] = "Type and Learn C";
puts(string);
strcpy(string, "Turbo C++");
puts(string);
```

The first line creates and initializes a 20-byte `char` array to the string `Type and Learn C`. The second line displays that string. The third line copies a new string, `Turbo C++`, to the `string` array. (The compiler automatically supplies a null terminator.) The last line displays the new string. On-screen, you see

```
Type and Learn C
Turbo C++
```

The `strcpy` function transfers a *source* string to a *destination,* which must be an array of `char` large enough to hold the transferred characters:

```
strcpy(destination, source);
```

You can also call `strcpy` to copy one string variable to another. Try these statements in a fresh copy of SHELL.CPP:

```
char s1[20] = "First string";
char s2[20] = "Second string";
puts(s1);
puts(s2);
strcpy(s1, s2);
puts(s1);
puts(s2);
```

The fifth line copies the characters (including a null terminator) from `s2` to `s1`. After that statement executes, the two `char` arrays contain the identical strings.

When the program is calling `strcpy`, it is your responsibility to ensure that the destination array is large enough to hold the characters from the source string.

In many programs, you'll need to prompt users to enter a string. There are several ways to accomplish that task, but some are better than others. In fact, some methods are downright dangerous. For example, try these statements in a copy of SHELL.CPP:

```
char string[80];
printf("Enter a string: ");
gets(string);  // ???
puts(string);
```

After defining an 80-byte `char` array (large enough for a 79-character string plus a null terminator), the program prompts you to enter a string. Function `gets` transfers each entered character into the `string` variable, which `puts` and then displays. Trouble is, the `gets` function does not prevent you from typing beyond the end of the memory allocated to `string`. If you enter more than 79 characters, the function merrily deposits them beyond the end of the allocated memory, obliterating whatever else happens to be at that location. If that memory contains code, the program is due for a colossal crash.

There is a relatively safe way to call `gets` — merely increase the length of the string variable beyond the size of the computer's line buffer, sometimes called the "type-ahead" buffer:

```
char string[255];
```

Assuming the buffer is about 128 characters, that will prevent errors caused by typing too many characters. Of course, the rest of the allocated memory is wasted. Also, it's possible for other software to increase the buffer length, reintroducing the same problem. So, what's the answer? The classic solution uses a function, `scanf`, to input strings limited to a specified length. As in `printf`, the f in `scanf` means "formatted." The `scanf` function inputs formatted objects.

Make a fresh copy of SHELL.CPP, then add these lines below the comment *Insert snippets here:*

```
char string[21];
printf("Enter a 20-character string: ");
scanf("%20s", string);
fflush(stdin);
puts(string);
```

The `scanf` function's literal string uses the notation *%20s* to limit input to 20 characters. A null terminator is automatically added after the final character. To allow space for the null, 21 bytes are allocated to the array. It is also necessary to call the auxiliary function, `fflush`, specifying the standard input file `stdin` to reset the system's input. If you don't flush the input, subsequent strings cannot be read because the end-of-line character produced by pressing Enter remains in the input stream, causing future calls to `scanf` to end immediately without pausing for new input.

One serious problem with the preceding method is that `scanf` treats a blank character as the end of the string. Also, `scanf` is an extensive function that takes great care to use properly. It can input all sorts of data, but its use requires you to understand topics not yet introduced.

Fortunately, there's another, and perhaps better, method for entering strings. Make a fresh copy of SHELL.CPP; then insert these two lines below the file's #include directives:

```
#include <string.h>
#define SIZE 21
```

As I mentioned, for safety, it's a good idea to use a symbolic constant like SIZE for specifying array sizes. The same rule goes for strings. Construct a string and a few other variables by adding these lines below the comment *Insert snippets here:*

```
char string[SIZE];
int i = 0;
int limit = SIZE;
char c;
```

The input method I'm about to show you requires a destination to hold characters (`string`), an array index (`i`), a limiting value equal to the array's size in bytes (`limit`), and a `char` variable to hold each character as it is typed (`c`). The technique limits the number of characters to one less than specified by `limit`. Finish the program by typing these lines below the preceding four:

```
printf("Enter a 20-character string: ");
while (--limit > 0) {
  c = getchar();
  if (c == EOF || c == '\n')
    limit = 0;
  else
    string[i++] = c;
}
string[i] = '\0';
fflush(stdin);
puts(string);
```

A while loop repeats as long as limit less one is greater than 0. (The -- operator decrements limit on each pass through the loop.) Function getchar is called to obtain a character entered at the keyboard. An if statement tests whether that character is an end-of-file system value (represented by constant EOF) or an end of line control code, represented as the character '\n'. In either case, limit is set to zero, ending the loop. Otherwise, the input character in c is inserted into string at index position i, which is incremented by the ++ operator. After inputting the string, fflush is called to flush the input of any leftover end-of-line characters, which can be left in the input by this technique if you enter more than limit-1 characters. Function puts displays the final result.

That may seem to be a lot of work to enter strings safely, but as you will learn in Chapter 9, you can wrap the programming up into a function that you can call to input a string — but more on that later. There are two other string functions I want to show you before moving on.

Concatenating strings

It is frequently necessary to join — or to use the fancy programming word, *concatenate* — two or more strings. For instance, suppose you have these two strings:

```
char first[80] = "George";
char second[80] = "Washington";
```

You can join those two strings by calling the strcat function like this:

```
strcat(first, second);
```

That attaches the characters from second to the end of the string in first. The resulting string is stored in first. The trouble with this approach is that the final name comes out as *GeorgeWashington,* with no space between the two names. So let's start over with first and second. A more acceptable way to concatenate the names into one string is to define a third char array:

```
char name[255];
```

Copy `first` to `name` by calling `strcpy`:

```
strcpy(name, first);
```

Attach a space to the end of that string by calling `strcat`:

```
strcat(name, " ");
```

Finally, add in the last name:

```
strcat(name, second);
```

The result in `name` is *George Washington,* properly spaced. Be sure to understand the preceding steps. In many cases, you begin a concatenation by first calling `strcpy` to initialize a string variable, after which you call `strcat` one or more times to build the final string.

Comparing strings

There are other string operations that I'll introduce in time, but there's one more you need to learn now. Programs can compare two strings alphabetically by calling the `strcmp` function. The function requires two string arguments — let's call them `stringA` and `stringB`. Use the function like this:

```
int result = strcmp(stringA, stringB);
```

That sets `result` to one of three values. If the two strings are exactly equal, `result` is set to 0. If `stringA` is alphabetically less than `stringB`, `result` is set to –1. If `stringA` is alphabetically greater than `stringB`, `result` is set to +1. An `if` statement can test `result` and take an appropriate action based on the string comparison:

```
if (result == 0)
  doSomething();
```

The program calls `doSomething` (not shown) if the two strings are equal. To call the function if `stringA` is less than `stringB`, you can write

```
if (result < 0)
  doSomething();
```

Or to call the function if `stringA` is greater than `stringB`, revise that to

```
if (result > 0)
  doSomething;
```

After you get used to using `strcmp`, you can call the function directly in `if` and other statements rather than store its value in a variable. For example, to call `doSomething` if the two strings are equal, you can write

```
if (strcmp(stringA, stringB) == 0)
  doSomething();
```

Use `< 0` or `> 0` in place of `== 0` to call `doSomething` depending on which string is alphabetically greater.

Storing Data in Structures

C has one more derived data type that you will find immensely useful. Like an array, a `struct` (short for *structure*) collects one or more elements into one housing. Unlike an array, however, in which all the elements must be of the same type, a `struct`'s elements (called *members*) may be of different types. Form a `struct` like this:

```
struct Coordinate {
  int x;
  int y;
};
```

That specifies a `struct` named `Coordinate` with two `int` members, `x` and `y`. Because the members are of the same type, you can also declare them like this:

```
struct Coordinate {
  int x, y;
};
```

 A `struct` declaration must end with a semicolon. The compiler should warn you if you forget, but some C compilers display cryptic error messages for missing semicolons. If you receive unusual messages, check that all `struct` declarations are properly terminated.

The members may be of the same or of different types. For example, `struct`s are useful for creating records, as might be stored in a database file:

```
struct Record {
  char name[40];
  char address[64];
  char cityStZip[80];
  int age;
  float weight;
};
```

The `struct Record` declares five members: three strings (of different lengths), an `int` value for a person's age, and a `float` variable for his or her weight.

Each of those `struct`s, `Coordinate` and `Record`, is a template for objects that a program may create. Structures are not objects themselves. They are data types that you may use to define one or more variables having the `struct`'s members. Think of `struct`s as schematics from which you can build objects, much as a carpenter uses a blueprint to construct a house. To define a `struct` variable, use its name in a definition, just as you define other variables:

```
struct Coordinate location;
```

C++ compilers (such as the one supplied with this book) permit you to delete the `struct` keyword:

```
Coordinate location;
```

Either way, the statements define a variable, `location`, with two `int` members, x and y. The two members are packed next to each other. To reference either one, use *dot notation,* specifying a member name after the variable:

```
location.x = 10;
location.y = 20;
```

That sets member x to 10 and y to 20 inside the `location` structure. Use similar programming to construct objects of more complex structures, such as `Record`. First, define a variable of that type:

```
struct Record rec;
```

The `rec` variable is an object of the `Record` data type. Insert a string into `rec`'s string members by calling the `strcpy` function. Also include the STRING.H header:

```
#include <string.h>
...
struct Record rec;
strcpy(rec.name, "Tom Swan");
strcpy(rec.address, "IDG Books Worldwide");
strcpy(rec.cityStZip, "San Mateo, CA 94402");
```

Assign values to the `age` and `weight` members as well:

```
rec.age = 43;
rec.weight = 145;
```

Try your hand at structures by typing the following statements into a fresh copy of SHELL.CPP, from the PART2 directory. First, add this `#include` directive under those already there:

```
#include <string.h>
```

Next, below that line, type the following `struct` declaration:

```
struct Phone {
  char name[80];
  char phone[13];
};
```

That declares `Phone` as a structure of two string members, `name` and `phone`, each an array of `char`, but of different lengths. Use the structure by defining a variable of type `Phone`, and then copy string data to its members. Add these lines below the comment *Insert snippets here:*

```
struct Phone rec;
strcpy(rec.name, "Your name");
strcpy(rec.phone, "215-555-1212");
```

The first line defines `rec` as a variable of the `struct Phone` data type. As I mentioned, with modern C++ compilers, you can delete the `struct` keyword. The next two statements assign string data to the `name` and `phone` members inside `rec`. Display that information by adding two more statements:

```
puts(rec.name);
puts(rec.phone);
```

Remember that all `struct`s are templates and, as such, may be used to create multiple variables. For example, to add another record to your database, define it and add some string data to its members:

```
struct Phone rec2;
strcpy(rec2.name, "Any name");
strcpy(rec2.phone, "401-555-1212");
```

Display the new record with two more `puts` statements:

```
puts(rec2.name);
puts(rec2.phone);
```

You could go on this way, defining `Phone` records and copying string data to them, but there's a better way to store multiple structures of the same type. Let's take a look.

Arrays of structures

Combining the forces of arrays and `struct`s creates truly powerful derived data types with several intriguing properties. Form an array of `struct` objects as you do any other array. For example, this creates an array of 100 `Phone` structures:

```
struct Phone database[100];
```

Add that line to the developing program just above function `main`. For reasons I'll get to later in the book, large variables such as the `database` array of 100 `Phone` structures are best stored globally — that is, outside of any functions. Defining `database` globally also causes it to be initialized to all zero bytes, eliminating the need to write initializing statements.

To refer to one of the structures in the array, use an integer index along with dot notation. For example, to copy a name to the first record, use a statement such as:

```
strcpy(database[0].name, "Your name");
```

The expression `database[0]` refers to the first `Phone` structure in full. The expression `database[0].name` refers to the `name` member of the first record in the `database` array. Feel free to change `Your name` to your name, or to any other string. Add a phone number to the first record with this statement:

```
strcpy(database[0].phone, "501-555-1212");
```

Use higher index values to refer to other records in the database array. Again, change the names and numbers to those from your little black book if you want. (In this computer age, does anybody actually keep a little black book anymore?) Also add as many additional records as you have, up to a total of 100 (indexed as database[99]). These statements add two more records to database:

```
strcpy(database[1].name, "Another name");
strcpy(database[1].phone, "717-555-1212");
strcpy(database[2].name, "Third name");
strcpy(database[2].phone, "201-555-1212");
```

To display the information in database, you could use individual puts statements as before, but it's more efficient to use a for loop. First, define two variables of type int:

```
int numRecs = 3;
int i;
```

Set numRecs to the total number of records you entered into database. Integer i is used by the loop and as the array index:

```
for (i = 0; i < numRecs; i++) {
  puts("");
  puts(database[i].name);
  puts(database[i].phone);
}
```

Nested structures

A structure may be nested inside another structure — in other words, one of a struct's members may be another struct. Suppose you need to store X and Y coordinate values. Declare a Point structure with two integer members, x and y:

```
struct Point {
  int x, y;
};
```

To define another structure for the upper-left and lower-right corners of a rectangle, you can nest two Point structures as struct members:

```
struct Rect {
  Point upperLeft;
  Point lowerRight;
};
```

The Rect structure has two members, upperLeft and lowerRight, each an object of the Point struct. You may create a variable of type Point and assign values to its members:

```
Point p;
p.x = 10;
p.y = 20;
```

You may also create a variable of type Rect and assign values to its nested structure members:

```
Rect r;
r.upperLeft = p;
r.lowerRight.x = 50;
r.lowerRight.y = 100;
```

The first line defines r as a variable of type Rect. The next line assigns Point p to the upperLeft member inside r. You can make this assignment because upperLeft and p are both of the same Point data type. The final two lines use double dot notation to assign values to the x and y members in the Point member, lowerRight, inside r.

Structures and typedef

Earlier, I explained how to use typedef with enumerated data types. A similar trick works with structs. In ANSI C, you must use the struct keyword to refer to a structure. For example, given the Point structure from the preceding section, ANSI C requires you to define a variable of that type as

```
struct Point myPoint;
```

C++ compilers do not require you to type struct before every instance of Point. With C++, you can simply write

```
Point myPoint;
```

With typedef, it's possible to acheive the same abbreviation with strict ANSI C compilers. As I explained, typedef uses the general form:

```
typedef <anytype> Name;
```

That gives <anytype> a symbolic *Name*, which can be used in place of that type. For example, <anytype> can be a struct declaration:

```
typedef struct tagPoint {
  int x, y;
} Point;
```

In that declaration, struct tagPoint is given the symbolic name Point by the typedef declaration. (It's traditional, though not required, to precede the structure name with *tag* as shown.) Given the preceding, you can now define variables of the alias Point without using the struct keyword:

```
Point myPoint;
```

With typedef, that works the same in C and C++. The compiler "sees" it as

```
struct tagPoint myPoint;
```

That about does it for derived data types. Next in the lineup is a subject I'm sure you've been waiting for — pointers. Perhaps you've heard that pointers are difficult to tame. If you've followed the text so far, however, I promise you'll have no trouble mastering pointers — a key subject in C programming. So don't miss the following chapter. It's one of the most important in this book.

Chapter 8

Pointers

If there's one subject that perplexes new C programmers, it's
pointers. That's because the benefits of pointers are difficult to
appreciate until you learn how to use them, and to get to that stage,
you have to memorize a bunch of rules that may seem to have little
rhyme or reason. But trust me. Experienced C programmers realize
that pointers are among their most important tools. In fact, much of
the world's software simply couldn't be written without them.

To the Point

So, what's a pointer? To comprehend the answer, you have to
understand that in memory, every byte has a unique location called
an *address.* Except in special circumstances, the internal structure of
an address doesn't matter to a C program. In PCs, for instance,
addresses might be composed of segment and offset values. In other
systems, addresses can be simple integer values. Usually, you can
ignore those differences in memory architecture. The vital fact is
that all bytes have *unique* addresses. By storing an address value in
a variable, *it points to a unique location in RAM.*

Really, pointers are that simple. A pointer is just a variable that
holds a memory address (see Figure 8-1). The byte at that address
may contain an ASCII character, or it could be the first byte of an
array or a structure. Using pointers, a program can address objects
of any type. What's more, storing pointer variables inside structures
creates objects that can address other objects, forming all sorts of
wonderments such as linked lists, trees, and other exotic castles in
the sand of memory's bits and bytes.

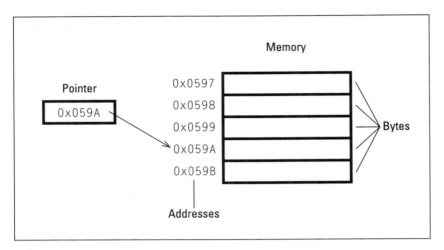

Figure 8-1 ▶ A pointer is a variable that holds a memory address.

Creating pointers

To create a pointer, define a variable as you normally do, but add an asterisk (C's *pointer symbol*) after the data type. For example, this creates a pointer to an `int` object:

```
int *ip;
```

That literal states that "variable `ip` is an `int` pointer." As such, the pointer can hold the address of any `int` object stored somewhere in memory. Like all variables, however, `ip` must be initialized before it is ready for use. Defining a pointer simply creates a variable that is capable of addressing another object. The pointer doesn't actually point to anything yet.

The placement of the asterisk in a pointer definition is somewhat controversial. You may type it immediately after the data type name, before the pointer variable's name, or between the type and pointer names with or without surrounding spaces. The following are equivalent definitions, but the first style is the most common:

```
int *ip;
int* ip;
int * ip;
int*ip;
```

You may create pointers to any objects of any type. Just supply whatever data type name you need. For example, this creates a `char` pointer named `cp`:

```
char *cp;
```

As I explain later in this chapter, `char` pointers are useful for addressing strings. Here's how to define a `float` pointer:

```
float *fp;
```

I often use *p* in pointer variable names, but you can name them anything you like. This defines `myPointer` as a pointer to a `float` object:

```
float *myPointer;
```

You may also create pointers to derived data types such as structures. Using the `Phone` structure from the preceding chapter:

```
struct Phone {
  char name[80];
  char phone[13];
};
```

the following creates a pointer, `recp`, to an object of the `Phone` type:

```
struct Phone *recp;
```

Here again, `recp` doesn't yet address any object in memory. To cause that to happen, you must initialize the pointer. Here's how.

Initializing pointers

Initializing a pointer gives it the address of an object in memory. After you initialize a pointer, you can use it to perform various operations on that object.

There are several ways to initialize pointers, but the most straightforward is to use C's address-of operator, &. Suppose that you have the following `int` definition somewhere in your program:

```
int count;
```

You can also define an `int` pointer:

```
int *ip;
```

Because `ip` is an `int` pointer, it can address an `int` object. A statement can therefore assign `count`'s address to `ip`:

```
ip = &count;
```

Applying the address-of operator to `count` forms an expression that C evaluates as the object's address. The assignment statement assigns `count`'s address to `ip`, after which `ip` points to `count`'s value in memory (see Figure 8-2). In other words, `ip` is an alias for `count`. Both `count` and `ip` *refer to the same value in RAM*.

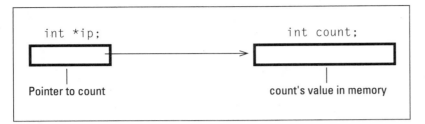

Figure 8-2 ▶ The `int` pointer `ip` addressing the `count` object in memory.

Defining and initializing pointers sets the stage for the next subject — using the addressed data, a process called *dereferencing the pointer.* Here's how that works.

Dereferencing pointers

A pointer refers to a location in memory where an object is stored. To use that object, you must *dereference* the pointer, usually as part of an expression that performs an operation on the object. A few sample statements demonstrate this important concept. I'll use the same two variables from the preceding sections:

```
int count;
int *ip;
```

Variable `count` is an integer object. It is stored somewhere in memory. Variable `ip` is an `int` pointer. It can address an object of type `int`. To cause `ip` to point to the location where `count`'s value is stored, a statement can assign `count`'s address to `ip`:

```
ip = &count;
```

As you know, you can assign values directly to `count`:

```
count = 123;
```

Because `ip` addresses `count`, however, you can also use the pointer to perform the identical operation:

```
*ip = 123;   // Same effect as preceding statement
```

Prefacing a pointer with an asterisk informs the compiler that you intend to use the addressed object in an expression — in this case, assigning the constant 123 (see Figure 8-3). The expression `*ip` is evaluated *as an object of the addressed type.* Because in this example `ip` is an `int` pointer, the expression `*ip` can be used at any place where an `int` variable such as `count` is allowed.

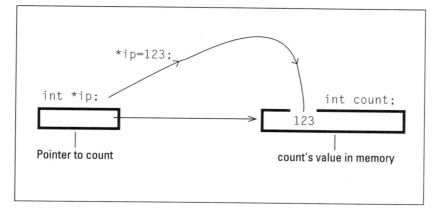

Figure 8-3 ▶ Assigning 123 to the dereferenced pointer stores that value in the addressed memory.

Here's another example. These lines define a float variable and a float pointer and also initialize each variable:

```
float pi;        // A float object
float *fp;       // A float pointer
pi = 3.14159;    // Assign PI to pi object
fp = &pi;        // Assign address of pi to fp
```

You can also perform the preceding four steps in two easy motions:

```
float pi = 3.14159;  // Define and initialize pi
float *fp = &pi;     // Assign pi's address to fp
```

The end result is a pointer fp that addresses the location in memory where pi is stored. To "get to" that object, dereference the pointer. For example, you can copy the addressed object to another variable. This assigns to copy the float value addressed by fp:

```
float copy = *fp;
```

Expressions such as *ip and *fp are treated as objects of the addressed types. Without the dereference operator, ip and fp are pointers — that is, they are address values. Be sure to understand the difference! You can, for example, assign one pointer to another. Start with two pointers:

```
int *ip1;  // Integer pointer 1
int *ip2;  // Integer pointer 2
```

You may initialize those pointers to address two integer objects (not shown):

```
ip1 = &intObject1;
ip2 = &intObject2;
```

To copy the *object* addressed by ip2 to the *object* addressed by ip1, dereference each pointer in an assignment statement:

```
*ip1 = *ip2;
```

That assigns the value addressed by ip2 to the location addressed by ip1. You may also assign one pointer to another:

```
ip1 = ip2;
```

That assigns the *address value* in ip2 to the *address value* in ip1. After that statement executes, ip1 addresses the same location in memory as ip2. To try your hand at creating and using pointers, complete Listing 8-1, POINT.CPP.

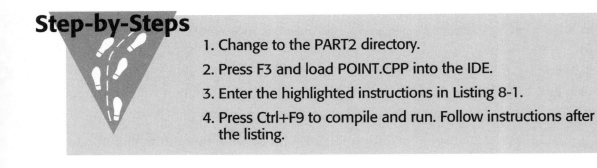

Step-by-Steps

1. Change to the PART2 directory.

2. Press F3 and load POINT.CPP into the IDE.

3. Enter the highlighted instructions in Listing 8-1.

4. Press Ctrl+F9 to compile and run. Follow instructions after the listing.

Listing 8-1. POINT.CPP

```
/* Creating and using pointers */

#include <stdio.h>
#include <conio.h>

char Pause()
{
  char c;
  printf("\nPress Enter to continue...");
  while ((c = getchar()) != '\n') { }
  return c;
}

int main()
{
  clrscr();

  int count;
  int *ip;
```

```
   count = 123;
   ip = &count;

   printf("count == %d\n", count);
   printf("*ip   == %d\n", *ip);

   Pause();
   return 0;
}
```

The first two lines you typed define an int object, count, and an int pointer, ip. The next two lines assign 123 to count and the address of count to ip. As the two output printf statements show, count and the dereferenced expression *ip are one and the same — each displays the same value because each refers to the same integer object in memory.

To prove that assumption, add the following line above the first printf statement:

```
   count = 451;
```

When you press Ctrl+F9 to compile and run the modified program, it displays:

```
count == 451
*ip   == 451
```

Because ip points to count, assigning a new value to count also affects the object addressed by ip. Delete the statement you just typed and replace it wit:

```
   *ip = 987;
```

Rather than assign a value to count, this time you assigned a value to the deferenced pointer. Again, the operation affects both values, proving that ip addresses count.

Dynamic Memory Allocation

Pointers are rarely used as I've shown so far. After all, rather than use an int pointer to address an int object such as count, you may as well use count directly. A more beneficial use for pointers is to address *dynamic objects* that are allocated memory at runtime. It's one of the most important techniques in C programming to learn. If programming methods were gourmet recipes, dynamic memory allocation would be right up there with Lobster Newburg and Chateaubriand.

When a C program runs, it has access to a relatively large area of memory variously referred to as the core, the heap, dynamic RAM, and a host of other names. Whatever you call it (I prefer the term *heap*), think of this memory resource as a pool from which you can dip buckets of bytes on demand. Taking a bucketful from the heap — that is, allocating some dynamic memory — reserves memory for your program's use. Pouring the bucketful back into the pool — in other words, deleting or freeing the allocated RAM — returns the reserved memory to the pool so that it can be reused by other operations.

Reserving dynamic memory

To reserve a block of memory, include the STDLIB.H or ALLOC.H header files (you may also include both files):

```
#include <alloc.h>
```

That makes two functions available: `malloc` (memory allocator) and `free`. Use `malloc` to request a block of memory from the heap. First, define a pointer:

```
float *fp;
```

Then call `malloc` to reserve enough space to store an object of the pointer's type. Assign the address returned by `malloc` to the pointer:

```
fp = malloc(sizeof(float));
```

Always use `sizeof` or another safe method to request the proper amount of memory for an object. In C++, you must also tack on a *type cast expression* in front of `malloc`:

```
fp = (float *)malloc(sizeof(float));
```

The type cast expression `(float *)` is needed because `malloc` returns a generic address value, called `void *`, that has no specific type. A *void pointer* is just an address. To assign a void pointer to a typed pointer such as `fp`, you must use a type cast expression, informing the compiler of your intentions. Prefacing `malloc` with `(float *)` tells the compiler to treat `malloc`'s return value as a `float` pointer. ANSI C is less strict than C++ in this regard, but you should use a type cast expression anyway so that your programs are compatible with C and C++ compilers.

If you want the memory bytes cleared to all zeros, call the similar function `calloc`:

```
fp = (float *)calloc(1, sizeof(float));
```

Unlike `malloc`, `calloc` requires two parameters — the number of objects to allocate (1 in this case) and the size in bytes of each object (`sizeof(float)` here). If successfully allocated, the memory is cleared to all zeros.

Use a dynamic object by dereferencing the pointer — exactly as you learned earlier in this chapter. For example, after allocating memory for a `float` object and assigning that memory's address to the `float` pointer `fp`, you can assign a value to the object like this:

```
*fp = 3.14159;
```

With an asterisk, the expression `*fp` is treated as the object addressed by `fp`. To copy that value to another variable, you can write

```
float copy = *fp;
```

If `malloc` cannot find enough memory to satisfy a memory request, it returns a *null pointer,* usually equal to zero. (Some compilers define null pointers differently, but they are the exceptions. The compiler supplied with this book defines a null pointer as zero.) You should always test whether a call to malloc succeeded, typically by using an if statement to check whether the resulting pointer is null. The following statements, for example, call a function Error (not shown) if malloc fails:

```
fp = (float *)malloc(sizeof(float));
if (fp == NULL)
  Error();
```

The if statement's control expression is often abbreviated as

```
if (!fp)
  Error();
```

Remember, zero represents false. A null pointer equals zero, and therefore, you may use pointers directly as true-false control expressions. The system constant NULL also equals zero, so the expressions (!fp) and (fp == NULL) are equivalent.

To perform an operation if a memory allocation succeeds, you can use a similar abbreviation. The following statements call DoSomething (not shown) if malloc successfully reserves space for a float object:

```
fp = (float *)malloc(sizeof(float));
if (fp)
  DoSomething();
```

That's identical to:

```
fp = (float *)malloc(sizeof(float));
if (fp != NULL)
  DoSomething();
```

It's OK to write (fp != NULL), but experienced C programmers realize that (fp) is equivalent because, if the pointer is nonzero, its value is logically true; if the pointer is zero, its value is logically false.

Mentally read the expression if (fp) as "if fp is valid" and the expression if (!fp) as "if fp is not valid," and you'll master this common trick of abbreviation in no time flat.

Freeing dynamic memory

When you are finished using a dynamic object, always free its memory. If you don't free unused dynamic memory, your program will run out of RAM if the pool of available bytes runs dry. Freeing allocated memory returns it to the pool for use by subsequent calls to malloc.

To free a pointer's memory, call free like this:

```
free(fp);
```

You may not free a null pointer, so this is safer:

```
if (fp != NULL)
  free(fp);
```

Or, using the pointer directly as a true-false value, use the abbreviated (and most common) form:

```
if (fp)
  free(fp);
```

After freeing a pointer's memory, you must be sure not to store new values there. Never, ever, upon pain of torture, do this:

```
free(fp);
*fp = 3.14159;  // ???
```

Ouch! That assigns a value to the freed pointer's memory, a very bad mistake because that memory, after being returned to the pool, is no longer reserved for the program's use. *The compiler does not warn you about this mistake.* You may reuse the pointer, however, in another call to malloc:

```
fp = (float *)malloc(sizeof(float));
```

After that, assuming fp is not null, it is again safe to store values in the newly allocated memory. But remember: it is *never OK* to use a pointer's memory after it has been freed.

Using C++ new and delete operators

Even though this book is about C programming, I can't resist adding a note about the C++ operators new and delete. These operators work much like malloc and free but are easier to use. Strict ANSI C compilers don't have them, but they are included with the compiler supplied with this book.

First, define a pointer:

```
float *fp;
```

Pointer fp can address a float object in memory. To allocate space for that object, use new like this:

```
fp = new float;
if (!fp)
  Error();
```

Some programmer's add parentheses after new, although they are not needed:

```
fp = new(float);
```

Use a pointer allocated memory by new the same as you do pointers allocated space by malloc:

```
*fp = 3.14159;
float copy = *fp;
```

To free memory allocated by `new`, use the `delete` operator:

```
delete fp;
```

Unlike with `free`, it is OK to delete null pointers, so there's no need to test whether `fp` is null beforehand.

You may use `malloc`, `free`, `new`, and `delete` in the same program, but you must always call `free` to free memory allocated by `malloc`. Similarly, you must always call `delete` to free memory allocated by `new`. Never mix the two techniques — calling `free` for memory allocated by `new`, for example, or using `delete` to free memory allocated by `malloc` or `calloc` may cause bugs. In practice, many C++ compilers define `new` and `delete` using `malloc` and `free`, so mixing the methods may seem to be safe. But C++ compilers are not required to implement `new` and `delete` in any specific way, and it is highly dangerous to ignore this warning.

Pointer Operations

Pointers are frequently used to address blocks of memory, called *buffers,* that may contain many objects. Buffers are commonly used as temporary holding pens for data on its way to and from other locations. When your're programming with buffers, it's often advantageous to use pointer arithmetic and related operations to simplify addressing buffered data.

Pointers also enjoy a close relationship with arrays. After all, an array is just a block of memory — a buffer, in other words — that contains one or more objects of the same type. Using a pointer to address the first byte of an array also gives you access to all of the array's other objects. A `char` pointer addressing a string is the most common instance of the technique, so let's begin there.

Pointers and strings

Up to now, I've defined all strings either literally in quotes or as arrays of `char`. Here are some samples of the various ways of defining strings covered so far:

```
#define NAME "Abraham Lincoln"
char string[81];
char city[64] = "Charleston";
char planet[] = "Venus";
```

Line one defines a symbolic constant NAME as an alias for a quoted literal string. Line two defines an uninitialized array of `char`, large enough to hold an 80-character string plus a null terminator. Line three defines an initialized 64-byte string, assigning it the city name *Charleston.* Line four lets the compiler choose the correct size for another initialized string.

Using dynamic memory allocation and a `char` pointer, there's another way to construct string objects that is often the best method of all. First, define the pointer. I'll name it `sp` for "string pointer":

```
char *sp;
```

Next, call `malloc` to allocate some memory and assign the address of the string buffer's first byte to `sp`:

```
sp = (char *)malloc(256);
```

To check whether `malloc` succeeded, you should also test whether `sp` is null:

```
if (!sp)
  Error();
```

To save space, from now on, I won't include similar error checking, but you should *always* test for null pointers in your own code. If `sp` is not null, it addresses a block of memory large enough to hold a 255-character string plus a null terminator (see Figure 8-4).

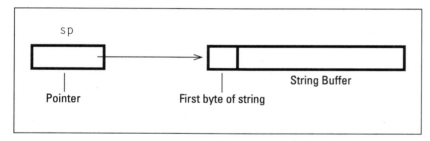

Figure 8-4 ▶ A `char` pointer addressing a block of memory.

You may use the pointer `sp` in two ways: as a pointer to `char` *or as an array of* `char`. For example, to assign a string to the memory addressed by `sp`, include the STRING.H header file and call the `strcpy` function:

```
#include <string.h>
...
strcpy(sp, "Red skies at night");
```

That copies the string `Red skies at night` to the memory buffer addressed by `sp`. Suppose that you need to inspect the second character of that string. You can do that by treating `sp` as an array:

```
char copy = sp[1];
```

Though `sp` is a pointer, it may be used with array brackets and an index, in this case referencing the string's second character. (`sp[0]` references the first.) Figure 8-5 illustrates the relationship between the pointer and its use as an array. The expression `s[0]` is equivalent to `sp+1` (one byte from the location addressed by `sp`). The expression `sp[1]` is equivalent to `sp+1`, and so on.

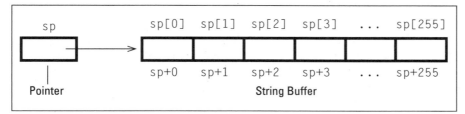

Figure 8-5 ▶ Pointers and arrays enjoy a close relationship.

After you are finished using the string, free its allocated memory by feeding sp to the free function:

```
free(sp);
```

Using char pointers to address strings is a vital C programming technique, one that you will use time and again. For practice, complete Listing 8-2, STRING.CPP.

Step-by-Steps

1. Change to the PART2 directory.

2. Press F3 and load STRING.CPP into the IDE.

3. Enter the highlighted instructions in Listing 8-2.

4. Press F2 to save the modified listing — you'll need it in the next section.

5. Press Ctrl+F9 to compile and run. Follow instructions after the listing.

Listing 8-2: STRING.CPP

```
/* String pointer */

#include <stdio.h>
#include <conio.h>
#include <alloc.h>
#include <string.h>

#define SIZE 256
```

```
char Pause()
{
  char c;
  printf("\nPress Enter to continue...");
  while ((c = getchar()) != '\n') { }
  return c;
}

int main()
{
  clrscr();

  char *sp;
  sp = (char *)malloc(SIZE);
  strcpy(sp, "Your name");
  puts(sp);
  free(sp);

  Pause();
  return 0;
}
```

Programs that use `char` pointers to address strings should include the header files ALLOC.H and STRING.H (in addition to any others needed). For safety, it's usually best to define a constant such as `SIZE` for the string's size. Remember to allow one byte for the string's null terminator.

Function `main` defines a string pointer `sp`, allocates `SIZE` bytes of memory, and assigns the memory's address to `sp`. You can replace the first two lines you typed into `main` with a single statement:

```
char *sp = (char *)malloc(SIZE);
```

Either method is fine — use the one that's most convenient for your application.

Function `strcpy` copies to `sp`'s addressed memory a literal string `Your name` (replace the string with another if you wish). Function `puts` displays the string. These and many other functions are designed to use `char` pointers.

After displaying the string, the program calls `free` to dispose of the allocated memory. Never forget this vital step — always match every call to `malloc` with a call to `free`.

Some compilers, including the one packed with this book, create code that automatically frees all allocated memory blocks when the program ends. So, technically speaking, the call to `free` in STRING.CPP isn't needed. It's a good idea to include the statement, however, as another compiler or operating system may *not* automatically free allocated memory.

Pointers and address operators

For some kinds of operations, it's useful to think of address values as integers that can be incremented, decremented, and compared using arithmetic expressions. You may, for example, apply the ++ and - - operators to pointers, incrementing and decrementing their address values. In that way, you can "walk" a pointer though memory, examining successive bytes. For an example of how this works, add the following snippets to the STRING.CPP program. (Go back to the preceding section and reenter the highlighted lines if you didn't do that already.)

To start a new output line, type this statement immediately above the call to `free` in function `main`:

```
puts("");  // Start new line
```

Next, define a `char` pointer to address the string, also addressed by `sp`. Enter these lines:

```
char *t;
t = sp;
```

Alternatively, in place of those two lines, you can type this single statement:

```
char *t = sp;
```

Either way, `t` and `sp` address the same string in memory. We'll use `t` as a temporary pointer to access each character in the string. Enter this `while` loop to display the string one character at a time:

```
while (*t != '\0') {
  putchar(*t);
  t++;
}
```

The loop's controlling expression dereferences `t` to examine the addressed character. The expression `*t` literally means "the character addressed by `t`." If that character is not null, the program assumes that `t` addresses a character inside the string, and it calls `putchar` to transfer that character to the standard output — that is, the display. Next, the expression `t++` *increments the pointer,* thus pointing the temporary pointer `t` to the next character. Eventually, the pointer finds the null byte at the end of the string, and the `while` loop ends.

When using pointers as demonstrated here, always make a copy of the original pointer. You need the original (`sp` in the example) to access the string for future operations, and more importantly, you need it so you can pass `sp` to `free`, disposing of the allocated memory.

Experienced C programmers usually shorten the preceding snippets as follows. After the `while` loop's closing brace, start a new display line:

```
puts("");
```

Then type these abbreviated statements:

```
t = sp;
while (*t != '\0')
  putchar(*t++);
```

The first line reassigns sp to t, making t again address the beginning of the string. Inside the while loop, the expression *t++ performs double duty — it has the value of the addressed character, and it also increments the pointer to the next string. In time, you'll learn to use shorthand expressions such as these, but there's nothing technically wrong with the longer version presented earlier.

You may also add and subtract integer values from pointers. For example, these are permissible statements (you may add them to the STRING.CPP program if you wish):

```
char *cp = "Abcdefg";
putchar(*cp);
cp = cp + 4;  // or cp += 4;
putchar(*cp);
```

The first line defines a string pointer, cp, that addresses the literal string Abcdefg. Function putchar displays the character addressed by sp — initially, *A*. The next statement adds 4 to cp, moving the pointer to character *e,* displayed by the second call to putchar. (Line three may also be written cp += 4;). You may also subtract integer values from pointers, but when using these techniques, be careful not to address locations outside the memory allocated to the pointer.

Two pointers to the same buffer or array may be subtracted (but not added) — a method commonly used to calculate the number of bytes between two locations. For example, define a string pointer, a len integer, and a temporary pointer:

```
char *string = "Any string";
int len;
char *temp = string;
```

The goal is to set len to the number of characters addressed by pointer string. There are many possible solutions. Here's one:

```
while (*temp != '\0')
  temp++;
len = temp - string;
```

Advancing the temp pointer to the string's null terminator and then subtracting the two pointers gives the number of bytes between (not including the null terminator).

It is also possible to compare two pointers for equality. Given pointers p1 and p2 of the same type, for example, you may compare them in a statement such as:

```
if (p1 == p2)
  DoSomething();
```

If the two pointers are the same, the program calls DoSomething (not shown). You may also compare pointers for inequality:

```
if (p1 != p2)
  DoSomething();
```

All other arithmetic operations on pointers not shown in this section or elsewhere in this chapter are strictly forbidden. Since the C language doesn't specify how memory bytes are arranged, it is senseless to test whether one pointer is greater or less than another. You may subtract two pointers, but you may not add them. You may not divide or multiply pointers, and you may not use floating-point values in pointer arithmetic expressions.

Even comparing pointers for equality may or may not work reliably on all computers. In PCs, for example, it's possible for two *different* pairs of segment and offset values to address the same location in memory. Pointers having those values would appear to be different, even though they address the same byte. For absolute safety, avoid using pointer comparisons.

Pointers and arrays

Though char pointers are probably the most common variety, pointers may address other kinds of objects. In past chapters, you learned how to define an array of int:

```
int ia[100];
```

That creates an integer array, ia, of 100 int values. You may do the same by using a pointer:

```
int *iap;
```

That defines a pointer to an int. Call malloc to define a memory buffer for the array:

```
iap = (int *)malloc(100 * sizeof(int));
```

The expression 100*sizeof(int) reserves enough memory for 100 int objects, regardless of how many bytes an int occupies. For the compiler supplied with this book, an int takes two bytes, so the resulting buffer is, in this case, 200 bytes long. Another compiler may define int to be larger or smaller, however, and it's wise to use sizeof as shown, rather than assume that integers occupy a fixed amount of space.

After allocating the buffer, you may use iap to address the buffered integer objects. These statements assign values to the first three array slots:

```
iap[0] = 123;
iap[1] = 456;
iap[2] = 789;
```

As with `char` pointers, the expression `iap[0]` is equivalent to `iap+0`. The expression `iap[1]` is equivalent to `iap+1`, and `iap[2]` is the same as `iap+2`. When adding or subtracting pointers and integer constants, the compiler takes the size of the addressed objects into account. Given two-byte `int` objects, the expression `iap+1` creates an address value that is *two* bytes beyond `iap`. The expression `iap+2` creates an address *four* bytes beyond `iap`. Address arithmetic is always computed in multiples of the sizes of addressed objects.

Storing pointers in arrays is another important technique that creates a table useful for addressing variable-size data. One of the most common examples of the method is an array of `char` pointers that form a table of strings, as demonstrated by Listing 8-3, SARRAY.CPP.

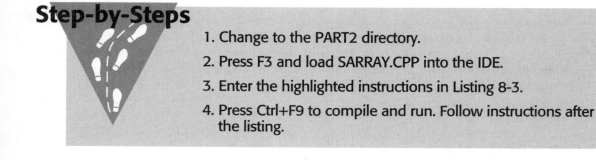

Step-by-Steps

1. Change to the PART2 directory.

2. Press F3 and load SARRAY.CPP into the IDE.

3. Enter the highlighted instructions in Listing 8-3.

4. Press Ctrl+F9 to compile and run. Follow instructions after the listing.

Listing 8-3: SARRAY.CPP

```
/* String pointer array */

#include <stdio.h>
#include <conio.h>
#include <ctype.h>
#include <string.h>

#define SIZE 10

char * sarray[SIZE];

char Pause()
{
  char c;
  printf("\nPress Enter to continue...");
  while ((c = getchar()) != '\n') { }
  return c;
}
```

```
int main()
{
  clrscr();

  sarray[0] = "Pennsylvania";
  sarray[1] = "California";
  sarray[2] = "Virginia";
  sarray[3] = "North Carolina";
  sarray[4] = "South Carolina";
  sarray[5] = "Georgia";
  sarray[6] = "Florida";
  sarray[7] = "Arizona";
  sarray[8] = "Rhode Island";
  sarray[9] = "Nevada";

  int i;

  for (i = 0; i < SIZE; i++)
    puts(sarray[i]);

  Pause();
  return 0;
}
```

As is usually best, a symbolic constant SIZE determines the size of the array. Study the array's definition closely:

```
char * sarray[SIZE];
```

Literally, that creates "an array named sarray of char pointers." It is, in other words, an array of ten pointers, each of which can address a string. The ten assignments you typed into main initialize the array's pointers, giving each the address of a literal string. (The compiler stores the strings in the compiled code file; the addresses are assigned at runtime.) It's especially important to understand that no characters are transferred into the array — only the addresses of the strings' initial characters are assigned to the array elements.

A simple for loop displays each string by passing its address to the puts function. The expression sarray[i] is "the char pointer at index i in the array."

There's another, and often more convenient, way to prepare a table of char pointers. To try the alternative method, delete the statements you added to SARRAY.CPP. Then insert this definition after the fourth (and final) #include directive near the top of the listing:

```
char * sarray[] = {
  "Pennsylvania",
  "California",
  "Virginia",
  "North Carolina",
  "South Carolina",
  "Georgia",
  "Florida",
  "Arizona",
  "Rhode Island",
  "Nevada"
};
```

This method does not require a SIZE constant. Instead, the compiler calculates the size of sarray based on the number of strings. Each string is separated by commas, and the list is delimited with braces, ending with a semicolon. Despite appearances, the construction is not an array of strings — it is an array of char pointers, each of which addresses a literal string constant stored in the compiled code file. For simplicity, it's useful to call this a string array, as long as you realize that only char pointers, not characters, are stored in the array. Figure 8-6 illustrates how sarray and its strings appear in memory.

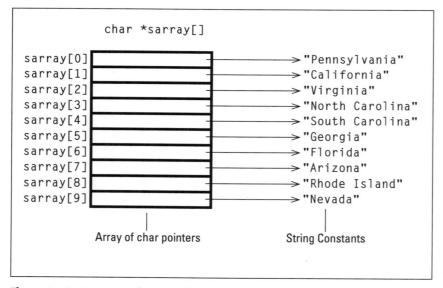

Figure 8-6 ▶ An array of char pointers to string constants.

To display the string array requires two integer variables — an index i and a limit set to the number of char pointers in the array. Insert these statements into main above Pause:

```
int i;
int limit = sizeof(sarray) / sizeof(char *);
```

Integer i is used in a `for` loop. Integer `limit` is assigned the array's size in bytes divided by the size of one `char` pointer. Obviously, the result is the number of pointers in the array. (Using `sizeof` as shown ensures that the program works correctly regardless of a pointer's size, which can differ among compilers.)

Using those two values, it's simple to write a `for` loop to display each string. Add these lines to the program:

```
for (i = 0; i < limit; i++)
  puts(sarray[i]);
```

Pointers and structures

You'll find many other uses for pointers. You can, for example, address structures with pointers, and you also can add pointer members to a structure's design. The number of possible combinations is truly mind-boggling — you can have arrays of structure pointers, each of which has one or more pointer members, which may address arrays or even other structures. I couldn't possibly describe all the combinations, but here are two for which you'll find countless uses.

You may address structure objects using pointers. Include the ALLOC.H header file and declare your structure. For example, here's another version of the `Phone` structure from the preceding chapter:

```
#include <alloc.h>
...
typedef struct tagPhone {
  char * name;
  char * phone;
} Phone;
```

Rather than use `char` arrays for `name` and `phone`, this time I defined the members as `char` pointers. Next, define a pointer to a `Phone` object:

```
Phone * recptr;
```

The `recptr` variable is a pointer to a `Phone` object. To create that object, you can call `malloc` like this:

```
recptr = (Phone *)malloc(sizeof(Phone));
```

That reserves enough memory for one `Phone` object and, if successful, assigns the address of the object to `recptr`. Again, I use `sizeof` to determine the correct number of bytes to allocate. Dereference `recptr` to gain access to the addressed object. These statements, for instance, assign the addresses of strings to the object's members:

```
(*recptr).name = "Your name";
(*recptr).phone = "432-555-1212";
```

Dereferencing `recptr` accesses the addressed structure; using dot notation accesses that structure's individual members. This method works, but since the dot in dot notation has a higher precedence order than the dereference operator, you must use parentheses as shown. Fortunately, there's a better way to accomplish the same task. These statements are equivalent to the preceding two:

```
recptr->name = "Your name";
recptr->phone = "432-555-1212";
```

The `->` operator, which resembles an arrow, may be used only with a structure pointer. It dereferences the structure pointer and accesses a member by name in one operation. Always use this preferred technique to access addressed structure members.

Another useful method uses an array of structure pointers to form a tightly packed database of strings with no wasted bytes. Listing 8-4 demonstrates the technique.

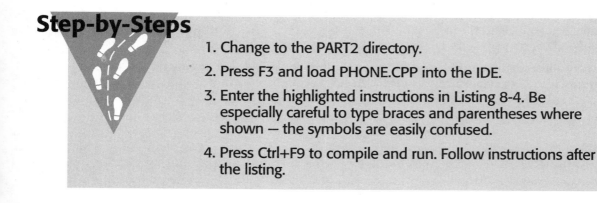

Step-by-Steps

1. Change to the PART2 directory.

2. Press F3 and load PHONE.CPP into the IDE.

3. Enter the highlighted instructions in Listing 8-4. Be especially careful to type braces and parentheses where shown — the symbols are easily confused.

4. Press Ctrl+F9 to compile and run. Follow instructions after the listing.

Listing 8-4: PHONE.CPP

```
/* Phone number database */

#include <stdio.h>
#include <conio.h>
#include <ctype.h>

typedef struct tagPhone {
  char * name;
  char * phone;
} Phone;

Phone database[] = {
  { "Tom Swan",     "717-555-1212" },
  { "Bill Clinton", "201-555-1212" },
  { "Your name",    "432-555-1212" },
  { "Another name", "876-555-1212" }
};
```

```
char Pause()
{
  char c;
  printf("\nPress Enter to continue...");
  while ((c = getchar()) != '\n') {  }
  return c;
}

int main()
{
  clrscr();

  int i;
  int limit = sizeof(database) / sizeof(Phone);

  for (i = 0; i < limit; i++) {
    puts("");
    puts(database[i].name);
    puts(database[i].phone);
  }

  Pause();
  return 0;
}
```

You first typed the Phone structure, containing two char pointer members, name, and phone. Next, you created a database of Phone objects, initializing each member of each object with the address of a literal string. Using char pointers rather than char arrays (as you did with the similar example in the preceding chapter) eliminates any wasted bytes at the ends of the arrays following the strings' null terminators.

Function main displays the database by first defining two integer variables — an index i and a limit equal to the number of records. Because the program calculates limit at runtime, you may add and subtract records in the database array without making any other adjustments. Just recompile and run.

By now, I hope you are comfortable creating and using pointers. They do seem odd at first, so if you are still fuzzy on this chapter's information, you might want to reread it before continuing. Future chapters will use pointers extensively. Next up are functions — key tools that you will use in virtually every program you write.

Chapter 9

Functions

A function encapsulates one or more statements, variables, and parameters into a unified package that you can call into action whenever needed. Functions come in all sizes and shapes. A function, for example, might perform a simple calculation. A more complex function might sort an array of strings or write file data to disk. Most programs written in C consist of dozens of functions, each designed to perform a particular service.

Functions operate like departments in a company, each having a unique job to perform. Each department performs its task more or less independently, but taken as a whole, all departments form the company's structure. In a similar way, a program's functions perform relatively simple tasks that, when combined, produce the program's output and actions.

All C programs have at least one function, `main`, which contains the program's initial statements. Some other functions come ready to use — the `puts` function, for example, is provided with the compiler. As you learn in this chapter, you can also write your own functions, dividing complex programs into manageable pieces that you can work on one at a time.

Basic Functions

Functions use a simple design that's easy to learn. The basic function looks like this:

```
int Square(int v)
{
}
```

First comes the function's data type, in this case, `int`. Next is the function's name, `Square`, followed by a pair of parentheses. Inside parentheses are any parameters used by the function. In this case, `Square` declares a single parameter, an `int` object named v. Lastly, the function's body is delimited by a pair of braces. Insert statements between the braces to perform the function's actions. Here, for example, is how you might complete `Square`:

```
int Square(int v)
{
   return v * v;
}
```

A `return` statement passes a value of the appropriate type back as the function's result. In this example, parameter v is multiplied by itself, and the resulting product is returned. Elsewhere in the program, you can use `Square` to double an integer value:

```
int k = 45;
k = Square(k);
```

The second statement calls `Square`, passing a copy of k to the function's integer parameter. The function returns the square of that value, which is then assigned back to k. As a result, k now equals 45*45, or 2025. After the function returns, the program continues where it left off with the next statement in line.

Using functions

One of the most common uses for a function is to perform repetitive tasks efficiently. Suppose, for example, that you need to calculate the length of a string. First, you define and initialize the string using a `char` pointer (add this and the next several statements to a copy of SHELL.CPP if you want to follow along):

```
char *string = "Abcdefg";
```

Next, using a temporary pointer as explained in the preceding chapter, you type these statements to compute the string's length:

```
char *temp = string;
while (*temp != '\0')
   temp++;
int length = temp - string;
```

That sets `length` to the number of characters addressed by `string`. Display the string and its length with these statements:

```
puts(string);
printf("length == %d\n", length);
```

Wrapping statements into functions

All of that works just fine, but it's mighty inconvenient to type the same commands over and over to find the lengths of strings. For better efficiency, you can wrap the statements into a function and use it as a string-length command. Listing 9-1, SLEN.CPP, demonstrates this technique.

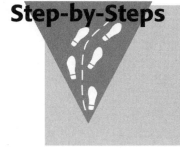

Step-by-Steps

1. Change to the PART2 directory.

2. Press F3 and load SLEN.CPP into the IDE.

3. Enter the highlighted instructions in Listing 9-1.

4. Press Ctrl+F9 to compile and run. Follow instructions after the listing.

Listing 9-1: SLEN.CPP

```
/* Find length of string */

#include <stdio.h>
#include <conio.h>
#include <ctype.h>

#define STRING_CONSTANT "Constant comment"

char Pause()
{
  char c;
  printf("\nPress Enter to continue...");
  while ((c = getchar()) != '\n') { }
  return c;
}
```

```c
int Length(char *s)
{
  if (!s) return 0;
  char *t = s;
  while (*t != '\0')
    t++;
  return t - s;
}

void ShowLength(char *s)
{
  puts("");
  if (s)
    puts(s);
  else
    puts("<null string>");
  printf(" length == %d\n", Length(s));
}

int main()
{
  clrscr();

  char MyName[] = "Tom Swan";
  char YourName[] = "Insert your name here";
  char *p = NULL;

  ShowLength("Abcdefghijklmnopqrstuvwxyz");
  ShowLength(MyName);
  ShowLength(YourName);
  ShowLength(STRING_CONSTANT);
  ShowLength(p);

  Pause();
  return 0;
}
```

 C compilers, including the one supplied with this book, provide a string-length function, strlen, in the STRING.H header file. It is a useful exercise, however, to write your own string-length function as described here.

The sample program has three functions. One, `Pause`, is already supplied. Function `Length` finds the length of a string. `ShowLength` displays a string and its length. Notice how simple the `main` program is. To display strings and their lengths, the program simply calls `ShowLength`, feeding it a literal string, a string variable, a constant, and so forth. The statement

```
ShowLength(MyName);
```

calls the function, causing its statements to run and operating on the passed data, `MyName`. Take a look at `ShowLength`'s statements. The function looks like a program, and, in fact, it is a kind of program in miniature. Ignoring its insides for the moment, the function has this basic design:

```
void ShowLength(char *s)
{
}
```

Using the word `void` as the function's data type indicates that this function does not return a value to its caller. (Think of `void` as meaning "nothing.") The name of the function, `ShowLength`, follows its type. After that comes a pair of parentheses with a single `char` pointer parameter. Finally, the function's body is delimited with a pair of braces.

Those same elements, in different forms, exist in all functions. If a function requires no input data, write empty parentheses after its name:

```
void f()
{
}
```

In strict ANSI C, you should insert the word `void` inside the parentheses, indicating that the function has no parameters:

```
void f(void)
{
}
```

C++ compilers, including the one packaged with this book, do not require you to insert `void` in parentheses, though you may do so if you wish. (I prefer not to use `void` since I normally use a C++ compiler.)

Inside the function's braces, insert the statements that perform the function's actions. Take another look at `ShowLength` in the sample listing. First, the function calls `puts` to display a blank line. It then calls `puts` again to display the string `s`, passed to the function's `char` pointer parameter. If `s` is null, however, an `if` statement displays *<null string>*. The final statement in `ShowLength` deserves a closer look. Here it is again:

```
printf(" length == %d\n", Length(s));
```

The statement calls the program's second function, `Length`, which computes the length of a string. You might also call `Length` like this:

```
int len;
len = Length(s);
```

That assigns to `len` the function's *return value,* in this case equal to the number of characters in the string. The name of the function operates like an object of its type. In other words, `Length` is said to be an `int` function.

Examine the `Length` function's statements in the sample listing. As with `ShowLength`, `Length` begins with a declaration line that gives the function's type, its name, and any parameters:

```
int Length(char *s)
```

The function's type, `int`, indicates the type of `Length`'s return value. The function's name comes next, followed by any parameters in parentheses. A pair of braces following the function's declaration delimit the function's statements. The first statement tests whether parameter `s` is null:

```
if (!s) return 0;
```

That says "if `s` is null, return the value 0." Using `return` immediately ends the function, skipping any statements that follow. Thus, if you pass a null string to `Length`, this is the only statement that runs. If `s` is not null, the next three statements execute. First, a temporary `char` pointer, `t`, is assigned a copy of the address held by `s`. Next, a `while` loop advances `t` to the string's null terminator. Then the function's final statement returns the string's length:

```
return t - s;
```

Subtracting the two pointers, `t` and `s`, gives the number of `char` objects between their addressed positions. That value is an integer, and therefore, it may be returned by the `int` function.

 All functions that declare a return data type other than `void` must return a value of that type for all possible exit paths from the function. Failing to execute a `return` statement causes the compiler to issue the error *Function should return a value.* If you receive that error message, be sure that your function executes `return` for every possible condition that might end the function. Or, if the function doesn't need to return a value, change its data type to `void`.

Functions may return values of just about any types, though most functions return simple values of type `int`, `float`, `double`, and so on. Functions may return pointers; they also may return structures but not arrays. (They may, however, return pointers to arrays.)

Automatic Variables

Inside a function, you may define *automatic variables* for use by the function's statements. They are "automatic" because they are defined each time the function is called to action. The variables exist in memory *only while the function is active.* When the function is not running, automatic variables do not exist, and they do not retain their values between calls to the function. Consider this function, which sums two integer values:

```
int Sum(int a, int b)
{
  int c;
  c = a + b;
  return c;
}
```

Function Sum returns an int value equal to the sum of two other integers, a and b. You probably wouldn't write a function like this — it is simpler to add values directly, but the function demonstrates some important concepts. Inside the function (that is, inside its delimiting braces) is the variable definition:

```
int c;
```

That variable is allocated memory *every time the function runs.* When the function ends, the allocated memory is deleted. Thus int c exists in memory only while the function is active. The variable is temporary — it is automatically created and deleted for use strictly inside the function. Due to this scheme, automatic variables efficiently use memory, allowing multiple functions to share limited memory space for their private variables.

Automatic demo

Listing 9-2, GETSTR.CPP, demonstrates automatic variables with a function, GetString, that you can use in your own programs. The function lets users safely enter text into char arrays, limiting the number of characters to the defined size of the array.

Step-by-Steps

1. Change to the PART2 directory.

2. Press F3 and load GETSTR.CPP into the IDE.

3. Enter the highlighted instructions in Listing 9-2.

4. Press Ctrl+F9 to compile and run. Follow instructions after the listing.

Listing 9-2: GETSTR.CPP

```
/* GetString function */

#include <stdio.h>
#include <conio.h>

char Pause()
{
  char c;
  printf("\nPress Enter to continue...");
  while ((c = getchar()) != '\n') { }
  return c;
}

void GetString(char *s, int size)
{
  int i = 0;
  char c;

  while (--size > 0) {
    c = getchar();
    if (c == EOF || c == '\n')
      size = 0;
    else
      s[i++] = c;
  }
  s[i] = '\0';
  fflush(stdin);
}

int main()
{
  clrscr();

  char s1[11];
  char s2[21];

  puts("Enter a 10-character string:");
  GetString(s1, sizeof(s1));
  puts("Enter a 20-character string:");
  GetString(s2, sizeof(s2));
```

```
    puts("");
    puts("Here are your two strings:");
    puts(s1);
    puts(s2);

    Pause();
    return 0;
}
```

Function GetString returns void — that is, it returns no value. The function requires two input parameters: a char pointer s and an int value size, equal to the size in bytes of the buffer addressed by s. Call the function like this:

```
char string[80];
GetString(string, sizeof(string));
```

That creates an 80-byte string and calls GetString to allow users to enter up to 79 characters into the buffer. A null terminator is inserted after the last character typed.

The function makes use of two automatic variables, an int value i and a char c. The function's statements were listed in Chapter 7, but packaged into a function, they are much more useful. Because the function type is void, no return statement is required. (You may use a return statement, however, to end a void function.)

It's especially important to realize that automatic variables do not retain their values between calls to a function. So, every time the program calls GetString, int i and char c are re-created, and the variables must be initialized each time before use. If you need to maintain values between function calls, use a global variable defined outside of a function. For example, study this fragment:

```
int global;
void f()
{
  int local;
  ...
}
```

The global integer is defined outside of any function. Because it's a global variable, it exists throughout the program's runtime life, and it retains any value assigned to it. The automatic local variable inside f exists only while f is active. Outside of f, local does not exist and it therefore cannot retain its value between function calls.

Scope

Another important aspect of global and local variables concerns their *scope,* a measure of access rights to variables and other items. A few fragments help explain the concept of scope. Start with a global variable defined outside of any function:

```
int count;
```

Any function defined afterwards may use `count`. The variable's scope is global — that is, it is accessible from all parts of the program following the variable's definition. A function, for example, may use `count` in a statement (the three-dot ellipsis indicates where other programming might go):

```
void f1()
{
  int temp = count + 1;
  ...
}
```

Because `count` is global, it is *visible* to function `f1`. That function defines an automatic variable, `temp`, that has local scope. Another function cannot access `temp`:

```
void f2()
{
  int copy = temp;  // ???
  ...
}
```

That example will not compile because `temp`'s scope is limited to its defining function. You receive the error message *Undefined symbol 'temp' in function* because `temp` is for `f1`'s private use; it isn't visible inside `f2`. That function could, however, define its own `temp`:

```
void f2()
{
  int temp;
  ...
}
```

Even though `temp` is already defined in `f1`, another distinct variable of the same name may be defined in `f2`. The two `temp`s are limited in scope to their defining functions. Each is a distinct object, even though they happen to have the same names. (Ten functions, in other words, may each define a variable `int i` without conflict.)

Here's another example that demonstrates a subtle variation on the theme of scope:

```
void f3()
{
  int count;
  ...
}
```

Function f3 defines a local, automatic variable count, the same name as the global variable. The local variable overrides the global one, and there are now two distinct counts: the global one and the automatic one inside the function. In general, you should avoid redefining global variables this way, but the technique is occasionally useful.

If a global variable doesn't have the value you think it should, check whether you have accidentally redefined it as a local variable inside a function.

In general terms, a variable's scope is limited to its defining block, which can be a function or any other compound statement. A while loop, for instance, may define a variable like this:

```
while (condition) {
   int i;
   i = count + 10;
   ...
}
```

The int i object is newly defined on each pass through the loop. Its scope is limited to the while statement; other statements may not use this instance of i. Other parts of the program may, however, define another int i within another scope.

Parameters and Arguments

Memorize these two rules: *A parameter is an object received by a function. An argument is a value passed to a function parameter.* When you define a function like this:

```
void f(int k)
{
   ...
}
```

the *parameter* int k operates like a local, automatic variable defined inside the function. When you call the function:

```
f(123);
```

the value 123 is said to be an *argument*. A copy of the argument's value is passed to the function parameter, as though the program executed the assignment:

```
k = 123;
```

The parameter receives the value of the passed argument. Inside the function, k is initialized to the argument value, 123. A sample program, Listing 9-3, RANDOM.CPP, generates random number sequences, and it helps explain the important concepts of parameters and arguments.

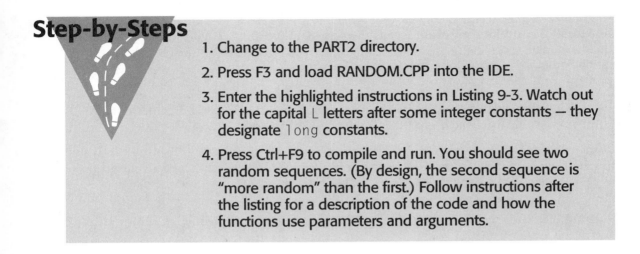

Step-by-Steps

1. Change to the PART2 directory.

2. Press F3 and load RANDOM.CPP into the IDE.

3. Enter the highlighted instructions in Listing 9-3. Watch out for the capital L letters after some integer constants — they designate long constants.

4. Press Ctrl+F9 to compile and run. You should see two random sequences. (By design, the second sequence is "more random" than the first.) Follow instructions after the listing for a description of the code and how the functions use parameters and arguments.

Listing 9-3: RANDOM.CPP

```c
/* Random Number Generator */

#include <stdio.h>
#include <conio.h>

#define M4 10000L       // 10 ^^ 4
#define M8 100000000L   // 10 ^^ 8
#define  B 31415621L    // Constant multiplier

long seed;

char Pause()
{
  char c;
  printf("\nPress Enter to continue...");
  while ((c = getchar()) != '\n') { }
  return c;
}

long LongMult(long p, long q)
{
  long p1, p0, q1, q0;
  p1 = p / M4;
  p0 = p % M4;
  q1 = q / M4;
  q0 = q % M4;
```

```
   return (((p0 * q1 + p1 * q0) % M4) *
      M4 + p0 * q0) % M8;
}

void RandomInit(long startingSeed)
{
   seed = startingSeed;
}

long RandomInt()
{
   seed = (LongMult(seed, B) + 1) % M8;
   return seed;
}

long RandomRange(long r)
{
   return ((RandomInt() / M4) * r) / M4;
}

int main()
{
   clrscr();

   int i;

   puts("\nLinear Congruential Random Number Generator\n");
   RandomInit(1234567L);
   for (i = 0; i < 32; i++)
      printf("%10ld", RandomInt());
   puts("");
   for (i = 0; i < 32; i++)
      printf("%10ld", RandomRange(32768L));

   Pause();
   return 0;
}
```

As you probably have realized, this chapter's listings are longer and more complex than others presented up to now. But don't let the *size* of a program throw you: RANDOM.CPP is composed of relatively short functions, each having a specific task. When reading a foreign listing, concentrate on its functions — you'll find the entire program easier to understand by focusing on its parts rather than trying to comprehend the whole at once.

First in RANDOM.CPP are a few miscellaneous definitions: three constants and a `long` variable, `seed`. The `seed` holds the most recent number in a randomized sequence. Subsequent numbers are formed using `seed`. The variable must be global because it must retain its value between calls to the program's functions.

The first function you typed, `LongMult`, multiplies two `long` integer parameters p and q, returning the rightmost eight digits of the result. There isn't time or space to explain every nuance of the math used here — in a nutshell, the statements multiply p and q in pieces to avoid overflow that might be caused by large products. The parameters p and q receive values from calls to `LongMult`. Inside the function, p and q are local variables, usable only inside the function.

A simpler example of function parameters occurs next in function `RandomInit`, which declares a single `long` parameter, `startingSeed`. The function assigns `startingSeed` to the global `seed` variable. Skip to this statement in `main`:

```
RandomInit(1234567L);
```

The argument `1234567L` is passed to `RandomInit`'s `startingSeed` parameter, exactly as though the program had executed an assignment:

```
startingSeed = 1234567L;
```

Function `RandomInt` is an example of a parameterless function. It returns a value but requires no input arguments. `RandomInt` calls `LongMult` to multiply `seed` times constant B. The rest of the expression implements an algorithm known as the *linear congruential method,* a popular random number generator. `RandomInt` assigns each successive random number to `seed`, and it also returns that value.

Another function, `RandomRange`, also returns a number at random, but in this case, the function limits the result to a parameter r. Call `RandomRange` like this:

```
long rand = RandomRange(32768L);
```

That assigns to `rand` a number selected at random between 0 and one less than the function's argument, 32768. Notice how the functions call each other, creating a hierarchy of function calls at runtime. Each function is relatively simple, but together, they perform magic — outputting random sequences in `main`'s two `for` loops.

 If you examine RANDOM.CPP's output closely, you'll notice that the rightmost digits of the first sequence are definitely nonrandom (they cycle repeatedly from 0 to 9). This is an expected characteristic of the linear congruential method. Function `RandomRange` returns "more random" sequences by using the leftmost digits of the values returned by `RandomInt`.

Function parameters may be of any types. You may declare float, double, long, int, char, and parameters of other types. You may also pass structures and arrays to functions, but an array is always passed by address (that is, by a pointer to its first element). You may also declare *pointer parameters,* a powerful technique that you will need time and again.

Pointer parameters

Listing 9-4, UPPER.CPP, shows how to use pointer parameters in a function that converts the characters in a string to all uppercase. The function is useful for preparing strings prior to sorting or searching, as it is generally faster to process single than mixed case text.

Step-by-Steps

1. Change to the PART2 directory.

2. Press F3 and load UPPER.CPP into the IDE.

3. Enter the highlighted instructions in Listing 9-4. The program uses the GetString function from GETSTR.CPP. Type only the new programming as highlighted.

4. Press Ctrl+F9 to compile and run. Follow instructions after the listing.

Listing 9-4: UPPER.CPP

```c
/* Uppercase String Function */

#include <stdio.h>
#include <conio.h>
#include <string.h>

char Pause()
{
  char c;
  printf("\nPress Enter to continue...");
  while ((c = getchar()) != '\n') { }
  return c;
}
```

```
void GetString(char *s, int size)
{
  int i = 0;
  char c;
  while (--size > 0) {
    c = getchar();
    if (c == EOF || c == '\n')
      size = 0;
    else
      s[i++] = c;
  }
  s[i] = '\0';
  fflush(stdin);
}

void Upper(char *s)
{
  int i;
  char c;
  if (!s) return;
  for (i = 0; i < strlen(s); i++) {
    c = s[i];
    if ('a' <= c && c <= 'z') {
      c -= 32;
      s[i] = c;
    }
  }
}

int main()
{
  clrscr();

  char input[80];

  puts("Enter a string:");
  GetString(input, sizeof(input));

  puts("\nYour original string is:");
  puts(input);
```

```
Upper(input);
puts("\nAfter calling Upper, the string is:");
puts(input);

Pause();
return 0;
}
```

Function `Upper` is declared as

```
void Upper(char *s)
```

Translated into English, that means `Upper` returns no value (`void`), and it operates on data passed as a `char` pointer, `s`. You can define a string and call the function like this:

```
char string[40] = "Abcdefg";
Upper(string);
```

The second statement passes `string` (an address value) to the function's `char` pointer parameter, `s`. The function uses the passed address to locate the string's characters and convert them to uppercase.

When you run the sample program, it prompts you to enter a string. It then displays the original string, calls `Upper` to convert the string's characters to uppercase, and then displays the final result.

Array parameters

Passing strings as `char` pointers to functions is a specific instance of a more general rule that applies to all arrays. As you know, a string is just an array of `char`. You may also pass arrays of other types to functions, but when you do, the compiler always generates code that passes the address of the array's first element. For example, suppose that you define an array of `float` values:

```
float farray[100];
```

You then write a function to arrange the values in the array, perhaps sorting them from low to high. The function could be declared like this:

```
void Sort(float fa[], int numItems)
{
}
```

Function `Sort` returns no value. It uses two parameters: an array of `float` object and an `int` value equal to the number of elements in the array. To sort an array, define it and pass it to the function:

```
float scores[100];
Sort(scores, 100);
```

Despite appearances, the scores array is passed to Sort as the address of the first float object in the array. That differs from the normal rule that arguments are passed as copies of their values to parameters. When you write a function like this:

```
void f(int x)
```

using the function in a statement passes a copy of a value to the parameter x:

```
int count = 123;
f(count);
```

Technically speaking, count is *passed by value* to the function. In other words, the function's parameter x is given a copy of the argument, as though the program had executed the assignment:

```
x = count;
```

Because x is just a copy of count, a statement inside the function can modify x *without changing count's original value:*

```
x++;  // Doesn't change count
```

But if you pass a function a pointer to a variable, the pointer addresses the original object. Consider a function declared as

```
void f(int *ip)
```

Calling this function requires you to pass the address of an integer object as an argument to the int pointer parameter:

```
int count;
f(&count);
```

Inside the function, ip now addresses count. A statement in the function that assigns a value to the dereferenced pointer *changes the original count value:*

```
*ip = 123;  // Changes count!
```

Now, let's get back to arrays as function parameters. Because arrays tend to be large, C *always passes arrays by address.* Listing 9-5, SORT.CPP, demonstrates the importance of this rule.

Step-by-Steps

1. Change to the PART2 directory.

2. Press F3 and load SORT.CPP into the IDE.

3. Enter the highlighted instructions in Listing 9-5. I furnished two of the program's functions. You can type the other two.

4. Press Ctrl+F9 to compile and run. Follow instructions after the listing.

Listing 9-5: SORT.CPP

```cpp
/* Sort an array */

#include <stdio.h>
#include <conio.h>
#include <stdlib.h>
#include <time.h>

#define SIZE 50  // Number of elements in array

void QuickSort(int a[], int l, int r)
{
  int i, j, x, t;

  i = l;
  j = r;
  x = a[(l + r) / 2];
  do {
    while (a[i] < x) i++;
    while (x < a[j]) j--;
    if (i <= j) {
      t = a[i];
      a[i] = a[j];
      a[j] = t;
      i++;
      j--;
    }
  } while (i <= j);
  if (l < j) QuickSort(a, l, j);
  if (i < r) QuickSort(a, i, r);
}

void Sort(int fa[], int numItems)
{
  QuickSort(fa, 0, numItems - 1);
}

void ShowArray(int fa[], int numItems)
{
  int i;

  puts("");
  for (i = 0; i < numItems; i++)
    printf("%8d", fa[i]);
}
```

```
char Pause()
{
  char c;
  printf("\nPress Enter to continue...");
  while ((c = getchar()) != '\n') { }
  return c;
}

int main()
{
  clrscr();

  int farray[SIZE];
  int i;

  randomize();
  for (i = 0; i < SIZE; i++)
    farray[i] = rand();
  puts("\nUnsorted array:");
  ShowArray(farray, SIZE);
  Pause();
  Sort(farray, SIZE);
  puts("\nSorted array:");
  ShowArray(farray, SIZE);

  Pause();
  return 0;
}
```

Functions QuickSort, Sort, and ShowArray each declare an array parameter of type int. To use the functions, main fills an array farray with values selected at random and then displays the unsorted data with the statement:

```
ShowArray(farray, SIZE);
```

That passes the address of farray's first element to the function. Similarly, to sort the data in the array, the program executes the statement

```
Sort(farray, SIZE);
```

Those are the same arguments passed to ShowArray, and again, the array is passed by address to the function. Examine how Sort works. It executes the single statement:

```
QuickSort(fa, 0, numItems - 1);
```

As you can see, Sort merely passes its duties on to another function, QuickSort, which does the actual sorting. The Quick Sort method, by the way, is widely accepted as one of the fastest general-purpose sorters around.

Top-Down Programming

One of the best methods for approaching the task of writing computer programs goes by the name *top-down programming*. In short, you state a problem that you need to solve — creating a phone-number database, for example. You then divide the problem into pieces, perhaps jotting areas of concern into a text file. Some of the program's duties might include

```
Input new data
Print reports
Search for numbers
Open database files
Save database files
```

Eventually, those items may become program commands, but it's too early to start writing code. Each item is too broad, and more dividing is needed to define what the program should do. The *Search for numbers* operation, for example, might be roughly segmented into these additional steps:

```
Get number to find
Search for number
if found, display number
else display error
```

You still aren't writing code — you are just outlining the program's design. Some of the text might *look* like code — the last two lines, for instance — but it's only a description that helps organize your thoughts. As you continue to design the program, you collect a list of relatively simple jobs that "solve" the problem of writing the program. Now, it's time to try converting some of your operations into functions:

```
int SearchForNumber(char *number)
{
  int i;
  for (i = 0; i < LIMIT; i++)
    if (Match(number, &database[i]))
      return i;
  return -1;
}
```

The SearchForNumber function is hypothetical, and it calls another function Match that is not yet completed. But no matter; you can fill in such details later. The important lesson is that, with the top-down method, you work on small, easily managed problems, building the final code one piece at a time.

As you divide the program into pieces, try writing some of the steps as functions. Don't hesitate to delete those that don't work out, and don't be surprised if, in writing a function, you discover a better way to organize the code, requiring you to toss out hours of work. Writing programs is like painting pictures — you are likely to erase more than you keep. The trick is to design each function carefully and to choose tasks for functions that can be used in many different places — jobs that are easier said than done. If you find yourself becoming overwhelmed by the tasks at hand, remember to *divide and conquer*. Functions make it possible to work on programs in sensible portions. No programmer, no matter how talented, can write a full blown database system in one sitting!

The top-down method brings up a subject that I've purposely avoided until now — how to organize a large program's files and headers. Large programs have hundreds of functions, far too many to keep in a single file, as in most of this book's relatively short sample listings. Here are some rules and examples that will help answer questions you may have about writing multiple-file programs. The key tool is a *function prototype*.

Function prototypes

A function prototype declares, but does not implement, a function. For example, here's what the prototype looks like for the Sort function from the preceding section:

```
void Sort(int fa[], int numItems);
```

The declaration is the same as it is in the real function, but it ends with a semicolon, and it does not have a body. When the compiler has seen a function prototype, it can compile statements that call the function without also needing the function's statements. Thus, a module can use Sort, which might be implemented in a separate file. The two files can be compiled independently of each other. A linker then can join the compiled object-code files to create the final executable code file. In a large program, this division of labor becomes essential as it avoids having to recompile functions that are already finished and tested.

Function prototypes are best stored in header files that can be included by modules needing those functions. For example, the Sort prototype might be stored in a file, QSORT.H. The function's implementation could be stored in another file, QSORT.CPP. That file can be compiled separately, creating an object-code file QSORT.OBJ, which can be linked into a program.

Other modules can include the QSORT.H header file and call the Sort function. For that, the function's implementation isn't required — only the prototype in the header file. Eventually, the linker is called to combine multiple object-code files to create the final code file.

Headers and prototypes

To demonstrate the organization of a large program and the use of function prototypes in this section, you divide the SORT.CPP program among multiple files. Though still pint-sized, the resulting files illustrate how you might organize a larger program in separate modules.

We'll do one module at a time. First, let's relegate the Pause function to its own module. Listing 9-6, PAUSE.H, stores the function's prototype. (You don't have to type any of the following listings; they are provided in finished form on disk in the PART2 directory.)

Listing 9-6: PAUSE.H

```
/* pause.h */

// Function prototype
char Pause();
```

The PAUSE.H header file contains a single function prototype. Any module can include the file in order to call Pause. A second file, Listing 9-7, PAUSE.CPP, contains the function's implementation.

Listing 9-7: PAUSE.CPP

```
/* pause.cpp */

#include <stdio.h>
#include <conio.h>
#include "pause.h"

char Pause()
{
  char c;
  printf("\nPress Enter to continue...");
  while ((c = getchar()) != '\n') { }
  return c;
}
```

As a separate module, PAUSE.CPP does not have a main function — only one module in any program may define main. Like a main program module, however, PAUSE.CPP includes any header files that it needs. You may compile the module separately by using the *Compile* menu's *Compile to OBJ* command. Most C compilers have similar commands to compile separate modules.

The PAUSE module merely contains a function — it is not a complete program. You cannot run PAUSE, and if you try to compile it to an .EXE code file, the linker issues the error *Undefined symbol _main in module.* This is expected — separately compiled object-code files such as PAUSE must be linked with a host program.

A second header file and module contains the program's sorting functions in Listings 9-8, QSORT.H, and 9-9, QSORT.CPP.

Listing 9-8: QSORT.H

```
/* qsort.h */

// Function prototypes

void Sort(int fa[], int numItems);
void ShowArray(int fa[], int numItems);
```

Listing 9-9: QSORT.CPP

```
/* qsort.cpp */

#include <stdio.h>
#include "qsort.h"

void QuickSort(int a[], int l, int r)
{
  int i, j, x, t;
  i = l;
  j = r;
  x = a[(l + r) / 2];
  do {
    while (a[i] < x) i++;
    while (x < a[j]) j--;
    if (i <= j) {
      t = a[i];
      a[i] = a[j];
      a[j] = t;
      i++;
      j--;
    }
  } while (i <= j);
  if (l < j) QuickSort(a, l, j);
  if (i < r) QuickSort(a, i, r);
}

void Sort(int fa[], int numItems)
{
  QuickSort(fa, 0, numItems - 1);
}
```

```
void ShowArray(int fa[], int numItems)
{
  int i;

  puts("");
  for (i = 0; i < numItems; i++)
    printf("%8d", fa[i]);
}
```

Here again, QSORT.CPP is a separate module. You may compile it to an object-code file QSORT.OBJ, but you cannot run it because it isn't a finished program.

The module's header file, QSORT.H, declares two function prototypes, Sort and ShowArray. The module, QSORT.CPP, however, defines *three* functions, demonstrating how a module can hide functions for its private use. Without the prototype, another module cannot easily access functions that you want to keep hidden. Those might be critical functions that would cause problems if used inappropriately. Or they could be functions such as QuickSort that aren't needed outside of the module.

Last comes the main program. For demonstration purposes, a header file defines a lone constant. Of course, one constant could just as well go in the main program file, but a large program typically uses dozens of constants, which are best stored in a header file. Listing 9-10, SORTDEMO.H, and Listing 9-11, SORTDEMO.CPP, complete the program.

Listing 9-10: SORTDEMO.H

```
/* sortdemo.h */

#define SIZE 50  // Number of elements in array
```

Listing 9-11: SORTDEMO.CPP

```
/* Multiple-file demonstration */

#include <stdio.h>
#include <conio.h>
#include <stdlib.h>
#include <time.h>'
#include "qsort.h"
#include "pause.h"
```

```
#include "sortdemo.h"

int main()
{
  clrscr();

  int farray[SIZE];
  int i;

  randomize();
  for (i = 0; i < SIZE; i++)
    farray[i] = rand();
  puts("\nUnsorted array:");
  ShowArray(farray, SIZE);
  Pause();
  Sort(farray, SIZE);
  puts("\nSorted array:");
  ShowArray(farray, SIZE);

  Pause();
  return 0;
}
```

As usual, the main program includes various header files. Notice, however, that this time it also includes the three headers for the program's separate modules:

```
#include "qsort.h"
#include "pause.h"
#include "sortdemo.h"
```

Double quotes surround the filenames because they are stored in the same directory as SORTDEMO.CPP. Because the QSORT.H and PAUSE.H headers declare function prototypes for Pause, Sort, and ShowArray, the program may call those functions even though their implementations are stored separately. Simply including the headers with their function prototypes makes the functions available to the program or to any other module.

Projects

That completes the program's organization. In general, declarations such as function prototypes and #define directives are best stored in .H header files. Function bodies and variable definitions should be stored in .CPP modules. The question remains — how do you put all these modules together to create the finished code?

The answer differs among various compilers and linkers. With the Turbo C++ compiler supplied with this book, you create a *project* file listing the program's modules. Follow these steps:

1. Use the *File\Change dir...* command to change to the PART2\SORTDEMO subdirectory.

2. Close all open windows (press Alt+F3 repeatedly until all windows are gone). Also close any open project by selecting the *Project\Close project...* command.

3. Select the *Project\Open project...* command.

4. Type a project filename into the *Load Project File* input box. For example, enter **sortdemo** and press Enter. The IDE automatically supplies the .PRJ file extension, creating SORTDEMO.PRJ in the current directory.

5. You now see an empty *Project* window. Select the Project|Add item... command, and select the three files SORTDEMO.CPP, PAUSE.CPP, and QSORT.CPP, one at a time (click the *Add* button for each, or just press Enter). The dialog stays open so that you can select multiple file names. When you are done, select the *Cancel* button (or press Esc). If you make any mistakes, delete the files from the *Project* window and repeat step 4.

6. That's it — you have completed the program's project. To compile and run the demonstration, press Ctrl+F9. Those keys compile each separate module to an object-code .OBJ file and then link the object modules to create the finished code file, SORTDEMO.EXE.

7. Before opening new files, select *Project\Close project. . .* to close and save the SORTDEMO.PRJ file on disk. The IDE also records any open windows in SORTDEMO.DSK. Restarting the IDE from the directory then restores the most recent environment so that you can continue to work on the project.

When you compile a project, the IDE issues only the minimum number of commands needed to compile and link the final code. If the PAUSE.OBJ and QSORT.OBJ object-code files are already up to date, these files are not recompiled. Instead, they are simply linked to the final code. As you write larger and larger programs, you'll appreciate the capability of the Turbo C++ IDE to compile only the bare minimum number of modules in a project, a feature that can save a lot of time when developing an application.

For best results, store each project and its files in a separate directory.

In Part 3, I return to functions, listing many provided in the standard library provided with the compiler packed with this book. Meanwhile, you may want to extract some of the functions in this chapter into your own library. Most programmers collect functions the way philatelists hoard stamps. Fortunately, you don't have to paste functions into an album — you can just store them in a disk directory and include them into your programs as needed.

The next chapter closes Part 2 with a variety of "Advanced Programming Techniques" that I've been saving for just the right moment. You won't need the information in Chapter 10 in every program you write, but the advanced techniques I'm about to describe are invaluable tools, and you'll want to at least skim the chapter so that you know what's there.

Advanced Programming Techniques

You won't use the methods in this chapter every day, but don't skip the following sections — they contain a wealth of material that, some day, may provide just what you need to solve a sticky problem. These tidbits and other techniques belong in every C programmer's grab bag.

Most programming examples in this chapter are in the form of snippets that you can insert into a shell file. Follow these instructions to try out this chapter's programming.

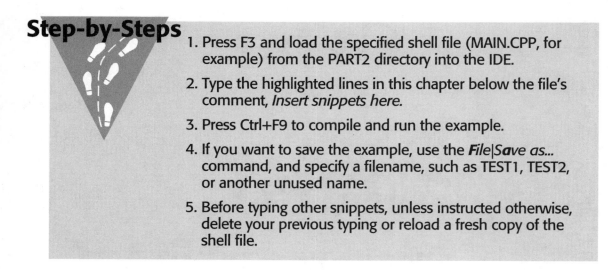

1. Press F3 and load the specified shell file (MAIN.CPP, for example) from the PART2 directory into the IDE.

2. Type the highlighted lines in this chapter below the file's comment, *Insert snippets here.*

3. Press Ctrl+F9 to compile and run the example.

4. If you want to save the example, use the *File|Save as...* command, and specify a filename, such as TEST1, TEST2, or another unused name.

5. Before typing other snippets, unless instructed otherwise, delete your previous typing or reload a fresh copy of the shell file.

More on *main*

As you know, every program begins running with the first statement in function `main`. Following are some additional techniques you can use with `main`.

Command-line arguments

Most operating systems can pass arguments to programs similar to the way statements in a C program can pass arguments to functions. From the DOS command line, for example, you can type commands, such as:

```
xcopy file.txt newfile.txt
```

The filenames *file.txt* and *newfile.txt* are *command-line arguments.* They are separated by spaces or commas and are passed to the XCOPY program exactly as typed. Arguments are also frequently used to select program options such as /F (Free Memory) in this DOS command:

```
mem /F
```

In a C program, function `main` can detect and access command-line arguments passed to a program. To do that, declare `main` with two parameters:

```
int main(int argc, char *argv[])
{
}
```

The first parameter, `int argc`, indicates the number of command-line arguments. You should There's always at least one argument, equal to the program's pathname. To display that name, add this snippet to MAIN.CPP:

```
printf("pathname = %s\n", argv[0]);
```

Arguments are stored in memory as null terminated strings addressed by `char` pointers in the `argv` array. The expression `argv[0]`, for example, addresses the program's pathname; `argv[1]` addresses the first command-line argument; `argv[2]` addresses the second argument; and so on. To list all arguments, add this `if` statement to MAIN.CPP:

```
int i;
for (i = 0; i < argc; i++)
  printf("Arg # %d == %s\n", i, argv[i]);
```

Select the *Run\Arguments...* command, and enter **the cat in the hat** (or any other list of sample arguments). When you press Ctrl+F9 to compile and run, the program displays

```
Arg # 0 == C:\TCLITE\PART2\MAIN.EXE
Arg # 1 == the
Arg # 2 == cat
Arg # 3 == in
Arg # 4 == the
Arg # 5 == hat
```

It's often useful to design programs to display instructions if no arguments are specified. Try this snippet in MAIN.CPP:

```
puts("Your Program by Your Name");
if (argc <= 1) {
  puts("");
  puts("This program displays instructions");
  puts("if no command-line arguments are");
  puts("specified.");
}
```

Select the *Run\Arguments...* command and press Del and then Enter to delete any current arguments before running other programs in the IDE.

Main's return statement

Function `main` usually ends with a `return` statement, which passes an integer value back to the process that ran the program. That process can be the DOS command-line processor, or it can be another program — an alternate DOS shell, for example —from which users select programs from a directory listing.

To return a value from `main`, declare the function with the `int` data type and end with a `return` statement:

```
int main()
{
  ...
  return 0;
}
```

The `return` statement ends `main` and, therefore, also ends the program. Returning zero indicates no errors. To tell the command processor that an error occurred during the program, you can return a nonzero value from `main`:

```
int main()
{
  ...
  return 1;  // Error!
}
```

Use the DOS `ERRORLEVEL` batch-file command to detect returned values. For example, this batch command, which you can use in a .BAT file that runs the program, transfers control to label `Error` if `ERRORLEVEL` is greater than or equal to 1 (DOS's == operator is equivalent to C's >=):

```
if ERRORLEVEL == 1 GOTO ERROR
...
:ERROR
```

Programs that do not return values to the operating system can declare `main` by using the `void` data type. In that case, no `return` statement is needed:

```
void main()
{
  ...
}
```

 Not all operating systems can use return values as described here for MS-DOS.

Exiting and error handling

Most often, `main` ends with a `return` statement. You can also end a program, however, by calling the `exit` function, either in `main` or in any other function. Include the STDLIB.H header file in any program that calls `exit`. For example, add this function to MAIN.CPP above function `main`:

```
void EndProgram()
{
  puts("Inside EndProgram");
  Pause();
  exit(1);
}
```

The value in parentheses is passed back to DOS's ERRORLEVEL (or a similar variable in another operating system). In addition, all open files are closed and other cleanup chores are executed, making exit a very safe way to end a program.

Then call EndProgram to exit the program. Add this snippet to function main:

```
EndProgram();
puts("This statement never executes!");
```

The sample program calls EndProgram, which ends the program by calling exit.

More on Preprocessor Directives

Preprocessor directives, such as #include and #define, are not programming statements, but commands to the compiler. In a classically written C compiler, a *preprocessor stage* scans all directives, creates a new temporary source code file with the translated directives, and then performs the real compilation on that final text. The complete text from an included header file, for instance, is inserted into the temporary source code at the location of the #include directive.

Modern compilers, such as Turbo C++, do not have a preprocessor stage. To achieve high compilation speeds, the compilers handle directives and compile the source code in one pass. But regardless of how directives are handled internally, they have the identical effects among compilers — directives are, in a sense, minilanguages built into C. Here are a few facts about using preprocessor directives that may come in handy from time to time.

Include files (#include)

As you know, an #include directive includes a file's text at the directive's location. You normally use #include like this:

```
#include <stdlib.h>
```

The angle brackets around the filename cause the compiler to look for STDLIB.H in a directory listed in a DOS PATH statement (or the equivalent in another operating system). To look for a file in the current directory, surround its name with double quotes:

```
#include "myhead.h"
```

In MS-DOS, you can also specify drive letters and pathnames:

```
#include "c:\headers\myheader.h"
```

It's probably best not to be so specific, however, because with explicit drive and path information, directives such as that one make it difficult to install source files in other directories and drives. Rather than fill up PATH with default directories, specify *partial* subdirectories like this:

```
#include <myheads\header.h>
```

That includes HEADER.H stored in the MYHEADS subdirectory in the default path for headers, usually C:\...\INCLUDE, where the ellipsis indicates the compiler's root directory (C:\TCLITE for this book).

Some programmers also use #include to insert common functions into their programs. You can, for example, include any text file, not only headers:

```
#include "fnlib.inc"
```

That includes the FNLIB.INC file into the source code at this location. The file (not shown here) can contain a set of commonly used functions or other declarations.

Macro substitution (#define)

A #define directive most commonly defines a symbolic constant. Here are some samples to refresh your memory:

```
#define MAX 100
#define TITLE "My Program"
#define PI 3.14159
```

It's important to realize that #define merely associates text with a symbol. The text 100 (not the value) is associated with MAX. The text "My Program", including the quotes, is associated with TITLE. The text 3.14159 (again, not the value) is associated with PI. The symbols are *text macros,* which the preprocessor replaces with the associated text. This statement, for instance:

```
puts(TITLE);
```

is translated by the preprocessor before compilation to

```
puts("My Program");
```

A common error (which I still make, even though I know better) is to end a #define directive with a semicolon. *Never do this:*

```
#define TITLE "My Program";  // ???
```

The semicolon is included in the text associated with TITLE; thus, the puts statement is translated to

```
puts("My Program";);
```

The misplaced semicolon drives the compiler crazy — or, at the very least, it results in a cryptic error message. You can, however, end #define directives with C or C++ comments, which the preprocessor ignores:

```
#define TITLE "My Program"   /* Title of program */
#define PI 3.14159           // Pi to 5 decimal places
```

Text macros also can make use of simple argument substitutions. For instance, insert this line after the final #include directive in a copy of SHELL.CPP:

#define ShowTitle(S) puts(S)

That associates the macro ShowTitle(S) with the text puts(S). The compiler understands S as a *replaceable argument.* Also insert this snippet inside main:

ShowTitle("Program Name");

The preprocessor substitutes the string "Program Name", including the quotes, for the macro's S parameter, translating that line into

```
puts("Program Name");
```

Of course, it's just as easy to call puts directly. Still, macros with replaceable arguments can be useful. The STDLIB.H header file, for instance, defines four macros:

```
#define random(num) (int)(((long)rand()*(num))/RAND_MAX)
#define randomize()  srand((unsigned)time(NULL))
#define max(a,b)     (((a) > (b)) ? (a) : (b))
#define min(a,b)     (((a) < (b)) ? (a) : (b))
```

Elsewhere in this book, I explained that randomize starts a new random sequence. Actually, randomize is not a function — it's a macro that is translated to a call to srand, passing the current time as an unsigned integer value. That's why you must include the TIME.H header file in programs that use randomize.

The max and min macros are especially valuable. Because their arguments are translated via simple substitution, you can use them with any data types. For example, define two int variables, as follows:

```
#include <stdlib.h>
...
int value1 = 123;
int value2 = 987;
```

Define a third variable and initialize it to the maximum of `value1` or `value2` with this statement:

```
int result = max(value1, value2);
```

Replace `max` with `min` to initialize `result` to the minimum of the two values. The preprocessor translates the statement to the following, which is obviously more difficult to type (and to read):

```
int result = (((value1) > (value2)) ? (value1) : (value2));
```

 If you cannot compile programs that use `max` and `min`, the macros cannot be defined in STDLIB.H. Borland's C++ compilers, for example, define the macros only for straight C programs (because there are other C++ techniques for creating similar capabilities, using methods beyond the scope of this book). If you receive errors for `max` and `min`, add these directives to your program:

```
#define max(a,b) (((a) > (b)) ? (a) : (b))
#define min(a,b) (((a) < (b)) ? (a) : (b))
```

Substitution macros are sometimes used by a compiler to emulate another compiler's function calls. For example, suppose that your working compiler defines `FileOpen` as a function that opens a file. One fine day, you need to compile your code with another compiler that defines a similar function but names it `OpenFile`. (Such incompatibilities are more common than you may imagine.) Rather than rewrite your code, define a macro for the new name:

```
#define FileOpen(A, B) OpenFile(A, B)
```

That causes the new compiler's preprocessor to translate statements like this:

```
FileOpen("myFile", handle);
```

to the new compiler's equivalent statement:

```
OpenFile("myFile", handle);
```

Undefined symbols (#undef)

You can undefine a symbol, removing it from the list of symbols the compiler recognizes. For example, suppose that you include a header file that defines these symbols:

```
#define YES 1L
#define NO 0L
```

Because your program doesn't need long integer constants, you decide to redefine the symbols as the following:

```
#define YES 1
#define NO 0
```

Unfortunately, you now receive the warning *Redefinition of 'YES' is not identical.* You receive a similar warning for NO. It's OK to redefine the same symbol exactly as it is already defined (which may happen, for example, if the same header file is included more than once during compilation). But it may be a mistake to redefine a symbol differently, so the compiler issues the warning.

To eliminate the warning, undefine the symbols before redefining them. To undefine a symbol, use the #undef directive, as follows:

```
#undef YES
#undef NO
```

That throws out any current definitions for YES and NO, as though they had never been defined.

A symbol is *defined* if it exists, regardless of that symbol's associated value. A symbol is *undefined* if it has never appeared in a #define directive or if it was undefined with #undef.

Conditional compilation (#ifdef and friends)

By testing whether a symbol is defined or undefined, a source code file can direct the compiler to process selected statements. This technique, called *conditional compilation,* makes it possible to write source code files that compile differently based on the existence or values of symbolic constants.

You can use the technique to create debugging versions of your code. Start by defining a symbol named DEBUG:

```
#define DEBUG
```

You don't need to associate a value with DEBUG. It is important only that the symbol is defined — that is, the symbol is *known* to the compiler. Elsewhere in the file, use #ifdef (if defined) to test whether DEBUG exists:

```
#ifdef DEBUG
  puts("Debugging Version");
  puts("0.16  12/20/96");
#endif
```

End the #ifdef section with #endif. If DEBUG is defined, the compiler processes the statements between the two directives. If DEBUG is not defined, *the compiler skips all text between.* Thus, to eliminate the two temporary puts statements, simply turn the symbol definition into a comment:

```
//#define DEBUG
```

You can delete the line, but then you'd have to retype it to again define DEBUG. Alternatively, you can undefine the symbol:

```
#undef DEBUG
```

Use #ifndef to test whether a symbol is *not* defined:

```
#ifndef DEBUG
   puts("Production Version 1.00");
   puts("(c) 1999 by Tom Duck Software");
#endif
```

Use #endif to end the section. The statements between the two directives are compiled only if DEBUG is not defined. Following either #ifdef or #ifndef, you can insert an #else section:

```
#ifdef DEBUG
   puts("Debugging Version");
#else
   puts("Production Version");
#endif
```

The first puts is compiled if DEBUG is defined. The second is compiled if DEBUG is not defined. An #endif must eventually follow #else. Multiple *else* sections are created by using #elif (else if):

```
#ifdef DEBUG
   puts("Debugging Version");
#elif defined(CUSTOM)
   puts("Custom Version");
#else
   puts("Production Version");
#endif
```

Defining DEBUG compiles the first puts statement. Defining a symbol CUSTOM compiles the second puts, but only if DEBUG is not defined. If neither symbol is defined, the third puts is compiled. An #endif directive finishes the construction. Use the defined *preprocessor operator* as shown to test whether a symbol is defined in #elif.

A more general directive, #if, selects a section of the source code for compilation if an expression evaluates to true (nonzero), but it isn't as popular as other conditional directives. Use #if with defined like this:

```
#if defined(DEBUG)
   puts("Debugging Version");
#else
   puts("Production Version");
#endif
```

The first line is equivalent to:

```
#ifdef DEBUG
```

Compiler directives (#pragma)

A recent addition to C, and one that is used by many C++ compilers, is the #pragma directive. Use it to give implementation-dependent commands to a compiler. All C and C++ compilers ignore unrecognized #pragma commands.

The Turbo C++ compiler packaged with this book responds to several #pragma commands. Insert this directive, for example, ahead of a function to eliminate a warning that one or more of the function's parameters are unused:

```
#pragma argsused
void f(int i)
{
  // Doesn't use i
}
```

The compiler normally warns you that function f doesn't use its integer parameter i, but the warning is temporarily disabled by the #pragma command. You can use the command to eliminate the warning for this and other unfinished functions under development. The command affects only the immediately following function.

    #pragma directives are compiler specific, so I'll stop explaining them here. For more information on Turbo C++ #pragmas, press Shift+F1 to bring up the IDE's help index, enter **#pragma,** and press Enter. Then use the Tab and Enter keys to read about each #pragma option.

Debugging (#error)

The #error directive is highly valuable for debugging. Use it to output a message during compilation. For example, suppose that you are writing a programmer's utility that requires a certain symbol to be defined. You can instruct the compiler to display a custom error message if the symbol doesn't exist by inserting statements such as:

```
#ifndef CLIMIT
  #error Constant CLIMIT not defined
#endif
```

The error message is treated in the same way as others issued by the compiler. While the error condition exists, a code file is not created. You can place the commands inside or outside a function (outside is the more common location).

Predefined symbols

All C and C++ compilers define several symbols that are useful, especially for debugging. Two are standard: __LINE__ and __FILE__. To avoid conflicts with program identifiers that are named LINE and FILE, each symbol is surrounded by two pairs of underscores. You can use them to display the current line and file if a certain symbol is or isn't defined:

```
#ifndef DEBUG
   puts("Error: This is a debugging module");
   printf("Line #%d  File:%s\n", __LINE__, __FILE__);
#endif
```

That displays the following message at runtime:

```
Error: This is a debugging module
Line #25  File:X.CPP
```

The ASSERT.H header

Of all the debugging aids in C, the ASSERT.H header is one of the most useful. Include the file in any module, as follows:

```
#include <assert.h>
```

You can now write *assertion statements* in files for performing logical tests at runtime. Suppose, for example, that inside a function, a global variable maximum is supposed to be greater than or equal to 100. Assert that rule with this line:

```
assert(maximum >= 100);
```

In effect, the directive states that "if the expression in parentheses is false, halt the program's execution immediately and display an error message." The message is written to the standard error output file stderr. If the preceding line is added to main, for example, and if the following global variable is also declared:

```
int maximum = 50;
```

running the program displays the assertion error:

```
Assertion failed: maximum >= 100, file TEST.CPP, line 24
Abnormal program termination
```

The message includes the test expresssion, the filename, and the line number where the assertion failed. If the tested expression is true (in this case, if maximum is greater than or equal to 100), no error is generated, and the program continues normally.

Assertion statements occupy space in the compiled code, so it's usually best to remove them in the program's production release. The easiest way to remove them is to define the symbol NDEBUG *before* including the ASSERT.H header:

```
#define NDEBUG
#include <assert.h>
```

This statement nullifies all uses of `assert` as though they were not present. To reenable the assertions, turn the #define directive into a comment:

```
// #define NDEBUG
#include <assert.h>
```

Nested comments

Although comments may seem to be part of the C language, they actually are ignored by the compiler. Normally, comments cannot be nested. You cannot, for example, insert one comment into another, such as:

```
/*
Start of outer comment
  /* Incorrect start of inner comment */
End of outer comment
*/
```

That won't compile because the comment actually ends at line three, causing the compiler to issue an error for the apparently undefined symbol, End, at line four. By using a C++ compiler, however, there is a way to nest comments that's useful for debugging. Suppose, for example, that you suspect these statements of causing trouble:

```
int max = 100;   // Define maximum value for loop
int i;           // Loop control variable
for (i = 0; i < max; i++)
  doSomething();
```

You decide that setting max to 100 is unnecessary. To test your theory, you can delete the line, but I find that it's best to surround it with C-style comment brackets that preserve the original line while using an alternate test statement:

```
/* DEBUG
int max = 100;   // Define maximum value for loop
*/
int max = 99;    // Alternate test
int i;
for (i = 0; i < max; i++)
  doSomething();
```

It's OK to nest a line that ends in a C++ comment (//) inside a C-style comment delimited with /* and */. I add the word DEBUG to the source code so that I can easily find the temporary sections by using a text editor's search command.

The preceding sample code doesn't really nest a comment because there's only one comment, not two. Some C compilers also permit comment nesting, which may also be useful for debugging as explained here without using C++ style comments. The technique is best used, however, only as a temporary measure because many C compilers prohibit nested comments.

More on Pointers

If you are still fuzzy on pointers, you may want to reread Chapter 8 before continuing. In this section, I explain some advanced pointer techniques that you may find useful.

Indirect pointers (pointers to pointers)

A pointer that addresses another pointer is called an *indirect pointer*. It is often used in memory management software to address blocks of RAM or other objects that may move at runtime. So that programs can always find the objects, the programs use an indirect pointer that is automatically updated with the object's address.

Figure 10-1 illustrates how indirect pointers can be used. The indirect pointer on the left addresses one of several other pointers in the center. The center pointer, in turn, addresses the object. (The indirect pointer belongs to the program; the pointers in the center belong to the operating system.) If the object moves, the center pointer's address value can be changed without affecting the indirect pointer.

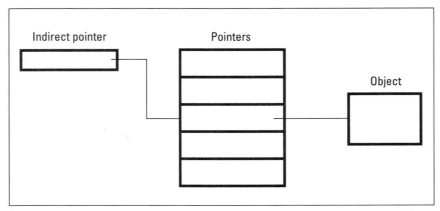

Figure 10-1 ▷ Indirect pointers.

Indirect pointers have more mundane uses in C programs, as the next snippets demonstrate. Add the following programming to a copy of SHELL.CPP in the PART2 directory. First, define an array of char pointers, initialized to the names of the days of the week. Insert these lines after the last #include directive, above function Pause:

```
char * days[7] = {
  "Sunday", "Monday", "Tuesday", "Wednesday",
  "Thursday", "Friday", "Saturday"
};
```

Array days contains seven char pointers, each of which addresses one of the strings in braces. An indirect pointer can address days and its char pointers. Define the pointer inside main:

```
char ** strPtr;
strPtr = days;
```

The pointer strPtr is literally an indirect pointer — it addresses an array of char pointers. The second line assigns to strPtr the address of the days array. You can then use strPtr as an array to display one of the day names:

```
puts(strPtr[3]);
```

Pointers to functions

Pointers normally address objects, but they also can address code. A pointer, for example, can address a function in memory. The program can use the pointer to call the function, a highly useful technique that permits programs to assign different function addresses to pointers, affecting how the program operates at runtime.

Try these snippets in a copy of SHELL.CPP. First, insert a simple test function that displays a message. Type these lines after the final #include directive, above function Pause:

```
void TestFunction()
{
  puts("Inside test function");
}
```

You can, of course, call TestFunction in the usual way by writing its name in a statement:

```
TestFunction();
```

But you also can address and call the function by using a pointer. The pointer's definition, however, may seem a bit odd until you get used to the syntax. Add this line to main:

```
void (*pf)();
```

That declares pf as "a pointer to a void function that requires no parameters." Note that eliminating the first set of parentheses has an entirely different effect:

```
void *pf();
```

That declares a function pf that returns a void pointer. To declare a pointer *to* a void function requires the extra parentheses.

Having declared the function pointer pf, you can use it *as though it were an actual function.* For example, to call the function addressed by pf, simply write the pointer's name followed by parentheses:

```
pf();
```

That may seem unusual, but if you consider that function names are represented internally as the addresses of the function code, it makes better sense. Without the parentheses, however, pf is just a pointer, and it can be used as such. You can assign pf to another pointer of a compatible type:

```
void (*anotherPtr)();
anotherPtr = pf;
anotherPtr();
```

Line one declares a second function pointer, anotherPtr, of the same type as pf. Line two assigns pf to anotherPtr. Now, both pointers address the same function in memory. Line three calls the function addressed by anotherPtr.

You will most often use the preceding method to pass a function pointer to another function, which can then call the addressed code. The technique permits statements to modify the functions called by other statements — an extremely valuable technique for writing general-purpose code, such as sorting and searching subroutines. Listing 10-1, FUNPTR.CPP, demonstrates one of the most useful instances of the technique and shows how to take advantage of a sorting function provided by the standard library. The function qsort requires a pointer to a comparison function that you are required to supply. Because of this design, qsort can sort arrays of any types. After the listing, I'll explain how the function works.

Step-by-Steps

1. Change to the PART2 directory.

2. Press F3 and load FUNPTR.CPP into the IDE.

3. Enter the highlighted instructions in Listing 10-1.

4. Press Ctrl+F9 to compile and run and then follow the instructions after the listing.

Listing 10-1: FUNPTR.CPP

```cpp
/* Function Pointers */

#include <stdio.h>
#include <stdio.h>
#include <conio.h>
#include <stdlib.h>
#include <time.h>

#define SIZE 50    // Number of elements in array

int array[SIZE];   // Array of integers

char Pause()
{
  char c;
  printf("\nPress Enter to continue...");
  while ((c = getchar()) != '\n') { }
  return c;
}

int Compare(const void *a, const void *b)
{
  int aint = *(int *)a;
  int bint = *(int *)b;
  if (aint < bint)
    return -1;
  else if (aint > bint)
    return +1;
  else
    return 0;
}

void DisplayArray(void)
{
  puts("");
  for (int i = 0; i < SIZE; i++)
    printf("%8d", array[i]);
}
```

```
main()
{
  clrscr();

  randomize();
  for (int i = 0; i < SIZE; i++)
    array[i] = rand();
  puts("\nUnsorted array:");
  DisplayArray();
  qsort((void *)array, SIZE, sizeof(array[0]), Compare);
  puts("\nSorted array:");
  DisplayArray();

  Pause();
  return 0;
}
```

To give the program some data to sort, you inserted a global array of integer values, and you defined a constant, SIZE, to specify the number of objects in the array. Next, you typed the comparison function, named Compare. (It could be called something else.) The function is declared as

```
int Compare(const void *a, const void *b)
```

The qsort function requires an int function of that design. The comparison function receives two arguments, each of type const void *. In other words, a and b are generic pointers to objects of unspecified types. They are declared const because Compare is not permitted to change the addressed values — if it did, sorting would not work.

The comparison function returns 0 (zero) if the two addressed objects are equal. It returns –1 if the object addressed by pointer a is less than the object addressed by b. It returns +1 if object a is greater than object b. It's up to you to decide how to write the function. In my version, I define two int variables, aint and bint, to which I assign the int values addressed by the two pointers. This statement may take some mental effort to decode:

```
int aint = *(int *)a;
```

Because a is a void pointer, a type cast expression (int *) is required to tell the compiler that a actually addresses an int object. The leftmost asterisk dereferences the cast pointer by providing access to the addressed integer, which is assigned to aint.

Now, ain't that sweet?

After doing the same to obtain the value addressed by b, the function compares the two values and returns the appropriate result. By the way, to sort the array from high to low, simply return the reverse values — that is, if object a is less than b, return +1; if object a is greater than b, return –1.

Finally, in `main`, you entered statements that use the comparison function. A `for` loop fills the global array with values selected at random. This information is displayed by function `DisplayArray`, after which `qsort` is called to sort the array. Study the statement that calls `qsort`:

```
qsort((void *)array, SIZE, sizeof(array[0]), Compare);
```

The function requires several arguments. The first argument is the address of the data to be sorted, which is type cast to a `void` pointer. The next argument is the number of objects in the array, followed by the size in bytes of one object. That size is most easily supplied by taking the `sizeof` the first element of the array. Finally, `Compare` is passed as a function pointer to `qsort`.

When you refer to a function by name *without* parentheses, as in `Compare`, the result is the address of that function. When you refer to a function by name *with* parentheses, as in `Compare()`, the compiler generates code that calls the function. Obviously, in this case you do not want to call the function; instead, you want to pass its address to `qsort` so *that* function can call it to sort the array.

More on Structures

In Chapter 7's discussions on derived data types, I left out three little-used structure techniques that can be valuable programming tools. You may want to review `struct` declarations before reading the following information on structures.

Incomplete structure declarations

You can declare the name of a `struct` without supplying its body by writing it like this:

```
struct Record;
```

That tells the compiler that you intend to provide a `struct` named `Record`, but you aren't ready to define that structure's contents. Meanwhile, the *incomplete structure declaration* permits other statements to refer to the structure by address. You can, for example, define a pointer to `struct Record`:

```
struct Record *recptr;
```

You cannot, however, create `Record` variables:

```
struct Record myData;  // ???
```

because, at this point, the compiler doesn't know `Record`'s size. To create a variable, the compiler must know how many bytes to reserve for the object.

Incomplete structure declarations are most often used to create structures that contain pointers to other structures. Suppose, for example, that you need two structures, each of which requires a pointer member that addresses an object of the other type. It's a Catch-22 situation: In order to declare the pointers, you have to declare each of the two structures ahead of the other, an apparent impossibility.

The solution is to use an incomplete structure declaration:

```
struct Record;
```

Follow the incomplete structure declaration with the other structure, including a pointer to a struct Record object:

```
struct Other {
  struct Record *p;
  int x;  // other data
};
```

Despite the fact that Record is unfinished, the compiler permits Other to declare the struct Record pointer, p. Finally, you can finish the declarations and supply a body for Record:

```
struct Record {
  struct Other *q;
  int y;  // other data
};
```

Unions

A *union* is a special structure with members that overlay one another, something like the acetate overlays in an encyclopedia — the ones that show you the organs inside a human body, for example, one gruesome layer at a time.

Declare a union as you do a structure, but use the union keyword in place of struct:

```
union TwoTimer {
  int i;
  unsigned u;
};
```

This statement looks like a struct, but as a union, the two members *are stored at the same location in memory*. In other words, i and u overlay each other and provide two interpretations of the same bytes in RAM. Define an object of a union as you do a structure:

```
union TwoTimer object;
```

Then you can assign and use the members of object as you do the members of a structure:

```
object.i = -25;
```

Because i and u are not distinct but are just different names for the same object, they can be used to view information in two different ways. Two printf statements, for instance, can display the value –24 assigned to member i as an unsigned value simply by referring to member u:

```
printf("object.i == %d\n", object.i);
printf("object.u == %u\n", object.u);
```

A more practical use for unions is to extract 8-bit bytes from 16-bit words, as long as you realize, however, that such operations are dependent on the sizes of data types and how their bytes are arranged in memory. Using unions in the way I'm about to explain works with the compiler supplied with this book, but the same method may fail with a different compiler.

For simplicity, start by defining an alias for a `char` (add the line to a copy of SHELL.CPP, after the last #include directive):

```
typedef unsigned char Byte;
```

That creates the symbol `Byte` as a new type, equivalent to `unsigned char`. Use `Byte` in a `struct` with two members (add the declaration after the preceding `typedef`):

```
typedef struct tagOverlay {
  Byte loByte;
  Byte hiByte;
} Overlay;
```

Next, declare a union, `Word`, with two overlaid members. The first member is an `unsigned` word, `w`. The second is an object of the `Overlay` structure (type it after the preceding declaration):

```
typedef union tagWord {
  unsigned w;
  Overlay bytes;
} Word;
```

Because the members of a union overlay each other, `Word` may be used to view a 16-bit value as an `unsigned` word or as two bytes. For example, these statements, which you can add to the `main` function after the comment *Insert snippets here,* define an object of type `Word` and assign it the value 5068:

```
Word value;
value.w = 5068;
```

To extract the high and low bytes of the value, follow the preceding two lines with these statements:

```
unsigned low = value.bytes.loByte;
unsigned high = value.bytes.hiByte;
```

Display the word and its two byte components by adding these statements to the program:

```
printf("Word value == %u\n", value.w);
printf("low byte == %u\n", low);
printf("high byte == %u\n", high);
```

On screen, you see

```
Word value == 5068
low byte == 204
high byte == 19
```

The expression `value.bytes` refers to the `bytes` member inside the union object `value`. That member is a structure with two additional members `loByte` and `hiByte`. The expression `value.bytes.loByte` therefore refers to the low-order byte of the member `w`. The expression `value.bytes.hiByte` refers to that value's high-order byte. Again, I stress that "high byte" and "low byte" are system-dependent terms — they may have the reverse meanings with other compilers and operating systems. Also, a C compiler may define the `unsigned` type as having more than two bytes, which causes the preceding examples to fail. Use unions with extreme caution!

Bit fields

Another system-dependent feature called a *bit field* resembles a structure but lets you specify the number of bits that each member occupies. The technique is often employed in software de-signed for a particular computer — a function that accesses a register, for example, or a hard-ware port on a device attached to the computer. Programs that use bit fields may work strangely or not at all when transferred to another compiler, so don't use this feature if your code must run on a variety of computers.

Declare a bit-field structure as you do other `struct`s, but make all members the `unsigned` type. Follow each member with a colon and the number of bits to use for that value. This statement, for example, defines a 16-bit, bit-field structure named `Bits`:

```
struct Bits {
   unsigned fourBits : 4;
   unsigned threeBits : 3;
   unsigned oneBit : 1;
   unsigned eightBits : 8;
};
```

`Bits` has four members, each occupying a different number of bits in the structure. If the sum of bits does not total 16, the structure can be padded with unused bits to make its size an even multiple of 16. (Take that rule with a grain of salt, however, as the exact effect depends on the compiler's specifications.)

Use a bit-field structure as you do any other. You can define an object of the `struct`'s type with the following:

```
struct Bits object;
```

You can then assign values to the `object`'s bit fields:

```
object.threeBits = 19;
object.oneBit = 1;
object.fourBits = 0x0f;
object.eightBits = 256;
```

I hesitate to walk farther along this tenuous limb — bit field structures are not for faint-hearted programmers. Bit fields can cause hard-to-find bugs. They work slowly (because the compiler has to generate time-consuming instructions to pack values into objects of arbitrary bit sizes), and they may cause programs to be highly system dependent. If you still have a good reason to use bit field structures, by all means do so. But expect to spend some extra time debugging your code!

More on Variables

The C language includes four *storage class specifiers* — auto, extern, static, and register — that you can use in variable definitions. Actually, there are five specifiers: Technically speaking, typedef is also a storage class specifier, even though it results in no memory allocations. (Fortunately, only compiler authors need to worry about syntactical quirks like these.)

The auto specifier has little practical value because variables in functions are auto by default. The two declarations inside a function, for example, are equivalent:

```
void f()
{
  int i;
  auto int i;  // Same as above
  ...
}
```

Either way, i is defined (allocated memory) automatically each time the function is called. You can use auto only inside a function. Global variables cannot be auto.

Use the extern specifier to indicate that a variable is defined elsewhere in the program, usually in another module. Suppose, for example, that a module defines this variable:

```
int count = 256;
```

Another module can access count by declaring it as an external object. To do that, preface the declaration with extern:

```
extern int count;
```

Most often, however, you'll use a declaration, such as the preceding example, inside a function that needs to access a variable in another module. The declaration tells the compiler that count is defined elsewhere. Eventually, an int named count *must* be defined, or the linker will refuse to construct the final code file.

A static variable is the exact opposite of an automatic one. A static variable is an object that occupies permanent space (permanent, that is, while the program runs) but is typically not globally available to statements. A function typically uses a static variable to retain information between function calls but also to hide the variable from other functions — a useful technique that can help prevent bugs caused by a function changing a variable it should leave alone.

Information hiding, as the subject is known, is especially important in the design of function libraries. A properly designed library uses such techniques as static variables to help prevent errors caused by sloppy programming. Of course, it's best not to write sloppy code in the first place, but nobody's perfect.

Try the following snippets in a copy of SHELL.CPP. First, insert this function after the last #include directive:

```
void f()
{
  static int count = 0;
  printf("count == %d\n", count);
  count++;
}
```

Because integer variable count is declared static, the compiler allocates permanent space for the object, which is initialized to the value 0. Even though that statement appears inside the function, it is executed only once before the function is first called. Unlike an automatic variable, the static count retains its value between function calls. Prove that by adding this code to main:

```
int i;
for (i = 0; i < 10; i++)
  f();
```

When you run the program, it calls function f ten times. On each call, the function displays count's value. Because count retains its value between function calls, the program displays

```
count == 0
count == 1
count == 2
. . .
count == 9
```

Static variables are especially useful in providing functions with objects that, like global variables, keep their values throughout the runtime life of the program. Static variables, however, cannot be accessed globally. Another function, for instance, can't gain access to the static count by declaring it extern:

```
void g()
{
  extern int count;  // ???
  count += 20;
}
```

This statement causes the linker to issue an error, and the code file is not created. If count were a global variable, function g could use extern to gain access to its value. Because count is static, only function f can modify the variable, a fact that contributes greatly to the program's health and stability.

The fourth and final storage class specifier, register, is more of a suggestion than a command. Use register to *request* that an object be stored directly in a processor register:

```
register int i;
```

The compiler attempts to store i directly in a processor register rather than allocate memory for the integer value. Because registers are easily accessible by compiled code, register variables may improve runtime performance. But then again, they may have little or no effect because most modern compilers already use registers to the best possible advantage.

You cannot specify which processor register to be used by a `register` variable. What's more, the object may not wind up inside an actual register at all. The compiler uses a register only if one is available. The `register` specifier is merely a request, not a demand. (And, no, writing `register please!` does not help at all.)

That brings Part 2 to a close — I hope you've enjoyed the ride so far. In Part 3, you dig more deeply into the standard C function library, a rich collection of well tested routines that you'll come to rely on time and again. It's hard to imagine a C program that doesn't use at least some functions in the standard library. There are input and output functions, math functions, time and date functions, string functions, and many others. You've already seen some library functions in action. Now, let's look at some more.

Part 3

Standard Function Library

The standard function library is often thought of as part of the C language, but it isn't. The standard library is actually a collection of modules written mainly in C with a bit of assembly language thrown in here and there. Using the library in a C program is optional, but it can save development and debugging time. For example, C has no native input and output commands. To read and write text and other file data, you could write your own I/O modules (no easy task), but you can more simply include a standard library header into your code and call its ready-made functions.

Because this book is an introduction to C, and not a complete reference, the following chapters exclude a few obscure library functions that even expert programmers rarely need. I did not, however, restrict chapters to functions defined only by ANSI C. If a Borland function seemed useful, I included it. Nonstandard functions are marked "Borland only."

 I discuss many more ANSI and Borland-specific functions in my book, *Mastering Borland C++,* which includes a complete alphabetic reference to the Borland C++ and Turbo C++ function libraries.

There's no single right way to organize a function reference, but I've tried to select chapters and headings to simplify hunting for specific functions, and to group them according to purpose. Sample programs are listed for most function groups. When you need a certain capability, look first at the beginning of this book in the table of contents under Part 3. For example, if you need a function that can search for words in strings, look under "Pattern-Matching Functions" in Chapter 14, "String Functions (STRING.H)." Or, you can look up functions by name in the alphabetic subject index at the end of this book.

Chapter 11 describes "Input and Output Functions (STDIO.H)," Chapter 12 lists "Utility Functions (STDLIB.H)," Chapter 13 goes into "Time and Date Functions (TIME.H)," Chapter 14 introduces "String Functions (STRING.H)," and Chapter 15 details "Math Functions (MATH.H)." To use a function, include its header file listed in the chapter title. For instance, to use the utility functions described in Chapter 11, insert this directive into your program:

```
#include <stdio.h>
```

Use the IDE's online help commands for more information on specific functions. Press Shift+F1 for an index, type the first few letters of a function's name (you normally don't have to type the entire name), and press Enter. Or, position the cursor on a function name in a program's text, and press Ctrl+F1. The IDE's online help lists complete program examples for every function. To run a sample program, select all lines by moving the cursor while holding down Shift (or click and drag the mouse pointer). Press Ctrl+Ins to copy the text to the clipboard, then press Esc to close the help window. Use the *File\New* command to create a new editing window, and press Shift+Ins to insert the clipboard text. Unhighlight selected lines by pressing Ctrl+KH. You can then compile and run the program (Ctrl+F9), modify it, save it to a disk file, and so on. Unlike the programs in this book, the IDE's examples do not pause for you to see their output. If a program ends before you can see what it is doing, press Alt+F5 to view the output screen. Press any key to return to the IDE.

Chapter 11

Input and Output Functions (STDIO.H)

A program without input and output is like a building without windows and doors. Perhaps that may appeal to the CIA, but most people need conventional means to get in and out of their dwellings and to see beyond their walls.

Likewise, most programs need commands to read information into memory and to write data to output devices such as disk drives and displays. That's why most C programs include the STDIO.H header, which defines input and output (I/O) functions plus a few related odds and ends. To use the functions in this chapter, add this directive to your program:

```
#include <stdio.h>
```

I divided the standard I/O functions into the following eight sections, each with a unique expertise:

▶ *File-handling functions* — For preparing to read and write data in files and for performing related utility operations. Included are functions for opening, closing, and seeking data in binary and text files.

▶ *Directory functions* — For removing and renaming file entries in a directory. There are only two functions in this section.

▶ *File I/O functions* — For general purpose reading and writing of file data of any type and size. The two functions in this section, `fread` and `fwrite`, are especially valuable tools in database applications.

▶ *Character I/O functions* — For character input and output using the standard input (`stdin`) and output (`stdout`) predefined files, normally associated with the keyboard and display, respectively. Use the functions in this section to read and write character and string data on the console.

▶ *Character I/O file functions* — For character input and output, similar to the functions in the preceding paragraph but with the added capability of working with any files. Use these functions, for example, to read and write characters and strings in disk text files.

▶ *Formatted output functions* — For writing formatted information to the standard output (`stdout`), to any other file, or to a string buffer. The infamous `printf` function is described here.

▶ *Formatted input functions* — For reading formatted information from the standard input (`stdin`), from any other file, or from a string buffer. The notorious `scanf` function is described in this section.

▶ *Error-handling functions* — For detecting and clearing error conditions during I/O operations and also for obtaining string descriptions of errors. Functions in this section can help you to write "user friendly" code that traps and explains runtime errors.

Definitions in STDIO.H

The STDIO.H header defines a few related data types and constants used by the functions in this section. Most functions, for example, accept pointer arguments of type `FILE*`, an internal structure with members that you do not need to access directly. (The members are likely to be different, or to be used differently, by various operating systems.) Define a `FILE` pointer like this:

```
FILE *fp;
```

You can then pass `fp` to one of the functions, or in some cases, you can assign a function's `FILE*` result to `fp`. You can use `fp` to read, write, and append data in files, and for other operations requiring a *file stream,* a term that refers to a file as a sequence of bytes.

The STDIO.H header also defines several constants, such as `SEEK_SET`, `EOF`, and `NULL`. You don't have to be concerned with the underlying values of these functions — just use them as described here.

File-Handling Functions

int fclose(FILE *stream) This function closes a file previously opened by fopen. Closing a file writes to disk any buffered data held in memory. It's usually wise to close all open files when you are done using them. The function returns zero if successful or EOF if the file could not be closed.

int feof(FILE *stream) Returns true (nonzero) if the designated file's internal read/write marker is positioned at the end of the file; false (0) if the file is not positioned at its end.

int fflush(FILE *stream) Flushes to disk any buffered information held in memory for the designated output file. Has no effect on input files. Call this function after writing data to a file to ensure that the information is actually transferred to the output device or disk file. Returns zero if successful or EOF if an error occurs.

int fgetpos(FILE *stream, fpos_t *pos) Copies the internal file position value to the fpos_t variable addressed by pointer pos. The fpos_t data type is provided because various operating systems use different types of values to record a file's position. You can pass the data in *pos to fsetpos. Returns zero if successful; nonzero if an error occurs.

FILE *fopen(const char *path, const char *mode) Opens a file for I/O. After opening a file, you can read and write data to it. Specify the file's name, drive, and directory in path. Specify an access mode as one of the strings listed in Table 11-1. The plus sign designates *update mode,* in which a file's contents can be read or written. Add the letter *b* to any access mode for binary I/O—"wb" or "r+b", for example. Without *b,* files are opened for character I/O. Assign the function result to a FILE pointer. Returns a pointer to an initialized FILE variable (of an internal structure), or NULL if an error occurs.

Table 11-1 ▶ Access Modes for Function fopen

Mode	Purpose
"a"	Opens file ready for appending data to its end
"r"	Opens existing file for reading only
"w"	Overwrites or creates a new file for writing only
"a+"	Opens file initially for appending, also reading and writing
"r+"	Opens existing file for reading and writing
"w+"	Overwrites or creates a new file for reading and writing

int fseek(FILE *stream, long offset, int origin) Attempts to change a file's internal position to a new location, a process traditionally called *seeking*. After seeking, read and write operations take place starting at the new location. Designate an open file in the first parameter. Set offset to a value according to the rules of the third variable, origin. If origin equals SEEK_SET, the file's position is moved to offset bytes from the beginning; if origin equals SEEK_CUR, the file is positioned plus or minus offset bytes from the current position; if origin equals SEEK_END, the file is positioned offset bytes backward from the end. Only binary files can use the preceding values. For text files, which contain strings of variable lengths, you can set offset only to zero or, if origin equals SEEK_SET, to a value returned by ftell. Returns zero if successful; nonzero if an error occurs.

int fsetpos(FILE *stream, const fpos_t *pos) Positions a file's internal read/write pointer to a value of type fpos_t, which must be obtained from fgetpos. Use this function to reset a file to a previously recorded location. For example, you can call fgetpos to record the current position and perform a read or write operation at that spot. You can then call fsetpos to return the file's position to the saved location. Returns zero if successful; nonzero if an error occurs.

long ftell(FILE *stream) Returns the file position as a long integer value, or –1L if an error occurs (if, for example, the designated file is not open).

void rewind(FILE *stream) Resets the file's internal read/write pointer to the beginning of the file and also clears any error conditions. Does not return a value.

See "Directory Functions" and "File I/O Functions" in this chapter for sample programs that demonstrate some of the functions in this section.

Directory Functions

int remove(const char *path) Deletes the named file from the specified path, or the current directory if no path information is supplied. Never use this function on a file that is currently open. Returns zero if successful or nonzero if the file cannot be removed (or if it doesn't exist).

int rename(const char *oldname, const char *newname) Changes the name of an existing file (oldname) to another name (newname). Returns zero if successful; nonzero if an error occurs (if the new name already exists, for example).

Listing 11-1, DIRFN.CPP, demonstrates the functions in this section. Follow these instructions to complete the example:

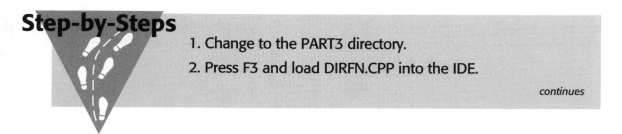

Step-by-Steps

1. Change to the PART3 directory.
2. Press F3 and load DIRFN.CPP into the IDE.

continues

> 3. Enter the highlighted instructions in Listing 11-1. (For
>   reference, and to help you locate typing errors, the
>   completed example is stored in PART3\FINISHED.)
>
> 4. Press Ctrl+F9 to compile and run. Repeat these steps for
>   all sample listings in this chapter, but substitute a different
>   filename in step 2.

Listing 11-1: DIRFN.CPP

```cpp
/* Directory Functions */

#include <stdio.h>
#include <stdlib.h>
#include <conio.h>

char Pause()
{
  char c;
  printf("\nPress Enter to continue...");
  while ((c = getchar()) != '\n') { }
  return c;
}

int main()
{
  clrscr();

// Define a file pointer and result variable
  FILE *fp;
  int ioresult;

// Create a temporary file named TEMP.$$$
  fp = fopen("temp.$$$", "w");
  if (!fp) {
    puts("Error creating file");
    exit(1);
  }

// Close the temporary file
  fclose(fp);
```

```
// Rename TEMP.$$$ to NEWTEMP.$$$
  ioresult = rename("temp.$$$", "newtemp.$$$");
  if (ioresult != 0) {
    puts("Error renaming file");
    exit(2);
  }

// Delete NEWTEMP.$$$ from the directory
  ioresult = remove("newtemp.$$$");
  if (ioresult != 0) {
    puts("Error removing file");
    exit(3);
  }

// Display final message
  puts("All file operations completed");

  Pause();
  return 0;
}
```

File I/O Functions

size_t fread(void *ptr, size_t size, size_t n, FILE *stream)
Although it looks complicated, fread performs a simple task. Use the function to read data from a file (usually a disk file) into a memory buffer. Pass the buffer's address in ptr, its size in bytes in size, the number of objects of that size in n, and a FILE pointer in stream. Typically, size is set to the size of the buffer and n is set to 1. If the buffer is an array of objects, however, you can set size to the size in bytes of one object and set n to the number of objects to read. The file must be opened by fopen by using a binary mode that permits reading. Returns the number of objects of size bytes successfully read from the file. This value can be less than the number of objects in the file without indicating an error (permitting, for example, reading an entire file by specifying a very large value for n). Call ferror to determine whether the read operation was successful.

size_t fwrite(const void *ptr, size_t size, size_t n, FILE *stream)
As you may expect, fwrite writes data to a file from a memory buffer. Pass the buffer's address in ptr, its size in bytes in size, the number of objects of that size in n, and a pointer to an open FILE. The file must have been opened by fopen using a binary mode that permits writing to the file. Returns the number of objects of size bytes successfully written. If fwrite returns a value less than n, an error occurred. You can also call ferror to determine whether the write operation was successful.

Listing 11-2, FILEIO.CPP, demonstrates the functions in this section.

Listing 11-2: FILEIO.CPP

```
/* File I/O Functions */

#include <stdio.h>
#include <stdlib.h>
#include <conio.h>

#define SIZE 100      // Number of values in array

int array[SIZE];      // Array of int values

char Pause()
{
  char c;
  printf("\nPress Enter to continue...");
  while ((c = getchar()) != '\n') { }
  return c;
}

int main()
{
  clrscr();

// Define file pointer and other variables
  FILE *fp;
  int ioresult, i;

// Fill array with sequential values
  for (i = 0; i < SIZE; i++)
    array[i] = i + 1;

// Create new file in write-binary mode
  fp = fopen("data.bin", "w+b");
  if (!fp) {
    puts("Error creating DATA.BIN");
    exit(1);
  }
```

```c
// Write the SIZE of the array to the file
  int size = SIZE;
  ioresult = fwrite(&size, sizeof(size), 1, fp);
  if (ioresult != 1) {
    puts("Error writing size");
    exit(2);
  }

// Write the arrayed data to the file
  ioresult = fwrite(array, sizeof(int), SIZE, fp);
  if (ioresult != SIZE) {
    puts("Error writing array");
    exit(3);
  }

// Close the file
  fclose(fp);

// Open the file again, this time for read-binary mode
  fp = fopen("data.bin", "rb");
  if (!fp) {
    puts("Error opening file for reading");
    exit(4);
  }

// Read the number of elements in the file
  ioresult = fread(&size, sizeof(size), 1, fp);
  if (ioresult != 1) {
    puts("Error reading size");
    exit(5);
  }

// Allocate memory to hold that many int values
  int *ip = (int *)malloc(size * sizeof(int));
  if (!ip) {
    puts("Error allocating memory for array");
    exit(6);
  }

// Read the file data into the allocated memory
  ioresult = fread(ip, sizeof(int), size, fp);
  if (ioresult != size) {
    puts("Error reading from file");
    exit(7);
  }
```

```
// Close the file
  fclose(fp);

// Display values read into allocated memory
  puts("Array values:");
  for (i = 0; i < size; i++)
    printf("%8d", ip[i]);

// Free the allocated memory
  free(ip);

  Pause();
  return 0;
}
```

Character I/O Functions

int getc(FILE *stream) Returns the next character from the designated file and is typically defined as a macro, which may cause the stream expression to be evaluated multiple times. If that seems to cause trouble in your program, use the equivalent fgetc described under "Character I/O File Functions." Returns the character value; EOF if attempting to read past the end of a file or if an error occurs.

int getchar(void) Returns the next character from the standard input file, stdin. Equivalent to getc(stdin). Returns the character value; EOF if attempting to read past the end of a file or if an error occurs.

char *gets(char *s) Reads a line of text (that is, a string terminated by the '\n' new-line escape code) from the standard input file, stdin, into the string buffer addressed by s. Replaces the newline character with a null. It is your responsibility to ensure that the buffer is large enough to hold the input line. Returns s if successful or NULL if an error occurs.

int putc(const int c, FILE *stream) Writes one character c onto the output file stream. Typically implemented as a macro, the function may cause the stream expression to be evaluated more than once. If that causes trouble, call the equivalent fputc function described under "Character I/O File Functions." Returns c if successful or EOF if an error occurs.

int putchar(const int c) Writes one character c onto the standard output file, stdout. Equivalent to putc(c, stdout). Returns c if successful or EOF if an error occurs.

int puts(const char *s) Writes the null-terminated string addressed by s to the standard output file, stdout, and appends a newline character to the end of the written string. Does not write the null terminator. Returns the last character written (always a nonzero value) if successful or EOF if an error occurs.

int ungetc(int c, FILE *stream) Returns one character to the designated file stream. That character will be read by the next call to an input function, such as `getc`. Use `ungetc` in code that needs to look ahead one character in the input — a special character value, for instance, or a control code. Only one character can be returned per file between input operations; you cannot, for example, use `ungetc` to return an entire string to a file. Returns `c` if successful or `EOF` if an error occurs.

Listing 11-3, CHAR.CPP, demonstrates some of the functions in this section.

Listing 11-3: CHAR.CPP

```
/* Character I/O Functions */

#include <stdio.h>
#include <conio.h>

int main()
{
  clrscr();

// Define character and string variables
  char c;
  char s[256];

// Display program title and a blank line
  puts("Character I/O Demonstrations");
  puts("");

// Prompt for a single character and display it
  printf("Enter a character: ");
  c = getc(stdin);
  printf("You typed: %c\n", c);
  fflush(stdin);

// Prompt for a string and display it
  printf("Enter a string: ");
  gets(s);
  printf("You typed: %s\n", s);

// Pause until user presses Enter
  printf("\nPress Enter to end program...");
  while ((c = getchar()) != '\n') { }

  return 0;
}
```

Character I/O File Functions

int fgetc(FILE *stream) Returns the next character from the designated file. Implemented as a true function (that is, not a macro). Returns the character value or EOF if attempting to read past the end of a file or if an error occurs.

char *fgets(char *s, int n, FILE *stream) Reads up to n-1 characters from the designated file stream into the character buffer addressed by s. Stops reading upon detecting a newline character in the input. Appends a null to the end of the string. Unlike gets, fgets inserts the newline character (if any) into the buffer. Returns s if successful; NULL if an error occurs or if attempting to read past the end of file.

int fputc(int c, FILE *stream) Writes one character c onto the output file stream. Implemented as a true function (that is, not a macro). Returns c if successful or EOF if an error occurs.

int fputs(const char *s, FILE *stream) Writes the null-terminated string addressed by s to the file designated by stream. Returns the last character written if successful or EOF if an error occurs.

Listing 11-4, CHARF.CPP, demonstrates some of the functions in this section.

Listing 11-4: CHARF.CPP

```
/* Character I/O File Functions */

#include <stdio.h>
#include <stdlib.h>
#include <conio.h>

#define SIZE 256  // Size of string buffer

char Pause()
{
  char c;
  printf("\nPress Enter to continue...");
  while ((c = getchar()) != '\n') { }
  return c;
}

int main()
{
  clrscr();
```

```cpp
// Define file, character, and string variables
  FILE *fp;
  char c;
  char s[SIZE];

// Display messages and pause
  puts("Read and display CHARF.CPP text file");
  puts("one line at a time.");
  Pause();
  clrscr();

// Open the program's text file, CHARF.CPP, for reading
  fp = fopen("charf.cpp", "r");
  if (!fp) {
    fputs("Error opening file", stderr);
    exit(1);
  }

// Read and display file, one line at a time
  while (!feof(fp)) {
    fgets(s, SIZE, fp);
    if (!feof(fp))
      fputs(s, stdout);
  }

// Display messages and pause
  puts("\n\nRead and display CHARF.CPP text file");
  puts("one character at a time.");
  Pause();
  clrscr();

// Rewind file to top; read and display one char at a time
  rewind(fp);
  while (!feof(fp)) {
    c = fgetc(fp);
    fputc(c, stdout);
  }

// Close the file
  fclose(fp);

  Pause();
  return 0;
}
```

Formatted Output Functions

int fprintf(FILE *stream, const char *format, ...) What may be called the granddaddy of functions in the standard library, `fprintf` is a remarkably capable, though sometimes cranky, subroutine. Its proper use requires a great deal of care — and often, an equal amount of trial and error. Essentially, `fprintf` and its cousins `printf` and `sprintf` convert binary arguments — integers, floating-point values, strings, and so on — into text representations that are manipulated and massaged according to an overwhelming array of options.

The first argument to `fprintf` is an output file, either a predefined one, such as `stdout`, or a disk file opened by `fopen`. (Use `printf` instead of `fprintf` to write to `stdout` by default; except for that difference, `fprintf` and `printf` are the same.) Formatting options are specified by a *formatting string,* passed as the function's second argument (`printf`'s first). The formatting string contains a series of instructions from a kind of minilanguage that describes how each argument value should be formatted. The ellipsis (...) in `fprintf`'s declaration indicates that one or more arguments can be specified following the formatting string. *Every instruction in the formatting string must have a corresponding argument.* To complicate matters further, the formatting string can also contain literal text (labels, punctuation, and so on) and such escape codes as '\n' that are written unchanged to the output file.

Whew! The `fprintf` function is nearly a full-fledged program in its own right. Later in this section is a sample listing that will help you understand more about how the function works, but if it takes a while to master `fprintf`, don't worry — *everybody* struggles over this one.

In its simplest form, `fprintf` can be used to write a string to an output file:

```
fprintf(stdout, "Write me to the stdout file.\n");
```

Usually, however, you won't use `fprintf` like that. Instead, you'll insert formatting instructions into the string, followed by one or more arguments. In the final output, `fprintf` replaces the formatting instructions with text representations of each argument value. Given an `int value` equal to 123, for example, this writes `Value==123` to the standard output:

```
fprintf(stdout, "Value==%d\n", value);
```

The text `Value==` in the formatting string is written unchanged to the output file, `stdout`. The formatting instruction `%d` tells `fprintf` to insert a decimal value at this location. The function converts the argument `value` to text and inserts that text into the final output. The '\n' escape code starts a new line on the output.

Get in the habit of picking apart text, instructions, and escape codes in formatting strings. For example, the preceding formatting string has three distinct parts: `Value==`, `%d`, and `\n`. Train your eye to distinguish between these parts.

You must supply an argument for each formatting instruction. The following statement, for example, writes two argument values, an `int count` and a `float balance`, to the standard output:

```
fprintf(stdout, "count==%d, balance=%f\n", count, balance);
```

The instruction `%d` is replaced with the value of `count`; `%f` is replaced with `balance`. It is your responsibility to provide arguments of the expected types. In the preceding example, `count` must be an integer, and `balance` must be a floating point. The compiler doesn't check those facts, and `fprintf`'s results will be unpredictable if you feed it the wrong kinds of argument values. *Double- and triple-check your typing when using this finicky function.*

Learning `fprintf`'s formatting language takes time and study. Each formatting instruction begins with a percent sign, and there may be zero, one, or more such instructions in a formatting string. Formatting instructions adhere strictly to the following design guide:

```
% [flags] [width] [.prec] [F|N|h|l] type
```

A percent sign is followed by one or more other specifiers, which must be written in the order shown. Optional items are encased in brackets. (Do not insert the brackets into the formatting string.) Because all formatting instructions must have at least a *type*, which tells the function how to interpret an argument, type specifiers are described first in Table 11-2. Table 11-3 describes *flag* options, which serve as additional modifiers — to specify left or right justification in a column, for example. Table 11-4 describes column *width* options. Table 11-5 descibes *.prec* values (which must be preceded by a period), specifying the precision of numerical values. Table 11-6 lists four *modifiers,* F, N, h, or l, which can be added to a formatting instruction, further affecting its result in ways that are determined by the value's type.

As you can tell, `fprintf` is a whopper of a function. It returns the number of characters written or `EOF` if an error occurs.

Many of the formatting characters in Tables 11-2 through 11-6 depend on one another, but not all combinations of characters are permissible. Many of the same options are used by the `fscanf`, `scanf`, and `sscanf` functions described under "Formatted Input Functions" in this chapter. Those options with unique effects are labeled *scanf* or *scanf only*.

Table 11-2 ▶ `fprintf` *type* Specifiers

type	Formatted Output
d	Signed decimal `int`
i	Signed decimal `int`
o	Unsigned octal `int`
u	Unsigned decimal `int`
x	`printf`: Unsigned hexadecimal `int` lowercase `scanf`: Hexadecimal `int`
X	`printf`: Unsigned hexadecimal `int` uppercase `scanf`: Hexadecimal `long`
f	Floating point [-]dddd.ddd
e	Floating point [-]d.ddd e [+/-]ddd
g	Same as e or f based on precision
E	Same as e but uses E for exponent
G	Same as g but uses E for exponent
c	Single character
s	Print characters up to '\0' or [.prec]
%	The % character
p	Pointer: near = YYYY; far = XXXX:YYYY
n	Stores in `*argument` count of characters written

Table 11-3 ▶ `fprintf` *flag* Specifiers

[flag]	Effect on Formatted Output
(none)	Right-justify; pad 0 or blank to left
-	Left-justify; pad spaces to right
+	Always begin numeric with + or -
blank	Preface negative numbers only with sign
# c, s, d, i, u o x or X e, E, f g or G	Convert using alternate form for type: (no effect) Prepend 0 to nonzero argument Prepend 0x or 0X to argument Always insert decimal point Same as e, E, or f less trailing 0s

Table 11-4 ▶ fprintf *width* Specifiers

[width]	Effect on Formatted Output
n	At least n characters, blank-padded
0n	At least n characters, 0 left-filled
*	Next argument specifies width

Table 11-5 ▶ fprintf *.prec* Specifiers

[.prec]	Effect on Output
(none)	Default precision
.0 　d, i, o, u, x: 　e, E, f:	For type: 　Default precision 　No decimal point
.n	At most n characters
*	Next argument specifies precision

Table 11-6 ▶ fprintf *modifier* Specifiers

Modifier	Type	Argument Interpreted As
F	(none)	far pointer
N	(none)	near pointer
h	d, i, o, u, x, X	short int
l	d, i, o, u, x, X	long int
l	e, E, f, g, G	double (scanf only)
L	e, E, f, g, G	long double

int printf(const char *format, ...) Writes formatted text to the standard output file, stdout. Equivalent to fprintf(stdout, ...). Use printf instead of fprintf to write formatted text to the standard output file (usually the display). Except for their initial arguments, both functions are the same. Returns the number of characters written or EOF if an error occurs.

int sprintf(char *buffer, const char *format, ...) Writes formatted text to a character buffer addressed by the first argument, which must be a char pointer. Appends a null terminator to the end of the output. The function is otherwise the same as fprintf or printf. Use sprintf to create formatted strings that you later write to files or use in another fashion. It is your responsiblity to ensure that the output buffer is large enough to hold the formatted text plus a null terminator. Returns the number of characters written (not including the null terminator); EOF if an error occurs.

Listing 11-5, PRINTF.CPP, demonstrates the functions in this section.

Listing 11-5: PRINTF.CPP

```
/* Formatted Output Functions */

#include <stdio.h>
#include <conio.h>

// Define objects of various types
int xint = 123;
long xlong = 12345678L;
char xchar = '@';
char *xstring = "Any port in a storm";
double xdouble = 3.14159;
long double xlongdouble = xdouble * 1000;

char Pause()
{
  char c;
  printf("\nPress Enter to continue...");
  while ((c = getchar()) != '\n') { }
  return c;
}

int main()
{
  clrscr();
```

```
// Format and write global objects
  printf("xint (decimal) == %d\n", xint);
  printf("xint (hex)     == %#x\n", xint);
  printf("xint (octal)   == %#o\n", xint);
  printf("xlong          == %ld\n", xlong);
  printf("xchar          == %c\n", xchar);
  printf("xstring        == %s\n", xstring);
  printf("xdouble        == %lf\n", xdouble);
  printf("xlongdouble(1) == %Le\n", xlongdouble);
  printf("xlongdouble(2) == %Lf\n", xlongdouble);

// Display a blank line
  fprintf(stdout, "\n");

// Use fprintf to display an error number to stderr
  int errnum = 99;  // Dummy error number
  fprintf(stderr, "Sample error message #%d\n", errnum);

// Define a buffer to hold formatted text
  char buffer[256];

// Insert formatted string into buffer and display
  sprintf(buffer, "\nValue of xint == %d", xint);
  printf("%s\n", buffer);

  Pause();
  return 0;
}
```

Formatted Input Functions

int fscanf(FILE *stream, const char *format, ...) The fscanf function and its cousins scanf and sscanf are the mirror images of functions fprintf, printf, and sprintf, described in the preceding section. The fscanf function reads characters from an input file stream and converts those characters into binary values according to rules specified by a formatting string, format. Each value is deposited in an argument that is written after the formatting string. The arguments must be pointers.

Remember: with no exceptions, every argument passed to fscanf, scanf, or sscanf *must* be a pointer. If you keep this simple rule in mind, you'll find these functions to be valuable tools; otherwise, they will give you nothing but trouble.

The formatting string uses the same options described for the `fprintf` family in Tables 11-2 through 11-6. Blanks and tabs in the string are ignored. Other text matches nonwhite-space text from the input (xxx, for instance, matches the next three characters). Newline characters are treated as "white space," as are blanks, tabs, carriage returns, vertical tabs, and form feed control codes. The function skips all such characters in the input source, and therefore, `fscanf` can process more than one input line in order to provide values for each listed argument.

If successful, `fscanf` returns the number of arguments (not the number of characters) converted from text to binary or `EOF` if an error occurs.

You can use `fscanf` to input values from the standard input file (normally the keyboard). The following, for example, uses `fscanf` to create a simple decimal to hexadecimal converter:

```
int value;
printf("Enter an integer value: ");
fscanf(stdin, "%d", &value);
fflush(stdin);  // Flush possible errors
printf("Your value in hex is: %X\n", value);
```

After prompting for an integer value, the program calls `fscanf` to read characters from `stdin` into the integer object, `value`, which is passed by address to the function. The call to `fflush` resets the input file in case of errors and also removes any pending end-of-line characters so that future input statements work as expected.

You can replace the call to `fscanf` with `scanf`, which by default reads from the standard input file:

```
scanf("%d", &value);
```

You can also test the result returned by `fscanf` or `scanf` for errors. First, add an integer variable to hold the function result:

```
int ioresult;
```

Next, call `fscanf` as before, but save the function's return value in the `ioresult` variable:

```
ioresult = fscanf(stdin, "%d", &value);
```

Flush the input file and then test whether `ioresult` equals one, which is the number of expected objects. If not, an error occured, and the program can display an error message and exit (or take another appropriate action). The program might exit, for example, if the user types ABC rather than a valid integer value:

```
fflush(stdin);
if (ioresult != 1) {
  puts("Input error");
  Pause();
  exit(1);
}
```

int scanf(const char *format, ...)   Reads formatted input from stdin.
Equivalent to fscanf(stdin, ...). Returns the number of arguments converted from text to
binary; EOF if an error occurs.

> Follow fscanf and scanf statements with a call to fflush, passing the same input file
> (stdin for example). Flushing the input file will clear the stream of errors that may
> prevent subsequent statements from working correctly.

int sscanf(const char *buffer, const char *format, ...)
Converts text in a string buffer to binary values according to the rules in the formatting string,
format. This version of fscanf is particularly useful for reading input lines from files and
inserting values in those lines into binary variables. Returns the number of arguments converted
from text to binary; EOF if an error occurs (attempting to read past the end of the input buffer,
for example).

Listing 11-6, SCANF.CPP, demonstrates the functions in this section.

Listing 11-6: SCANF.CPP

```
/* Formatted Input Functions */

#include <stdio.h>
#include <stdlib.h>
#include <conio.h>

char Pause()
{
  char c;
  printf("\nPress Enter to continue...");
  while ((c = getchar()) != '\n') { }
  return c;
}

int main()
{
  clrscr();

// Define character buffer and other variables
  char buffer[256] = "0x89FC";
  int value;
  int ioresult;
```

```
// Convert buffer to integer value
  ioresult = sscanf(buffer, "%x", &value);
  if (ioresult != 1) {
    puts("Error scanning buffer");
    exit(1);
  }

// Display value in hex and decimal
  printf("Value in hex     == 0x%X\n", value);
  printf("Value in decimal == %d\n", value);

// Use scanf to input a string from stdin
  printf("\nEnter a string: ");
  scanf("%s", buffer);
  fflush(stdin);

// Display string (note: input stops at first blank)
  printf("Your string is: %s\n", buffer);

// Use fscanf to input an integer value
  printf("\nEnter an integer value: ");
  fscanf(stdin, "%d", &value);
  printf("Your value in is: %8d\n", value);
  printf("Your value in hex is: 0x%X\n", value);
  fflush(stdin);

// Display messages and pause
  puts("\nRead SCANF.CPP text file using fscanf,");
  puts("skipping white space characters.");
  Pause();
  clrscr();

// Define file pointer and open SCANF.CPP for reading
  FILE *fp = fopen("scanf.cpp", "r");
  if (!fp) {
    fprintf(stderr, "Error opening file");
    exit(1);
  }
```

```
// Use fscanf to input text less white space from file
  while (!feof(fp)) {
    fscanf(fp, "%s", buffer);
    if (!feof(fp))
      puts(buffer);
  }

// Close the file
  fclose(fp);

  Pause();
  return 0;
}
```

Error-Handling Functions

void clearerr(FILE *stream) Resets (clears) any error flags and end-of-file indicators from the specified file `stream`. Call this function after detecting and responding to an I/O error. You can then perform additional I/O operations on the file. Returns nothing.

int ferror(FILE *stream) Use `ferror` to check for errors that may have occurred during a preceding I/O operation. Returns zero if no errors are detected on the specified file `stream`; a nonzero value if an error occurred.

void perror(const char *s) Writes to the standard error output file, `stderr`, the string s plus an error message corresponding to a global `errno` value, defined in ERRNO.H (and also by STDDEF.H and STDLIB.H). You do not need to include those headers, however, to use `perror`. Calls `fprintf`. Returns nothing.

char *strerror(int errnum) Also defined in STRING.H, `strerror` returns the address of an error-message string for the error number `errnum`. Error messages are system dependent — they differ among compilers and operating systems. The function returns address of error-message string constant, or address of string `Unknown error` for unrecognized `errnum` values.

Listing 11-7, FERROR.CPP, demonstrates the functions in this section.

Listing 11-7: FERROR.CPP

```
/* Error-Handling Functions */

#include <stdio.h>
#include <stdlib.h>
#include <conio.h>

char Pause()
{
  char c;
  printf("\nPress Enter to continue...");
  while ((c = getchar()) != '\n') { }
  return c;
}

int main()
{
  clrscr();

// Define file pointer
  FILE *fp;

// Display messages
  puts("Attempting to open nonexistent file");
  puts("named NOFILE.XXX. This should produce");
  puts("an expected I/O error\n");

// Force error and display error message
  puts("Opening NOFILE.XXX...");
  fp = fopen("nofile.xxx", "r");
  if (!fp)
    perror("Error detected");

// Get address of error message and display
  char *es = strerror(errno);
  puts("\nError string addressed by es:");
  puts(es);

// Clear any pending errors on stdin file
  clearerr(stdin);

  Pause();
  return 0;
}
```

Chapter 12

Utility Functions (STDLIB.H)

The functions in STDLIB.H are as varied as the Halloween candy in a young goblin's trick-or-treat bag. No matter what kind of programs you write, you'll want to stuff your code with many of the goodies in this do-everything module.

To use the functions in this chapter, add this directive to your program:

```
#include <stdlib.h>
```

For ease in identifying functions according to their purposes, I divided the functions in STDLIB.H among the following nine sections:

▶ *Flow-Control Functions* — For exiting programs and for attaching code that is called automatically just before a program ends. The exit function in this section permits any function at any time to end a program.

▶ *ASCII to Binary Functions* — For converting ASCII strings to binary values. In many cases, the functions in this section are simpler to program than the `fscanf` and related functions described in the preceding chapter, which also can convert ASCII text to binary.

▶ *Binary to ASCII Functions* — For converting binary values to ASCII strings. These functions are simpler to use than the `sprintf` function described in the preceding chapter, which can also convert binary values to ASCII strings.

▶ *Memory Management Functions* — For allocating and freeing dynamic memory. Use these functions to reserve dynamic objects that share a global memory pool set aside for the program's use.

▶ *Environment Functions* — For accessing operating system environment strings. The functions in this section are standard among all ANSI C compilers, but specific environment strings differ widely among operating systems, so use these functions with care if you want your programs to be portable.

▶ *Sorting and Swapping Functions* — For sorting arrays and for swapping byte values. The `qsort` function in this section is optimized for speedy in-memory sorting.

▶ *Search Functions* — For quickly searching arrays using one of several techniques. The standard library defines only one seach function, `bsearch`. The other two functions in this section are available only on Borland C and C++ compilers.

▶ *Mathematical Functions* — For common math operations. See also Chapter 15, "Math Functions (MATH.H)," for many more mathematical functions.

▶ *Random Number Functions* — For seeding a random number generator and producing random sequences. These functions are not intended for use in critical applications, but they are valuable nonetheless, especially for filling test arrays with random values, for game software, and so on.

Definitions in STDLIB.H

Like most headers in the standard library, STDLIB.H defines a few miscellaneous constants and structures. Some of the standard items are.

▶ `errno` — Include STDLIB.H to gain access to this global variable, which holds I/O error codes set by many functions, including I/O functions described in the preceding chapter.

▶ `NULL` — Though technically defined in STDLIB.H, the compiler recognizes `NULL` even if STDLIB.H is not included.

▶ `RAND_MAX` — Set to `0x7FFF` for the C compiler supplied with this book. Use the constant in programs that need to determine the maximum possible value returned by function `rand`.

▶ `size_t` — A useful data type that helps eliminate conflicts among programs to be used with different C compilers in which integer objects might have different binary sizes. Defined as equivalent to the `unsigned` integer type that operator `sizeof` returns.

The STDLIB.H header defines other Borland-specific items, as well as some additional structures I'll explain as needed by specific functions.

Flow-Control Functions

void abort(void)   Ends the program with a forced error, the exact effects of which may differ among compilers and operating systems. Calling abort in programs created with the compiler packed with this book prints the message *Abnormal program termination* on the standard error output file, stderr.

int atexit(atexit_t func)   Designates a function to be called automatically when a program ends by normal means, either by function main returning (or ending) or by a statement that calls exit. You may name the function as you wish, but it must be of the type atexit_t, a void function that has no parameters, for example:

```
void myExit(void);
```

To register that function for automatic execution when the program ends, pass its name to atexit:

```
atexit(myExit);
```

This returns zero if the function is successfully registered; nonzero if an error occurs.

Do not call exit from inside the function registered by atexit.

void exit(int status)   Ends the program immediately, returning a status value to the operating system or other task that ran the program. Under MS-DOS, status is assigned to ERRORLEVEL, which you may examine in a batch file. Any exit function registered by atexit is called before the program ends. Returns nothing.

int system(const char *command)   Passes a command string to the operating system for execution, just as though you typed the command at a DOS prompt (or its equivalent on another operating system). If command is null, however, system returns zero (0) if a command processor is not available; nonzero (1) if the system can accept commands. If command is non-null, system passes it to the command processor (COMMAND.COM under MS-DOS). In that case, system returns zero for success; nonzero if an error occurs. For example, this statement lists a directory:

```
system("DIR");
```

You may also use system to execute another program or a batch file. Just supply the program's name, along with a directory path if necessary:

```
system("C:\\mydir\\myapp.exe");
```

Because DOS is not a multitasking operating system, the system command does not work properly for programs run under control of the IDE. You must execute programs directly from DOS or another command processor. The compiler supplied with this book cannot create stand-alone executable code files; to use system, you must compile the program using a commercial version of Turbo or Borland C++.

Listing 12-1, FLOW.CPP, demonstrates some of the functions in this section. Follow these instructions to complete the example.

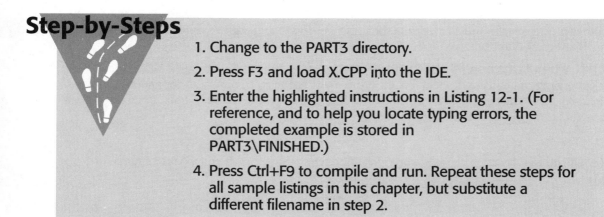

Step-by-Steps

1. Change to the PART3 directory.

2. Press F3 and load X.CPP into the IDE.

3. Enter the highlighted instructions in Listing 12-1. (For reference, and to help you locate typing errors, the completed example is stored in PART3\FINISHED.)

4. Press Ctrl+F9 to compile and run. Repeat these steps for all sample listings in this chapter, but substitute a different filename in step 2.

Listing 12-1: FLOW.CPP

```
/* Flow-Control Functions */

#include <stdio.h>
#include <stdlib.h>
#include <conio.h>

char Pause()
{
  char c;
  printf("\nPress Enter to continue...");
  while ((c = getchar()) != '\n') { }
  return c;
}

// Custom exit function
void fexit(void)
{
  puts("Inside custom exit function");
  Pause();
}

int main()
{
  clrscr();
```

```
// Register a custom exit function
  atexit(fexit);

// Exit program immediately
  exit(0);

// Following statements do not execute
  puts("This message is not written!");
  Pause();
  return 0;
}
```

ASCII to Binary Functions

double atof(const char *s) The "ASCII to floating point" function, atof, returns the double binary equivalent of string s; zero if s cannot be converted.

int atoi(const char *s) The "ASCII to integer" function, atoi, returns the int binary equivalent of string s; zero if s cannot be converted.

long atol(const char *s) The "ASCII to long" function, atol, returns the long binary equivalent of string s; zero if s cannot be converted.

The preceding three functions, atof, atoi, and atol, are simplified versions of strtod, strtol, and strtoul. Use the preceding functions unless you need the extra capabilities of the following three functions.

double strtod(const char *s, char **endptr) The "String to decimal" function, strtod, returns the double binary equivalent of the initial characters in string s, ignoring leading white space (blanks, tabs, and so on). The string must be in the form:

`[ws] [sn] [ddd] [.] [ddd] [fmt[sn]ddd]`

Bracketed items are optional, *ws* stands for white space, *sn* is a minus or plus sign, *ddd* are decimal digits, a period represents the decimal point, and *fmt* is the character e or E.

If the second argument to strtod is a char* variable, strtod stores in that pointer the address where the function stopped converting text to binary. Note that this address points *into* the string addressed by s. You may use endptr to *parse* (take apart, piece by piece) multiple values in strings. For informal string to double conversions, call the simpler atof function. Returns the converted value; zero if an error occurs.

long strtol(const char *s, char **endptr, int radix) The "string to long" function, strtol, returns the long binary equivalent of the initial characters in string s, ignoring leading white space. The string must be in the form:

    [ws] [sn] [O[x|X]] [ddd]

Bracketed items are optional, a vertical bar means "or," *ws* stands for white space, *sn* is a minus or plus sign, *x* or *X* indicate a value in hexadecimal, and *ddd* are decimal, hexadecimal, or octal digits. Hex values may be prefaced with 0x or 0X. Octal values may be prefaced with 0.

You may pass a char* variable to endptr, in which case strtol stores the address in string s where the function stopped converting text to binary. Pass NULL to endptr if you don't want the function to perform this service. Pass a number base from 2 to 36 in radix (2 for binary digits, 8 for octal, 10 for decimal, or 16 for hexadecimal). Returns the converted value; zero if an error occurs.

unsigned long strtoul(const char *s, char **endptr, int radix) The "string to unsigned long" function, strtoul, is similar to strtol but returns an unsigned long binary value. Returns the converted value; zero if an error occurs.

Listing 12-2, ATOB.CPP, demonstrates some of the functions in this section.

Listing 12-2: ATOB.CPP

```
/* ASCII to Binary Functions */

#include <stdio.h>
#include <stdlib.h>
#include <conio.h>

#define SIZE 80   // Size of input string

char Pause()
{
  char c;
  printf("\nPress Enter to continue...");
  while ((c = getchar()) != '\n') { }
  return c;
}

// Prompt for and input a line of text
void GetLine(char *s, const char *msg)
{
  printf(msg);
  fgets(s, SIZE, stdin);
  fflush(stdin);
}
```

```
int main()
{
  clrscr();

// Define a few variables
  char s[SIZE];
  double dv;
  int iv;
  long lv;

// Get and convert a floating point value
  GetLine(s, "Enter a floating point value: ");
  dv = atof(s);
  printf("Value == %f\n", dv);

// Get and convert an integer value
  GetLine(s, "Enter an integer value: ");
  iv = atoi(s);
  printf("Value == %d\n", iv);

// Get and convert a long integer value
  GetLine(s, "Enter a long integer value: ");
  lv = atol(s);
  printf("Value == %ld\n", lv);

// Parse multiple values in a string
  char *multi = "3.5 9.77 123.32";
  char *p = multi;
  puts("\nParsing 3 values from a string.\n");
  printf("Input string == %s\n", multi);
  while (*p) {
    dv = strtod(multi, &p);
    printf("Value = %f\n", dv);
    multi = p;
  }

  Pause();
  return 0;
}
```

Binary to ASCII Functions

char *itoa(int value, char *string, int radix)   The "integer to ASCII" function, itoa, converts a binary int value to a string. Stores the resulting string at the address given by the string argument, using the number base specified by radix (2 for binary, 8 for octal, 10 for decimal, or 16 for hexadecimal). Returns string for convenience in assigning that address to other variables, passing it to function parameters, and so forth. You may, however, ignore the function result.

char *ltoa(long value, char *string, int radix)
Borland only   The "long to ASCII" function, ltoa is similar to itoa, but converts a long value to a string. Returns string.

char *ultoa(unsigned long value, char *string, int radix)
Borland only   The "unsigned long to ASCII" function, ultoa, is similar to ltoa but converts an unsigned long value to a string. Returns string.

Listing 12-3, BTOA.CPP, demonstrates the functions in this section.

Listing 12-3: BTOA.CPP

```
/* Binary to ASCII Functions */

#include <stdio.h>
#include <stdlib.h>
#include <conio.h>

char Pause()
{
  char c;
  printf("\nPress Enter to continue...");
  while ((c = getchar()) != '\n') { }
  return c;
}

int main()
{
  clrscr();
```

```
// Define a few variables
  char s[80];
  int iv;
  long lv;
  unsigned long ulv;

// Assign values to variables
  iv = 0xF6A9;
  lv = 75891L;
  ulv = 2456190245UL;

// Convert integer to ASCII
  itoa(iv, s, 16);
  printf("iv  == %x\n", iv);
  printf("s   == %s\n\n", s);

// Convert long integer to ASCII
  ltoa(lv, s, 10);
  printf("lv  == %ld\n", lv);
  printf("s   == %s\n\n", s);

// Convert unsigned long integer to ASCII
  ultoa(ulv, s, 10);
  printf("ulv == %lu\n", ulv);
  printf("s   == %s\n\n", s);

  Pause();
  return 0;
}
```

Memory Management Functions

void *calloc(size_t nitems, size_t size)   Allocates memory for a number of objects (nitems), each of a specified size in bytes (size). Sets all allocated bytes to zero. Returns the address of the first allocated byte; NULL if enough memory is not available.

void free(void *block)   Returns to the memory pool a block allocated by calloc, malloc, or realloc, making the block available for future allocations. The address passed to block must be a value returned by one of those three functions. Has no effect if block is NULL. After passing the address of a memory block to free, that block must not be used. The block pointer, however, may be reused to address another memory block allocated by calloc, malloc, or realloc. Returns nothing.

void *malloc(size_t size)   Allocates `size` bytes of memory. Does not initialize the allocated memory. Returns the address of the allocated memory's first byte; `NULL` if `size` bytes are not available.

void *realloc(void *block, size_t size)   Adjusts the size of allocated memory addressed by `block`, which must be a value returned by `calloc`, `malloc`, or `realloc`. Specify the number of bytes in `size`, which may be larger or smaller than the block's current size. The returned address may or may not be different from `block`. Returns the address of the newly allocated block; `NULL` if the reallocation request cannot be fulfilled (in which case `block` and the originally addressed memory are unchanged).

Listing 12-4, MEMORY.CPP, demonstrates the functions in this section.

Listing 12-4: MEMORY.CPP

```
/* Memory Management Functions */

#include <stdio.h>
#include <stdlib.h>
#include <conio.h>

#define SIZE 10     // Number of objects to allocate
#define RESIZE 20   // Number of objects to reallocate

char Pause()
{
  char c;
  printf("\nPress Enter to continue...");
  while ((c = getchar()) != '\n') { }
  return c;
}

void ShowBuffer(int *buf, size_t size, const char *msg)
{
  printf("%s\n", msg);
  for (int i = 0; i < size; i++)
    printf("%8d", buf[i]);
  puts("");
}

void UseBuffer(int *buf, size_t size, const char *msg)
{
  printf(msg);
```

```
  ShowBuffer(buf, size, " -- before initialization:");
  for (int i = 0; i < size; i++)
    buf[i] = i;
  printf(msg);
  ShowBuffer(buf, size, " -- after initialization:");
}

int main()
{
  clrscr();

// Define point to int buffer
  int *ibuffer;

// Allocate buffer of SIZE int objects with malloc
  ibuffer = (int *)malloc(SIZE * sizeof(int));
  if (ibuffer == NULL) {
    puts("Error calling calloc");
    exit(2);
  }

// Fill and display the buffer, then free it
  UseBuffer(ibuffer, SIZE, "malloc");
  free(ibuffer);

// Allocate buffer of SIZE int objects with calloc
  ibuffer = (int *)calloc(SIZE, sizeof(int));
  if (ibuffer == NULL) {
    puts("Error calling calloc");
    exit(1);
  }

// Fill and display the buffer, do NOT free it
  UseBuffer(ibuffer, SIZE, "calloc");

// Expand size of buffer with realloc
  int *temp = (int *)realloc(ibuffer, RESIZE);
  if (!temp) {
    puts("Error calling realloc");
    exit(3);
  } else {
    ibuffer = temp;
  }
```

```
    // Fill and display the buffer, then free it
    UseBuffer(ibuffer, RESIZE, "realloc");
    free(ibuffer);

    Pause();
    return 0;
}
```

Environment Functions

char *getenv(const char *name) Searches the operating system environment for a variable addressed by name. The function is provided in the standard library, but its use depends on the operating system's requirements. Under MS-DOS, for example, this sets path to the address of the system PATH environment variable:

```
    char *path = getenv("PATH");
```

That may produce meaningless results, however, under a different operating system. Returns the address of the environment string; NULL if the environment does not define name.

int putenv(const char *name)

Borland only Inserts a new string into a copy of the operating system environment, created for the private use of the program. Similar in effect to the MS-DOS SET command. The string addressed by name must be in the form:

```
    [variable=[value]]
```

where *variable* and *value* may be any characters. You might, for example, specify a temporary pathname with the command:

```
    putenv("TMP=C:\MYDIR");
```

Or you can alter the system PATH like this:

```
    putenv("PATH=C:\DOS;C:\MYDIR");
```

Strings inserted with putenv may be found by calling getenv. When the program ends, the copied environment is deleted from memory, along with any inserted strings. This function does not affect the DOS master environment. Returns zero if the string is successfully inserted; –1 if an error occurs.

The environment copy given to an MS-DOS program normally has little or no room for additional entries. To reserve space for putenv strings, add a command such as the following to a CONFIG.SYS text file in the boot directory. Change 512 to the number of bytes to reserve for the total environment in multiples of 16, in the range 160 to 32768. The default environment size is 256 bytes. Obviously, this note applies only to MS-DOS programs that use COMMAND.COM as the command shell.

```
SHELL=C:\DOS\COMMAND.COM C:\DOS\ /e:512 /p
```

Listing 12-5, ENVY.CPP, demonstrates the functions in this section.

Listing 12-5: ENVY.CPP

```
/* Environment Functions */

#include <stdio.h>
#include <stdlib.h>
#include <conio.h>

char Pause()
{
  char c;
  printf("\nPress Enter to continue...");
  while ((c = getchar()) != '\n') { }
  return c;
}

int main()
{
  clrscr();

// Define variables
  char *result;
  int k;

// Search for PATH environment variable
  result = getenv("PATH");
  if (!result)
    puts("No PATH defined");
  else
    printf("PATH == %s\n", result);
```

```
// Attempt to insert a new variable
  k = putenv("XTMP=any value");
  if (k != 0)
    puts("Cannot insert new variable");

// Search for the new XTMP variable
  result = getenv("XTMP");
  if (!result)
    puts("No XTMP defined");
  else
    printf("XTMP == %s\n", result);

  Pause();
  return 0;
}
```

Sorting and Swapping Functions

void qsort(void *base, size_t nelem, size_t width, int(*fcmp)(const void *, const void *)) Sorts two or more objects adjacently stored in an array addressed by `base`. Uses an optimized version of the *quicksort* (or "quicker sort") algorithm, which is generally recognized as the fastest all-around sorter for most kinds of data. The quicksort algorithm was first proposed by C. A. R. Hoare in the *Computer Journal, No. 5 (1962), pp. 10–15.* The `qsort` implementation supplied with this book's compiler is recursive, but the function copies certain data elements to static memory storage, minimizing stack use.

Specify the number of objects in `nelem`. Set `width` to the object size in bytes. (All objects must be the same size.) You must also write and provide a comparison function, `fcmp`, that receives the addresses of two objects and returns an `int` value: –1 if object A is less than object B; 0 if the objects are equal; or +1 if object A is greater than object B. The meanings of "less than," "equal," and "greater than" are up to you to define — to sort a database of records, for example, you might compare fields in structures addressed by the comparison function's parameters. See the sample code later in this section for an example of how to use `qsort` and how to write a comparison function. Returns nothing.

void swab(char *from, char *to, int nbytes)
Borland only Swaps `nbytes` bytes in buffers addressed by `from` and `to`. The value of `nbytes` must be even. Bytes are swapped using this formula:

```
to[0] = from[1]
to[1] = from[0]
to[2] = from[3]
...
to[n-2] = from[n-1]
to[n-1] = from[n-2]
```

The swab function is intended for converting file data to be shared between computers that store bytes in words in different orders. On PCs, for example, which use Intel and compatible processors, the most significant byte of a word is stored second. On Macintosh systems, which use Motorola processors, the most significant byte in a word is stored first. The swab function can be used to convert data for use by both systems. Returns nothing.

A few sample statements demonstrate how to use swab. Consider these two strings:

```
char s[] = "abcdefgh";
char t[] = "         ";
```

Applying swab to s and t swaps the letter pairs *ab, cd, ef,* and *gh.* For example, these statements

```
printf("before:\n s == %s\n t == %s\n\n", s, t);
swab(s, t, strlen(s));
printf("after:\n s == %s\n t == %s\n\n", s, t);
```

display the following results:

```
before:
 s == abcdefgh
 t == 
after:
 s == abcdefgh
 t == badcfehg
```

Listing 12-6, SORTER.CPP, demonstrates the qsort function in this section.

Listing 12-6: SORTER.CPP

```
/* Sorting Function */

#include <stdio.h>
#include <stdlib.h>
#include <conio.h>

#define SIZE 10  // Number of records in array

// Structure for objects to sort
typedef struct tagCoord {
  int x, y;
} Coord;

// Array of Coord objects
Coord array[SIZE];
```

```
char Pause()
{
  char c;
  printf("\nPress Enter to continue...");
  while ((c = getchar()) != '\n') { }
  return c;
}

// Fill array's x and y members at random
void FillArray()
{
  for (int i = 0; i < SIZE; i++) {
    array[i].x = rand();
    array[i].y = rand();
  }
}

// Display global array of Coord objects
void ShowArray(const char *msg)
{
  char buffer[20];

  puts(msg);
  for (int i = 0; i < SIZE; i++) {
    sprintf(buffer, "(%d,%d)", array[i].x, array[i].y);
    printf("%20s", buffer);
  }
  puts("\n");   // Start new line twice
}

// Compare two Coord objects on their x members
int onx(const void *a, const void *b)
{
  int x1, x2;

  x1 = ((Coord *)(a))->x;
  x2 = ((Coord *)(b))->x;
  return (x1 - x2);
}
```

```
// Compare two Coord objects on their y members
int ony(const void *a, const void *b)
{
  int y1, y2;
  y1 = ((Coord *)(a))->y;
  y2 = ((Coord *)(b))->y;
  return (y1 - y2);
}

int main()
{
  clrscr();

// Initialize and display array of Coord objects
  FillArray();
  ShowArray("Before sorting:");

// Sort array on x members and display
  qsort(array, SIZE, sizeof(Coord), onx);
  ShowArray("After sorting on x:");

// Sort array on y members and display
  qsort(array, SIZE, sizeof(Coord), ony);
  ShowArray("After sorting on y:");

  puts("(Note: Read data from left to right.)");
  Pause();
  return 0;
}
```

Search Functions

**void *bsearch(const void *key, const void *base,
size_t nelem, size_t width,
int(*fcmp)(const void *, const void *))**

Searches an array of two or more objects stored adjacently in an array, using the binary search algorithm. The objects must be sorted in ascending order. Set key to the the address of the object to find. Set base to the address of the first object in the array to be searched. Set nelem to the number of objects in the array. Set width to the size in bytes of one object. (All objects must be of the same size). You must also write and provide a comparison function, fcmp, that receives the addresses of two objects. The function should return –1 if object A is less than object B, 0 if the two objects are equal, or +1 if object A is greater than object B. You may use the same comparison function passed to qsort (typically called to sort an array before searching). Returns the address of an object found in the array; NULL if no object matches key*.

```
void *lfind(const void *key, const void *base,
 size_t *nelem, size_t width,
 int(*fcmp)(const void *, const void *))
```

Borland only Searches an array of objects, similar in results to bsearch, but with several significant differences. Set key to the address of an object to find. Set base to the address of the first object in the array. Pass the address of a size_t integer, nelem, that holds the number of objects in the array. (In lfind, nelem must be a *pointer* to an integer variable — in bsearch, nelem may be an integer value or constant.) Set width to the size in bytes of one object. All objects must be the same size. You also must provide a comparison function, fcmp, that receives the addresses of two objects. The function must return zero if the objects are equal; nonzero if not. (You may use the same comparison function passed to qsort or bsearch.) Unlike bsearch, the objects in the array do not need to be sorted. Returns the address of an object found in the array; NULL if no object matches key*.

```
void *lsearch(const void *key, void *base,
 size_t *nelem, size_t width,
 int(*fcmp)(const void *, const void *))
```

Borland only Identical to lfind in every way except that, if the object addressed by key is *not* found in the array, a copy of that object is added to the end of the array, which must have enough free space available for that insertion. If an insertion is made, lsearch increments the size_t variable addressed by nelem by one. Returns the address of an object found in the array. If no matching object is found, lsearch returns the address of the inserted object's copy.

Listing 12-7, SEARCH.CPP, demonstrates the bsearch function in this section. The other two functions are used similarly.

Listing 12-7: SEARCH.CPP

```
/* Search Functions */

#include <stdio.h>
#include <stdlib.h>
#include <conio.h>

#define SIZE 20  // Number of elements in array

int array[SIZE];
```

```
char Pause()
{
  char c;
  printf("\nPress Enter to continue...");
  while ((c = getchar()) != '\n') { }
  return c;
}

// Initialize array with values selected at random
void FillArray()
{
  for (int i = 0; i < SIZE; i++)
    array[i] = rand();
}

// Display array's contents
void ShowArray(const char *msg)
{
  puts(msg);
  for (int i = 0; i < SIZE; i++)
    printf("%8d", array[i]);
  puts("");
}

// Comparison function for qsort and bsearch
int icomp(const void *a, const void *b)
{
  int i, j;
  i = *(int *)(a);
  j = *(int *)(b);
  return i - j;
}

int main()
{
  clrscr();

// Define variables
  int key;
  int *result;
```

```
// Initialize and display array
  FillArray();
  ShowArray("Before sorting:");

// Sort and again display array
  qsort(array, SIZE, sizeof(int), icomp);
  ShowArray("After sorting:");

// Prompt for an integer value to find in array
  printf("Enter integer to find: ");
  scanf("%d", &key);
  fflush(stdin);

// Search for requested value; display if found
  result = (int *)bsearch(&key, array, SIZE, sizeof(int), icomp);
  if (!result)
    printf("\nError: %d not found in array\n", key);
  else
    printf("\nSuccess: key %d found in array\n", *result);

  Pause();
  return 0;
}
```

Mathematical Functions

int abs(int x) Returns the absolute (nonnegative) value of x. If x equals 123, for example, abs(x) equals 123; if x equals –456, abs(x) equals 456.

div_t div(int numer, int denom)   Divides numer/denom and returns the quotient and remainder of that division as a structure defined in STDLIB.H as

```
typedef struct {
  long int quot;    /* quotient */
  long int rem;     /* remainder */
} div_t;
```

To use div, define an object of type div_t and assign the function result to that object. Returns the structure result; or if denom equals zero, under MS-DOS, aborts the program and displays the message *Divide error.*

long labs(long x) Same as abs but returns the absolute (nonnegative) equivalent of a long value x.

ldiv_t ldiv(long numer, long denom)   Same as div but divides the long
arguments numer/denom. Returns a structure of type ldiv_t, defined in STDLIB.H as

```
typedef struct {
    long int quot;      /* quotient */
    long int rem;       /* remainder */
} ldiv_t;
```

To use ldiv, define an object of type ldiv_t and assign the function result to that object.
Returns the structure result; or if denom equals zero, under MS-DOS, aborts the program and
displays the message *Divide error.*

Listing 12-8, MATH.CPP, demonstrates some of the functions in this section.

Listing 12-8: MATH.CPP

```
/* Mathematical Functions */

#include <stdio.h>
#include <stdlib.h>
#include <conio.h>

char Pause()
{
  char c;
  printf("\nPress Enter to continue...");
  while ((c = getchar()) != '\n') { }
  return c;
}

// Return an integer value from stdin
int GetInt()
{
  int v;

  scanf("%d", &v);
  fflush(stdin);
  return v;
}

// Return a long value from stdin
long GetLong()
{
  long v;
```

```c
    scanf("%ld", &v);
    fflush(stdin);
    return v;
}

int main()
{
  clrscr();

// Define a few variables
  int iv;
  long lv;
  ldiv_t divResult;

// Demonstrate abs function
  printf("Enter an integer value: ");
  iv = GetInt();
  printf("iv        == %d\n", iv);
  printf("abs(iv)   == %d\n", abs(iv));

// Demonstrate labs function
  printf("\nEnter a long integer value: ");
  lv = GetLong();
  printf("lv        == %ld\n", lv);
  printf("labs(lv)  == %ld\n", labs(lv));

// Prompt for two long integer values
  printf("\nEnter a long numerator: ");
  long numer = GetLong();
  printf("Enter a long denominator: ");
  long denom = GetLong();

// Divide two longs with ldiv function
  divResult = ldiv(numer, denom);

// Display quotient and remainder of division
  printf("\n%ld / %ld == %ld\n", numer, denom, divResult.quot);
  printf("remainder == %ld\n", divResult.rem);

  Pause();
  return 0;
}
```

Random Number Functions

`int rand(void)` Returns the next number in a pseudo-random sequence in the range of 0 to RAND_MAX. Because ANSI C does not specify the algorithm used by rand, the function cannot be expected to produce equivalent results on different compilers — not even among different versions of the *same* compiler. The version of rand supplied with this book's compiler is adequate for informal random number generation but is not intended for use in critical applications (secure password encryption, for instance). Returns the same sequence each time the program is run unless srand is first called to "seed" the generator.

`void srand(unsigned seed)` Seeds the random number generator to begin a new sequence. Pass zero or another integer to srand to regenerate the same sequence. Or pass the current time or another indeterminate value to generate different sequences on each program run. Returns nothing.

Listing 12-9, RAND.CPP, demonstrates the functions in this section.

Listing 12-9: RAND.CPP

```
/* Random Number Functions */

#include <stdio.h>
#include <stdlib.h>
#include <time.h>
#include <conio.h>

char Pause()
{
  char c;
  printf("\nPress Enter to continue...");
  while ((c = getchar()) != '\n') { }
  return c;
}

// Display n ints selected at random
void ShowRands(int n)
{
  int next;

  for (int i = 0; i < n; i++) {
    next = rand();
    printf("%8d", next);
  }
}
```

```
int main()
{
  clrscr();

// Display predefined RAND_MAX constant
  printf("RAND_MAX == %u\n", RAND_MAX);

// Display default random sequence (unseeded)
  puts("\nDefault random sequence:");
  ShowRands(10);

// Display random sequence seeded with 1 (default)
  srand(1);
  puts("\nAfter seeding with srand(1):");
  ShowRands(10);

// Display random sequence seeded with 123
  puts("\nAfter seeding with srand(123):");
  ShowRands(10);

// Display random sequence seeded with time
  srand((unsigned)time(NULL));
  puts("\nAfter seeding with current time:");
  ShowRands(10);

  Pause();
  return 0;
}
```

Chapter 13

Time and Date Functions (TIME.H)

The group Chicago sang, "Does anybody really know what time it is? Does anybody really care?" Well, yes, most of us *do* care to know the time, though it's a pleasure to stretch out on the beach every once in a while and forget about clocks, calendars, and schedules.

Computer programs also need to know the time, not only to display it on-screen, but also to seed random number generators, to compute software performance, and to perform time-related calculations. The functions in this chapter access the system's date and time through a standard function interface, which you can add to programs by inserting the directive:

```
#include <time.h>
```

The functions in TIME.H are conveniently arranged into three categories. These are

- ▶ *Fundamental Date and Time Functions* — For obtaining the time in two ways: as the current calendar time and as the elapsed processor time since the program started. It also includes a function to compute the number of seconds between two time values.

- ▶ *Binary Conversion Functions* — For time conversions among local, calendar, and Greenwich Mean Time (GMT) values.

- ▶ *ASCII Conversion Functions* — For converting binary time values into ASCII strings.

Definitions in TIME.H

The TIME.H header defines two data types, `time_t` and `clock_t`, for representing times as integer values. This book's compiler defines `time_t` and `clock_t` as equivalent to type `long`:

```
typedef long time_t;
typedef long clock_t;
```

Other compilers may define the two variables as another type — or, possibly, as two different types — so don't assume that `time_t` and `clock_t` will always be `long` integers. Generally, `clock_t` represents the time in *clock ticks,* meaning processor cycles or equivalent units. The `time_t` data type represents calendar times as integer values, usually in seconds.

The TIME.H header also defines two symbolic constants:

```
#define CLOCKS_PER_SEC 18.2
#define CLK_TCK        18.2
```

Both constants are set to the same values, equal to the number of clock ticks per second on PCs and compatibles. (Technically speaking, a subroutine in the PC's BIOS is called 18.2 times per second, providing a limited timer, but most PCs today also have hardware clocks that give more accurate times.) Processor times expressed in `clock_t` clock units can be divided by `CLK_TCK` to obtain the time in seconds.

For representing the components of calendar dates and times, TIME.H defines structure `tm` with several `int` members. The following declaration copied from TIME.H describes each member and gives its value ranges in parentheses (I added the comments):

```
struct tm {
  int tm_sec;    // Seconds (0-59)
  int tm_min;    // Minutes (0-59)
  int tm_hour;   // Hours (0-23)
  int tm_mday;   // Day of month (1-31)
  int tm_mon;    // Month (0-11)
  int tm_year;   // Year (0 == 1900)
  int tm_wday;   // Day of week (0-6)
  int tm_yday;   // Day of year (1-366)
  int tm_isdst;  // True (1) for daylight savings time
};
```

The `tm_mon` member represents January as 0, February as 1, and so on. The `tm_year` member equals the number of years *since* 1900. The `tm_wday` member represents Sunday as 0, Monday as 1, and so on.

Fundamental Date and Time Functions

`clock_t clock(void)`   Returns the number of clock ticks that have elapsed since the program started. Divide the function result by `CLK_TCK` to convert to seconds.

`double difftime(time_t time2, time_t time1)` Subtracts two calendar times `time2-time1`. Note that the later time is given first. Returns the number of seconds between the two times as a `double` value.

`time_t time(time_t *timer)`   Returns the current calendar time as a `time_t` value, equal to the number of elapsed seconds since GMT 00:00:00 (January 1, 1970). Ignores parameter `timer` if the pointer is `NULL`. If `timer` is not null, `time` stores its result–in the variable addressed by `timer`. Returns the time value; -1 if the time is unavailable.

Listing 13-1, DATETIME.CPP, demonstrates most of the functions in this section. Follow these instructions to complete the example:

Step-by-Steps

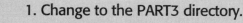

1. Change to the PART3 directory.

2. Press F3 and load DATETIME.CPP into the IDE.

3. Enter the highlighted instructions in Listing 13-1. (For reference, and to help you locate typing errors, the completed example is stored in PART3\FINISHED.)

4. Press Ctrl+F9 to compile and run. Repeat these steps for all sample listings in this chapter, but substitute a different filename in step 2.

Listing 13-1: DATETIME.CPP

```
/* Fundamental Date and Time Functions */

#include <stdio.h>
#include <time.h>
#include <conio.h>
```

```
char Pause()
{
  char c;
  printf("\nPress Enter to continue...");
  while ((c = getchar()) != '\n') { }
  return c;
}

int main()
{
  clrscr();

// Define program variables
  clock_t begin, end;
  time_t beginSec, endSec;
  int i, j;
  double f;

// Compute time to perform 1 million operations
  begin = clock();
  puts("Performing 1 million floating point operations");
  puts("Please wait...");
  for (i = 1; i <= 1000; i++)
    for (j = 1; j <= 1000; j++)
      f = i / j;  // Operation to time
  end = clock();
  printf("time: %f secs\n", (end - begin) / CLK_TCK);

// Pause and calculate elapsed seconds
  beginSec = time(NULL);
  Pause();
  endSec = time(NULL);
  f = difftime(endSec, beginSec);
  printf("You paused for %0.2f secs\n", f);

  Pause();
  return 0;
}
```

Binary Conversion Functions

struct tm *gmtime(const time_t *timer) Converts a time_t value addressed by pointer parameter timer to Greenwich Mean Time (GMT). Returns the address of an internal tm structure that contains the function results; NULL if unable to convert the time to GMT.

The `gmtime` and `localtime` functions in this section return the address of a static `tm` structure that is overwritten by subsequent function calls. For reliable results, always copy the addressed structure to another `tm` variable.

struct tm *localtime(const time_t *timer)

Converts a `time_t` value addressed by pointer parameter `timer` to the local time. Returns the converted time as a pointer to an internal `tm` structure.

time_t mktime(struct tm *timeptr)

Converts the `tm` structure addressed by pointer parameter `timeptr` into a `time_t` value. The standard function returns the converted time value; –1 if the `tm` structure members contain any out-of-range values.

The `mktime` function supplied with this book's compiler automatically adjusts any out-of-range members in the `tm` structure argument — it does not return –1 for errors. The supplied function also recalculates the `tm_wday` and `tm_yday` members based on the values of the other structure members — you do not have to supply values for those two fields.

Listing 13-2, BINTIME.CPP, demonstrates the functions in this section.

Listing 13-2: BINTIME.CPP

```
/* Binary Conversion Functions */

#include <stdio.h>
#include <stdlib.h>
#include <time.h>
#include <conio.h>

// Array of day-name string pointers
char *daystr[] = {
  "Sunday", "Monday", "Tuesday", "Wednesday",
  "Thursday", "Friday", "Saturday"
};

char Pause()
{
  char c;
  printf("\nPress Enter to continue...");
  while ((c = getchar()) != '\n') { }
  return c;
}
```

```
int main()
{
  clrscr();

// Define time variables and structures
  time_t rawt;
  struct tm localt;
  struct tm gmt;

// Get and display local and GMT times
  rawt = time(NULL);
  localt = *localtime(&rawt);
  gmt = *gmtime(&rawt);
  printf("Local time: %s", asctime(&localt));
  printf("GMT time:   %s", asctime(&gmt));

// Define structure and time value
  struct tm t;
  time_t timeValue;

// Fill structure with date and time components
  t.tm_sec   = 45;
  t.tm_min   = 15;
  t.tm_hour  = 7;
  t.tm_mday  = 12;
  t.tm_mon   = 8;
  t.tm_year  = 96;
  t.tm_wday  = 0;    // Calculated
  t.tm_yday  = 0;    // Calculated
  t.tm_isdst = 1;    // True

// Use structure to make a time value; display it
  timeValue = mktime(&t);
  printf("Calculated time: %s", ctime(&timeValue));

// Show week day and number of days past this year
  rawt = time(NULL);
  t = *localtime(&rawt);
  mktime(&t);  // Ignore function result
  printf("Today is: %s\n", daystr[t.tm_wday]);
  printf("Days past this year: %d\n", t.tm_yday);

  Pause();
  return 0;
}
```

ASCII Conversion Functions

char *asctime(const struct tm *tblock)   Converts a `tm` structure addressed by pointer parameter `tblock` to an ASCII string. The addressed structure is not changed. Returns the address of a static string buffer that is overwritten on subsequent calls to the function. For best results, use the `strcpy` function or similar from STRING.H to copy the addressed string to another `char` array. The returned string is formatted as follows, and is ended with a new line (`'\n'`) and a null:

```
Thu Dec 22 09:30:01 1956
```

char *ctime(const time_t *time)   Converts a local calendar `time_t` value addressed by pointer parameter `time` to an ASCII string. Equivalent to

```
asctime(localtime(time));
```

Like `asctime`, the addressed string returned by `ctime` is a static buffer that is overwritten by subsequent function calls. For best results, copy the addressed string to another `char` array.

size_t strftime(char *s, size_t maxsize,
** const char *fmt, const struct tm *t)**   Constructs a formatted string using date and time values in a `tm` structure addressed by pointer parameter `t`. Inserts up to `maxsize` characters into the `char` buffer addressed by parameter `s`. Uses a formatting string, addressed by `fmt`, similar in style to the formatting strings passed to `sprintf` (see Chapter 11).

Each instruction in `strftime`'s formatting string consists of a percent sign and a character. The function replaces each instruction with a component of the `tm` structure. Other text is copied unchanged to the result. If, for example, it happens to be the eleventh hour, the formatting string *Hour:%H* is translated to *Hour:11*. Table 13-1 lists the formatting instructions recognized by function `strftime`. Returns the number of characters inserted into the string result, not including the null terminator attached to the end of the string.

Table 13-1 ▶ Formatting Commands for strftime

Command	Description	Example
%a	Weekday name (abbreviated)	Fri
%A	Weekday name (full length)	Friday
%b	Month name (abbreviated)	Dec
%B	Month name (full length)	December
%c	Local date and time *	Fri Dec 10 14:42:29 1993
%d	Day of month	10
%H	Hour (24-hour time)	14

(continued)

Table 13-1 ▶ *(continued)*

Command	Description	Example
%I	Hour (12-hour time)	2
%j	Day of year	344
%m	Month number	12
%M	Minutes	42
%p	AM or PM	PM
%S	Seconds	29
%U	Year week number *	49
%w	Week day number	5
%W	Year week number *	49
%x	Local date only	Fri Dec 10, 1993
%X	Local time only	14:42:29
%y	Year minus century	93
%Y	Year including century	1993
%Z	Name of local time zone	PST
%%	The % character *	%

*The %c command inserts a carriage return into the output (an effect that may be implementation dependent). The %U command considers Sunday to be the first day of the week. The %W command considers Monday to be the first day. The %% command inserts a percent sign into the output.

Listing 13-3, STRTIME.CPP, demonstrates the strftime function in this section. See Listing 13-2, BINTIME.CPP, for samples of the asctime and ctime functions.

Listing 13-3: STRTIME.CPP

```cpp
/* ASCII Conversion Functions */

#include <stdio.h>
#include <time.h>
#include <conio.h>

#define SIZE 80   // Size of output string

char Pause()
{
  char c;
  printf("\nPress Enter to continue...");
  while ((c = getchar()) != '\n') { }
  return c;
}

// Call strftime for various commands
void ShowEffectOf(const char *command,
  const struct tm *theTime)
{
  char result[SIZE];

  strftime(
    result,
    SIZE - 1,
    command,
    theTime);
  printf("%s = = %s\n", command, result);
}

int main()
{
  clrscr();

// Define variables
  time_t rawt;
  struct tm theTime;
  char buffer[SIZE];

// Get current time into theTime
  rawt = time(NULL);
  theTime = *localtime(&rawt);
```

```
// Show effect of each strftime command
  ShowEffectOf("%a", &theTime);
  ShowEffectOf("%A", &theTime);
  ShowEffectOf("%b", &theTime);
  ShowEffectOf("%B", &theTime);
  ShowEffectOf("%c", &theTime);
  ShowEffectOf("%d", &theTime);
  ShowEffectOf("%H", &theTime);
  ShowEffectOf("%I", &theTime);
  ShowEffectOf("%j", &theTime);
  ShowEffectOf("%m", &theTime);
  ShowEffectOf("%M", &theTime);
  ShowEffectOf("%p", &theTime);
  ShowEffectOf("%S", &theTime);
  ShowEffectOf("%U", &theTime);
  ShowEffectOf("%w", &theTime);
  ShowEffectOf("%W", &theTime);
  ShowEffectOf("%x", &theTime);
  ShowEffectOf("%X", &theTime);
  ShowEffectOf("%y", &theTime);
  ShowEffectOf("%Y", &theTime);
  ShowEffectOf("%Z", &theTime);
  ShowEffectOf("%%", &theTime);

// Use strftime to display date and time information
  puts("");
  strftime(buffer, SIZE - 1, "time: %X\n", &theTime);
  puts(buffer);
  strftime(buffer, SIZE - 1, "date: %x\n", &theTime);
  puts(buffer);
  strftime(buffer, SIZE - 1, "Month & day: %B, %A", &theTime);
  puts(buffer);

  Pause();
  return 0;
}
```

Chapter 14

String Functions (STRING.H)

Although many programmers think of strings as data types, strings are just arrays of `char` terminated with a null byte equal to zero. Each `char` in a string occupies one eight-bit byte, making strings efficient places for storing labels, prompts, error messages, or any other text.

Arrays of `char` can also be used as general-purpose buffers. You might, for example, allocate memory for a 1024-byte buffer into which you insert one or more structures. You could then write the buffer to disk along with its data. Simply reverse the steps to read the records back into memory. This form of *buffered I/O* helps limit the number of accesses to relatively slow disk drives, thus improving overall program performance.

The standard function library provides a gaggle of functions for manipulating strings and `char` buffers. To use the functions described in this chapter, add this directive to your program:

```
#include <string.h>
```

The functions prototyped in the STRING.H header fall into several unique categories:

▶ *Utility functions* — For determining string lengths and initializing string characters to an ASCII value.

▶ *Upper- and lowercase functions* — For converting strings to upper- or lowercase.

▶ *Copy functions* — For copying strings, or portions of strings, to other `char` arrays.

▶ *Comparison functions* — For alphabetically comparing two strings or portions of strings.

▶ *Concatenation functions* — For joining two strings.

▶ *Pattern-matching functions* — For searching strings, looking for one or more characters.

▶ *Miscellaneous functions* — For an error function and one oddball subroutine that reverses a string's characters.

▶ *Buffer functions* — For moving, comparing, copying, and performing other operations' `char` buffers, which may hold string or other kinds of data. The string functions in this chapter use many of C's buffer functions to perform their jobs; you can use them too on buffers containing various kinds of objects. With most C compilers, buffer functions are written in optimized assembly language and are therefore likely to be faster than equivalent operations written in C.

Definitions in STRING.H

Other than function prototypes, there's only one significant declaration in STRING.H — the `size_t` type, used for defining variables that hold buffer sizes, character counts, and so on. The `size_t` type (actually, it's an alias for another type) is defined in Turbo and Borland C++ as

```
typedef unsigned size_t;
```

Another compiler might define `size_t` differently. It must, however, be the same type returned by the `sizeof` operator. The `size_t` type is declared in other headers (STDLIB.H, for instance), but is also declared in STRING.H so you don't have to include STDLIB.H just to use that one type. (It's always OK to redefine a type name such as `size_t` as long as it is redefined *exactly* the same. Thus a program may include STDLIB.H and STRING.H, declaring `size_t` twice, without harm.)

 All of the string functions in this chapter use or return pointers of type `char*` or `const char*` to address strings. A `char*` parameter indicates that the function may modify the addressed string; a `const char*` parameter indicates that the function makes no changes to the addressed string. Buffer functions use and return `void*` or `const void*` pointers — that is, pointers to no specific type of data.

Utility Functions

size_t strlen(const char *s)   Counts the number of characters in the string addressed by s. The result might be smaller than the size of the addressed char buffer. Returns the number of non-null characters in the string up to, but not including, the terminating null; returns zero if the first byte addressed by s equals null.

char *strnset(char *s, int ch, size_t n)
Borland only Inserts character ch into the first n bytes of the string addressed by char pointer s. Stops inserting characters upon detecting a null terminator in the addressed string or after inserting n characters. Returns s.

char *strset(char *s, int ch)
Borland only Inserts character ch into all bytes of the string addressed by char pointer s. Stops inserting characters upon detecting a null terminator in the addressed string. Equivalent to strnset(s, ch, strlen(s)). Returns s.

Listing 14-1, STRUTIL.CPP, demonstrates the functions in this section. Follow these instructions to complete the example.

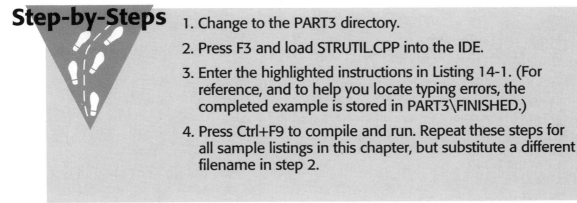

Step-by-Steps

1. Change to the PART3 directory.

2. Press F3 and load STRUTIL.CPP into the IDE.

3. Enter the highlighted instructions in Listing 14-1. (For reference, and to help you locate typing errors, the completed example is stored in PART3\FINISHED.)

4. Press Ctrl+F9 to compile and run. Repeat these steps for all sample listings in this chapter, but substitute a different filename in step 2.

Listing 14-1: STRUTIL.CPP

```
/* Utility Functions */

#include <stdio.h>
#include <string.h>
#include <conio.h>
```

```
char Pause()
{
  char c;
  printf("\nPress Enter to continue...");
  while ((c = getchar()) != '\n') { }
  return c;
}

int main()
{
  clrscr();

// Define string and length variables
  char title[] = "Go Tell It on the Mountain";
  char author[] = "James Baldwin";
  int len;

// Display title string and its length
  len = strlen(title);
  printf("%s (%d characters)\n", title, len);

// Display author string and its length
  len = strlen(author);
  printf("%s (%d characters)\n", author, len);

// Set first six characters in author string to blanks
  strnset(author, ' ', 6);
  printf("\nAuthor's last name == %s\n\n", author);

// Display title, replace with dashes, and display
  puts(title);
  strset(title, '-');
  puts(title);

  Pause();
  return 0;
}
```

Upper- and Lowercase Functions

char *strupr(char *s)

Borland only Converts to uppercase all lowercase letters in the string addressed by char pointer s. Leaves other characters unchanged. Returns s.

char *strlwr(char *s)   Converts to lowercase all uppercase letters in the string addressed by char pointer s. Leaves other characters unchanged. Returns s.

Listing 14-2, STRUL.CPP, demonstrates the functions in this section.

Listing 14-2: STRUL.CPP

```
/* Upper- and Lowercase Functions */

#include <stdio.h>
#include <string.h>
#include <conio.h>

char Pause()
{
  char c;
  printf("\nPress Enter to continue...");
  while ((c = getchar()) != '\n') { }
  return c;
}

int main()
{
  clrscr();

// Define and display a string
  char s[] = "Upper and Lowercase String";
  puts("\nOriginal string");
  puts(s);

// Convert string to uppercase and display
  puts("\nConvert to all uppercase");
  strupr(s);
  puts(s);

// Convert string to lowercase and display
  puts("\nConvert to all lowercase");
  puts(strlwr(s));

  Pause();
  return 0;
}
```

Copy Functions

char *stpcpy(char *dest, const char *src)

Borland only Same as strcpy, described next, but returns dest + strlen(src) — that is, the address in dest *after* the last character copied from src.

char *strcpy(char *dest, const char *src)

Copies all characters from the string addressed by src to the string addressed by dest. It is your responsibility to ensure that the size of the destination buffer is large enough to hold the copied string. Does not change the string addressed by src. Adds a null terminator to the end of the copied string. Returns dest.

char *strdup(const char *s)

Borland only Allocates a memory block large enough to hold the string addressed by s and then copies the addressed string into the block. When you are finished using the duplicated string, call free in the STDLIB.H header to delete the allocated memory. Returns the address of the duplicated string; null if enough memory is not available.

char *strncpy(char *dest, const char *src, size_t maxlen)

Copies up to maxlen characters from the string addressed by src to the char buffer addressed by dest. Does *not* end the resulting string with a null terminator. Pads the resulting string with nulls if the source string has fewer than maxlen characters. Returns dest.

Listing 14-3, STRCOPY.CPP, demonstrates the functions in this section.

Listing 14-3: STRCOPY.CPP

```
/* Copy Functions */

#include <stdio.h>
#include <stdlib.h>
#include <string.h>
#include <conio.h>

#define SIZE 80  // Size of destination string

char Pause()
{
  char c;
  printf("\nPress Enter to continue...");
  while ((c = getchar()) != '\n') { }
  return c;
}
```

```c
int main()
{
  clrscr();

// Define variables
  char src[] = "I'd Rather be Programming";
  char dest[SIZE];
  int i;
  char *dup, *copy;  // Two char pointers

// Copy source string to destination
  strcpy(dest, src);
  printf("dest == %s\n", dest);

// Create a duplicate string
  dup = strdup(src);
  if (!dup) {
    puts("Out of memory");
    exit(1);
  }

// Fill string with nulls
  for (i = 0; i < SIZE; i++)
    dup[i] = 0;

// Copy characters to *dup and display
  strncpy(dup, src, 13);
  printf("but %s Sailing!\n", dup);

// Duplicate a string and attach new ending
  copy = (char *)malloc(strlen(src) + 1);
  char *t = stpcpy(copy, src); // Copy and find end
  strcpy(t, " or Sailing");    // Attach new ending
  puts(copy);  // Display modified string

// Free the memory allocated by strdup
  free(dup);
  free(copy);

  Pause();
  return 0;
}
```

Comparison Functions

int strcmp(const char *s1, const char *s2)   Compares two strings alphabetically. The strings are addressed by `const char` pointers `s1` (string 1) and `s2` (string 2). Returns a value less than zero if string 1 is less than string 2; zero if the two strings are exactly the same; or a positive value if string 1 is greater than string 2.

int stricmp(const char *s1, const char *s2)   Same as `strcmp` but ignores any differences in upper- or lowercase letters in the two addressed strings. (The *i* in `stricmp` stands for "ignore case.")

int strncmp(const char *s1, const char *s2, size_t maxlen) Same as `strcmp` but compares up to the first `maxlen` characters in the addressed strings.

int strnicmp(const char *s1, const char *s2, size_t maxlen) **Borland only** Same as `strncmp` but ignores any differences in upper- or lowercase letters in the two addressed strings.

Listing 14-4, STRSORT.CPP, demonstrates the functions in this section.

Listing 14-4: STRSORT.CPP

```
/* Comparison Functions */

#include <stdio.h>
#include <stdlib.h>
#include <string.h>
#include <conio.h>

// Define an array of string pointers
// (Strings randomly sampled from Moby Words
//  database of 21,400 proper names)

char *names[] = {
  "Jenne",
  "Burnside",
  "Allerie",
  "Vinn",
  "Arly",
  "Coshow",
  "Georgine",
  "Gudren",
  "Augustine",
  "Matilde",
  "Demitria",
  "Papotto",
  "Amii",
  "Janis",
  "Chadwick"
};
```

```
// Calculate number of char pointers in array
   int num = sizeof(names) / sizeof(char *);

char Pause()
{
   char c;
   printf("\nPress Enter to continue...");
   while ((c = getchar()) != '\n') { }
   return c;
}

// Display numbered list of names
void DisplayArray()
{
   int i;

   for (i = 0; i < num; i++)
     printf("%2d: %s\n", i, names[i]);
}

// String comparison function
int StrCompare(const void *s1, const void *s2)
{
// Case-sensitive comparison
   return strcmp(*(const char **)s1, *(const char **)s2);

// Case-insensitive comparison
//   return stricmp(*(const char **)s1, *(const char **)s2);

// Compare first 8 characters only
//   return strncmp(*(const char **)s1, *(const char **)s2, 8);
}

int main()
{
   clrscr();

// Display strings before sorting
   puts("\nBefore sorting:\n");
   DisplayArray();
   Pause();

// Display strings after sorting
```

```
    puts("\nAfter sorting:\n");
    qsort(names, num, sizeof(char *), StrCompare);
    DisplayArray();

    Pause();
    return 0;
}
```

Concatenation Functions

char *strcat(char *dest, const char *src) Concatenates (joins) the
string addressed by pointer src onto the end of the string addressed by dest. The function
requires the string addressed by dest to be initialized. If the destination string is a null string,
strcat works the same as strcpy. Returns dest.

char *strncat(char *dest, const char *src, size_t maxlen)
Same as strcat but copies at most maxlen characters from the source string addressed by src
onto the end of the string addressed by dest. As with strcat, strncat requires the string
addressed by dest to be initialized. Returns dest.

Listing 14-5, STRCAT.CPP, demonstrates the functions in this section.

Listing 14-5: STRCAT.CPP

```
/* Concatenation Functions */

#include <stdio.h>
#include <string.h>
#include <conio.h>

#define SIZE 80   // Size of destination string

char Pause()
{
    char c;
    printf("\nPress Enter to continue...");
    while ((c = getchar()) != '\n') { }
    return c;
}

int main()
{
    clrscr();
```

```
// Define string variables and result buffer
  char first[] = "Abraham";
  char last[] = "Lincoln";
  char result[SIZE];

// Join first and last strings using strcat
  strcpy(result, first);
  strcat(result, " ");
  strcat(result, last);
  printf("\nstrcat result == %s\n", result);

// Join first and last strings using strncat
  strcpy(result, last);
  strcat(result, ", ");
  strncat(result, first, 1);
  strcat(result, ".");
  printf("\nstrncat result == %s\n", result);

  Pause();
  return 0;
}
```

Pattern-Matching Functions

char *strchr(const char *s, int c)   Searches for character c in a string addressed by char pointer s. Returns the address of the first c character found in s; null if the string does not have that character.

size_t strcspn(const char *s1, const char *s2)   Returns the length of the initial portion of the string addressed by s1 that contains characters *not* in the string addressed by s2. (In other words, strcspn determines the number of characters beyond the beginning of s1 where one or more characters in s2 are found.) Returns strlen(s1) if no characters in s2 match those in s1.

char *strpbrk(const char *s1, const char *s2)   Returns a pointer to the first character in the string addressed by s1 that matches *any* character in the string addressed by s2. Returns null if no characters from s2 match those in s1.

char *strrchr(const char *s, int c)   The reverse of strchr. Returns a pointer to the last occurrence of character c in the string addressed by s; null if character c is not in the string.

size_t strspn(const char *s1, const char *s2) Returns the length of the initial segment in the string addressed by s1 consisting of characters *entirely* from the string addressed by s2. In other words, strspn searches a string for a subset composed of characters from another string.

char *strstr(const char *s1, const char *s2) Returns the address in the string addressed by s1 of the first occurrence of the string addressed by s2. Use this function to search one string (s1) for the existence of another string (s2). Returns null if the string at s2 cannot be found in s1.

char *strtok(char *s1, const char *s2) Tokenizes the string addressed by s1 into a series of substrings, separated by the characters in the string addressed by s2. If, for example, s1 addresses a series of words separated by commas, and if s2 addresses a string with a comma character (the separator), strtok inserts a null into the original string at s1 in place of the first comma located. Pass NULL as the first argument to continue replacing separator characters in the original string. (See the sample listing in this section for more information on using strtok — this one takes some practice to use properly.) Returns each tokenized string's address; null when the original string (s1) has no more separator characters from s2.

The strtok function modifies the string addressed by s1. To preserve the original string data, operate on a copy of the string or save its characters in a temporary buffer.

Listing 14-6, STRPAT.CPP, demonstrates the functions in this section.

Listing 14-6: STRPAT.CPP

```
/* Pattern-Matching Functions */

#include <stdio.h>
#include <string.h>
#include <conio.h>

#define SIZE 80  // Size of char buffer

char Pause()
{
  char c;
  printf("\nPress Enter to continue...");
  while ((c = getchar()) != '\n') { }
  return c;
}
```

```c
int main()
{
  clrscr();

// Define string and other variables
  char *alpha = "abcdefghijklmnopqrstuvwxyz";
  char *digit = "0123456789";
  char *telephone = "205-555-1212";
  char buffer[SIZE];
  char *t;
  int k;

// Display original strings
  puts("Original strings:");
  printf("*alpha == %s\n", alpha);
  printf("*digit == %s\n", digit);
  printf("*telephone == %s\n\n", telephone);

// Find substring in alpha starting with 'q'
  t = strchr(alpha, 'q');
  if (t)
    printf("strchr : *t == %s\n", t);

// Count chars in telephone up to first '-'
  k = strcspn(telephone, "-");
  strncpy(buffer, telephone, k);
  buffer[k] = 0;
  printf("strcspn: area code == %s\n", buffer);

// Find location in telephone of first '-'
  t = strpbrk(telephone, "-");
  if ((t) && (strlen(t) > 1))
    t++;
  printf("strpbrk: local number == %s\n", t);

// Find last occurrence in telephone of '-'
  t = strrchr(telephone, '-');
  if ((t) && (strlen(t) > 1))
    t++;
  printf("strrchr: last digits == %s\n", t);
```

```
// Find length of preface in telephone with digits
  k = strspn(telephone, digit);
  strncpy(buffer, telephone, k);
  buffer[k] = 0;
  printf("strspn : area code == %s\n", buffer);

// Search for pattern in telephone
  t = strstr(telephone, "1212");
  printf("strstr : telephone ");
  if (t)
    puts("contains 1212");
  else
    puts("does not contain 1212");

// Tokenize telphone into components
  puts("\nstrtok : Telephone number tokens:");
  strcpy(buffer, telephone);
  t = strtok(buffer, "-");
  while (t) {
    puts(t);
    t = strtok(NULL, "-");
  }

  Pause();
  return 0;
}
```

Miscellaneous Functions

char *strerror(int errnum)   Returns the address of a static error message string for errnum. Also defined in STDIO.H. For more information, see the section in Chapter 11 called, "Error-Handling Functions."

char *strrev(char *s)
Borland only Reverses the characters in the string addressed by s — changing, for example, *ABCD* to *DCBA*. This oddball function's value is questionable (it's implementation is often posed as an exercise to first-year computer programming students), but strrev is occasionally useful for repeatedly searching long strings for characters or substrings at their ends. Reversing the strings before searching may improve the program's performance. Returns s.

Listing 14-7, STRMISC.CPP, demonstrates the functions in this section.

Listing 14-7: STRMISC.CPP

```
/* Miscellaneous Functions */

#include <stdio.h>
#include <string.h>
#include <conio.h>

#define SIZE 80  // Size of char buffer

char Pause()
{
  char c;
  printf("\nPress Enter to continue...");
  while ((c = getchar()) != '\n') { }
  return c;
}

int main()
{
  clrscr();

// Define string and other variables
  char *alpha = "abcdefghijklmnopqrstuvwxyz";
  char buffer[SIZE];
  int i;

// Call strerror to display sample error messages
  puts("First 10 error messages:\n");
 for (i = 1; i <= 10; i++)
   printf("%2d: %s", i, strerror(i));

// Call strrev to reverse a string's characters
  puts("");
  strcpy(buffer, alpha);
  printf("before strrev: %s\n", buffer);
  strrev(buffer);
  printf("after strrev : %s\n", buffer);

  Pause();
  return 0;
}
```

Buffer Functions

void *memchr(const void *s, int c, size_t n) Searches n bytes of a buffer addressed by s for character c. Returns a pointer to that character in the buffer; null if c is not found.

int memcmp(const void *s1, const void *s2, size_t n) Alphabetically compares n characters of two string buffers addressed by s1 (string 1) and s2 (string 2). (The function provides the raw power behind string comparison functions such as strcmp.) Returns a value less than zero if string 1 is less than string 2; zero if the two strings are exactly the same; or a positive value if string 1 is greater than string 2.

void *memcpy(void *dest, const void *src, size_t n) Copies n bytes from the buffer addressed by src to the buffer addressed by dest. It is your responsibility to ensure that dest addresses a buffer at least n bytes long. Results may be unexpected if the two buffers overlap (if, for example, src addresses a byte *inside* the buffer addressed by **dest**). See memmove for a function that works correctly for overlapping buffers. Use memcpy to copy data only between nonoverlapping buffers. Returns dest.

int memicmp(const void *s1, const void *s2, size_t n) **Borland only** Same as memcmp but ignores differences in upper- and lowercase letters in the addressed buffers.

void *memmove(void *dest, const void *src, size_t n) Same as memcpy but works correctly even if the src pointer addresses a byte inside the dest buffer — that is, if the two buffers overlap. You may use memcpy or memmove to copy bytes between nonoverlapping buffers. Returns dest.

void *memset(void *s, int c, size_t n) Inserts n characters of value c into the buffer addressed by s. It is your responsibility to ensure that s addresses a buffer at least n bytes long. Returns s.

Listing 14-8, BUFFER.CPP, demonstrates the functions in this section.

Listing 14-8: BUFFER.CPP

```
/* Buffer Functions */

#include <stdio.h>
#include <string.h>
#include <conio.h>

#define SIZE 256  // Buffer size
```

```
char Pause()
{
  char c;
  printf("\nPress Enter to continue...");
  while ((c = getchar()) != '\n') { }
  return c;
}

// Display memcmp comparison results
void ShowComparison(const char *s1, const char *s2, int result)
{
  char op[] = "==";

  if (result < 0)
    op[0] = '<';
  else if (result > 0)
    op[0] = '>';
  printf("%s %s %s\n", s1, op, s2);
}

int main()
{
  clrscr();

// Define string and other variables
  char dest[SIZE];
  char src[SIZE];
  char *t;
  int k;

// Initialize source string
  strcpy(src, "ABCDEFGH*IJKLMNOP*QRSTUVWXYZ*");

// Use memchr to replace * in source with new lines
  puts("BEFORE:");
  puts(src);
  do {
    t = (char *)memchr(src, '*', strlen(src));
    if (t)
      *t = '\n';
  } while (t);
  puts("\nAFTER:");
  puts(src);
```

```
// Initialize strings for next section
  strcpy(src, "Perot, Ross");
  strcpy(dest, "Perot");

// Compare using source length
  k = memcmp(src, dest, strlen(src));
  puts("memcmp using first string length:");
  ShowComparison(src, dest, k);

// Compare using dest length
  k = memcmp(src, dest, strlen(dest));
  puts("memcmp using second string length:");
  ShowComparison(src, dest, k);

// Copy a buffer using memcpy
  puts("");
  strcpy(src, "abcdefghijklmnopqrstuvwxyz");
  memset(dest, 0, SIZE);  // Set to all zeros
  memcpy(dest, src, strlen(src) + 1);
  printf("memcpy: dest == %s\n", dest);

// Demonstrate memcpy on overlapping buffer
  memcpy(dest + 1, dest, 12);
  puts("\nmemcpy on overlapping buffer:");
  printf("memcpy: dest == %s\n", dest);

// Use memmove to delete leading blanks from string
  strcpy(dest, "        <<—Delete these blanks");
  printf("\nmemmove: Before == %s\n", dest);
  k = strspn(dest, " ");
  if (k > 0)
    memmove(dest, dest + k, 1 + strlen(dest) - k);
  printf("memmove: After  == %s\n", dest);

  Pause();
  return 0;
}
```

Chapter 15

Math Functions (MATH.H)

Fortunately for those who didn't pay attention in math class, you don't have to be a mathematical genius to use C's math functions. On the other hand, if higher math is your forte, you'll find the functions in MATH.H helpful, though somewhat rudimentary. To use them, insert this directive into your program:

```
#include <math.h>
```

Functions prototyped in MATH.H fall into several categories. These are

▶ *Trigonometric Functions* — For calculating sines, cosines, tangents, and so on.

▶ *Logarithmic Functions* — For natural and base 10 logarithms.

▶ *Power Functions* — For raising values to a specified power or to a power of ten.

▶ *Miscellaneous Functions* — For performing various mathematical calculations such as square roots and floating-point absolute values, and also for taking `double` values apart, defining a math error handler, and more.

All floating-point parameters and function results in MATH.H are of type `double`. Trigonometric function arguments and results are expressed in radians.

Definitions in MATH.H

The MATH.H header defines a few constants and structures used by functions in this chapter. Three important constants are

▶ HUGE_VAL — Overflow value equal to the maximum positive `double` value permitted for function arguments. Larger arguments set the global `errno` variable to `EDOM`.

▶ EDOM — Domain error (value is outside of domain defined for the function) assigned to `errno`.

▶ ERANGE — Range error (value cannot be represented using the `double` data type) assigned to `errno`.

The Borland MATH.H header also defines a nonstandard enumerated data type, listing possible error values carried by an `exception` structure. The _mexcep data type is defined as

```
typedef enum {
  DOMAIN = 1,  /* argument domain error  -- log (-1)       */
  SING,        /* argument singularity   -- pow (0,-2))    */
  OVERFLOW,    /* overflow range error   -- exp (1000)     */
  UNDERFLOW,   /* underflow range error  -- exp (-1000)    */
  TLOSS,       /* total loss of significance -- sin(10e70) */
  PLOSS,       /* partial loss of signif. -- not used      */
  STACKFAULT   /* floating point unit stack overflow       */
} _mexcep;
```

The `exception` structure, intercepted by a user-defined `matherr` function, carries one of the preceding values, identifying the type of error that occurred. (See "Miscellaneous Functions" for more information on `matherr`.) The `exception` structure also carries additional information about an error. It is defined as:

```
struct exception {
  int type;
  char *name;
  double arg1, arg2, retval;
};
```

The `type` member is set to one of the _mexcep constants. The `name` member addresses an error message string. The three `double` arguments equal the function's two parameters (if any) and its return value.

In addition to those definitions, MATH.H also provides a set of symbolic constants that come in handy. All are preceded by M_. (Other C compilers usually define similar constants, but unfortunately, not always using the same spellings.) Table 15-1 lists Borland's math constants defined in MATH.H. Keep in mind that these constants are unique to Turbo and Borland C++.

For better portability, define your own constants using the values listed in Table 15-1.

Table 15-1 ▶ Symbolic Constants in MATH.H

Constant	Value
M_1_PI	0.318309886183790671538
M_1_SQRTPI	0.564189583547756286948
M_2_PI	0.636619772367581343076
M_2_SQRTPI	1.12837916709551257390
M_E	2.71828182845904523536
M_LN10	2.30258509299404568402
M_LN2	0.693147180559945309417
M_LOG10E	0.434294481903251827651
M_LOG2E	1.44269504088896340736
M_PI	3.14159265358979323846
M_PI_2	1.57079632679489661923
M_PI_4	0.785398163397448309616
M_SQRT_2	0.707106781186547524401
M_SQRT2	1.41421356237309504880

Trigonometric Functions

double acos(double x)   Returns arccosine of x in radians.

`double asin(double x)` Returns arcsine of x in radians.

`double atan(double x)` Returns arctangent of x in radians.

`double atan2(double y, double x)` Returns arctangent of y / x in the range of – Π to Π.

`double cos(double x)` Returns cosine of x in radians.

`double cosh(double x)` Returns hyperbolic cosine of x in radians.

`double sin(double x)` Returns sine of x in radians.

`double sinh(double x)` Returns hyperbolic sine of x in radians.

`double tan(double x)` Returns tangent of x in radians.

`double tanh(double x)` Returns hyperbolic tangent of x in radians.

Listing 15-1, TRIG.CPP, demonstrates the `cos` function in this section. Other math functions are used similarly. Follow these instructions to complete the example:

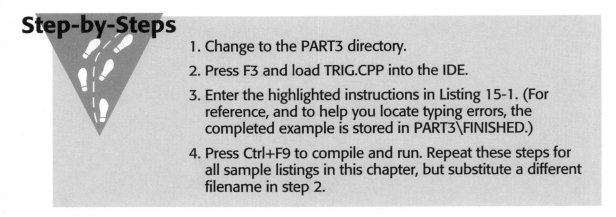

Step-by-Steps

1. Change to the PART3 directory.

2. Press F3 and load TRIG.CPP into the IDE.

3. Enter the highlighted instructions in Listing 15-1. (For reference, and to help you locate typing errors, the completed example is stored in PART3\FINISHED.)

4. Press Ctrl+F9 to compile and run. Repeat these steps for all sample listings in this chapter, but substitute a different filename in step 2.

Listing 15-1: TRIG.CPP

```
/* Trigonometric Functions */

#include <stdio.h>
#include <conio.h>
#include <math.h>
```

```
char Pause()
{
  char c;
  printf("\nPress Enter to continue...");
  while ((c = getchar()) != '\n') { }
  return c;
}

// Return an angle converted to radians
double Radians(double angle)
{
  return (angle * M_PI) / 180.0;
}

int main()
{
  clrscr();

  puts("Cosines of angles from 0 to 360 degrees");
  puts("");

// Display table of cosines
  double a;
  for (a = 0; a <= 360; a += 10)
    printf("a == %3.0f -- cos(a) == %+1.8f\n",
      a, cos(Radians(a)));

  Pause();
  return 0;
}
```

Logarithmic Functions

double log(double x)   Returns the natural logarithm of x.

double log10(double x)   Returns the base 10 logarithm of x.

Listing 15-2, LOG.CPP, demonstrates the functions in this section.

Listing 15-2: LOG.CPP

```
/* Logarithmic Functions */

#include <stdio.h>
#include <conio.h>
#include <math.h>

char Pause()
{
  char c;
  printf("\nPress Enter to continue...");
  while ((c = getchar()) != '\n') { }
  return c;
}

int main()
{
  clrscr();

// Define variables;
  double x = 5.45679;
  double result;

// Demonstrate log function
  result = log(x);
  printf("Natural log of %lf == %lf\n", x, result);

// Demonstrate log10 function
  result = log10(x);
  printf("Base 10 log of %lf == %lf\n", x, result);

  Pause();
  return 0;
}
```

Power Functions

double pow(double x, double y)   Returns the value of x raised to the y power.

double pow10(int p)
Borland only Returns 10 to the p power.

Listing 15-3, POW.CPP, demonstrates the functions in this section.

Listing 15-3: POW.CPP

```
/* Power Functions */

#include <stdio.h>
#include <conio.h>
#include <math.h>

char Pause()
{
  char c;
  printf("\nPress Enter to continue...");
  while ((c = getchar()) != '\n') { }
  return c;
}

int main()
{
  clrscr();

// Define variables;
  double x = 2.0;
  double y = 7.0;
  double result;

// Demonstrate pow function
  result = pow(x, y);
  printf("%1.3lf to the %1.3lf power == %lf\n", x, y, result);

// Demonstrate pow10 function
  result = pow10(y);
  printf("10 to the %1.3lf power == %lG\n", y, result);

  Pause();
  return 0;
}
```

Miscellaneous Functions

int abs(int i) Returns the absolute (nonnegative) value of i. For convenience, this function is defined in MATH.H and STDLIB.H. (Use fabs to find the absolute value of floating-point arguments.)

double ceil(double x) Returns the smallest integer (as a double value) greater than or equal to x. See also floor.

double exp(double x) Returns *e* to the x power.

double fabs(double x) Returns the absolute (nonnegative) value of x. (Use abs to find the absolute value of integer arguments.)

double floor(double x) Returns the largest integer (as a double value) less than or equal to x.

double fmod(double x, double y) Returns x modulo y, equal to the remainder of x/y.

double frexp(double x, int *exponent) Spits a floating-point value into a mantissa and exponent. Pass the value in x. The function result equals that value's mantissa. The exponent is stored in the int object addressed by the exponent pointer. See also modf.

double hypot(double x, double y)
Borland only Returns the hypotenuse of a right triangle with sides of lengths x and y.

double ldexp(double x, int exponent) Returns x times two raised to the specified exponent. Equivalent to x*pow(2, exponent).

int matherr(struct exception *e) Define a function of this type to trap math errors, or *exceptions,* raised by improper arguments or return values by various functions in this chapter. Return any nonzero value to indicate that the error has been successfully handled; zero otherwise.

double modf(double x, double *ipart) Spits a floating-point value into its integer and fractional parts. Pass the value in x. The function returns that value's fractional part as a double value and stores the integer part in the double object addressed by pointer ipart.

double sqrt(double x) Returns the square root of x.

Listing 15-4, MISC.CPP, demonstrates most of the functions in this section.

Listing 15-4: MISC.CPP

```
/* Miscellaneous Functions */

#include <stdio.h>
#include <conio.h>
#include <math.h>

char Pause()
{
  char c;
  printf("\nPress Enter to continue...");
  while ((c = getchar()) != '\n') { }
  return c;
}
```

```
// Define a matherr function
// Ignore linker warning about redefinition
// Delete this function to see standard result
int matherr(struct exception *e)
{
  puts("\nMath error received!");
  printf("type == %d\n", e->type);
  printf("name == %s\n", e->name);
  printf("arg1 == %lf\n", e->arg1);
  printf("arg2 == %lf\n", e->arg2);
  printf("return value == %lf\n", e->retval);
  return 1;
}

int main()
{
  clrscr();

// Define a target variable
  double x = M_PI;

// Demonstrate some miscellaneous functions:
  printf("x == %lf\n", x);
  printf("ceil(x) == %lf\n", ceil(x));
  printf("exp(x) == %lf\n", exp(x));
  printf("fabs(x) == %lf\n", fabs(x));
  printf("floor(x) == %lf\n", floor(x));
  printf("fmod(x, 2) == %lf\n", fmod(x, 2));
  printf("ldexp(x, 4) == %lf\n", ldexp(x, 4));
  printf("sqrt(x) == %lf\n", sqrt(x));

// Define variables for frexp function
  double mantissa;
  int exponent;

// Demonstrate frexp function
  mantissa = frexp(x, &exponent);
  printf("\nx == %lf\n", x);
  printf("mantissa == %lf\n", mantissa);
  printf("exponent == %d\n", exponent);

// Define variables for modf function
```

```
    double fractpart, intpart;

// Demonstrate modf function
    fractpart = modf(x, &intpart);
    printf("\nx == %lf\n", x);
    printf("integer part == %lf\n", intpart);
    printf("fractional part == %lf\n", fractpart);

// Define variables for hypot function\
    double sideA = 4.5;
    double sideB = 9.3;
    double hypotenuse;

// Demonstrate hypot function
    hypotenuse = hypot(sideA, sideB);
    printf("\nSide A == %lf\n", sideA);
    printf("Side B == %lf\n", sideB);
    printf("Hypotenuse == %lf\n", hypotenuse);

// Force a math error
    puts("\nForce an overflow error to occur");
    double bad = pow(HUGE_VAL, 7);
    printf("bad == %lf\n", bad);

    Pause();
    return 0;
}
```

Part 4

Algorithms

As houses begin with blueprints, computer programs arise from *algorithms* — step-by-step plans that describe solutions to problems. Algorithms explain in general terms techniques for sorting arrays, for searching records, for creating data structures, and for performing countless other tasks that can be converted to statements in C or other programming languages.

The study of algorithms can occupy a lifetime, but most programmers simply use them as building blocks in a program's construction. In Part 4, you learn about classic algorithms in several categories, and you learn how to translate them into C. After reading the next three chapters, you'll be ready to tackle more sophisticated algorithms published in books, magazines, and journals. (You can find more algorithms every month in my column, "Algorithm Alley," published in *Dr. Dobb's Journal.*)

Chapter 16 describes algorithms for "Self-Referential Data Structures" — methods you can use to form lists, trees, and other efficient data structures composed of objects that address one another in memory. Chapter 17 focuses on "Sorting and Searching" — two classic themes in the study of algorithms. Chapter 18 looks into "File Processing" — techniques for managing database files. The chapter includes the complete source code for a mailing list and phone-number database manager, composed of seven individual programs. You can use the demonstration programs directly, or you can convert them into a general-purpose database management system.

By the way, the word *algorithm* comes from an unlikely source — it originates from the name of a Persian textbook author, Abu Ja'far Mohammed ibn Mûsâ al-Khowârizmî.

Chapter 16

Self-Referential Data Structures

Everyone has seen circus elephants parading around the ring, trunks and tails twisted together like jungle vines. If you mentally replace elephants with objects in memory, and if you substitute trunks and tails with pointers, you arrive at a fairly good representation of a *linked list*, one of the most important data structures you can learn how to tame.

In this chapter, you learn about algorithms for creating and managing lists and trees, which are formed with linked lists. The resulting data structures efficiently use memory, and they organize data in ways that simplify sorting and searching.

Lists

Objects in a linked list are *self-referential*. That means they contain one or more pointers that refer to other objects of the same type. In programs, the objects are most easily constructed as structures that have one or more pointer members. When those pointers address objects of the same structure type, the result is a *self-referential list* — that is, a list of objects that address one another.

Designing a self-referential list immediately poses a chicken and egg problem. Which do you create first, the pointer or the structure? The answer relies on a rule that permits a structure to have a pointer member of the structure's own type, even though that structure isn't yet completely declared. For instance, you can design a structure `Record` that contains a member pointer of type `struct Record*`:

```
struct Record {
  int data;              // Other data in object
  struct Record *next;   // Pointer to Record object
};
```

The structure's first member, `data`, represents any information to be stored in `Record` objects. (The structure could have other fields in any order.) The second member, `next`, is a pointer to a `Record` object, one that also has a `next` member. The `next` member can be named anything you like, and it doesn't have to be the last item. For clarity, it's usually best to declare a type alias for `struct Record*` and use that name as the pointer's type:

```
typedef struct Record * RecordPtr;
```

That tells the compiler to recognize `RecordPtr` as an alias for a pointer to an object of the `Record` type. (In other words, `RecordPtr` is equivalent to `struct Record*`.) You can then use `RecordPtr` as the type of the structure's `next` member:

```
struct Record {
  int data;            // Other data in object
  RecordPtr next;      // Pointer to Record object
};
```

The `next` member is sometimes called a *link field*. In a `Record` object, if `next` is non-null, it addresses another `Record` object. If `next` is null, the object does not address another object — it is the end of the line. To use the structure, define a record pointer `rp` and allocate memory for a `Record` object using statements like these (you also have to include the STDLIB.H header, which declares the `malloc` function):

```
#include <stdlib.h>
...
RecordPtr rp;
rp  = (RecordPtr)malloc(sizeof(Record));
```

Pointer rp (if non-null) now addresses an object of type Record. Initialize that object's fields with programming such as:

```
rp->data = 123;
rp->next = NULL;
```

The first line assigns 123 to the addressed object's data member — you could also assign other information to other fields. The last line is critical. It sets the object's next pointer to NULL, indicating that the field does *not* address another object.

Figure 16-1 illustrates how the pointer and object appear in memory. Pointer rp addresses the object of type Record. Inside the object are two members — the data field (representing any data contained by the object) and the next pointer, set to NULL. In this and other drawings in this chapter, a NULL pointer is represented as an electrical grounding symbol.

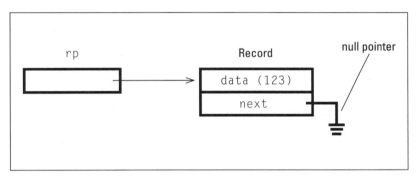

Figure 16-1 ▶ Pointer rp addresses a Record object.

Setting the next member in a Record object to the address of another object creates a list of two objects. This constructs another Record structure and links it to the first:

```
rp->next = (RecordPtr)malloc(sizeof(Record));
```

The statement allocates memory for a Record object and assigns the object's address to the next member inside the *other* object addressed by rp. Now the first object addresses another. (For clarity, I ignore allocation errors. In a real program, however, you should *always* check whether malloc returns null.)

You can now assign values to the second object addressed by the first object's next member:

```
rp->next->data = 456;
rp->next->next = NULL;
```

The two objects now appear as illustrated in Figure 16-2. Pointer rp still addresses the first Record. But now that record's next member addresses the second object. *That* object's next member is set to NULL, marking the end of the two-object list.

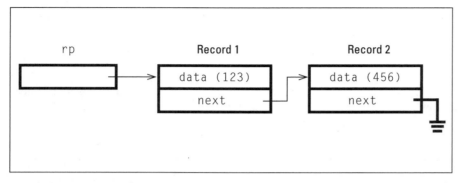

Figure 16-2 ▶ A linked list of two objects.

You could continue to allocate Record objects and assign their addresses to next members of preceding objects, expanding the list in Figure 16-2 until you have as many objects as you need or until you run out of memory. It's mighty inconvenient, however, to use statements like the following to refer to objects deep inside the list:

```
rp->next->next->next->next = ...
```

That's just too rigid to be of practical use. Instead, we need general-purpose algorithms for inserting objects into linked lists, for removing objects from linked lists, and for freeing memory allocated to those objects. The next sections explore algorithms for managing objects stored in linked lists.

At this point, you might question the value of linked lists. Why not use an array to store objects in memory? The answer depends on the application, and in some cases, an array may be a better choice. A linked list, however, can store objects *anywhere* in memory. In Figure 16-2, for example, the two objects do not have to be adjacent as they would if stored in an array. A linked list also can grow and shrink under control of the program — it doesn't have to be a fixed size. On the downside, programming linked lists is more difficult. I can't say which structure is "better." It's up to you to choose the best method for your application.

Single-linked list

A single-linked list consists of objects each with a single pointer member that addresses the next object in line. Figure 16-2 illustrates how a single-linked list appears in memory. Three algorithms describe the steps for creating, managing, and disposing single-linked lists:

▶ Push object onto a single-linked list

▶ Pop object from a single-linked list

▶ Traverse a single-linked list

The resulting list operates as a *stack* — a data structure that expands by *pushing* and *popping* objects to and from one end of the list. Think of a stack as a set of dishes in a spring-loaded bin. To add a dish, you "push" one onto the top of the stack. To remove one, you "pop" it off the top.

Push onto list

To add a new object to a list, we need three items:

▶ Item pointer (ip)

▶ Item reference (iref)

▶ List pointer (list)

Pointer ip addresses the new object. To push it onto the list, the object's next member is set to the address of the object now on the top of the list (or null if the list is empty). Then the list pointer is set to the object's address. Mentally work through the algorithm's steps for pushing objects onto a stack:

1. Create item to be inserted onto list. Assign item's address to ip.

2. Assign list pointer to ip.next field.

3. Set list to ip.

To convert the algorithm to C statements, we need two type aliases — one for an item pointer and one for a reference to an item (that is, a pointer to an item pointer):

```
typedef Item *ItemPtr;
typedef ItemPtr *ItemRef;
```

The algorithm can now be written in C, using a function Push as shown in Listing 16-1.

Listing 16-1: Algorithm in C for pushing an item onto a stack

```
// Push newitem onto list
void Push(ItemPtr newitem, ItemRef list)
{
  newitem->next = *list;
  *list = newitem;
}
```

Pop from list

The reverse operation removes an object from a list. If the list is empty, we state that the program creates a new object and returns its address. (A variation on this theme could halt the program or call an error function.) Using the declarations from the preceding section, the algorithm's steps are

1. If list is null, create a new item and return its address.

2. Else return the address of the list's first item.

3. Set the list pointer to the item's next field.

As a C function, the algorithm appears as shown in Listing 16-2.

Listing 16-2: Algorithm in C for popping an item from a stack

```
// Pop newitem from list
ItemPtr Pop(ItemRef list)
{
  ItemPtr p;
  if (*list == NULL)
    p = NewItem();
  else {
    p = *list;
    *list = (*list)->next;
  }
  return p;
}
```

Traverse list

Traversing a list *visits* its objects, using the list and object next pointers to walk from item to item until reaching the end — like a clown jumping from the back of one elephant to the next until falling into the sawdust at the end of the chain.

Traversing a list uses a pointer p of type ItemPtr. The algorithm's steps follow:

1. Set a pointer p equal to list.

2. If p is null, end the algorithm.

3. Perform operation on object addressed by p.

4. Set p to p->next and repeat from step 2.

Step 4 indicates a repeated operation. Listing 16-3 uses a while loop to implement the algorithm, and it calls a function DoSomething (not shown), representing the operation performed on the addressed object.

Listing 16-3: Algorithm for traversing a stack

```
// Visit each object in list addressed by p
void Traverse(Itemptr p)
{
  while (p != NULL) {
    DoSomething(p);
    p = p->next;
  }
}
```

Sample list program

Listing 16-4, LIST.CPP, puts into action the algorithms in the preceding sections. The program displays a growing and shrinking list of objects, each containing an integer value (the objects could, of course, contain other kinds of data). The sample program also shows how to free memory allocated to a linked list.

Step-by-Steps

1. Change to the PART4 directory.

2. Press F3 and load LIST.CPP into the IDE.

3. Enter the highlighted instructions in Listing 16-4.

4. Press Ctrl+F9 to compile and run.

Listing 16-4: LIST.CPP

```
/* List Algorithms */

#include <stdio.h>
#include <stdlib.h>
#include <conio.h>

// Declare Item alias so we can define next two aliases
typedef struct tagItem Item;

// Declare pointer and reference aliases
typedef Item *ItemPtr;    // Pointer to struct item
typedef ItemPtr *ItemRef; // Pointer to item pointer
```

```c
// Declare the structure
typedef struct tagItem {
  int data;              // Data to store in objects
  ItemPtr next;          // Link field
} Item;

// Wait for use to press Enter
char Pause()
{
  char c;
  printf("\nPress Enter to continue...");
  while ((c = getchar()) != '\n') { }
  return c;
}

// Create and return address of an Item object
ItemPtr NewItem()
{
  ItemPtr p = (ItemPtr)malloc(sizeof(Item));
  if (!p) {
    fprintf(stderr, "\nERROR: Out of memory\n");
    exit(1);
  }
  p->data = rand();   // Assign data to object
  p->next = NULL;     // Initialize link field
  return p;           // Return object address
}

// Push newitem onto list
void Push(ItemPtr newitem, ItemRef list)
{
  newitem->next = *list;
  *list = newitem;
}

// Pop newitem from list
ItemPtr Pop(ItemRef list)
{
  ItemPtr p;
  if (*list == NULL)
    p = NewItem();
  else {
    p = *list;
    *list = (*list)->next;
  }
  return p;
}
```

```c
// Display object's data
void ShowItem(ItemPtr p)
{
  if (!p) return;  // Exit if p is null
  printf("%8d", p->data);
}

// Display contents of list at p
void Traverse(ItemPtr p)
{
  while (p != NULL) {
    ShowItem(p);
    p = p->next;
  }
  puts("");  // Start new line
}

int main()
{
  clrscr();

// Define and initialize variables;
  ItemPtr list = NULL;  // List pointer
  ItemPtr p;            // Item object pointer
  int i;                // For-loop control variable

// Add and display objects
  puts("\nPushing objects onto list");
  for (i = 0; i < 7; i++) {
    p = NewItem();
    Push(p, &list);
    Traverse(list);
  }

// Remove and free objects
  puts("\nPopping objects from list");
  while (list != NULL) {
    Traverse(list);
    p = Pop(&list);
    free(p);
  }

  Pause();
  return 0;
}
```

Trees

Adding a second pointer to a list structure creates an object that can address two other objects, creating a *double-linked list.* You might think of the two pointers as addressing information to the "left" and to the "right." Although such directions are physically meaningless (there are no "lefts" and "rights" in memory), the concepts may help you visualize the organization of a data structure, called a *tree.*

On the left side of the tree are objects with data in decreasing order. On the right side are objects with data in increasing order. For example, Figure 16-3 shows a tree of objects, each containing data elements which might be strings. The object pointers (shown as small boxes to the left and right of each string) address strings alphabetically less than (left) or greater than (right) any given object's data. Objects in a tree are sometimes called *nodes.*

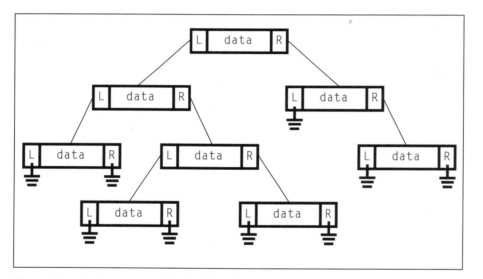

Figure 16-3 ▶ A tree uses a list of objects having two pointers each.

As in a linked list, a tree's objects are most easily programmed as structures. Using the ItemPtr type alias from before, the Item structure might look like this:

```
typedef struct tagItem {
  char *data;      // Pointer to object's data
  ItemPtr left;    // Pointer to left branches
  ItemPtr right;   // Pointer to right branches
} Item;
```

This time, `data` is a string pointer, but you can store other information in the structure. Two pointers, `left` and `right`, are shown in Figure 16-3. The `left` pointer addresses an object with data alphabetically less than a given object's information. The `right` pointer addresses data alphabetically greater. Either or both pointers may be null.

Using the structure's `left` and `right` pointers, a program can access all the tree's data in one of three ways. We can follow all the left pointers, process the data, and then follow the right pointers until visiting all objects in the tree. We can process a node's information and then follow its left and right pointers to other nodes. Or we can follow all left and right pointers and process only nodes at the ends of each branch.

In algorithm form, each tree traversal method uses recursion — that is, the steps repeat themselves from the top until reaching an object's null pointer, `p`. Each algorithm is described as a function, `Traverse`, that calls itself using `left` or `right` pointers in the object structures.

Pre-order tree traversal

First comes the algorithm for *pre-order traversal,* so named because the information at each node is processed *before* other nodes are searched:

1. If p is null exit

2. Process node at p

3. Traverse(p->left)

4. Traverse(p->right)

To `Traverse` a node means to start the algorithm over from the top. The position of each restart is remembered; thus when step 3 reaches a null `left` pointer, step 1 exits, causing step 4 to execute for that node. The recursion may be difficult to follow mentally, so don't worry if the algorithm doesn't make perfect sense as yet. Later, when you implement the algorithm in C, the steps will become clearer. For now, just concentrate on the fact that step 2 processes data *before* steps 3 and 4 search other nodes — it is the position of step 2 that gives this algorithm its "pre-order" name.

In-order tree traversal

Altering when a node is processed creates a different path through the tree's objects. The *in-order traversal* algorithm searches all the left branches, processes a node at the end of the branch, and then searches the right branches:

1. If p is null exit

2. Traverse(p->left)

3. Process node at p

4. Traverse(p->right)

Again, to Traverse a node means to stop the current search and restart the algorithm from the top. When step 1 exits for a null pointer in a node, the algorithm continues at step 3 *for that same node.* The position of each such restart is remembered so that the program first traverses all the left pointers until reaching a null one, and then it processes that object before picking up the search to all the right pointers.

You may also search all right pointers before searching the left ones, walking the tree in reverse order. An in-order search of string data walks the tree in alphabetical order.

Post-order traversal

The third algorithm, *post-order traversal,* searches all left and right pointers before processing each node:

1. If p is null exit

2. Traverse(p->left)

3. Traverse(p->right)

4. Process node at p

The only difference between that algorithm and the preceding two is the position of *Process node at p.* In post-order traversal, all nodes are searched before processing.

You should use post-order traversal to free memory allocated to object nodes. For example, step 4 could free the node at p.

Sample tree program

Listing 16-5 demonstrates the three algorithms for traversing a tree. It also includes a Search function that hunts for an object in the tree and, if not found, inserts that object at the appropriate position.

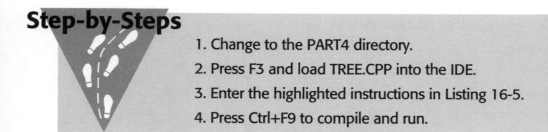

Step-by-Steps

1. Change to the PART4 directory.

2. Press F3 and load TREE.CPP into the IDE.

3. Enter the highlighted instructions in Listing 16-5.

4. Press Ctrl+F9 to compile and run.

Listing 16-5: TREE.CPP

```
/* Tree Algorithms */

#include <stdio.h>
#include <stdlib.h>
#include <string.h>
#include <conio.h>

#define SIZE 21  // Input string size

// Declare Item alias so we can define next two aliases
typedef struct tagItem Item;

// Declare pointer and reference aliases
typedef Item *ItemPtr;   // Pointer to struct item
typedef ItemPtr *ItemRef; // Pointer to item pointer

// Declare the structure
typedef struct tagItem {
  char *data;              // Pointer to data in objects
  ItemPtr left;            // Link field to items < data
  ItemPtr right;           // Link field to items > data
} Item;

// Wait for user to press Enter
char Pause()
{
  char c;
  printf("\nPress Enter to continue...");
  while ((c = getchar()) != '\n') { }
  return c;
}

// Input string from stdin
void GetString(char *s, int size)
{
  int i = 0;
  char c;
```

```
  while (--size > 0) {
    c = getchar();
    if (c == EOF || c == '\n')
      size = 0;
    else
      s[i++] = c;
  }
  s[i] = '\0';
  fflush(stdin);
}

// Create and return address of an Item object
ItemPtr NewItem()
{
  ItemPtr p = (ItemPtr)malloc(sizeof(Item));
  if (!p) {
    fprintf(stderr, "\nERROR: Out of memory\n");
    exit(1);
  }
  p->data = NULL;    // Initialize data pointer
  p->left = NULL;    // Initialize link field
  p->right = NULL;   // Initialize link field
  return p;          // Return object address
}

// Display data in object at node
void Process(ItemPtr node)
{
  printf("%s   ", node->data);
}

// Search for or insert object in tree
void Search(ItemRef tree, const char *s)
{
  ItemPtr p;
  int cmpresult;
```

```
  if (*tree == NULL) {
    p = NewItem();
    p->data = strdup(s);
    p->left = NULL;
    p->right = NULL;
    *tree = p;
  } else {
    p = *tree;
    cmpresult = strcmp(s, p->data);
    if (cmpresult < 0)
      Search(&p->left, s);
    else if (cmpresult > 0)
      Search(&p->right, s);
    else {
      puts("Duplicate data!");
      Process(p);
      puts("");
    }
  }
}


// Traverse tree using pre-order algorithm
void PreOrder(ItemPtr node)
{
  if (node != NULL) {
    Process(node);
    PreOrder(node->left);
    PreOrder(node->right);
  }
}


// Traverse tree using in-order algorithm
void InOrder(ItemPtr node)
{
  if (node != NULL) {
    InOrder(node->left);
    Process(node);
    InOrder(node->right);
  }
}
```

```
// Traverse tree using post-order algorithm
void PostOrder(ItemPtr node)
{
  if (node != NULL) {
    PostOrder(node->left);
    PostOrder(node->right);
    Process(node);
  }
}

// Free memory allocated to tree
// Uses post-order traversal algorithm
void FreeTree(ItemPtr root)
{
  if (root != NULL) {
    FreeTree(root->left);
    FreeTree(root->right);
    free(root);
  }
}

int main()
{
  clrscr();

// Define and initialize variables
  ItemPtr root = NULL;
  int done = 0;
  char s[SIZE];

// Prompt for tree data
  puts("Tree demonstration");
  while (!done) {
    printf("Data (Enter to quit): ");
    GetString(s, SIZE);
    done = (strlen(s) == 0);
    if (!done)
      Search(&root, s);
  }
```

```
// Display tree using three traversal algorithms
  puts("\nPREORDER:\n");
  PreOrder(root);
  puts("\n\nINORDER:\n");
  InOrder(root);
  puts("\n\nPOSTORDER:\n");
  PostOrder(root);
  puts("");

// Free memory allocated to tree nodes
  FreeTree(root);

  Pause();
  return 0;
}
```

There are many more kinds of lists and trees — the ones shown in this chapter are rudimentary, and I include them only to whet your appetite for more sophisticated algorithms. In the next chapter, you'll look at other classic methods for searching and sorting data — two operations that practically every program needs to do.

Chapter 17

Sorting and Searching

Career programmers probably spend more time writing code to search and sort data than any other task, and it pays to have more than one method up your sleeve. You've already checked out several examples of the Quick Sort algorithm, generally recognized as the fastest and most capable sorting method around. But the Quick Sort isn't necessarily the best choice for all sorting jobs. In cases where only a small amount of data needs to be sorted, or if the data is already nearly in order, other methods may perform as well or better than the so-called "quicker" sort.

This chapter explains two relatively simple, though useful, sorting methods you may find handy. Also included are methods for searching an array of objects. In addition to providing some useful functions, the chapter introduces terms that you'll need before digging into more sophisticated sorting and searching algorithms published in books and journals.

Sorting

For simplicity, the sample programs in this section sort an array of integer values from low to high. You can, however, adapt the techniques to other kinds of data using programming methods described elsewhere in the book. To sort strings, for instance, just call a string comparison routine such as `strcmp` in the STRING.H standard-library header. Except for minor adjustments like that, the following methods can sort any kind of data, but they are particularly good at putting small arrays in order.

Don't be fooled, though, into judging a sorting routine's value solely on speed. Other considerations such as stack space and use of memory are equally important — or more so, depending on the application and other circumstances. When selecting a sorting function, weigh all considerations before you choose your weapon.

Some terms

The sorting methods in this section are *internal algorithms* — that is, they sort arrays of data stored entirely in memory. External methods for sorting data in large disk files are too extensive for this chapter, but they are discussed in most advanced books on sorting.

The two sorting algorithms here are *stable,* meaning that equal records remain in their relative positions. *Unstable* sorting algorithms may rearrange the orders of equal records. If, for example, you sort the characters in the string *DCAAQ,* a stable sort keeps the two *A*s in the same order. An unstable sort may reverse the *A*s. When sorting records on their *keys* (individual members), it might be important to use a stable sort so that records with equal keys remain in their original relative positions, in which case a stable sorter might be required. (An unstable sorter can gain stability by adding unique suffixes to keys, in which case the relative order of records will remain the same after sorting.)

Selection sort

The selection sort uses an intuitive method to arrange an array of elements from low to high. It repeatedly scans the array looking for the smallest value less than the one being examined. If such a value is found, it is swapped with the item currently under examination. The method repeats, starting with the first array element, then with the second, the third, and so on, until the array is sorted.

Listing 17-1, SELECT.CPP, implements the selection sort algorithm for an array of integers.

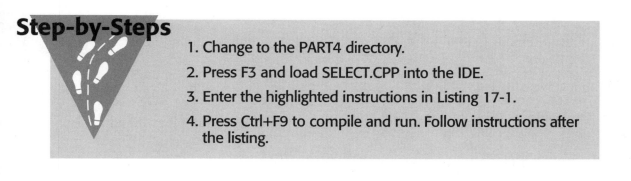

Step-by-Steps

1. Change to the PART4 directory.
2. Press F3 and load SELECT.CPP into the IDE.
3. Enter the highlighted instructions in Listing 17-1.
4. Press Ctrl+F9 to compile and run. Follow instructions after the listing.

Listing 17-1: SELECT.CPP

```c
/* Selection Sort Algorithm */

#include <stdio.h>
#include <stdlib.h>
#include <time.h>
#include <conio.h>

#define SIZE 50    // Number of elements in array

int array[SIZE];  // Array of elements to sort

// Wait for user to press Enter
char Pause()
{
  char c;
  printf("\nPress Enter to continue...");
  while ((c = getchar()) != '\n') { }
  return c;
}

// Fill array with values selected at random
void FillArray()
{
  int i;
  for (i = 0; i < SIZE; i++)
    array[i] = rand();
}
```

```
// Display array contents
void ShowArray(const char *msg)
{
  int i;
  printf("\n\n%s\n", msg);
  for (i = 0; i < SIZE; i++)
    printf("%8d", array[i]);
}

// Exchange items in array at indexes a and b
void Exchange(int a, int b)
{
  int t = array[a];
  array[a] = array[b];
  array[b] = t;
}

// Sort array using Selection Sort algorithm
void SortArray()
{
  int i, j, smallest;

  for (i = 0; i < SIZE; i++) {
    smallest = i;
    for (j = i + 1; j < SIZE; j++)
      if (array[j] < array[smallest])
        smallest = j;
    Exchange(smallest, i);
  }
}

int main()
{
  clrscr();

// Seed the random number generator
  srand((unsigned)time(NULL));

// Fill, show, sort, and again show the array
  FillArray();
  ShowArray("Before sorting");
  SortArray();
  ShowArray("After sorting");

  Pause();
  return 0;
}
```

Function `SortArray` shows how the selection sort algorithm works. A `for` loop examines each element of the array from index 0 to `SIZE-1`. Inside the `for` loop, a second loop sets `smallest` to the index of the smallest value less than the value under consideration. The two values are then swapped by another function, `Exchange`. Performing the operation on the entire array puts the values in order.

Insertion sort

The selection sort algorithm is one of the simplest and is among the easiest to understand. A somewhat more complex, but possibly faster, method is less intuitive. Called the *insertion sort,* the method works the way you might rearrange a deck of cards. Rather than exchange out-of-order elements (as in the selection sort), an insertion sort *inserts* items where they should go in the final array.

Seeing the insertion sort in action will help you understand how the method works. Listing 17-2, INSERT.CPP, demonstrates the algorithm in function `SortArray`. (The rest of the program is nearly indentical to SELECT.CPP.)

Step-by-Steps

1. Change to the PART4 directory.

2. Press F3 and load INSERT.CPP into the IDE.

3. Enter the highlighted instructions in Listing 17-2.

4. Press Ctrl+F9 to compile and run. Follow instructions after the listing.

Listing 17-2: INSERT.CPP

```
/* Insertion Sort Algorithm */

#include <stdio.h>
#include <stdlib.h>
#include <time.h>
#include <conio.h>

#define SIZE 50   // Number of elements in array

int array[SIZE];  // Array of elements to sort
```

```
// Wait for user to press Enter
char Pause()
{
  char c;
  printf("\nPress Enter to continue...");
  while ((c = getchar()) != '\n') { }
  return c;
}

// Fill array with values selected at random
void FillArray()
{
  int i;
  for (i = 0; i < SIZE; i++)
    array[i] = rand();
}

// Display array contents
void ShowArray(const char *msg)
{
  int i;
  printf("\n\n%s\n", msg);
  for (i = 0; i < SIZE; i++)
    printf("%8d", array[i]);
}

// Sort array using Insertion Sort algorithm
void SortArray()
{
  int i, j, k;

  for (i = 1; i < SIZE; i++) {
    k = array[i];
    j = i;
    while (j > 0 && array[j - 1] > k) {
      array[j] = array[j - 1];
      j--;
    }
    array[j] = k;
  }
}
```

```
int main()
{
  clrscr();

// Seed the random number generator
  srand((unsigned)time(NULL));

// Fill, show, sort, and again show the array
  FillArray();
  ShowArray("Before sorting");
  SortArray();
  ShowArray("After sorting");

  Pause();
  return 0;
}
```

As in the selection algorithm, the insertion sort uses a `for` loop to examine each value in the array. This time, however, the `for` loop starts with the second item at index 1. Inside the loop, `k` is set to the value under examination, and a control variable, `j`, is set to the current index, `i`. A `while` loop then scans backward (at successfully smaller `j` indexes), while `j` is greater than zero and while the next element toward the beginning of the array (at `j-1`) is greater than `k`. Inside this inner loop, an assignment statement moves the item at index `j-1` to position `j`, similar to the effect of inserting a card in a deck, which moves all the other cards down one position. After the inner loop finishes, element `k` is dropped into its final resting place in the slot made available by the preceding shuffle.

The main drawback of both the selection and insertion sorting algorithms is that they require data to be moved in the array. That's not a problem for sorting small objects like integers or floating-point values. But for sorting structures or strings, you may want to use a Quick Sort or sort an indirect array of pointers to data objects instead of the objects themselves.

Searching

Computers are great at searching files, arrays, databases, and other information sources looking for *keys* — target strings, that is, or other values that you need to find. Now, if I could only get my computer to find my *car keys,* I'd be happy. But, anyway, here's one of the easiest, and probably the most generally useful, search algorithms known.

The technique is called the *Binary Search* because of the way it divides an array of values into two halves repeatedly until the target key is or is not found. It requires that the array be sorted, which in practice isn't much of a problem since most databases are usually sorted anyway. Listing 17-3 demonstrates the technique.

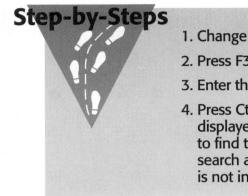

Step-by-Steps

1. Change to the PART4 directory.

2. Press F3 and load BINARY.CPP into the IDE.

3. Enter the highlighted instructions in Listing 17-3.

4. Press Ctrl+F9 to compile and run. Note a few values in the displayed array, and then enter those values one by one to find their positions. Enter nonexistent values to test the search algorithm's ability to determine that a certain value is not in the array.

Listing 17-3: BINARY.CPP

```c
/* Binary Search Algorithm */

#include <stdio.h>
#include <stdlib.h>
#include <time.h>
#include <conio.h>

#define SIZE 50    // Number of elements in array

int array[SIZE];   // Array of elements to sort

// Wait for user to press Enter
char Pause()
{
  char c;
  printf("\nPress Enter to continue...");
  while ((c = getchar()) != '\n') { }
  return c;
}

// Fill array with values selected at random
void FillArray()
{
  int i;
  for (i = 0; i < SIZE; i++)
    array[i] = rand();
}
```

```c
// Display array contents
void ShowArray(const char *msg)
{
  int i;
  printf("\n\n%s\n", msg);
  for (i = 0; i < SIZE; i++)
    printf("%8d", array[i]);
}

// Sort array using Selection Sort algorithm
void SortArray()
{
  int i, j, k;
  for (i = 1; i < SIZE; i++) {
    k = array[i];
    j = i;
    while (array[j - 1] > k) {
      array[j] = array[j - 1];
      j--;
    }
    array[j] = k;
  }
}

// Search array; return index or -1 for failure
int SearchArray(int key)
{
  int left = 0;
  int right = SIZE - 1;
  int i;

  while (right >= left) {
    i = (left + right) / 2;
    if (key == array[i])
      return i;
    if (key < array[i])
      right = i - 1;
    else
      left = i + 1;
  }
  return -1;
}
```

```
int main()
{
  clrscr();

  int i, key = 0;

// Seed the random number generator
  srand((unsigned)time(NULL));

// Initialize, sort, and display array
  FillArray();
  SortArray();
  ShowArray("Sorted values:");

// Prompt for values to find in array
  while (key != -1) {
    printf("\nFind what value (-1 to quit)? ");
    scanf("%d", &key);
    fflush(stdin);
    if (key >= 0) {
      i = SearchArray(key);
      if (i >= 0)
        printf("Found it! array[%d] == %d\n", i, array[i]);
      else
        printf("Key %d is not in array\n", key);
    }
  }

  Pause();
  return 0;
}
```

Before you examine how the binary search algorithm works, it's useful to take a look at the obvious way to search an array of values. You might call it the "brute force method" because it uses sheer brawn to examine every array value, looking for a specified key.

To try out the noncerebral technique, make a copy of BINARY.CPP and replace function `SearchArray` with the programming from Listing 17-4.

Listing 17-4: Brute force search

```
// "Brute force" linear search
int SearchArray(int key)
{
  int i;
  for (i = 0; i < SIZE; i++)
    if (key == array[i])
      return i;
  return -1;
}
```

The brute force search method is as obvious as a full moon. A for loop examines each element in the array, comparing it to the key that you want to find. If the key is found, the function returns its index value. If the for loop ends, the key is not in the array, and the function returns the error value –1.

You probably don't need me to explain how brute force searching works. You also don't need me to tell you that this method is probably the slowest you can write. But how do you know that fact? It isn't enough to decide such questions by intuition. The selection of good algorithms requires analysis to determine which is the best in a given situation.

One way to compare methods against the brute force algorithm is to count the number of comparisons made during the search. Though the brute force method works well enough, it requires an average of N/2 comparisons to find a key in an array of N objects. Worse, it always takes N comparisons to determine that a certain key doesn't exist. The binary search algorithm greatly reduces the number of comparisons required, thus improving the search function's performance. In general, a sorting or searching algorithm that uses fewer comparison operations runs faster than the competition; therefore, you can compare the algorithms by calculating their maximum numbers of comparisons.

The binary search algorithm is simple, but it may take some effort to comprehend. It works by first examining the object in the middle of an array. If that object is less than the key (the value to be found), then the object to be found must be in the upper half of the array. (Remember, the array is sorted.) If the object is greater than the key, the target object must be in the lower half of the array. Of course, if the object equals the key, the search ends successfully. Imagine — a single comparison eliminates the need to examine half of the remaining values! Repeating this process of dividing the array and examing the values in the remaining upper or lower halves locates the target key or quickly determines that the key doesn't exist.

BINARY.CPP implements the binary search algorithm in function SearchArray. Two index values, left and right, mark the portion of the array that may contain the search key. A while loop tests whether the right index is greater or equal to the left, in which case there are no more values left to examine, and therefore, the key is not in the array. Inside the loop, i is set to the index of the middle value — the object to be compared on this pass. If the key equals the object, the function returns the index value. If the key is less than the object, the right index is set to one less than the middle index i. If the key is greater than or equal to the object, the left index is set to one greater than the middle index.

Best of all, the maximum number of comparisons required to find a key using the binary search algorithm becomes relatively smaller when the array grows larger. An array of 100 elements takes at most six comparisons. An array of 1000 elements takes at most eight comparisons to find any key! In general, the binary search never requires more than $\log(N)+1$ comparisons, where N equals the number of elements in the array. Listing 17-5, NCOMPARE.CPP, uses that formula to compute the maximum number of comparisons for an array of a specified size.

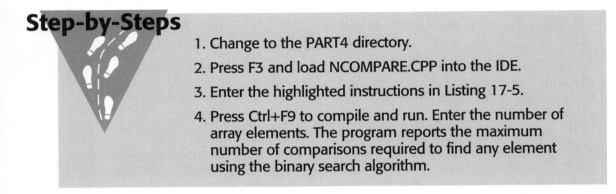

Step-by-Steps

1. Change to the PART4 directory.

2. Press F3 and load NCOMPARE.CPP into the IDE.

3. Enter the highlighted instructions in Listing 17-5.

4. Press Ctrl+F9 to compile and run. Enter the number of array elements. The program reports the maximum number of comparisons required to find any element using the binary search algorithm.

Listing 17-5: NCOMPARE.CPP

```
/* Binary Search Comparisons */

#include <stdio.h>
#include <conio.h>
#include <math.h>

char Pause()
{
  char c;
  printf("\nPress Enter to continue...");
  while ((c = getchar()) != '\n') { }
  return c;
}

int main()
{
  clrscr();

  puts("This program computes the maximum number");
  puts("of comparisons required by the binary");
  puts("search algorithm.");
```

```
// Number of elements in array
  int n;

// Prompt for number of elements
  printf("\nNumber of elements in array? ");
  scanf("%d", &n);
  fflush(stdin);

// Compute and display result
  double result = ceil(log(n) + 1);
  printf("Maximum number of comparisons == %0.0f\n",
    result);

  Pause();
  return 0;
}
```

Many published algorithms have similar formulas for computing their performance or other statistics. Take advantage of this valuable information by incorporating performance formulas into small programs such as NCOMPARE.CPP. Save your programs and use them to help select the best algorithms for the job.

The next, and last, chapter has more source code than any other. Get your fingers warmed up; then turn the page to dig into file processing algorithms. As you study the subject, you complete a mailing list management system that you can use as the basis of a more general database manager.

Chapter 18

File Processing

When computer disk drives are healthy, they are marvelous for storing databases and other information. But when disks break down, they can make grown managers wish they had never thrown away their Rolodexes and manila folders from ages past. At least a folder can't suffer a head crash, but just try to create a mailing list from a roomful of file cabinets stuffed with old clippings, coffee stains, and chewing gum, and it's easy to see why computers have taken over file management chores in businesses large and small. After all, disks are fairly reliable, and a regular backup strategy prevents most disasters.

No, there's no going back to the old days of gummy labels and hand-written lists of phone numbers, though, at times, even hard-core computer fanatics like me revert to pecking out a mailing label on the manual typewriter. Worse, I sometimes *write and address a letter by hand.* Maybe you do the same every so often when the boss isn't watching.

Don't get me wrong. I keep my little black book on disk just as you probably do. But some database files are too darn inconvenient to open, or the software doesn't do what I want, or I have to wade through thick instruction manuals just to figure out how to locate a friend's number, and so on. Certainly, there's a place in the world for high-powered products like Paradox and dBASE, but using one of those sophisticated database managers to maintain a simple list of names and addresses is like chartering a Boeing 727 to visit your next door neighbor. If the ticket price doesn't turn you off, the noise certainly won't win you any friends on the block.

What's the answer? For programmers versed in C, the solution is easy: You can write your own programs to store names, addresses, or other information in files. You don't have to be fancy. Simple I/O and text editing features do just fine for most purposes. In this chapter, you examine file-processing algorithms while building a seven-program mailing list manager. There's nothing sacred about the formats of the records as listed here. You can modify them however you like, and you can write many other programs to perform the database operations you need.

The chapter also demonstrates how to organize a nontrivial multifile program. All separate programs use projects, and much of the programming is stored in separate modules that need to be linked to host programs. Working through the *Type and Learn* examples in this chapter will give you an excellent start in organizing other multifile software projects.

Throughout the chapter, I explain algorithms for handling file-processing tasks, but the purpose of this chapter, unlike the preceding two, is not academic. Sometimes it's easier to learn algorithms by examining them in working code. So, in this chapter, the focus is on source code — lots of source code. Counting header files, the system occupies about 1800 lines. That's actually small as software goes (major programs can easily run 30,000 lines or more). Even so, the database system is large enough to give you a taste of how to write complex software using C.

Along the way, I also make suggestions for future improvements. You should consider the following programs mostly as starting places. It may be a good idea to begin a text file for jotting down possible additions that occur to you as you read through the chapter.

All finished files are stored in directory PART4\PHONEDB. The *Type and Learn* files, with sections that you must complete by typing highlighted statements, are stored in PART4. Use the IDE's *Project\Open project...* command to open any of the project files (ending in .PRJ) in either of those two directories. I also give complete instructions for compiling each separate program, but if you want to "wing it," just open each .PRJ file, compile, and go.

Files and Headers

Table 18-1 lists all files in the database system. Header files end with .H, project files with .PRJ, and source code files with .CPP. Database files created by the software end in .DB. There are no database files until you create them.

Table 18-1 ▶ Database Files and Headers

File	Description
DB.H	Structure and other common declarations
DBAPPEND.CPP	Appends records to a database file
DBAPPEND.PRJ	Project file for DBAPPEND.CPP
DBCHANGE.CPP	Edits and marks records for deletion
DBCHANGE.PRJ	Project file for DBCHANGE.CPP
DBEDIT.CPP	Functions for editing database records
DBEDIT.H	Header file for DBEDIT.CPP module
DBENTRY.CPP	Creates database files and enters new records
DBENTRY.PRJ	Project file for DBENTRY.CPP
DBGEN.CPP	Randomly generates test database files
DBGEN.PRJ	Project file for DBGEN.CPP
DBLIB.CPP	Functions used by various programs
DBLIB.H	Header file for DBLIB.H module
DBLIST.CPP	Lists records in mailing label form
DBLIST.PRJ	Project file for DBLIST.CPP
DBPURGE.CPP	Purges records marked for deletion
DBPURGE.PRJ	Project file for DBPURGE.CPP
DBRECORD.CPP	Functions for reading and writing records
DBRECORD.H	Header file for DBRECORD.CPP module
DBSHOW.CPP	Functions for displaying records
DBSHOW.H	Header file for DBSHOW.CPP
DBSORT.CPP	Sorts database records by name
DBSORT.PRJ	Project file for DBSORT.CPP

File Format and Support Functions

Any complex software system requires a variety of headers and function modules. Various pieces of the system share these external modules.

Listing 18-1 shows the system's main header file. In it are symbolic constants, enumerated constants, structures, and other declarative items that all parts of the system share.

Step-by-Steps

1. Change to the PART4 directory.

2. Press F3 and load DB.H into the IDE.

3. Enter the highlighted instructions in Listing 18-1. Press F2 to save the finished file. For more information about the file, read the text following the listing.

4. *This is not a program. Do not compile this listing.*

Listing 18-1: DB.H

```
// db.h -- Common header file
// Type and Learn C
// (c) 1994 by Tom Swan; All rights reserved

#ifndef DB_H           // Prevent multiple includes
#define DB_H           // Define symbol for possible next time

#ifndef TIME_H         // Check if time.h already included
#include <time.h>      // If not, include the header
#endif                 // End of time.h include directives

// - - - - - - - - - - - - - - - - - - - - - - - - - - - - - - - -
// String field lengths (including punctuation and null term)
// - - - - - - - - - - - - - - - - - - - - - - - - - - - - - - - -

#define FNAME_SIZE    81  // ex. C:\mydir\myfile.db
#define NAME_SIZE     41  // ex. Leon, Ponce de
#define COMPANY_SIZE  41  // ex. Fountain of Youth, Ltd.
#define ADDRESS_SIZE  51  // ex. 12 Young Road; Suite 200
#define CITY_SIZE     41  // ex. Bimini
#define STATE_SIZE    3   // ex. FI
```

```
#define ZIP_SIZE      11  // ex. 12345-6789
#define PHONE_SIZE    13  // ex. 123-555-1234
#define DATE_SIZE     11  // ex. mm/dd/yyyy

// -----------------------------------------------------------
// Error codes
// -----------------------------------------------------------

typedef enum {
  ERR_FIRST,        // Must be first!
  ERR_UNKNOWNCMD,   // Unknown command
  ERR_NOTOPEN,      // File not open
  ERR_ISOPEN,       // File is already open
  ERR_NOTFOUND,     // File not found
  ERR_EXISTS,       // File already exists
  ERR_CLOSE,        // Cannot close file
  ERR_CREATE,       // Cannot create file
  ERR_SAVE,         // Cannot save file
  ERR_OPEN,         // Cannot open file
  ERR_INSERT,       // Cannot insert file
  ERR_WRITE,        // Error writing to disk
  ERR_READ,         // Error reading from disk
  ERR_RECNUM,       // Bad record number
  ERR_EMPTY,        // File is empty
  ERR_SEEK,         // Seek operation failed
  ERR_TEMP,         // Cannot create temporary file
  ERR_LAST          // Must be last!
} ErrorCode;

// -----------------------------------------------------------
// Miscellaneous type definitions
// -----------------------------------------------------------

typedef enum {FALSE, TRUE} Boolean;
typedef unsigned char Byte;
typedef unsigned int Word;

// -----------------------------------------------------------
// Database structures
// -----------------------------------------------------------

// Dates
typedef struct tagDate {
```

```
    Byte month;       // 1-Jan, 2-Feb, ... 12-Dec
    Byte day;         // 1 ... 31
    Word year;        // dddd (full year)
} Date;

// Telephone numbers
typedef struct tagPhone {
  Word areaCode;   // ddd-000-0000
  Word exchange;   // 000-ddd-0000
  Word number;     // 000-000-dddd
} Phone;

// Database records as stored on disk
typedef struct tagRecord {

  // String fields
  char name[NAME_SIZE];          // Person's name (last first)
  char company[COMPANY_SIZE];    // Company name (if any)
  char address1[ADDRESS_SIZE];   // First address line
  char address2[ADDRESS_SIZE];   // Second address line
  char city[CITY_SIZE];          // City name
  char state[STATE_SIZE];        // State abbreviation
  char zip[ZIP_SIZE];            // Zip code

  // Telephone number fields
  Phone homePhone;               // Home telephone number
  Phone workPhone;               // Work telephone number

  // Date fields
  Date birthDate;                // Date of birth
  Date editDate;                 // Date of most recent edit

  // True or false fields
  Boolean married;               // True if married
  Boolean divorced;              // True if divorced
  Boolean single;                // True if not married or divorced
  Boolean deleted;               // True if record is inactive

} Record;

#endif  // DB_H  // End of "is db.h included?" test
```

The first two lines you typed implement a useful trick that can speed compilation times in multifile programs. The first line (be sure to type an underscore between B and H, not a period) tests whether symbol DB_H exists:

```
#ifndef DB_H
```

If the symbol does not exist, the compiler processes the rest of the file normally. But if DB_H exists, *the rest of the file is ignored.* Thus, if two or more modules include this same header, its contents are compiled only once, saving time. The second line you typed defines DB_H so that, if this same file is included again, the compiler will recognize the symbol and it won't recompile what it already has processed.

The next three lines take advantage of this timesaving mechanism, but from the other side of the coin. Carefully examine the following lines:

```
#ifndef TIME_H
#include <time.h>
#endif
```

The first line tests whether TIME_H exists. If not, the next line includes the TIME.H header. That header, provided in C's standard library, defines TIME_H. The last line ends this conditional section. As a result, TIME.H is included only if not already included by a previous module.

In general, I use these tricks only in header files, not in .CPP modules. The tricks are more valuable in headers because many modules may include the same header files, wasting time if those headers are accidentally included more than once during compilation.

You also typed a few #define directives that give sizes in bytes of various database string fields. In general, I use the word SIZE to refer to the *total* size of an object. I use LEN or LENGTH to refer to the length of a string in characters, *not* including a null terminator. For clarity, try to adopt similar naming conventions in your own code.

The header file defines several enumerated constants, such as ERR_NOTOPEN and ERR_SAVE for use by an Error function, listed later in the chapter. So that other parts of the system can know how many error messages there are, I define two constants, ERR_FIRST and ERR_LAST, which must be first and last in the ErrorCode list.

The file has several other typedef aliases that you do not have to type. Boolean is given the enumerated names FALSE and TRUE. A Byte is equivalent to an unsigned char. A Word is equivalent to an unsigned int. I find that similar aliases help me to write robust code, making perfectly clear the intent and range of variables.

Finally, in DB.H are several struct declarations that are used for the design of database records. The Date and Phone structures have obvious purposes (you don't have to type them). The Record structure defines the database file structure. All records in a database file are of this design. The structure is multilevel -- it contains substructures of the Date and Phone types. It also contains Boolean fields, such as married and deleted, which hold true or false values.

The last line of DB.H ends the conditional directive started at the beginning of the file.

Resist any urge to modify the Record structure. Compile and test the entire system before making changes. Later on, if you do add new fields, be sure to define appropriate symbolic constants for string sizes.

Next is another header, but this time, it is one that declares only function prototypes. I could have inserted these prototypes into DB.H, but I prefer to keep common declarations and prototypes in separate files as shown here.

Step-by-Steps

1. Change to the PART4 directory.

2. Press F3 and load DBLIB.H into the IDE.

3. Enter the highlighted instructions in Listing 18-2. Press F2 to save the finished file. For more information about the file, read the text following the listing.

4. *This is not a program. Do not compile this listing.*

Listing 18-2: DBLIB.H

```
// dblib.h -- Function library header file
// Type and Learn C
// (c) 1994 by Tom Swan; All rights reserved

#ifndef DBLIB_H    // Prevent multiple includes
#define DBLIB_H

#ifndef DB_H
#include "db.h"
#endif

// Clear screen and home cursor
void ClearDisplay();

// Wait for user to press Enter
char Pause();

// Display error message and pause
void Error(ErrorCode e);
```

```
// Return true if the named file exists
int FileExists(const char *path);

// Return true or false answer to Yes/No question
int Yes(const char *question);

// Return true if low <= n <= high
int InRange(long n, long low, long high);

// Insert date in time into Date struct addressed by dt
void InsDate(time_t time, Date *dt);

// Zero members in record addressed by rp
void ZeroRecord(Record *rp);

// Convert string to Phone structure
void StrToPhone(char *s, Phone *ph);

// Convert string to Date structure
void StrToDate(char *s, Date *dt);

// Convert string to Boolean (null == False)
void StrToBool(char *s, Boolean *b);

// Prompt for and get file name into buffer fs
// Input buffer (fs) must be FNAME_SIZE bytes long
// Automatically append ext(ension) onto name unless
// one is entered.
void GetFileName(const char *prompt,
  const char *ext, char *fs);

// Welcome user to the program
void Welcome();

#endif // DBLIB_H
```

The DBLIB.H header file begins with the same conditional compilation trick used in DB.H. If symbol DBLIB_H exists, the file is skipped, thus speeding compilation if the same header is included by more than one module.

File DB.H is included only if not already included by another module. The DB.H header file must be included by DBLIB.H because several functions use some of the data types declared in DB.H.

Beginning programmers often wonder whether a header file should include another header, or if only .CPP modules should have #include directives. As a rule, I include headers in *all* files that use something in that header. In this case, DBLIB.H prototypes the functions that use declarations in DB.H — the Date struct in function StrToDate, for example. So DBLIB.H should include DB.H. Because I use conditional compilation to prevent the same header from being compiled more than once, I can freely include all necessary headers in all headers and modules without significantly increasing compilation times.

For practice in creating function prototypes, you typed three prototypes for functions ClearDisplay, Pause, and Error. The other prototypes use a similar format. Remember always to end function prototypes with semicolons. Except for that difference, a prototype is identical to a real function's header.

Other modules may include DBLIB.H to use the functions prototyped in the header. Unlike standard library functions, however, you must also link the resulting code to the DBLIB module. That module contains the completed functions, listed here in Listing 18-3, DBLIB.CPP. Every function prototype in a header *must* have a corresponding implementation. Naturally, it's easiest to name the header and module the same — DBLIB.H and DBLIB.CPP, for instance. This is why I keep other declarations separate in DB.H. Just from their names, I know that DBLIB.H and DBLIB.CPP are related, but that DB.H contains declarations of a more general nature.

Step-by-Steps

1. Change to the PART4 directory.

2. Press F3 and load DBLIB.CPP into the IDE.

3. Enter the highlighted instructions in Listing 18-3. Press F2 to save the modified file. For more information about DBLIB.CPP, see the text following the listing.

4. *This is not a complete program. Do not attempt to compile and run it. To use DBLIB's functions, you must link the module to a host program, as explained later in this chapter.*

Listing 18-3: DBLIB.CPP

```cpp
// dblib.cpp -- Library of common functions and variables
// Type and Learn C
// (c) 1994 by Tom Swan; All rights reserved

#include <stdio.h>
#include <stdlib.h>
#include <string.h>
#include <conio.h>    // Non-standard header
#include <ctype.h>

#include "dblib.h"
#include "db.h"

// Global variables

char *errorString[] = {
/* ERR_FIRST       */ "No error",
/* ERR_UNKNOWNCMD */ "Unknown command",
/* ERR_NOTOPEN    */ "File not open",
/* ERR_ISOPEN     */ "File already open",
/* ERR_NOTFOUND   */ "File not found",
/* ERR_EXISTS     */ "File already exists",
/* ERR_CLOSE      */ "Cannot close file",
/* ERR_CREATE     */ "Cannot create file",
/* ERR_SAVE       */ "Cannot save file",
/* ERR_OPEN       */ "Cannot open file",
/* ERR_INSERT     */ "Cannot insert file",
/* ERR_WRITE      */ "Error writing to disk",
/* ERR_READ       */ "Error reading from disk",
/* ERR_RECNUM     */ "Bad record number",
/* ERR_EMPTY      */ "File is empty",
/* ERR_SEEK       */ "Seek operation failed",
/* ERR_TEMP       */ "Cannot create temporary file",
/* ERR_LAST       */ "No error"
};

// NOTE: The following function contains a call to a non-ANSI
// standard subroutine, clrscr, defined in conio.h. Replace
// this function with the equivalent clear screen statement
// that works on your system. The function should leave the
// display clear and position the cursor at upper left.
```

```c
// Clear display and home cursor
void ClearDisplay()
{
  clrscr();
}

// Wait for user to press Enter
char Pause()
{
  char c;
  printf("\nPress Enter to continue...");
  while ((c = getchar()) != '\n') { }
  return c;
}

// Return pointer to error message string
char *GetErrorMessage(ErrorCode e)
{
  if (ERR_FIRST <= e && e <= ERR_LAST)
    return errorString[e];
  else
    return NULL;
}

// Display error message and pause
void Error(ErrorCode e)
{
  char *s = GetErrorMessage(e);
  if (!s)
    s = "Unknown error code";
  fprintf(stderr, "\nError %d: %s\n", e, s);
  if (errno != 0) {
    perror("Reason ");
    errno = 0;
  }
  Pause();
}

// Return true if the named file exists
int FileExists(const char *path)
{
  FILE *f = fopen(path, "rb");
  int result = (f != NULL);
  if (f)
    fclose(f);
  return result;
}
```

```
// Return true or false answer to Yes/No question
int Yes(const char *question)
{
  int c;
  for (;;) {
    printf("%s ", question);
    c = toupper(getchar());
    fflush(stdin);
    if (c == 'Y')
      return TRUE;
    else if (c == 'N')
      return FALSE;
  }
}

// Return true if low <= n <= high
int InRange(long n, long low, long high)
{
  return (low <= n && n <= high);
}

// Insert date in time into Date struct addressed by dt
void InsDate(time_t time, Date *dt)
{
  struct tm *t = localtime(&time);
  dt->day = t->tm_mday;
  dt->month = t->tm_mon + 1;
  dt->year = t->tm_year + 1900;
}

// Zero members in record addressed by rp
void ZeroRecord(Record *rp)
{
  memset(rp, 0, sizeof(Record));
  InsDate(time(NULL), &rp->birthDate);
  InsDate(time(NULL), &rp->editDate);
}

// Convert string to Phone structure
void StrToPhone(char *s, Phone *ph)
{
  memset(ph, 0, sizeof(Phone));
  sscanf(s, "%d-%d-%d",
    &ph->areaCode, &ph->exchange, &ph->number);
}
```

```c
// Convert string to Date structure
void StrToDate(char *s, Date *dt)
{
  memset(dt, 0, sizeof(Date));
  sscanf(s, "%d/%d/%d",
    &dt->month, &dt->day, &dt->year);
  if (dt->year < 100)
    dt->year += 1900;
}


// Convert string to Boolean (null == False)
void StrToBool(char *s, Boolean *b)
{
  char c;

  if (strlen(s) == 0)
    *b = FALSE;
  else {
    c = tolower(s[0]);
    if (c == 'y' || c == 't')  // e.g. Yes or True
      *b = TRUE;
    else
      *b = FALSE;
  }
}


// Prompt for and get filename into buffer fs
// Input buffer (fs) must be FNAME_SIZE bytes long
// Automatically append ext(ension) onto name unless
// one is entered.
void GetFileName(const char *prompt,
  const char *ext, char *fs)
{
  char *cp;  // Miscellaneous char pointer
  printf("\n%s ", prompt);
  fgets(fs, FNAME_SIZE, stdin);
  fflush(stdin);
  cp = strchr(fs, '\n');
  if (cp)
    *cp = '\0';  // Replace newline with null
  if (strlen(fs) == 0)
    return;  // No name entered
  cp = strchr(fs, '.');  // Look for extension separator
  if (!cp && strlen(fs) + strlen(ext) < FNAME_SIZE)
    strcat(fs, ext);  // Add extension if necessary
}
```

```
// Welcome user to the program
void Welcome()
{
  ClearDisplay();
  puts("Phone and Mailing List Database");
  puts("Type and Learn C");
  puts("(c) 1994 by Tom Swan. All rights reserved.");
  Pause();
}
```

Like most modules and programs, DBLIB.CPP begins with several #include directives that you typed for practice. As usual, standard library headers are angle bracketed like this: <stdio.h>. Those in the current directory are quoted like this: "dblib.h".

 The DBLIB module uses one nonstandard header, CONIO.H, provided only with Borland compilers. To compile the program with another ANSI C compiler, delete that #include directive or change it to one that provides a function for clearing the screen and homing the cursor (positioning it at upper left). This is the *only* nonstandard header used, and it is included *only* at this position. To keep your own programs as portable as possible, try to minimize the number of nonstandard headers and functions or, at the least, banish them to a single module as I've done here.

The DBLIB module also defines global variables. Generally, I try to use as few globals as possible, and I never define them in a header. Define global variables, such as the error strings here, only in a code-producing module.

For practice, you also typed the three functions that you prototyped earlier in the DBLIB.H header. Function ClearDisplay calls the clrscr function in the nonstandard CONIO.H header. *This is the only non-ANSI function call in the system.* I could have used clrscr directly throughout the program, but by inserting it into my own ClearDisplay function, I can more easily port the code to another compiler simply by rewriting this one common subroutine.

The Pause function, which you have seen throughout this book's examples, is next. The third, and last, function you typed displays an Error message that uses an ErrorCode enumerated constant declared in DB.H. The function calls another function, GetErrorMessage, to obtain the address of the global error-message string associated with the constant held in parameter e. Look just above Error for the source code to GetErrorMessage. That function does not have a corresponding prototype in DBLIB.H because it is unlikely that other modules need to call it. This demonstrates that a module can have both public (prototyped) functions and others that are for the module's private use.

You also typed a function, FileExists, that returns true if a specified file exists on disk. The function calls fopen and, if successful, returns true. The file is closed before the function ends. Such functions as FileExists are useful in any program that accesses disk files.

A bit farther down, function ZeroRecord initializes an object of the Record structure declared in DB.H. All database programs need a similar function to erase records to a clean slate. Calling memset to set the entire object to zero bytes effectively inserts a null into the first character of all string fields. Other fields, however, such as the two Date objects here, may require additional initialization.

The module has many other functions, some of a general nature and others particular to this program. In hindsight, I might have separated these functions — placing such functions as Yes and InRange, for example, in a common module. Other functions, such as StrToDate and StrToBool, are specific to this program, and they probably would require changes in another setting. Experience teaches, however, that creating truly general function libraries is extremely difficult, so storing general and not-so-general functions together isn't a serious mistake.

Highly specific functions, however, that are obviously for this software project are best placed in their own modules. The first of these, like all modules in the system, prototypes its functions in a header file, as shown in Listing 18-4, DBEDIT.H. You've had enough practice typing function prototypes, so there's nothing to complete this time.

Listing 18-4: DBEDIT.H

```
// dbedit.h -- Edit record module header file
// Type and Learn C
// (c) 1994 by Tom Swan; All rights reserved

#ifndef DBEDIT_H   // Prevent multiple includes
#define DBEDIT_H

// Prompt for and return string entry
int GetString(const char *label, char *s, int size);

// Prompt for and return phone number
void GetPhone(const char *label, Phone *ph);

// Prompt for and return date
void GetDate(const char *label, Date *dt);

// Prompt for and return Boolean
void GetBool(const char *label, Boolean *b);

// Edit members in record addressed by rp
// Returns TRUE if record is to be saved
void EditRecord(Record *rp);

#endif  // DBEDIT_H
```

To use the functions prototyped in DBEDIT.H, another module simply includes that header. You also have to link the resulting code to the module that contains the function implementations. That code is listed in Listing 18-5, DBEDIT.CPP. As you can see, there's a pattern here. DB.H declares general items. Other headers declare function prototypes, implemented in separate modules. In this case, the DBEDIT module provides functions for editing records. As mentioned, the database system uses only simple I/O. You may want to consider improving the program's interface by writing an interactive string editor or by incorporating one purchased from a tools vendor.

Step-by-Steps

1. Change to the PART4 directory.

2. Press F3 and load DBEDIT.CPP into the IDE.

3. Enter the highlighted instructions in Listing 18-5. Press F2 to save the modified file. For more information about DBEDIT.CPP, see the text following the listing.

4. *This is not a complete program. Do not attempt to compile and run it. To use DBEDIT's functions, you must link the module to a host program as explained later in this chapter.*

Listing 18-5: DBEDIT.CPP

```
// dbedit.cpp -- Edit record module
// Type and Learn C
// (c) 1994 by Tom Swan; All rights reserved

#include <stdio.h>
#include <string.h>

#ifndef DBLIB_H
#include "dblib.h"
#endif

#ifndef DB_H
#include "db.h"
#endif

// Prompt for and return string entry
// No change if user presses Enter
// String erased if user types Space and presses Enter
// Return TRUE if string is edited or erased
// Return FALSE if string is not changed
```

```c
int GetString(const char *label, char *s, int size)
{
  char buffer[256];   // Input buffer
  char *cp;           // Pointer to new line if entered

  memset(buffer, 0, sizeof(buffer));
  printf("%s ", label);
  fgets(buffer, size, stdin);
  fflush(stdin);
  cp = strchr(buffer, '\n');
  if (cp)
    *cp = '\0';   // Delete any new line from entry
  if (strlen(buffer) > 0 && buffer[0] != ' ') {
    strncpy(s, buffer, size - 1);
    return TRUE;   // String edited
  } else if (buffer[0] == ' ') {
    memset(s, 0, size);
    return TRUE;   // String erased
  } else
    return FALSE;  // String not changed
}

// Prompt for and return phone number
void GetPhone(const char *label, Phone *ph)
{
  char buffer[PHONE_SIZE];
  memset(buffer, 0, sizeof(buffer));
  if (GetString(label, buffer, PHONE_SIZE))
    StrToPhone(buffer, ph);
}

// Prompt for and return date
void GetDate(const char *label, Date *dt)
{
  char buffer[DATE_SIZE];
  memset(buffer, 0, sizeof(buffer));
  if (GetString(label, buffer, DATE_SIZE))
    StrToDate(buffer, dt);
}
```

```
// Prompt for and return Boolean
void GetBool(const char *label, Boolean *b)
{
  char buffer[2];
  memset(buffer, 0, sizeof(buffer));
  if (GetString(label, buffer, 2))
    StrToBool(buffer, b);
}

// Edit members in record addressed by rp
void EditRecord(Record *rp)
{
  puts("");
  GetString("Name .........?", rp->name, NAME_SIZE);
  GetString("Company ......?", rp->company, COMPANY_SIZE);
  GetString("Address 1 ....?", rp->address1, ADDRESS_SIZE);
  GetString("Address 2 ....?", rp->address2, ADDRESS_SIZE);
  GetString("City .........?", rp->city, CITY_SIZE);
  GetString("State ........?", rp->state, STATE_SIZE);
  GetString("Zip ..........?", rp->zip, ZIP_SIZE);
  GetPhone ("Home phone ...?", &rp->homePhone);
  GetPhone ("Work phone ...?", &rp->workPhone);
  GetDate  ("Birth date ...?", &rp->birthDate);
  InsDate  (time(NULL), &rp->editDate);
  GetBool  ("Married ......?", &rp->married);
  GetBool  ("Divorced .....?", &rp->divorced);
  rp->single = (Boolean)(!rp->married);
  rp->deleted = FALSE;
}
```

When designing an editing module, I like to write individual functions for each type of information to be edited. There should be separate functions for entering phone numbers, dates, and so on. The trick in writing these functions is to choose a design that's most likely to be generally useful. In this case, I decided to use a general GetString function that works according to the following rules:

▶ The input string is required to be initialized. New entries must pass the address of a null string buffer of an appropriate size to GetString.

▶ While editing, press Enter to make no changes to a string.

▶ To erase a string, type a single space and press Enter. GetString deletes the lone space.

▶ To edit a string's contents, retype it. (A more interactive string editor is beyond this chapter's scope but would be more friendly than requiring new strings to be reentered. For simple editing jobs, however, this method is easy to implement and doesn't pose as great a hardship as you may imagine. After all, most names and addresses, once entered, do not change.)

After writing the individual editing functions, wrap them up into one grand editor such as the `EditRecord` function here. The function requires the address of an initialized `Record` object. Not all fields are directly available for editing. The `single` member, for example, is set to `TRUE` or `FALSE`, depending on the value of the `married` field. This is an example of a *calculated field* (though a simple one). The `deleted` field is also preset to false. If true, the record is only marked for deletion — it is still stored in the database (more on this later).

The flip side of editing is, of course, displaying information on-screen. Again, various functions for displaying record fields are best implemented in a separate module for other parts of the system to share. Listing 18-6, DBSHOW.H, prototypes the module's functions. To call the functions, other modules include the DBSHOW.H header, and the resulting code is linked to the module's implementation in Listing 18-7, DBSHOW.CPP. There's nothing to type in either of these modules, so you can give your fingers a rest.

Listing 18-6: DBSHOW.H

```
// dbshow.h -- Show record module header file
// Type and Learn C
// (c) 1994 by Tom Swan; All rights reserved

#ifndef DBSHOW_H    // Prevent multiple includes
#define DBSHOW_H

#ifndef DB_H
#include "db.h"
#endif

// Display phone number and start new line
void ShowPhone(Phone *ph);

// Display date and start new line
void ShowDate(Date *dt);

// Display Boolean and start new line
void ShowBool(Boolean tf);

// Display a record's members
void ShowRecord(Record *rp);

#endif  // DBSHOW_H
```

Listing 18-7: DBSHOW.CPP

```cpp
// dbshow.h -- Show record module
// Type and Learn C
// (c) 1994 by Tom Swan; All rights reserved

#include <stdio.h>
#include "dbshow.h"

// Display phone number and start new line
void ShowPhone(Phone *ph)
{
  if (ph->areaCode == 0)
    puts("(none)");
  else
    printf("%03d-%03d-%04d\n",
      ph->areaCode, ph->exchange, ph->number);
}

// Display date and start new line
void ShowDate(Date *dt)
{
  printf("%02d/%02d/%04d\n",
    dt->month, dt->day, dt->year);
}

// Display Boolean and start new line
void ShowBool(Boolean tf)
{
  if (tf)
    puts("Yes");
  else
    puts("No");
}

// Display a record's members
void ShowRecord(Record *rp)
{
  puts("\nCurrent record:");
  printf("Name .........: %s\n", rp->name);
  printf("Company ......: %s\n", rp->company);
  printf("Address 1 ....: %s\n", rp->address1);
  printf("Address 2 ....: %s\n", rp->address2);
  printf("City .........: %s\n", rp->city);
```

```
    printf("State ........: %s\n", rp->state);
    printf("Zip ..........: %s\n", rp->zip);
    printf("Home phone ...: "); ShowPhone(&rp->homePhone);
    printf("Work phone ...: "); ShowPhone(&rp->workPhone);
    printf("Birth date ...: "); ShowDate(&rp->birthDate);
    printf("Last edited ..: "); ShowDate(&rp->editDate);
    printf("Married ......: "); ShowBool(rp->married);
    printf("Divorced .....: "); ShowBool(rp->divorced);
    printf("Single .......: "); ShowBool(rp->single);
    printf("DELETED ......: "); ShowBool(rp->deleted);
}
```

The programming in the DBSHOW module performs no file-processing operations, and you should be able to understand the functions by reading the source and comments. It's time to move on to the next and final separate module in the database system.

Any database needs the capability of reading and writing records. In this case, Listing 18-8, DBRECORD.H, prototypes three functions that count the number of records in a file and that read and write individual records. You don't have to type any lines in the header. The header file's functions are implemented in Listing 18-9, DBRECORD.CPP.

Listing 18-8: DBRECORD.H

```
// dbrecord.h -- Record I/O module header file
// Type and Learn C
// (c) 1994 by Tom Swan; All rights reserved

#ifndef DBRECORD_H    // Prevent multiple includes
#define DBRECORD_H

#ifndef DB_H
#include DB_H
#endif

// Return number of records in database file f
long CountRecords(FILE *f);

// Seek and read record rn into *rp
int ReadRecord(FILE *f, long rn, Record *rp);

// Seek and write record rn from *rp
int WriteRecord(FILE *f, long rn, Record *rp);

#endif // DBRECORD_H
```

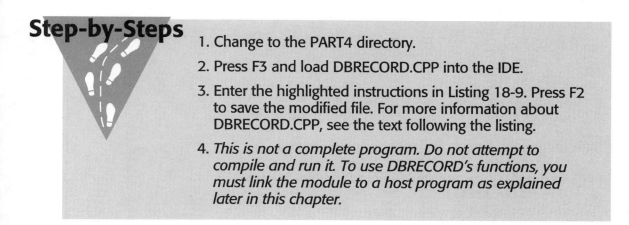

Step-by-Steps

1. Change to the PART4 directory.

2. Press F3 and load DBRECORD.CPP into the IDE.

3. Enter the highlighted instructions in Listing 18-9. Press F2 to save the modified file. For more information about DBRECORD.CPP, see the text following the listing.

4. *This is not a complete program. Do not attempt to compile and run it. To use DBRECORD's functions, you must link the module to a host program as explained later in this chapter.*

Listing 18-9: DBRECORD.CPP

```cpp
// dbrecord.cpp -- Record I/O module
// Type and Learn C
// (c) 1994 by Tom Swan; All rights reserved

#include <stdio.h>

#ifndef DBLIB_H
#include "dblib.h"
#endif

#ifndef DB_H
#include "db.h"
#endif

// Return number of records in database file f
long CountRecords(FILE *f)
{
  fseek(f, 0, SEEK_END);
  long n = ftell(f);
  rewind(f);
  return n / sizeof(Record);
//
// Alternate method: slow but bulletproof
/*
  long n = 0;
  Record rec;
  rewind(f);
  while (!feof(f)) {
    if (fread(&rec, sizeof(Record), 1, f) == 1)
      n++;
  }
```

```
      rewind(f);
      return n;
*/
}


// Seek and read record rn into *rp
// Handle all errors
// Return True on success
int ReadRecord(FILE *f, long rn, Record *rp)
{
  if (fseek(f, rn * sizeof(Record), SEEK_SET) != 0) {
    Error(ERR_SEEK);
    return FALSE;
  }
  if (fread(rp, sizeof(Record), 1, f) != 1) {
    Error(ERR_READ);
    return FALSE;
  }
  return TRUE;
}


// Seek and write record rn from *rp
// Handle all errors
// Return True on success
int WriteRecord(FILE *f, long rn, Record *rp)
{
  if (fseek(f, rn * sizeof(Record), SEEK_SET) != 0) {
    Error(ERR_SEEK);
    return FALSE;
  }
  if (fwrite(rp, sizeof(Record), 1, f) != 1) {
    Error(ERR_WRITE);
    return FALSE;
  }
  return TRUE;
}
```

Take a look at the last two functions first. ReadRecord requires three arguments: a FILE pointer f (the file must be open), a record number rn, and a pointer rp to a Record structure. The function returns true (nonzero) if it can successfully read the requested record; otherwise, it returns false. A true result indicates that the Record object holds the record from the file. A false result means that the Record is undefined.

Reading a database record at random requires two simple steps. First, *seek* to the record's position in the file, which means to position the file's internal read/write pointer where the next I/O operation will take place. After seeking, read the record into the object addressed by `rp`.

Two functions play key roles in the process. Function `fseek` positions the file's internal pointer. Function `fread` reads the record's bytes from disk. Reading a record leaves the internal pointer at the next record or at the end of the file.

Notice that each of those two operations is followed by a test for any errors. Function `Error` (see DBLIB.CPP) displays an error message, and the function returns false. Only if both functions succeed does `ReadRecord` return true.

Function `WriteRecord` is nearly the same as `ReadRecord`. First, it seeks to the record's position. Then it calls `fwrite` to write a record's bytes to disk. Again, careful checks for all possible error conditions are included.

It is often difficult to decide whether a function should handle an error conditon (by calling `Error`, for example, to display a message), or whether it should report an error condition back to its caller and let *that* code deal with the problem. I mix the methods here: handling the error where it occurs and returning an indication about the success or failure of the function. The caller in this case is not expected to display an error message if, for instance, `WriteRecord` returns false. Error handling code is frequently messy, but don't leave it out!

`ReadRecord` and `WriteRecord` are examples of random-access functions — those that read and write records at any place in a file. For these operations to work, all records must be of the same size. Notice how `sizeof(Record)` is used to compute that size. Any change to the `Record` structure in DB.H is automatically accounted for when you recompile the functions.

A third function, `CountRecords`, near the beginning of the DBRECORD module is partially completed on disk. The function's four statements, which you typed, compute the number of records in a file. First, `fseek` positions the internal read/write pointer to the end of the file. Function `ftell` is then called to find that position's value, assigned to a `long` integer n. After that, `rewind` resets the file to its beginning. Finally, the number of records is returned as the file's byte position divided by the size of one `Record` object.

Functions that arbitrarily change the file read/write position should reset the file. Follow the admonishment posted in many video stores: "Be kind; Rewind."

The statements listed for `CountRecords` should work for most ANSI C compilers. Some operating systems, however, define the end of a file differently, causing the value returned by `ftell` to differ. If the listed code doesn't work correctly, you can use the alternate statements listed as a comment. This programming counts a file's records the "hard way" by reading each record and incrementing a variable in a loop. The technique is foolproof but slow.

Leave your alternate programming, tests, and other unused statements in your files, converted to comments. That way, you can implement the statements simply by modifying a few lines.

File Fundamentals

That finishes the database's separate modules and headers. Next up are seven programs that you can use to create, edit, purge, sort, and perform other operations on database files.

Each program has an accompanying project file ending in .PRJ. Of course, you can use these files only with Borland's IDE, but other compilers offer similar methods for creating programs that use multiple modules. The project files automatically link the preceding separate modules to host programs, creating finished code files that you can run.

Finished project files are stored in the PART4\PHONEDB directory. You must re-create the project files for the *Type and Learn* sample listings that you complete in the PART4 directory. If you don't want to re-create the projects, however, you can copy their .PRJ files from PART4\PHONEDB.

The first project creates the DBENTRY program, which you can use to create new database files, to open existing files, and to enter new records. The project file is simply a list of filenames (see Listing 18-10). The project listings, however, do not show the real contents of a .PRJ file, which stores additional IDE settings in a binary form. *Never use a text editor to edit a .PRJ file — you will destroy it!* Instead, use the printed listings to create project files by following these steps:

1. Use the *File\Change dir...* command to change to the PART4 directory.

2. Close any open project by selecting the *Project\Close project* command. Always close a project before opening a new one.

3. Close all open files by pressing Alt+F3 repeatedly. (Closing the project closes all associated files, so this step may be unneccessary.)

4. Select the *Project\Open project...* command. You see a list of current .PRJ files (if any) in the current directory.

5. Type the name of the project you want to create, in this case, DBENTRY.PRJ. If the project exists, this step opens it; if not, the IDE creates a new project file.

6. Use the Project\Add item... command to enter or select each of the filenames listed in this chapter for each project. The order of the names is not important.

7. Compile the program by pressing F9 or compile and run by pressing Ctrl+F9. This step also compiles all separate modules used by the program, unless the modules are already compiled. Projects are smart. They help the IDE to compile only the minimum number of modules required to keep a program up to date.

You can also use projects to open, inspect, and edit source files used by a program. To open a module, for example, select its name from the *Project* window. (You may have to press F6 a few times to bring the window to the front.) You can also press F3 to open files, even those that don't belong to the project. For instance, I keep a file TODO.TXT in my directories listing jobs that I need to finish.

Remember to close a project after you are done using it. The Project|Close project command asks you whether you want to save any files you forgot to save manually. It also creates and saves the .PRJ file. *Always close your projects.*

In addition to the .PRJ file, the IDE stores the names, positions, and sizes of open windows, plus related information in a .DSK (desktop) file named the same as the project. The DBENTRY.DSK file, for example, stores the desktop for the DBENTRY.PRJ project. When you reopen a project, all open windows, cursor positions, and so on are restored automatically.

To save space, you can delete all .DSK files from the PART4 and PART4\PHONEDB directories. When you reopen a project that has no .DSK file, only the project window is shown. You can then open other files in the project. Deleting a .DSK file is a good way to start with a clean desktop — it's easier than closing multiple windows in the IDE. Also, in the unlikely event that you are unable to open a project file, first try deleting that project's .DSK file (if any). This may allow the project to be opened successfully. If not, you can always re-create the .PRJ file by using the filenames listed in this chapter.

Compiling a project locates any typing errors you may have made when completing the separate modules listed earlier in this chapter. If you receive errors, use the printed listings as guides to finding your mistakes. Correct the faulty lines and press F2 to save the file. The IDE automatically opens files as needed to help you find typing errors. You can leave these files open or close them as you wish. (Multiple projects can have the same files opened without harm.) If you still can't get a project to compile, you can use the finished files in PART4\PHONEDB for reference or just copy them to the PART4 directory.

Listing 18-10, DBENTRY.PRJ, lists the files in the DBENTRY project.

Listing 18-10: DBENTRY.PRJ

```
dbentry.cpp
dbshow.cpp
dbedit.cpp
dblib.cpp
```

Every project must have one, and only one, main module with the `main` function. The main module for the DBENTRY project is shown in Listing 18-11, DBENTRY.CPP.

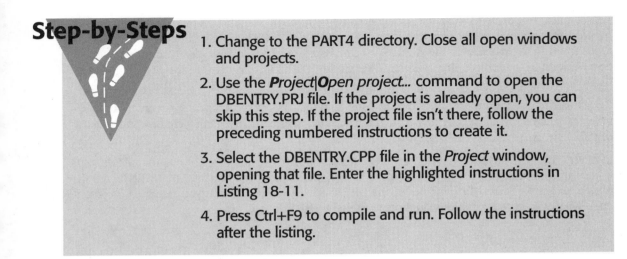

Step-by-Steps

1. Change to the PART4 directory. Close all open windows and projects.

2. Use the *Project|Open project...* command to open the DBENTRY.PRJ file. If the project is already open, you can skip this step. If the project file isn't there, follow the preceding numbered instructions to create it.

3. Select the DBENTRY.CPP file in the *Project* window, opening that file. Enter the highlighted instructions in Listing 18-11.

4. Press Ctrl+F9 to compile and run. Follow the instructions after the listing.

Listing 18-11: DBENTRY.CPP

```
// dbentry.cpp -- Enter new database records
// Type and Learn C
// (c) 1994 by Tom Swan; All rights reserved

#include <stdio.h>
#include <string.h>
#include <ctype.h>

#include "db.h"
#include "dblib.h"
#include "dbshow.h"
#include "dbedit.h"

// Global variables

FILE *dbf;
Boolean fileOpen = FALSE;
char fname[FNAME_SIZE];
```

```
// Display menu
void ShowMenu()
{
  char *prompt;    // Pointer to menu prompt string
  if (fileOpen)
    prompt = "DBENTRY> C.lose H.elp I.nsert S.ave Q.uit: ";
  else
    prompt = "DBENTRY> H.elp N.ew O.pen Q.uit: ";
  ClearDisplay();   // Clear display
  printf(prompt);  // Display prompt
}

// Return menu selection character
int GetMenuSelection()
{
  ShowMenu();            // Display command menu
  fflush(stdin);         // Flush input in case of I/O error
  int c = toupper(getchar());  // Get response
  fflush(stdin);         // Cancel any unread end-of-line chars
  return c;
}

// Close open database file
//
// 1. Close file
// 2. Report any errors
// 3. Set fileOpen flag false
//
void CloseFile()
{
  if (!fileOpen) {
    Error(ERR_NOTOPEN);
    return;
  }
  printf("\nClosing %s\n", fname);
  int result = fclose(dbf);
  if (result != 0) {
    Error(ERR_CLOSE);
    return;
  } else {
    fileOpen = FALSE;
    puts("\nFile closed");
  }
  Pause();
}
```

```
// Display instructions
void Help()
{
  puts("\nHelp with commands");
  puts("------------------");
  puts("C.lose  --Close an open database file");
  puts("H.elp   --Display this help text");
  puts("I.nsert --Insert a new record");
  puts("N.ew    --Create a new database file");
  puts("O.pen   --Open an existing database file");
  puts("Q.uit   --End program");
  puts("S.ave   --Flush any in-memory data to disk");
  puts("");
  puts("Close, Insert, and Save commands are available");
  puts("only when a file is open. New and Open commands");
  puts("are available only when a file is not open. Help");
  puts("and Quit commands are always available.");
  Pause();
}


// Insert new record into database file
//
// 1. Prompt for new record information
// 2. Verify and request permission to save
// 3. If permission given, append record to database file
// 4. Report any errors writing to disk
//
void InsertRecord()
{
  Record rec;
  size_t result;

  if (!fileOpen) {
    Error(ERR_NOTOPEN);
    return;
  }
```

```
    ZeroRecord(&rec);
    EditRecord(&rec);
    puts("\nConfirming entry...\n");
    ShowRecord(&rec);
    puts("");
    if (Yes("Save this record?")) {
      result = fwrite(&rec, sizeof(Record), 1, dbf);
      if (result != 1) {
        Error(ERR_INSERT);
        return;
      }
      puts("\nRecord inserted");
    } else
      puts("\nRecord not inserted");
    Pause();
}


// Start new database file
//
// 1. Prompt for filename
// 2. Add .DB extension if none supplied
// 3. Reject command if file already exists
// 4. Create empty file on disk
// 5. Report any errors
// 6. Leave file open and set fileOpen flag true
//
void NewFile()
{
  if (fileOpen) {
    Error(ERR_ISOPEN);
    return;
  }
  GetFileName("Create what file?", ".db", fname);
  if (strlen(fname) == 0)
    return;
  printf("\nCreating %s\n", fname);
  if (FileExists(fname)) {
    Error(ERR_EXISTS);
    return;
  }
```

```
  dbf = fopen(fname, "w+b");
  if (!dbf) {
    Error(ERR_CREATE);
    return;
  }
  fileOpen = TRUE;
  puts("\nFile created");
  Pause();
}


// Open existing database file
//
// 1. Prompt for filename
// 2. Add .DB extension if none supplied
// 3. Reject command if file does not exist
// 4. Open file for reading and writing
// 5. Report any errors
// 6. Leave file open and set fileOpen flag true
//
void OpenFile()
{
  if (fileOpen) {
    Error(ERR_ISOPEN);
    return;
  }
  GetFileName("Open what file?", ".db", fname);
  if (strlen(fname) == 0)
    return;
  printf("\nOpening %s\n", fname);
  if (!FileExists(fname)) {
    Error(ERR_NOTFOUND);
    return;
  }
  dbf = fopen(fname, "a+b");
  if (!dbf) {
    Error(ERR_OPEN);
    return;
  }
  fileOpen = TRUE;
  puts("\nFile opened");
  Pause();
}
```

```c
// Save changes to open database file
//
// 1. Flush file to disk
// 2. Report any errors
//
void SaveFile()
{
  if (!fileOpen) {
    Error(ERR_NOTOPEN);
    return;
  }
  printf("\nSaving %s\n", fname);
  int result = fflush(dbf);
  if (result != 0) {
    Error(ERR_SAVE);
    return;
  }
  puts("\nFile saved");
  Pause();
}

int main()
{
  Boolean done = FALSE;
  int selection;

  Welcome();

  while (!done) {

    selection = GetMenuSelection();

    switch (selection) {

      case 'C':
        CloseFile();
        break;

      case 'H':
        Help();
        break;

      case 'I':
        InsertRecord();
        break;
```

```
        case 'N':
          NewFile();
          break;

        case 'O':
          OpenFile();
          break;

        case 'Q':
          done = TRUE;
          break;

        case 'S':
          SaveFile();
          break;

        default:
          Error(ERR_UNKNOWNCMD);
          break;

      }

    }
    return 0;
  }
```

DBENTRY uses a simple interface that displays a menu at the top of the screen. (If the menu doesn't appear on top, check that the function `ClearScreen` in DBLIB.CPP erases the display and positions the cursor in the upper-left corner, called the *home* position.) The menu looks like this:

```
DBENTRY> H.elp N.ew O.pen Q.uit:
```

Type the first letter of a command and press Enter. Press H+Enter, for example, to display instructions. Commands are displayed with the letter you should type followed by a period.

Use the *N.ew* command to create a new database file. You are not permitted to overwrite an existing file (try to do this to see the resulting error message). To re-create a file, first use an operating system command or utility to delete the file. A new file is empty, and its directory size is zero. Use the *O.pen* command to open an existing file. If the file doesn't exist, the program displays an error. Use *Q.uit* to end the program and return to the IDE.

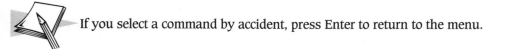 If you select a command by accident, press Enter to return to the menu.

Creating a new file, or opening an existing one, changes the program's menu to:

```
DBENTRY> C.lose H.elp I.nsert S.ave Q.uit:
```

Use *C.lose* to close the current file. Use *S.ave* to flush any in-memory data to disk. Records are written directly to the file, so you can always close it safely. If you want to preserve a file before entering new records, make a backup copy before running DBENTRY.

The *I.nsert* command presents a series of prompts for entering a new record. Here's a sample of the display copied after I entered a new record:

```
Name .........? Swan, Tom
Company ......? IDG Books
Address 1 ....? 155 Bovet Road
Address 2 ....? Suite 310
City .........? San Mateo
State ........? CA
Zip ..........? 94402
Home phone ...? 691-555-1212
Work phone ...? 785-555-1212
Birth date ...? 4/3/50
Married ......? y
Divorced .....? n
```

The name and address are real; the phone numbers are fictitious to protect innocent operators (and my sanity). After the last field is entered, the program displays "Confirming entry..." and shows the record in its final form, including all fields:

```
Current record:
Name .........: Swan, Tom
Company ......: IDG Books
Address 1 ....: 155 Bovet Road
Address 2 ....: Suite 310
City .........: San Mateo
State ........: CA
Zip ..........: 94402
Home phone ...: 691-555-1212
Work phone ...: 785-555-1212
Birth date ...: 04/03/1950
Last edited ..: 12/27/1993
Married ......: Yes
Divorced .....: No
Single .......: No
DELETED ......: No
```

Notice that some fields are entered automatically — for example, the *Last edited* entry, which is set to today's date. Date fields are also formatted differently than as originally entered. At this point, the program asks "Save this record?" Answer Yes (press Y+Enter) to write it to disk; answer No (press N+Enter) to throw away the new record. All records are saved by appending them to the end of the file.

Text Files

The second program in the database system also appends new records to a database file, but it uses a *batch-file technique.* This is often faster than entering records one by one using DBENTRY. It's amazing that many sophisticated database systems lack batch-file entry commands — one reason I prefer to write my own software.

The DBAPPEND program demonstrates text-file programming techniques. The program reads a text file containing new records. It converts those records from text form to `Record` structures and appends them to the end of a specified database file. The input text must be in the form:

```
Last name, First name; Company name;
Address 1; Address 2; City; ST; Zip;
Home Phone; Work Phone; Date of birth; Married?; Divorced?;
```

Fields, including the last, are teminated with semicolons. All fields must be included. Leading blanks are ignored. Separate multiple records with a single blank line. Here's a sample record as it might appear in the input batch file:

```
Holding, G.; Anchor Corp;
34 West Ave; Suite 21B; New York; NY; 18976;
210-555-1212; 210-555-1212; 7/4/42; N; Y;
```

The input file can have as many records as you need. You might use a text editor to create it, or you could use a *database front end editor* — in other words, a text editor that creates a file in the correct form. Perhaps you should consider writing that program, or you might use a commercial utility purchased from a third-party vendor. (You may have to write an auxiliary program to convert their file format to the one shown here, but that's probably easier than writing your own editor from scratch.)

Text files are simple, easily edited, and you can write your own programs to massage them in any way you like. You could even use a spreadsheet such as Excel for Microsoft Windows as an editor. Write the output to a text file, and either convert it to DBAPPEND's expected format, or modify DBAPPEND to recognize the delimited text files that Excel (and other programs) can create.

As with DBENTRY, DBAPPEND uses a project file, but this time, with only two files shown in Listing 18-12, DBAPPEND.PRJ. Create it as you did DBENTRY.PRJ, or you can copy the finished file from PART4\PHONEDB.

Listing 18-12: DBAPPEND.PRJ

```
dbappend.cpp
dblib.cpp
```

The DBAPPEND program uses a different interface from DBENTRY. I purposely used different interface techniques throughout this chapter to demonstrate various approaches to program designs. You may want to consider adopting one interface technique for all programs. Listing 18-13, DPAPPEND.CPP, lists the program's source code.

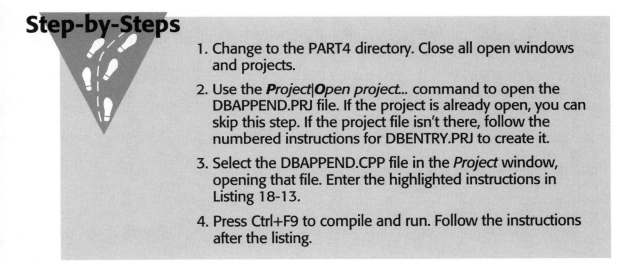

Step-by-Steps

1. Change to the PART4 directory. Close all open windows and projects.

2. Use the *Project|Open project...* command to open the DBAPPEND.PRJ file. If the project is already open, you can skip this step. If the project file isn't there, follow the numbered instructions for DBENTRY.PRJ to create it.

3. Select the DBAPPEND.CPP file in the *Project* window, opening that file. Enter the highlighted instructions in Listing 18-13.

4. Press Ctrl+F9 to compile and run. Follow the instructions after the listing.

Listing 18-13: DBAPPEND.CPP

```cpp
// dbappend.cpp -- Append records from text file
// Type and Learn C
// (c) 1994 by Tom Swan; All rights reserved

#include <stdio.h>
#include <string.h>
#include <ctype.h>

#include "dblib.h"
#include "db.h"

/* Input format (separate records with blank line)
Last name, First name; Company name;
Address 1; Address 2; City; ST; Zip;
Home Phone; Work Phone; Date of birth; Married; Divorced;
*/
```

```
// Global definitions

#define NUM_FIELDS 12  // Text-file fields per record
FILE *inf, *outf;      // Input and output files
long numWritten;       // Number of records written

// Open text and binary files; return true for success
// Files are closed if any errors are detected
int OpenFiles(const char *fromName, const char *toName)
{
  printf("\nOpening input file:\n%s\n", fromName);
  inf = fopen(fromName, "r");
  if (!inf) {
    Error(ERR_OPEN);
    return FALSE;
  }
  printf("\nOpening output file:\n%s\n", toName);
  outf = fopen(toName, "ab");
  if (!outf) {
    Error(ERR_OPEN);
    fclose(inf);
    return FALSE;
  }
  return TRUE;
}

// Read field from f into buffer, skipping white space
void GetField(FILE *f, char *buffer, size_t size)
{
  int i = 0, c;

  while (isspace(c = fgetc(f)) && c != EOF)
    ;              // Skip white space
  ungetc(c, f);  // Prepare to reread last char
  while ((c = fgetc(f)) != ';' && c != EOF && i < size)
    buffer[i++] = c;  // Build string from file
  if (i >= size)      // Adjust string index
    i = size - 1;
  buffer[i] = '\0';   // Insert null terminator
  return;
}
```

```
// Insert field in text form into record
// Assumes all string fields are zeroed
void InsertField(int n, char *buffer, Record *rp)
{
  switch (n) {

  // Name
    case 1:
      strncpy(rp->name, buffer, NAME_SIZE - 1);
      break;

  // Company
    case 2:
      strncpy(rp->company, buffer, COMPANY_SIZE - 1);
      break;

  // Address 1
    case 3:
      strncpy(rp->address1, buffer, ADDRESS_SIZE - 1);
      break;

  // Address 2
    case 4:
      strncpy(rp->address2, buffer, ADDRESS_SIZE - 1);
      break;

  // City
    case 5:
      strncpy(rp->city, buffer, CITY_SIZE - 1);
      break;

  // State
    case 6:
      strncpy(rp->state, buffer, STATE_SIZE - 1);
      break;

  // ZIP
    case 7:
      strncpy(rp->zip, buffer, ZIP_SIZE - 1);
      break;

  // Home phone
    case 8:
      StrToPhone(buffer, &rp->homePhone);
      break;
```

```c
    // Work phone
      case 9:
        StrToPhone(buffer, &rp->workPhone);
        break;

    // Date of birth
      case 10:
        StrToDate(buffer, &rp->birthDate);
        break;

    // Married
      case 11:
        StrToBool(buffer, &rp->married);
        break;

    // Divorced
      case 12:
        StrToBool(buffer, &rp->divorced);
        break;
    }

    // Edit-date, single, and deleted fields

    InsDate(time(NULL), &rp->editDate);
    rp->single = (Boolean)(!rp->married && !rp->divorced);
    rp->deleted = FALSE;

}

// Write record to output file; return True for success
int WriteRecord(FILE *f, Record *rp)
{
  int result = fwrite(rp, sizeof(Record), 1, f);
  if (result != 1)
    Error(ERR_INSERT);
  else
    numWritten++;
  return result;
}
```

```
// Append text to database; return True for success
int AppendText()
{
  Record rec;
  char buffer[256];
  int i;

// Give user last chance to bail out
  puts("\nReady to append records\n");
  if (!Yes("Continue?"))
    return FALSE;

  while (!feof(inf)) {
    ZeroRecord(&rec);  // Initialize record fields
    puts("");          // Start new line onscreen
    for (i = 1; i <= NUM_FIELDS; i++) {
      GetField(inf, buffer, 256);   // Read field from file
      InsertField(i, buffer, &rec); // Insert field into rec
      puts(buffer);  // Optional onscreen feedback
      if (feof(inf))           // Check if end of file reached
        i = NUM_FIELDS + 1;  // If at eof, end for-loop now
    }
    if (strlen(rec.name) > 0)      // Zero len == no record
      if (!WriteRecord(outf, &rec)) // Write rec to disk
        return FALSE;
  }
  return TRUE;
}

// Display instructions
void Instruct()
{
  puts("");
  puts("DBAPPEND");
  puts("");
  puts("This program appends records from a text file");
  puts("onto the end of a binary database file. Enter");
  puts("the two file names--text file first. For example,");
  puts("to add the records in a text file NEWRECS.TXT to");
  puts("a database file MYDATA.DB, enter the command");
  puts("");
  puts("    dbappend newrecs.txt mydata.db");
```

```
      puts("");
      puts("For safety, keep a backup copy of MYDATA.DB before");
      puts("giving the command. In the IDE, use the Run");
      puts("Arguments command to enter the two file names");
      puts("separated with a single space. Delete the arguments");
      puts("from the IDE before running other programs.");
   }

   int main(int argc, char *argv[])
   {
      int result = 0;  // Batch-file result
      Welcome();
      if (argc < 3)
        Instruct();      // Insruct if filenames absent
      else {
        result = OpenFiles(argv[1], argv[2]);
        if (result) {
          result = AppendText();
          fclose(inf);
          fclose(outf);
          printf("\n%ld record(s) appended\n", numWritten);
        }
      }
      Pause();
      return result;
   }
```

To run DPAPPEND, you must supply the names of two files. If you don't supply two filenames, the program displays instructions. From DOS or a similar operating system, run DPAPPEND like this:

```
dbappend newrecs.txt mydata.db
```

To run DBAPPEND from the IDE, use the *Run\Arguments...* command to enter the two filenames, separated with a single space. The program appends the records from NEWRECS.TXT onto the end of the database file MYDATA.DB. (Use DBENTRY to create the database file before running DPAPPEND.)

The program uses a few global definitions, including NUM_FIELDS, which equals the number of input fields — not necessarily the same as the number of members in the Record structure. Two file variables, inf and outf, designate the input and output files. Variable numWritten counts the number of appended records.

 DBAPPEND does not prevent you from appending the same records twice to the same database file. Keep a backup copy of your .DB file before adding files to it using DBAPPEND. (Perhaps you can improve the program to check for duplicate records and solve this problem.)

Function `OpenFiles` does the expected — it opens the input text and output database files. Many file-processing programs operate on two files, one supplying input and the other holding the program's output. You should be able to extract `OpenFiles` with minimal changes for other file-handing programs.

Function `GetField` reads a field in text format, ending in a semicolon but skipping leading blanks — called *white space*. This function might also be generally useful for reading other kinds of batch-entry text files.

The function `InsertField`, which you don't have to type, converts text input in a `char` buffer to binary form, stored in a `Record` field. Each field is numbered, and a large `switch` statement selects which field to convert based on the value of parameter n.

Function `WriteRecord` appends a new record onto the end of the output file. The records are appended because that file was opened using the `"ab"` (append binary) option (see function `OpenFiles`). Function `AppendText` is the program's main controlling function — it reads the input text, assembles a `Record` structure, and writes the record to disk.

The `main` function demonstrates a simple, but effective, interface for batch-file processing. If an incorrect number of arguments is supplied (`argc < 3`), function `Instruct` displays instructions; otherwise, the program opens both files and calls `AppendText` to run the show.

Binary Files

Testing a complex software package is always difficult. You can never test all possible input values; all you can do is test how the software behaves for average and way-out cases. One useful tool in the testing battle is a program that generates data at random. In this section, you develop a program that creates sample database files, which you can use to test other programs in the chapter. Files are generated directly in binary form.

Another way to write a file generator would be to output records in text file format that you could feed to DPAPPEND. You might want to consider writing this program.

Listing 18-14, DBGEN.PRJ, gives the files required by the program. As before, use this list to create a project file with the IDE or just copy DBGEN.PRJ from PART4\PHONEDB to the PART4 directory.

Listing 18-14: DBGEN.PRJ

```
dbgen.cpp
dblib.cpp
```

Listing 18-15, DBGEN.CPP, lists the program's source code. Again, I used a different interface — this time, prompting for a filename and the number of records to create. Enter the name of a file. The program will not overwrite an existing file. Enter the number of records to create. You can then use the resulting file with other programs in this chapter.

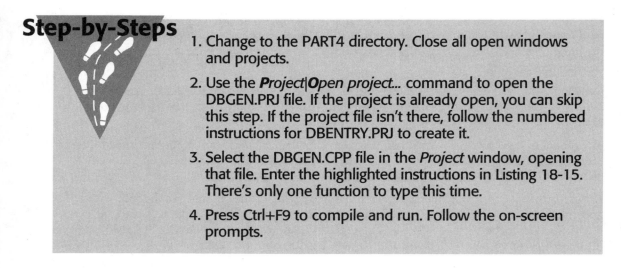

Step-by-Steps

1. Change to the PART4 directory. Close all open windows and projects.

2. Use the *Project|Open project...* command to open the DBGEN.PRJ file. If the project is already open, you can skip this step. If the project file isn't there, follow the numbered instructions for DBENTRY.PRJ to create it.

3. Select the DBGEN.CPP file in the *Project* window, opening that file. Enter the highlighted instructions in Listing 18-15. There's only one function to type this time.

4. Press Ctrl+F9 to compile and run. Follow the on-screen prompts.

Listing 18-15: DBGEN.CPP

```cpp
// dbgen.cpp -- Randomly generate test records
// Type and Learn C
// (c) 1994 by Tom Swan; All rights reserved

#include <stdio.h>
#include <stdlib.h>
#include <time.h>
#include <string.h>

#include "dblib.h"
#include "db.h"

// Return random number in range low to high
int RandRange(int low, int high)
{
  return low + (rand() % ((high - low) + 1));
}

// Create randomized string in s of size bytes
void RandomizeString(char *s, int size)
{
  int i;
  for (i = 0; i < size - 1; i++)
    s[i] = RandRange('a', 'z');
  s[i] = '\0';
}
```

```c
// Create randomized Phone structure in *ph
void RandomizePhone(Phone *ph)
{
  ph->areaCode = RandRange(123, 890);
  ph->exchange = RandRange(123, 890);
  ph->number = RandRange(1234, 7890);
}

// Create randomized Date structure in *dt
void RandomizeDate(Date *dt)
{
  dt->month = RandRange(1, 12);
  dt->day = RandRange(1, 30);
  dt->year = RandRange(1925, 1994);
}

// Create randomized Boolean value in *b
void RandomizeBool(Boolean *b)
{
  *b = (Boolean)RandRange(0, 1);
}

// Insert randomly generated info into *rp's fields
void RandomizeFields(Record *rp)
{
  ZeroRecord(rp);
  RandomizeString(rp->name, NAME_SIZE);
  RandomizeString(rp->company, COMPANY_SIZE);
  RandomizeString(rp->address1, ADDRESS_SIZE);
  RandomizeString(rp->address2, ADDRESS_SIZE);
  RandomizeString(rp->city, CITY_SIZE);
  RandomizeString(rp->state, STATE_SIZE);
  RandomizeString(rp->zip, ZIP_SIZE);
  RandomizePhone (&rp->homePhone);
  RandomizePhone (&rp->workPhone);
  RandomizeDate  (&rp->birthDate);
  RandomizeDate  (&rp->editDate);
  RandomizeBool  (&rp->married);
  RandomizeBool  (&rp->divorced);
  rp->single = (Boolean)(!rp->married && !rp->divorced);
  RandomizeBool  (&rp->deleted);
}
```

```c
// Create the database file
long CreateFile(const char *fs)
{
  Record rec;
  long numRecords, i;
  size_t result;
  FILE *outf;

  printf("\nReady to create: %s\n", fs);
  printf("\nHow many records? ");
  scanf("%ld", &numRecords);
  fflush(stdin);
  if (numRecords <= 0)
    return 0;
  outf = fopen(fs, "wb");
  if (!outf) {
    Error(ERR_CREATE);
    return 0;
  }
  for (i = 0; i < numRecords; i++) {
    RandomizeFields(&rec);
    result = fwrite(&rec, sizeof(Record), 1, outf);
    if (i % 10 == 0)
      printf(".");          // Display "progress feedback"
    if (result != 1) {
      Error(ERR_WRITE);     // Handle writing errors
      fclose(outf);         // Close output file
      remove(fs);           // Delete partial file (if any)
      return 0;             // Exit function
    }
  }
  puts("");               // Start new line
  fclose(outf);           // Close output file
  return numRecords;      // Return function result
}

// Start new random sequence
void Randomize()
{
  time_t t;
  srand((unsigned)time(&t));
}
```

```
int main()
{
  char fname[FNAME_SIZE];
  long numRecords;

  Welcome();
  puts("\nDBGEN\n");
  puts("This program creates a binary database of");
  puts("randomly generated records.");

  Randomize();
  GetFileName("Create what file?", ".db", fname);
  if (strlen(fname) > 0) {
    if (FileExists(fname)) {
      printf("\nFile %s\n", fname);
      Error(ERR_EXISTS);
    } else {
      numRecords = CreateFile(fname);
      printf("\n%ld records written to %s\n",
        numRecords, fname);
      Pause();
    }
  }
}
```

The CreateFile function that you typed returns the number of records written to the output file. That file is created using mode "wb" (write binary), and as in other programs, fwrite writes each newly generated record to disk.

As written, DBGEN works well enough, but the records it generates are unsophisticated. Each field is a fixed length, for example, and "name" fields are simply filled with random characters. A better program (and an excellent project for a rainy weekend) would generate lifelike files with fields that more closely resemble those in real records.

Writing good random-data generators requires an artist's touch. You could use *another* database, for example, from which to select first and last names. Phone numbers could be generated with real area codes, and ZIP codes should correspond to real cities.

I'll leave the changes to you — the resulting code could easily fill this chapter! Keep in mind, however, that complex software benefits from equally complex testing. A data generator is just one piece in the testing puzzle, but it may be the most important.

Serial Access Methods

I started this chapter by complaining about mailing lists, so let's finish off that problem right now. Listing 18-16, DBLIST.PRJ, lists the files for the DBLIST project. Listing 18-17, DBLIST.CPP, shows the program's source code. This time, we'll use *serial-access methods* to list all records in a database file.

Step-by-Steps

1. Change to the PART4 directory. Close all open windows and projects.

2. Use the *Project|Open project...* command to open the DBLIST.PRJ file. If the project is already open, you can skip this step. If the project file isn't there, follow the numbered instructions for DBENTRY.PRJ to create it.

3. Select the DBLIST.CPP file in the *Project* window, opening that file. Enter the highlighted instructions in Listing 18-17.

4. Press Ctrl+F9 to compile and run. Follow instructions after the listing.

Listing 18-16: DBLIST.PRJ

```
dblist.cpp
dblib.cpp
```

Listing 18-17: DBLIST.CPP

```
// dblist.cpp -- List database records
// Type and Learn C
// (c) 1994 by Tom Swan; All rights reserved

#include <stdio.h>
#include <string.h>

#include "dblib.h"
#include "db.h"

long numRecords;
```

```c
// Write record to stdout
void ListRecord(Record *rp, long rn)
{
  printf("\nRecord #%ld\n", rn);
  printf("%s\n", rp->name);
  printf("%s\n", rp->company);
  printf("%s\n", rp->address1);
  printf("%s\n", rp->address2);
  printf("%s, %s %s\n", rp->city, rp->state, rp->zip);
}

int main()
{
  Record rec;
  char fname[FNAME_SIZE];

// Get filename, or you can
// use strcpy(fname, "name.db") for silent running
  Welcome();
  GetFileName("List what file?", ".db", fname);
  if (strlen(fname) == 0)
    return 0;

  FILE *f = fopen(fname, "rb");
  if (!f) {
    Error(ERR_OPEN);
    return 1;
  }
  while (!feof(f)) {
    if (fread(&rec, sizeof(Record), 1, f) == 1) {
      ListRecord(&rec, numRecords);
      numRecords++;
    }
  }
  fclose(f);

// Display number of records listed
// Delete these statements for silent running
  printf("\n%ld record(s) listed\n", numRecords);
  Pause();

  return 0;
}
```

Function `ListRecord` writes one record to the standard output file in mailing label form. The selection of fields and their relative positions may not work for your labels. If not, just modify this function to write records any way you want.

> When printing mailing labels, I always direct output to a temporary text file. I then print that file on the labels. This two-step process prevents having to start the job over from the top if the labels get jammed or tear — which inevitably happens a few names from the end. With the formatted labels on disk, you can load that text file into an editor (the IDE works fine), delete the names already printed, and start over from that point, wasting relatively few labels in the process.

This time, the `main` function accesses the file in serial fashion. After opening the file using the `"rb"` (read binary) option, a `while` loop tests whether function `feof` returns true. If so, we have reached the end of the file, and the loop ends. If not, `fread` reads the next record, which is passed to `ListRecord` for printing.

The serial-access `while` loop is often written incorrectly. Not only must you test for the end of the file by calling `feof`, you also must test whether `fread` returns the number of expected records. Never write this loop as

```
while (!feof(f)) {
  fread(...);        // ???
  ListRecord(...);
}
```

In many operating systems, `feof` returns true only *after* attempting to read past the end of the file. It is possible, then, for `feof` to return false but for `fread` to fail to read a record. Guard against this problem by testing `fread`'s result:

```
while (!feof(f)) {
  if (fread(...) == n)
    ListRecord(...);
}
```

Only if `fread` returns the expected number of records (1 in DBLIST) should you use that record. The `while` loop ends after accessing all records in the file.

Random-Access Methods

You've already seen random-access methods in the DBRECORD module. You've also accessed files using serial methods in DBLIST. The *same* file can be used with either method — to pluck out records randomly, for example, or to process records in serial fashion from the first to the last.

Any database system needs a program to edit existing records. The technique is simple: prompt for a record number, read that record using random-access methods, allow the user to edit its fields, and then write the record back to the file in the same position. The program's execution, however, is another matter. Here again, due to space limitations, I use only simple I/O methods — to edit a field, you must retype it. Press Enter to skip over a field and make no changes to it. Press Space+Enter to erase a field. Obviously, this bare-minimum editor could be more user friendly, but it does nicely in a pinch. (The editor could also work via modem using only simple communication software — it doesn't require cursor positioning commands.)

Listing 18-18, DBCHANGE.PRJ, lists the files in this project. Listing 18-19, DBCHANGE.CPP, lists the program's source code.

Step-by-Steps

1. Change to the PART4 directory. Close all open windows and projects.

2. Use the *Project|Open project...* command to open the DBCHANGE.PRJ file. If the project is already open, you can skip this step. If the project file isn't there, follow the numbered instructions for DBENTRY.PRJ to create it.

3. Select the DBCHANGE.CPP file in the *Project* window, opening that file. Enter the highlighted instructions in Listing 18-19.

4. Press Ctrl+F9 to compile and run. Follow instructions after the listing.

Listing 18-18: DBCHANGE.PRJ

```
dbchange.cpp
dbshow.cpp
dbedit.cpp
dbrecord.cpp
dblib.cpp
```

Listing 18-19: DBCHANGE.CPP

```cpp
// dbchange.cpp -- Edit, delete, and undelete records
// Type and Learn C
// (c) 1994 by Tom Swan; All rights reserved

#include <stdio.h>
#include <stdlib.h>
#include <string.h>
#include <ctype.h>

#include "dblib.h"
#include "dbshow.h"
#include "dbedit.h"
#include "dbrecord.h"
#include "db.h"

// Global variables

char fname[FNAME_SIZE];
FILE *dbf;
long numRecords;

// Prompt for and return a record number
long GetRecordNumber()
{
  long rn;
  printf("\nRecord number? ");
  scanf("%ld", &rn);
  fflush(stdin);
  if (InRange(rn, 0, numRecords - 1))
    return rn;
  else {
    Error(ERR_RECNUM);
    return -1;
  }
}

// Change record members
//
// 1. Prompt for record number
// 2. Read and display that record
// 3. Modify record contents
// 4. Write record back to database
//
```

```
void ChangeRecord()
{
  Record rec;
  long rn = GetRecordNumber();
  if (rn < 0)
    return;
  if (!ReadRecord(dbf, rn, &rec))
    return;
  ShowRecord(&rec);
  puts("");
  if (Yes("Change this record?")) {
    EditRecord(&rec);
    puts("\nConfirming entry...\n");
    ShowRecord(&rec);
    if (Yes("\nSave changes?")) {
      if (!WriteRecord(dbf, rn, &rec))
        return;
      puts("\nChanges saved");
    } else
      puts("\nChanges not saved");
    Pause();
  }
}

// Mark and unmark records for deletion
//
// 1. Prompt for record number
// 2. Read and display that record
// 3. Request permission to delete/undelete
// 4. Toggle delete flag if permission given
// 5. Write record back to database
//
void DeleteRecord()
{
  int saveFlag = FALSE;  // True to save modified record
  Record rec;
  long rn = GetRecordNumber();
  if (rn < 0)
    return;
  if (!ReadRecord(dbf, rn, &rec))
    return;
  ShowRecord(&rec);
  puts("");
  if (rec.deleted) {
    puts("Record is already marked for deletion\n");
    saveFlag = Yes("Unmark this record?");
```

```
      } else
        saveFlag = Yes("Mark this record for deletion?");
      if (saveFlag) {
        rec.deleted = (Boolean)!rec.deleted;  // Toggle deleted flag
        if (!WriteRecord(dbf, rn, &rec))
          return;
        puts("\nChanges saved");
      } else
        puts("\nNo changes made");
      Pause();
}

// Display instructions
void Help()
{
  puts("\nHelp with commands");
  puts("------------------");
  puts("C.hange --Modify a record's fields");
  puts("D.elete --Mark or unmark a record for deletion");
  puts("H.elp   --Display this help text");
  puts("Q.uit   --End program");
  puts("");
  puts("Use the Delete command to mark or unmark records");
  puts("for eventual deletion from the file using the");
  puts("DBPURGE program. The Delete command does not");
  puts("remove records from the file. If you delete a");
  puts("record by mistake, use Delete again to unmark it.");
  puts("");
  puts("When editing records, retype new fields or press");
  puts("Enter to make NO change to a field. To erase a");
  puts("field, type a space and then press Enter.");
  Pause();
}

// Initialize global variables
// Program ends if file cannot be opened
void Initialize()
{
  GetFileName("Edit what file?", ".db", fname);
  if (strlen(fname) == 0)
    exit(0);  // Exit: no error
  printf("\nOpening %s\n", fname);
  dbf = fopen(fname, "r+b");
  if (!dbf) {
    Error(ERR_OPEN);
    exit(1);  // Exit: report error
  }
```

```
    numRecords = CountRecords(dbf);
    printf("\n%ld record(s) in file\n", numRecords);
    if (numRecords <= 0) {
      Error(ERR_EMPTY);
      fclose(dbf);
      exit(2);   // Exit: report error
    }
    Pause();
}

int main()
{
  int quitting = FALSE;   // Program ends when TRUE
  int cmd;                 // Menu command character

  Welcome();      // Display welcome message
  Initialize();   // Initialize global variables

  while (!quitting) {

    ClearDisplay();
    printf("DBCHANGE> C.hange D.elete H.elp Q.uit: ");
    cmd = toupper(getchar());
    fflush(stdin);

    switch (cmd) {

      case 'C':
        ChangeRecord();
        break;

      case 'D':
        DeleteRecord();
        break;

      case 'H':
        Help();
        break;

      case 'Q':
        quitting = TRUE;
        break;
```

```
          default:
            Error(ERR_UNKNOWNCMD);
            break;

        }
    }

    fclose(dbf);
    return 0;
}
```

Function `ChangeRecord` prompts for a record number, calls `ReadRecord` (defined in the DBRECORD module), and displays its contents. If you answer yes to the question "Change this record?," the program calls `EditRecord` to modify the record's fields. This is the same `EditRecord` function used by DBENTRY to enter new records. When a function can serve double duty, so much the better.

After you enter your changes, the program redisplays the record for confirmation. If you answer yes to "Save changes?," `WriteRecord` writes the modified record back to the file.

Despite its name, function `DeleteRecord` does not delete records from the file. Instead, it takes the safer course of marking records for later deletion. As you may recall from DB.H, each `Record` structure has a `deleted` field of type `Boolean`. Function `DeleteRecord` merely toggles this field true or false. Another program, DBPURGE (described in the next section), removes all records marked for deletion. Using DBCHANGE, you can mark and unmark a record as many times as you like. You can also edit marked records, which also resets their `deleted` flags to false.

A lot of the programming in DBCHANGE performs error checking and carefully requests permission from users before carrying out critical operations. The general rule is: If an operation can destroy information, *ask the user for permission.* Unfortunately, users get lazy (as do programmers), and even the most carefully written interface can lead to a loss of records. A better DBCHANGE program might provide an *undo* service, permitting saved records to be recovered (perhaps from a temporary file). But, in the end, there is *nothing* you can do to prevent all possible mishaps. Be sure to do as much as you can, however, to give users the chance to recover from most accidents.

Directories

The standard ANSI C library provides only two directory-related functions: `rename` and `remove`. As you can probably imagine, `rename` changes a file's directory name; `remove` deletes a file from a directory. ANSI C provides no other directory functions because operating systems differ drastically. Even so, all file systems have the capability of renaming and removing files, and there's a lot you can do with only these two functions.

Most compilers, including the one packaged with this book, provide function libraries for calling nonstandard operating system directory functions (and many others). See the DOS.H and DIR.H headers, for example, in the compiler's INCLUDE directory. I have purposely avoided discussing these functions because of their system-dependent nature. The programs in this chapter (and most in this book) should work under all ANSI C compilers with only minor revisions.

DBPURGE uses standard directory functions to maintain a backup copy of a database. The program deletes all records that have `deleted` fields set to true. Obviously, this is a drastic operation that, if misused, could result in a massive loss of records. Keeping a backup file is essential.

Listing 18-20, DBPURGE.PRJ, shows the files used by this project. Listing 18-21, DBPURGE.CPP, lists the program's source code. Run the program and enter the name of a file to purge. It is OK to purge a file that has no deleted records. The original file is saved in a file ending with .BAK.

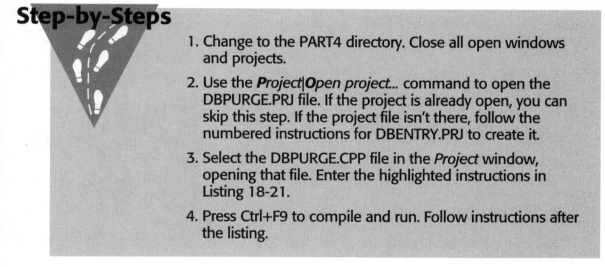

Step-by-Steps

1. Change to the PART4 directory. Close all open windows and projects.

2. Use the *Project|Open project...* command to open the DBPURGE.PRJ file. If the project is already open, you can skip this step. If the project file isn't there, follow the numbered instructions for DBENTRY.PRJ to create it.

3. Select the DBPURGE.CPP file in the *Project* window, opening that file. Enter the highlighted instructions in Listing 18-21.

4. Press Ctrl+F9 to compile and run. Follow instructions after the listing.

Listing 18-20: DBPURGE.PRJ

```
dbpurge.cpp
dbrecord.cpp
dblib.cpp
```

Listing 18-21: DBPURGE.CPP

```cpp
// dbpurge.cpp -- Purge records marked for deletion
// Type and Learn C
// (c) 1994 by Tom Swan; All rights reserved

#include <stdio.h>
#include <stdlib.h>
#include <string.h>

#include "dblib.h"
#include "dbrecord.h"
#include "db.h"


// Global variables

char fname[FNAME_SIZE];       // Input filename
char backname[FNAME_SIZE];    // Backup filename
char tempname[FNAME_SIZE];    // Temporary outpuf filename
FILE *dbf;                    // Input file variable
FILE *tf;                     // Temporary output file variable
long numRecords;              // Number of recs in file
long numDeleted;              // Number of recs purged


// Remove records marked for deletion from inf
// Return True for success
// Closes input file
//
// 1. create temporary file to hold output
// 2. copy unmarked records from input to output
// 3. close temporary file
// 4. close input file
// 5. delete old backup file if any
// 6. rename input file to backup filename
// 7. rename temporary file to input filename
//
int PurgeRecords(FILE *inf)
{
  Record rec;
```

```
    printf("\nPurging");
    rewind(inf);
    while (!feof(inf)) {
      if (fread(&rec, sizeof(Record), 1, inf) == 1) {
        putchar('.');      // Display activity feedback
        if (rec.deleted)
          numDeleted++;    // Count deleted recs
        else if (fwrite(&rec, sizeof(Record), 1, tf) != 1) {
          fclose(inf);
          fclose(tf);
          puts("");
          Error(ERR_WRITE);
          return FALSE;
        }
      }
    }
    puts("");
    fclose(inf);
    if (fclose(tf) != 0) {
      Error(ERR_CLOSE);
      return FALSE;
    }
    remove(backname);          // Delete old name.BAK
    rename(fname, backname);    // Rename name.DB to name.BAK
    rename(tempname, fname);    // Rename tmp?.$$$ to name.DB
    return TRUE;
}

// Initialize global variables
// Program ends if file cannot be opened
void Initialize()
{
    char *cp;     // Pointer to filename '.' if any

// Prompt for and open input file
    GetFileName("Purge what file?", ".db", fname);
    if (strlen(fname) == 0)
      exit(0);   // Exit: no error
    printf("\nOpening %s\n", fname);
    dbf = fopen(fname, "r+b");
    if (!dbf) {
      Error(ERR_OPEN);
      exit(1);   // Exit: report error
    }
```

```c
// Count records in file; exit if file is empty
  numRecords = CountRecords(dbf);
  printf("\n%ld record(s) in file\n", numRecords);
  if (numRecords <= 0) {
    Error(ERR_EMPTY);
    fclose(dbf);
    exit(2);  // Exit: report error
  }

// Create backup filename
  strcpy(backname, fname);
  cp = strchr(backname, '.');  // Look for extension char
  if (cp)
    *cp = '\0';  // Delete filename extension
  strcat(backname, ".bak");

// Create and open temporary output file
  strncpy(tempname, tmpnam(NULL), FNAME_SIZE - 1);
  tf = fopen(tempname, "wb");
  if (!tf) {
    fclose(dbf);
    Error(ERR_TEMP);
    exit(3);
  }
}

int main()
{
  Welcome();
  Initialize();
  if (Yes("\nPurge deleted records from file?")) {
    if (PurgeRecords(dbf)) {
      printf("\n%ld record(s) purged\n", numDeleted);
      printf("\nOriginal file saved as %s\n", backname);
    } else
      puts("\nFile not purged. Recover from backup!");
    Pause();
  }
  remove(tempname);  // Ignore errors
  return 0;
}
```

In programs like DBPURGE, I prefer to create all filenames in advance, storing them in global variables such as fname, backname, and tempname. There are many ways to create backup files; I use these steps:

1. Make no changes to the directory names until the program is finished operating on the original data.

2. Write all new data to a temporary file, using a temporary filename provided by the standard tmpnam function. The old data remains unchanged in its original file, and the new data (in this case, minus deleted records) is stored in a temporary file.

3. Delete any existing file named .BAK. Existing backup files are always OK to delete in advance, but your documentation should warn users not to use .BAK as an extension for their own files.

4. Rename the original file to use the extension .BAK. *The original file isn't modified; only its name is changed!*

5. Rename the temporary output file to the name of the original file.

Function Initialize prepares the program to carry out those steps. It opens the file to be purged, and it creates a backup filename in the global backname buffer. The function also calls tmpnam to create a temporary output file. This file is guaranteed to have a name that does not already exist. (Hint: Add printf statements to Initialize to display the backname and tempname buffers so you can see the generated filenames.)

Function PurgeRecords reads each record from the input file in serial fashion. If a record's deleted field is true, global numDeleted is incremented. If deleted is false, the record is transferred to the temporary output file. After the program processes the files, they are closed, and functions remove and rename change their names as explained in the preceding steps. Never call remove or rename for files that are open! Always close the files before removing them or changing their names.

You might want to modify DBPURGE to save deleted records in yet another file, perhaps ending in .DEL. To do that, create another temporary output file, write the deleted records to it, and rename the file when finished. This change permits you to keep archives of deleted records, which might be useful for later studies or for recovering from accidental deletions.

Sorting

The preceding chapter covered sorting methods, and you've also seen several examples of the qsort library function elsewhere in this book. But no database system would be complete without a program to sort records alphabetically.

Listing 18-22, DBSORT.PRJ, lists the files in the database sort project. Listing 18-23, DBSORT.CPP, gives the source code. The program is not fancy — it merely arranges records alphabetically by name. A more sophisticated program would permit sorting on any field or, perhaps, on a combination of structure members — ordering the file, for example, by name for all single individuals. Consider DBSORT in its present form as a mere shell for future expansions.

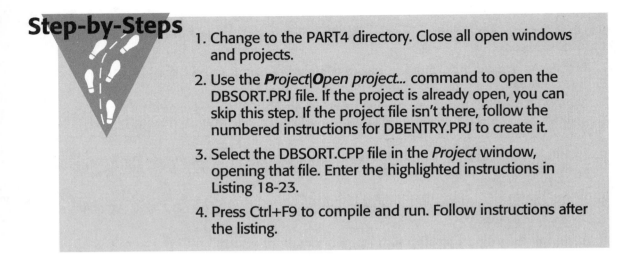

Step-by-Steps

1. Change to the PART4 directory. Close all open windows and projects.

2. Use the *Project|Open project...* command to open the DBSORT.PRJ file. If the project is already open, you can skip this step. If the project file isn't there, follow the numbered instructions for DBENTRY.PRJ to create it.

3. Select the DBSORT.CPP file in the *Project* window, opening that file. Enter the highlighted instructions in Listing 18-23.

4. Press Ctrl+F9 to compile and run. Follow instructions after the listing.

Listing 18-22: DBSORT.PRJ

```
dbsort.cpp
dblib.cpp
dbrecord.cpp
```

Listing 18-23: DBSORT.CPP

```cpp
// dbsort.cpp -- Sort database records
// Type and Learn C
// (c) 1994 by Tom Swan; All rights reserved

#include <stdio.h>
#include <stdlib.h>
#include <string.h>
#include <limits.h>

#include "dblib.h"
#include "dbrecord.h"
#include "db.h"

// Global variables

char fname[FNAME_SIZE];      // Input filename
char backname[FNAME_SIZE];   // Backup filename
FILE *dbf;                   // Input file variable
FILE *bakf;                  // Backup file variable
long numRecords;             // Number of recs in file
Record **rps;                // Array of record pointers
```

```
// Read records into memory
int ReadRecords(FILE *f)
{
  Record *rp;  // Pointer to dynamic Record objects
  unsigned n = 0;  // Number of records (and rps index)

  rewind(f);

  // Allocate memory for array of Record pointers
  // Use calloc so all pointers are nulled
  rps = (Record **)calloc(sizeof(Record *),
    (unsigned)numRecords);  // Okay because numRecords <= UINT_MAX
  if (!rps)
    return FALSE;    // Memory allocation failed

  // Read records into memory and save pointers in array
  while (!feof(f)) {
    rp = (Record *)malloc(sizeof(Record));
    if (!rp)
      return FALSE;  // Memory allocation failed
    rps[n] = rp;      // Save pointer to record in memory
    if (fread(rp, sizeof(Record), 1, f) == 1) {
      putchar('.');  // Display activity feedback
      n++;            // Increment array index
    }
  }
  return TRUE;
}

// Write records back to disk from beginning of file
// Return True for success
int WriteRecords(FILE *f)
{
  unsigned n;  // Array index

  rewind(f);
  for (n = 0; n < numRecords; n++) {
    if (fwrite(rps[n], sizeof(Record), 1, f) != 1) {
      puts("");
      Error(ERR_WRITE);
      return FALSE;
    }
```

```c
      putchar('.');  // Display activity feedback
    }
    return TRUE;
}


// Compare two Records on their name fields
int Compare(const void *a, const void *b)
{
  return strcmp(
    (*(const Record **)a)->name,
    (*(const Record **)b)->name  );
}


// Sort records in memory
void SortRecords()
{
  if (numRecords < 2)
    return;  // Not enough data to sort
  qsort(rps, (unsigned)numRecords, sizeof(Record *), Compare);
}


// Free allocated memory
void FreeMemory()
{
  unsigned n;  // Array index

  if (!rps) return;  // Nothing allocated
  for (n = 0; n < numRecords; n++) {
    if (rps[n])
      free(rps[n]);  // Free individual records
  }
  free(rps);          // Free array of Record pointers
}


// Close files; delete backup file; exit with error
void AbortSort()
{
  fclose(dbf);
  fclose(bakf);
  remove(backname);
  FreeMemory();
  exit(-1);
}
```

```
// Return True if database isn't too large
// System dependent due to 64K maximum on dynamic object size
int LimitsOkay()
{
  if (numRecords > UINT_MAX) {
    fprintf(stderr, "\nDatabase file is too large to sort\n");
    fprintf(stderr, "due to 64K memory allocation limit with\n");
    fprintf(stderr, "this compiler and operating system.\n");
    return FALSE;
  }
  return TRUE;
}

// Initialize global variables
// Program ends if file cannot be opened
void Initialize()
{
  char *cp;   // Pointer to filename '.' if any

// Prompt for and open input file
  GetFileName("Sort what file?", ".db", fname);
  if (strlen(fname) == 0)
    exit(0);  // Exit: no error
  printf("\nOpening %s\n", fname);
  dbf = fopen(fname, "r+b");
  if (!dbf) {
    Error(ERR_OPEN);
    exit(1);  // Exit: report error
  }

// Count records in file; exit if file is empty
  numRecords = CountRecords(dbf);
  printf("\n%ld record(s) in file\n", numRecords);
  if (numRecords <= 0) {
    Error(ERR_EMPTY);
    fclose(dbf);
    exit(2);  // Exit: report error
  }
```

```
// Create backup file
  strcpy(backname, fname);
  cp = strchr(backname, '.');  // Look for extension char
  if (cp)
    *cp = '\0';   // Delete filename extension
  strcat(backname, ".bak");
  bakf = fopen(backname, "wb");
  if (!bakf) {
    Error(ERR_WRITE);
    fclose(dbf);
    exit(3);  // Exit: report error
  }
}

int main()
{
  Welcome();
  Initialize();
  if (LimitsOkay() && Yes("\nSort file?")) {
    puts("\nReading records into memory");
    if (!ReadRecords(dbf))
      AbortSort();
    puts("\nCopying records to backup file");
    if (!WriteRecords(bakf))
      AbortSort();
    if (fclose(bakf) != 0) {
      Error(ERR_WRITE);
      AbortSort();
    }
    puts("\n\nSorting records in memory");
    SortRecords();
    puts("\nWriting sorted records to disk");
    if (WriteRecords(dbf))
      puts("\n\nDatabase sorted");
    else
      puts("\n\nDatabase not sorted. Recover from backup!");
    Pause();
  }
  fclose(dbf);
  FreeMemory();
  return 0;
}
```

There are many ways to sort a file, but some methods are too involved to discuss here. DBSORT takes the easy way out, reading all records into an array, sorting the array, and then writing the records back to disk. The program cannot sort large files that don't fit into memory, but it should still prove useful.

Function `ReadRecords` shows how to allocate an array of pointers to hold the records. Rather than store records directly in the array, the program prepares an array of `Record` pointers, each of which addresses an individual record in memory. This data structure combines the best of both worlds — it operates in list fashion but stores links in the array. The program can use the array to find each record, just as though they were stored in a list. Even better, *the program can sort the pointers, greatly reducing sorting times.*

The main difficulty in correctly sorting an array of object pointers is in writing the `qsort` comparison function. Function `Compare`, for instance, returns the string comparison result of the `name` members of two `Record` structures. The parameters passed by `qsort` to `Compare`, however, are not `Record` pointers; they are pointers *to* `Record` pointers. To gain access to the records using the double indirect pointers a and b, each must be cast to the type (const `Record**`), which is dereferenced with a leading asterisk. Finally, the `->` operator locates the `name` field in each record. The expressions may look odd, but because only pointers are shuffled rather than full records, sorting is very fast.

Epilogue

All good things must come to an end, and I hope that you have found this book to be a *good* introduction to C. Enjoy your new language. *You are only at the beginning of a lifelong experience in programming, and there are many more exciting times ahead.* It's been a pleasure writing *Type and Learn C* and working with all the fine folks at IDG and Borland International. I join them in wishing you success, fast compiles, and few bugs in all your programs to come.

Precedence and Evaluation Order

Table A-1 ▶ Precedence and Evaluation Order

Operators in Precedence Order	Evaluation Order
() [] -> .	left-right
! ~ ++ -- + - * & (type) sizeof	right-left *
* / %	left-right *
+ -	left-right *
<< >>	left-right
< <= > >=	left-right
== !=	left-right
&	left-right
^	left-right
|	left-right
&&	left-right
||	left-right
?:	right-left
= += -= *= /= %= &= ^= |= <<= >>=	right-left
,	left-right

Note to Table A-1: Unary operators +, -, and * (pointer dereference) have higher precedence than the same binary symbols.

Index